GW01418914

Building Community Resiliency and Sustainability With Tourism Development

Viana Hassan
University of Malta, Malta

Anna Staszewska
Katowice School of Economics, Poland

Shivam Bhartiya
Jain University, India

A volume in the Advances in
Hospitality, Tourism, and the
Services Industry (AHTSI) Book
Series

Published in the United States of America by
    IGI Global
    Business Science Reference (an imprint of IGI Global)
    701 E. Chocolate Avenue
    Hershey PA, USA 17033
    Tel: 717-533-8845
    Fax: 717-533-8661
    E-mail: cust@igi-global.com
    Web site: http://www.igi-global.com

Copyright © 2024 by IGI Global. All rights reserved. No part of this publication may be reproduced, stored or distributed in any form or by any means, electronic or mechanical, including
photocopying, without written permission from the publisher.
Product or company names used in this set are for identification purposes only. Inclusion of the
names of the products or companies does not indicate a claim of ownership by IGI Global of the
trademark or registered trademark.

Library of Congress Cataloging-in-Publication Data

CIP Data Pending

ISBN: 9798369354056
eISBN: 9798369354070

British Cataloguing in Publication Data
A Cataloguing in Publication record for this book is available from the British Library.

All work contributed to this book is new, previously-unpublished material.
The views expressed in this book are those of the authors, but not necessarily of the publisher.

For electronic access to this publication, please contact: eresources@igi-global.com.

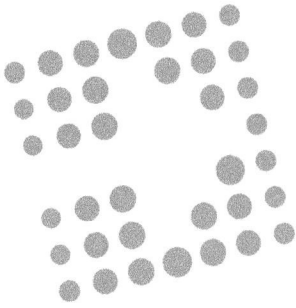

Advances in Hospitality, Tourism, and the Services Industry (AHTSI) Book Series

Maximiliano Korstanje
University of Palermo, Argentina

ISSN:2475-6547
EISSN:2475-6555

MISSION

Globally, the hospitality, travel, tourism, and services industries generate a significant percentage of revenue and represent a large portion of the business world. Even in tough economic times, these industries thrive as individuals continue to spend on leisure and recreation activities as well as services.

The Advances in Hospitality, Tourism, and the Services Industry (AHTSI) book series offers diverse publications relating to the management, promotion, and profitability of the leisure, recreation, and services industries. Highlighting current research pertaining to various topics within the realm of hospitality, travel, tourism, and services management, the titles found within the AHTSI book series are pertinent to the research and professional needs of managers, business practitioners, researchers, and upper-level students studying in the field.

Interlinking SDGs and the

Coverage

- Customer Service Issues
- Health and Wellness Tourism
- Hotel Management
- Leisure & Business Travel
- Service Management

IGI Global is currently accepting manuscripts for publication within this series. To submit a proposal for a volume in this series, please contact our Acquisition Editors at Acquisitions@igi-global.com or visit: http://www.igi-global.com/publish/.

Bottom-of-the-Pyramid Through Tourism

The (ISSN) is published by IGI Global, 701 E. Chocolate Avenue, Hershey, PA 17033-1240, USA, www.igi-global. com. This series is composed of titles available for purchase individually; each title is edited to be contextually exclusive from any other title within the series. For pricing and ordering information please visit http://www.igi-global.com/ book-series/advances-hospitality-tourism-services-industry/121014. Postmaster: Send all address changes to above address. Copyright © IGI Global. All rights, including translation in other languages reserved by the publisher. No part of this series may be reproduced or used in any form or by any means – graphics, electronic, or mechanical, including photocopying, recording, taping, or information and retrieval systems – without written permission from the publisher, except for non commercial, educational use, including classroom teaching purposes. The views expressed in this series are those of the authors, but not necessarily of IGI Global.

Titles in this Series

For a list of additional titles in this series, please visit: www.igi-global.com/book-series

Marco Valeri (Niccolò Cusano University, Italy) and Shekhar (University of Delhi, India)
Business Science Reference • copyright 2024 • 315pp • H/C (ISBN: 9798369331668) •
US $255.00 (our price)

Special Interest Trends for Sustainable Tourism
Kittisak Jermsittiparsert (University of City Island, Cyprus) and Pannee Suanpang (Suan
Dusit University, Thailand)
Business Science Reference • copyright 2024 • 463pp • H/C (ISBN: 9798369359037) •
US $345.00 (our price)

Cultural, Gastronomy, and Adventure Tourism Development
Rui Alexandre Castanho (WSB University, Poland) and Mara Franco (University of Madeira, Portugal)
Business Science Reference • copyright 2024 • 407pp • H/C (ISBN: 9798369331583) •
US $325.00 (our price)

Dimensions of Regenerative Practices in Tourism and Hospitality
Pankaj Kumar Tyagi (Chandigarh University, India) Vipin Nadda (University of Sunderland,
UK) Kannapat Kankaew (Burapha University International College, Thailand) and Kaitano
Dube (Vaal University of Technology, South Africa)
Business Science Reference • copyright 2024 • 338pp • H/C (ISBN: 9798369340424) •
US $295.00 (our price)

AI Innovations for Travel and Tourism
Ricardo Correia (Instituto Politécnico de Bragança, Portugal & CiTUR, Portugal) Márcio
Martins (Instituto Politécnico de Bragança, Portugal and CiTUR, Portugal) and Ruta Fontes
(Aveiro University, Portugal and GOVCOPP, Portugal)
Business Science Reference • copyright 2024 • 266pp • H/C (ISBN: 9798369321379) •
US $265.00 (our price)

IGI Global
PUBLISHER of TIMELY KNOWLEDGE

701 East Chocolate Avenue, Hershey, PA 17033, USA
Tel: 717-533-8845 x100 • Fax: 717-533-8661
E-Mail: cust@igi-global.com • www.igi-global.com

Table of Contents

Detailed Table of Contents

Chapter 1

> *Wasswa Shafik, Digital Circularity and Resilience Laboratory*
> *(DCRLab), Kampala, Uganda & School of Digital Science,*
> *Universiti Brunei Darussalam, Brunei*

Economic success, social equality, and environmental protection are needed to change global standards for sustainable development. Understanding and executing sustainable entrepreneurship is complicated, as this chapter shows. Sustainable service versions are evaluated globally for environmental and social health. Actual prototypes demonstrate sustainable solutions beyond revenue margins and a big service standard departure. CSR shows sustainable entrepreneurship's complicated campaign network. It examines firm, activities, and society's CSR motivations and effects on online reputation and sustainable development. Phase examined industry-specific issues and potential to improve sustainability across industries. The impact of eco-friendly technologies on IT business is examined. Ecological responsibility trends are examined for organizational change. Knowledge is used to create dependable, flexible, and sustainable enterprise plans and identify improvement opportunities.

Chapter 2

> *Mohamad Knio, Lebanese International University, Lebanon*

The chapter emphasizes the vital role of sustainability in the global landscape and businesses' role in driving sustainable practices. It advocates for a holistic approach, considering environmental, social, and governance factors, and highlights the benefits of transitioning to circular economies for a more environmentally friendly and economically viable future. Through case studies and insights, the chapter provides a comprehensive overview of sustainability's significance and actionable steps for organizations to embrace sustainable practices.

Chapter 3

Mohammad Badruddoza Talukder, International University of Business Agriculture and Technology, Bangladesh
Musfiqur Rahoman Khan, Daffodil Institute of IT, Bangladesh
Sanjeev Kumar, Lovely Professional University, India

Sustainable tourism initiatives can help address socioeconomic disparities and promote inclusive growth. These initiatives prioritize social tourism, sustainable consumption, and responsible business practices. By doing so, resource entities can benefit local communities, preserve cultural and natural resources, and contribute to sustainable development. The study involved a literature review, conceptual framework development, research design, data collection, analysis, policy implications, and conclusion. The study considers economic, social, and environmental impacts. However, unplanned tourism growth can have negative consequences, highlighting the need for sustainable tourism strategies. Ongoing monitoring and participation of all stakeholders are crucial to achieve sustainable tourism. Sustainable tourism practices can attract environmentally conscious tourists and contribute to economic growth. The values address socioeconomic gaps, promoting inclusive growth, stakeholder engagement, policy-led changes, a balanced approach, ongoing monitoring, and strategic collaborations.

Chapter 4
Exploring the Role of Sustainable Tourism in Building Environmental and

Gaurav Bathla, CT University, India
Ashish Raina, CT University, India
Amit Kumar, Central University of Haryana, India
Ranjeeta Tripathi, Amity University, Lucknow, India
Dalwinder Kaur, Manipal GlobalNxt University, Malaysia

This chapter delves into the critical intersection between sustainable tourism and the cultivation of environmental and social resilience. In an era marked by escalating environmental challenges and social disparities, understanding the potential of sustainable tourism as a catalyst for positive change is paramount. Through an interdisciplinary lens, this chapter navigates the intricate dynamics at play, examining how sustainable tourism practices can contribute to the preservation of natural ecosystems while simultaneously fostering community empowerment and social cohesion. From promoting biodiversity conservation and mitigating climate change impacts to enhancing livelihood opportunities and cultural preservation, the chapter unravels the intricate web of benefits that sustainable tourism offers. Moreover, it delves into the complexities of stakeholder engagement, policy formulation, and innovative strategies necessary for realizing the full potential of sustainable tourism in building resilient societies.

Chapter 5
Community-Based Tourism Development in Gurez Valley: A Planning

Hafizullah Dar, Lovely Professional University, India
Mudasir Ahmad Dar, Indira Gandhi National Open University, India

This study examined diverse tourism potentials and possibilities of community-based tourism development (CBTD) in Gurez valley. Desk research approach was adopted in which various theories and cases, apart from the other sources, were reviewed to accomplish the study purpose. The results, based on natural, socio-cultural, symbiotic, and event-based tourism resources, paved a way to design community-based tourism (CBT) model for Gurez valley. The hexagonal CBT model constitutes 1) involvement of local people, 2) training local people, 3) developing cooperative ownership, 4) developing local products, 5) creating partnership, and 6) product marketing. Applications of this model will help tourism planners and decision-makers in developing the community-based tourism and encouraging the local community to participate in CBT activities. Its applications will have direct positive impacts on the local economy, tourism resources, tourist experience, business, infrastructure, jobs, and other related aspects in the area.

The study aims to investigate the experiences of the tourists at Raghurajpur and employed netnographic study approach to extract the tourists' experience from TripAdvisor website. Raghurajpur in Indian state of Odisha is a popular rural tourism destination known for its different kinds of traditional art forms including paintings, engravings, and craft making. On thematic analysis of the data, the study came out with identification of four components of tourists' experience at Raghurajpur, namely travel motives, positive experience, negative experience, and concern for art and artisans. The study explains the reasons to visit Raghurajpur and sheds light on other aspects of tourists' experiences. This will help the stakeholders better understand the nature and status of Raghurajpur village so that they can take corrective actions to serve the exact needs of the tourists along with preserving its rich culture, heritage, and art.

India is rich in culture and well-known for its mythological knowledge. It has plenty of architectural marvels recognized by UNESCO and maintained by the Archaeological Survey of India (ASI). For this chapter, two of the cultural UNESCO sites, Mahabalipuram and Pattadakal, have been taken as the scope of the chapter. The introduction section talks about the history of the monuments and provides a brief overview of the tourism infrastructure. The following section, evaluation of tourism infrastructure, aims to analyze Mahabalipuram and Pattadakal's tourism infrastructure using four parameters: transportation and connectivity, accommodation, gastronomical facilities, and tourist amenities. An observational study of the sites was conducted between December 2023 and January 2024. This is followed by the recommendations provided by the authors to improve the tourism infrastructure in these sites and, finally, the chapter's conclusion and future scope for researchers.

This chapter explores how Egypt, Greece, Mexico, and India use sustainable tourism
to revive ancient sites and promote local communities. It looks at historical tourism
trends, initiatives for preservation, and community involvement. Strategies include
site management, education, and community partnerships. Economic benefits like
revenue and jobs, waste management, and cultural impacts on indigenous groups
are assessed. Challenges and lessons learned provide insights for sustainability.
Comparative analysis shows diverse approaches to balancing tourism and heritage
preservation. Responsible tourism is advocated for site protection and community
empowerment.

The nexus of the soft tourism development model must serve the concepts of
sustainability, resilience, and participation of the destination community. The
chapter explores the case study of a diving tourism destination and how it responds
to challenges for tourism development and environmental management, promoting
natural resources conservation, cultural heritage, and inclusive community well-being.
It provides the structural framework of the synergies that realize and the prospects
that offered to realize a unique proposal, an expanded tourism product that increases
the beneficial impact of tourism both locally and nationally.

Chapter 10

Edip Örücü, Bandırma Onyedi Eylül University, Turkey
Itir Hasirci, Inependent Researcher, Turkey
Ramazan Özkan Yildiz, Bandırma Onyedi Eylül University, Turkey

The aim of this research is to identify the effects of organisational agility and electronic human resource management (E-HRM) on sustainable competitive advantage. The population of the research consists of 471,000 employees working in hotels in Turkey. Data were collected through an online survey. Therefore, the sample of the research is 421 employees working in these hotels. Frequency, factor, reliability, normality, correlation, and regression analysis were performed. When the regression analysis was analysed, it was determined that organisational agility and E-HRM have significant effects on sustainable competitive advantage. When the result of the regression analysis is evaluated, it is seen that organisational agility affects sustainable competitive advantage more than E-HRM. Therefore, in this sample, recommendations are presented in order to bring the importance of organisational agility to all employees.

Chapter 11

Muhammed A. Yetgin, University of Karabük, Turkey
Kasım Yılmaz, University of Karabük, Turkey
Volkan Temizkan, University of Karabük, Turkey

On the UNESCO World Heritage List, Safranbolu is an essential tourist city in Turkey and internationally. Visited by thousands of tourists from Europe, the Far East, and other regions every year, Safranbolu is an attractive cultural tourism destination with its historic mansions, fountains, inns, baths, mosques, remarkable nature, traditional handicrafts, and local cuisine. Developing a city's tourism potential depends on the cooperation and coordination of stakeholders. Strategic cooperation increases efficiency and performance. The primary purpose of this study is to understand and reveal the importance of collaborative action styles of independent actors in expanding the potential of Safranbolu tourism destinations. In the study, data was collected through the qualitative interview method. According to the data obtained, it has been observed that stakeholders' collaborative action styles and techniques in Safranbolu tourism could be more effective at the expected level. For this reason, stakeholders need to act in coordination with an ordinary mind and develop effective strategies.

Selecting the ideal location for regenerative tourism is vital for environmental preservation and sustainable progress. Destination choice significantly impacts regenerative initiatives' effectiveness, affecting ecological benefits and socio-economic outcomes. A well-selected site fosters ecosystem restoration and positive engagement with indigenous communities, leveraging tourism as a force for biodiversity preservation, carbon capture, and local empowerment. In this chapter, the fuzzy multi-attributive border approximation area comparison (MABAC) approach is utilized to select the optimal site for regenerative tourism initiatives, considering six criteria each with five alternatives and input from three decision-makers. Normalization occurs after forming the initial decision matrix, followed by weight normalization. Performance index and rank are determined using the fuzzy multi-attributive border approximation area comparison (MABAC) procedure. Ultimately, after careful evaluation and consideration, it becomes evident that the fifth alternative stands out as the most suitable location for implementing regenerative practices in the field of tourism.

Electronic commerce has changed travel product distribution and buyer behavior. Internet usage drives the online travel market's fast development and commercial potential. Online travel booking operators now account for many global travel sales. It is feasible to do this as a result of the fast development of high-speed internet and smart phones, both of which are readily available to any person in today's world.

Preface

Communities play a crucial role in promoting resilience and sustainability amidst current global challenges. The book, *Building Community Resiliency and Sustainability With Tourism Development* serves as a guiding light for understanding the complex relationship between tourism, community well-being, and environmental stewardship. The need to create resilient and sustainable communities is more critical than ever due to climate change, socio-economic inequities, and the aftermath of a worldwide pandemic.

This book delves deeply into the interconnectedness between tourism growth and community building. It explores innovative solutions that leverage the tourism sector to enhance the resilience of local communities, recognizing tourism as a powerful driver of economic growth. Through meticulous analysis of case studies and exemplary methods from around the world, readers will discover how tourism can act as a catalyst for positive transformation, fostering employment, cultural exchange, and infrastructure development. Our approach transcends the conventional view of tourism, advocating for a holistic strategy that integrates social, economic, and environmental dimensions.

We aim to redefine sustainability in tourism by promoting responsible practices that prioritize the preservation of natural resources, cultural heritage, and community well-being. The book addresses the urgent need for a paradigm shift in the tourism sector, moving away from exploitative practices towards regenerative and inclusive alternatives. By incorporating insights from experts, policymakers, and community leaders, we present a compelling case for a new era of tourism that emphasizes resilience and sustainability.

A notable feature of this book is its emphasis on community involvement and empowerment. Through vivid narratives and real-life examples, it highlights the transformative potential of engaging local populations in the decision-making processes related to tourism development. By fostering a sense of ownership and pride, communities can harness the benefits of tourism while preserving their unique identity and natural assets. We offer practical frameworks and toolkits for community-led initiatives, demonstrating how collaboration among stakeholders can amplify the positive impact of tourism on both local and global scales.

As the global community strives to balance economic growth with environmental conservation, this book emerges as an essential guide. It challenges traditional notions about the role of tourism in our societies, presenting a blueprint for harnessing its potential as a force for good. *Building Community Resiliency and Sustainability With Tourism Development* is not merely a book; it is a call to action—a manifesto for a more thoughtful and harmonious future where communities thrive, and the beauty of our planet endures.

Chapter 1: Sustainable Development

This chapter delves into the essential pillars of sustainable development: economic success, social equality, and environmental protection. By exploring the complexities of sustainable entrepreneurship, the chapter evaluates various global sustainable service models that prioritize environmental and social health beyond mere profitability. Through actual prototypes and case studies, it highlights a departure from traditional business standards, emphasizing the importance of corporate social responsibility (CSR). The chapter examines CSR's multifaceted motivations and impacts on firms, activities, and society, particularly in online reputation and sustainable development. Industry-specific issues are discussed, along with the potential of eco-friendly technologies to foster organizational change and promote sustainability across various sectors.

Chapter 2: The Relevance of Sustainability in the 21st Century

This chapter underscores the critical importance of sustainability in the contemporary global landscape and the pivotal role of businesses in championing sustainable practices. Advocating for a holistic approach, it integrates environmental, social, and governance (ESG) factors and highlights the advantages of transitioning to circular economies. Through detailed case studies and insights, the chapter offers a comprehensive overview of sustainability's significance, outlining actionable steps for organizations to embrace and implement sustainable practices for a more environmentally friendly and economically viable future.

Chapter 3: Socioeconomic Gaps and Fostering Inclusive Growth: Sustainable Tourism Initiatives

This chapter explores how sustainable tourism initiatives can address socioeconomic disparities and promote inclusive growth. It emphasizes the importance of social tourism, sustainable consumption, and responsible business practices in benefiting local communities and preserving cultural and natural resources. The chapter includes a literature review, conceptual framework development, and an analysis of economic, social, and environmental impacts. Highlighting the necessity for sustainable tourism strategies, it calls for ongoing monitoring and stakeholder participation to ensure positive outcomes. Sustainable tourism practices are shown to attract environmentally conscious tourists and contribute to economic growth.

Chapter 4: Exploring the Role of Sustainable Tourism in Building Environmental and Social Resilience

This chapter examines the critical intersection of sustainable tourism and the development of environmental and social resilience. In light of escalating environmental challenges and social disparities, it explores how sustainable tourism can serve as a catalyst for positive change. The chapter discusses the preservation of natural ecosystems, community empowerment, and social cohesion through sustainable tourism practices. It addresses the complexities of stakeholder engagement, policy formulation, and innovative strategies necessary to harness the full potential of sustainable tourism in building resilient societies.

Chapter 5: Community-Based Tourism Development in Gurez Valley: A Planning Perspective

This chapter investigates the potential for Community-Based Tourism Development (CBTD) in Gurez Valley through a desk research approach. By reviewing theories and cases, it proposes a community-based tourism (CBT) model for the area, focusing on local involvement, training, cooperative ownership, product development, partnerships, and marketing. The application of this model is expected to have direct positive impacts on the local economy, tourism resources, infrastructure, and overall community well-being.

Chapter 6: A Netnographic Analysis of Tourists' Experiences in the Rural Tourism Village of India

This chapter employs a netnographic study approach to investigate tourist experiences in Raghurajpur, a rural tourism destination in Odisha, India. By analyzing data from TripAdvisor, the study identifies four key components of tourists' experiences: travel motives, positive experiences, negative experiences, and concern for art and artisans. The findings aim to help stakeholders better understand and address the needs of tourists while preserving the village's rich cultural heritage.

Chapter 7: Evaluation of Tourism Infrastructure Around the Ancient Marvels of Mahabalipuram and Pattadakal

This chapter evaluates the tourism infrastructure surrounding the UNESCO World Heritage sites of Mahabalipuram and Pattadakal. Through an observational study conducted between December 2023 and January 2024, the chapter analyzes four parameters: transportation and connectivity, accommodation, gastronomical facilities, and tourist amenities. It provides recommendations for improving the tourism infrastructure and discusses future research opportunities.

Chapter 8: Revitalizing Ancient Sites: Sustainable Tourism Strategies for Preservation and Community Development

This chapter explores how countries like Egypt, Greece, Mexico, and India utilize sustainable tourism to revive ancient sites and promote local communities. It examines historical tourism trends, preservation initiatives, and community involvement strategies. The chapter assesses economic benefits, waste management, and cultural impacts, offering insights for balancing tourism and heritage preservation. It advocates for responsible tourism to protect sites and empower communities.

Chapter 9: Dive into the Wreck of Peristera, Greece: A Study of Collaborative and Sustainable Tourism Development in the Blue Economy Framework

This chapter explores the case study of a diving tourism destination in Peristera, Greece, within the blue economy framework. It discusses the soft tourism development model that emphasizes sustainability, resilience, and community participation. The chapter highlights the synergies and prospects of promoting natural resource conservation, cultural heritage, and inclusive community well-being through sustainable tourism practices.

Chapter 10: A Research on Factors Affecting Sustainable Competitive Advantage in the Tourism Sector

This chapter investigates the impact of organizational agility and electronic human resource management (E-HRM) on achieving sustainable competitive advantage in the tourism sector. Based on data collected from 421 hotel employees in Turkey, the study employs various statistical analyses to determine the significance of these factors. The findings reveal that while both organizational agility and E-HRM positively influence sustainable competitive advantage, organizational agility has a more pronounced effect, underscoring the need for its emphasis in hotel management strategies.

Chapter 11: The Importance of Organizational Collaborative Strategic Actions of Independent Actors in Enhancing the Potential of Tourism Destination Management: Organizational Collaborative Strategic Actions of Independent Actors

This chapter explores the role of collaborative strategic actions among independent actors in enhancing the tourism potential of Safranbolu, a UNESCO World Heritage site. Through qualitative interviews, the study highlights the need for better coordination and strategic cooperation among stakeholders to improve efficiency and performance in managing this cultural tourism destination. The findings emphasize the critical importance of stakeholder collaboration for maximizing the tourism potential of historic cities like Safranbolu.

Chapter 12: Selecting the Best Place for Regenerative Practices in Tourism Using the Fuzzy MABAC Method

This chapter employs the fuzzy MABAC approach to select the optimal site for regenerative tourism initiatives. Considering six criteria with five alternatives and input from three decision-makers, the method ranks sites based on their overall performance. The chapter discusses the implications of the case study and sensitivity analysis, emphasizing the importance of destination choice for environmental preservation and sustainable progress.

Chapter 13: A Bibliometric Examination of Online Hotel Booking via OTA: An AI and Tech-Driven Travel Solution

This bibliometric analysis examines the trend of online hotel bookings through Online Travel Agencies (OTA), focusing on the roles of AI and technological advancements. The study discusses how AI and technology enhance the online booking experience, offering convenience and efficiency for travelers and hoteliers. The chapter identifies key trends and future directions for OTA in the tourism industry.

In conclusion, *Building Community Resiliency and Sustainability With Tourism Development* stands as a vital resource in navigating the intricate dynamics between tourism, community welfare, and environmental stewardship. Amidst the pressing challenges of climate change, socio-economic disparities, and the lingering effects of a global pandemic, the imperative to build resilient and sustainable communities has never been more urgent.

This compendium of knowledge offers a thorough examination of the symbiotic relationship between tourism growth and community development. Through an array of case studies and innovative approaches, it underscores the transformative power of tourism as a driver of economic progress, cultural exchange, and infrastructure enhancement. The chapters within advocate for a holistic and responsible approach to tourism, integrating economic, social, and environmental dimensions to foster sustainability.

A cornerstone of this book is its advocacy for sustainable practices that safeguard natural resources, cultural heritage, and community well-being. It challenges the traditional exploitative models of tourism, proposing instead a shift towards regenerative and inclusive strategies. By drawing on insights from experts, policymakers, and community leaders, the book presents a compelling vision for a new era of tourism—one that prioritizes resilience and sustainability.

Community involvement and empowerment emerge as pivotal themes, with vivid narratives illustrating the profound impact of local engagement in tourism-related decision-making. Practical frameworks and toolkits provided herein empower communities to leverage tourism for their benefit, while maintaining their unique identities and natural assets.

As we strive for a balance between economic growth and environmental conservation, this book serves as an essential guide and a clarion call for a more thoughtful and harmonious future. It invites readers to reimagine the role of tourism as a force for good, promoting thriving communities and preserving the planet's beauty. *Building Community Resiliency and Sustainability With Tourism Development* is more than a collection of scholarly insights—it is a manifesto for a sustainable future where tourism enriches lives and fortifies the resilience of communities worldwide.

Preface

Viana Hassan
University of Malta, Malta

Anna Staszewska
Katowice School of Economics, Poland

Shivam Bhartiya
Jain University, India

Chapter 1
Sustainable Development

Wasswa Shafik
https://orcid.org/0000-0002-9320-3186

*Digital Circularity and Resilience Laboratory (DCRLab), Kampala, Uganda &
School of Digital Science, Universiti Brunei Darussalam, Brunei*

ABSTRACT

Economic success, social equality, and environmental protection are needed to change global standards for sustainable development. Understanding and executing sustainable entrepreneurship is complicated, as this chapter shows. Sustainable service versions are evaluated globally for environmental and social health. Actual prototypes demonstrate sustainable solutions beyond revenue margins and a big service standard departure. CSR shows sustainable entrepreneurship's complicated campaign network. It examines firm, activities, and society's CSR motivations and effects on online reputation and sustainable development. Phase examined industry-specific issues and potential to improve sustainability across industries. The impact of eco-friendly technologies on IT business is examined. Ecological responsibility trends are examined for organizational change. Knowledge is used to create dependable, flexible, and sustainable enterprise plans and identify improvement opportunities.

1. INTRODUCTION

In the vibrant landscape of the modern international economic climate, the need for sustainable company techniques has become an indisputable need, driven by the immediate requirement to resolve financial development with ecological preservation and social equity (Danilov, 2022). Quick automation, population growth, and source deficiency have placed unmatched pressures on the world, motivating a standard change in international organization ideologies such as sustainable development

DOI: 10.4018/979-8-3693-5405-6.ch001

Copyright © 2024, IGI Global. Copying or distributing in print or electronic forms without written permission of IGI Global is prohibited.

goals[1]. Environment modification, social inequality, and source deficiency are no longer remote problems; however, they prompt hazards that require positive action from services (Liengpunsakul, 2021). Against this background, the fostering of sustainable organization techniques comes to be not simply a company obligation but a tactical necessity, as businesses acknowledge the connection of ecological, social, and financial consider protecting long-sustainable feasibility and adding to a resistant and growing worldwide area (Glavič, 2020).

The intensifying ecological situation emphasizes the necessity for smart service practices. Environment adjustment, driven mostly by anthropogenic tasks, presents a considerable risk to environments, biodiversity, and human cultures (Duvnjak & Kohont, 2021). The exhaustion of natural deposits, logging, and contamination are not just ecological worries but additionally powerful difficulties to the security of supply chains and the long-sustainable practicality of services (Clark et al., 2016). As firms progressively acknowledge their duty in these ecological difficulties, accepting sustainable methods becomes crucial for alleviating environmental influence, ensuring source strength is available, and contributing to a much healthier earth for future generations.

The call for sustainable organization methods is elaborately connected to changing social characteristics and increased stakeholder assumptions; other forms are demonstrated in Figure 1. In an age of extraordinary connection, details circulation, and social network impact, customers are much more notified and critical than ever before (Jilcha & Kitaw, 2017). They require openness, moral sourcing, and business obligation from the business they sustain. Additionally, staff members look for purpose-driven workplaces, and financiers focus on firms with durable ecological, social, and governance (ESG) methods. Subsequently, sustainable company methods have ended up being critical in structuring and keeping trust funds, brand name track records, and long-sustainable partnerships with stakeholders (Chauhan et al., 2022).

Figure 1. Forms of Sustainable Development

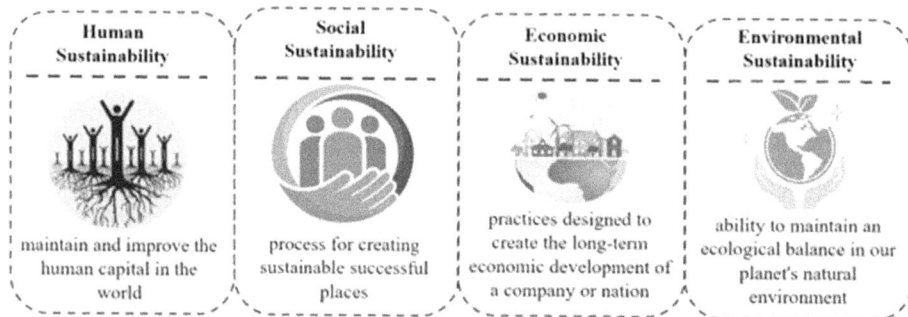

Human Sustainability	Social Sustainability	Economic Sustainability	Environmental Sustainability
maintain and improve the human capital in the world	process for creating sustainable successful places	practices designed to create the long-term economic development of a company or nation	ability to maintain an ecological balance in our planet's natural environment

Beyond ethical considerations, sustainability is significantly acknowledged as a keystone of financial stability and strength. Organizations are exposed to expanding dangers related to climate-related occasions, governing modifications, and supply chain disturbances (Bolton, 2021). Taking on sustainable techniques is not just an action to govern stress but a positive technique to boost functional performance, decrease prices, and provide future-proofing against rising dangers (Scheyvens et al., 2021). Investments in renewable resources[2], round economic situation techniques, and social duty not only minimize ecological influence but likewise place businesses to prosper in a developing financial landscape, cultivating development and versatility.

As services browse this facility's international landscape, the assimilation of sustainable methods is no longer an optional selection but a calculated necessity. Accepting sustainability not only addresses pushing ecological and social difficulties but likewise lines up companies with advancing customer assumptions, regulative landscapes, and sustainable financial factors to consider (Lee, 2020). By recognizing the connection between financial, ecological, and social variables, companies can create a course toward durability, advancement, and a favorable social influence. The trip in the direction of sustainable organization methods is not without obstacles (Khan et al., 2021). However, it stands for an essential action in developing an extra-sustainable and fair international future.

1.1. Chapter Contributions

This chapter provides the following contributions as summarized.

- The chapter explores diverse models that prioritize environmental conservation and social well-being, illustrating productive integration and its broader impacts.
- Evaluate the impact of corporate social responsibility[3] (CSR) initiatives on shaping sustainable entrepreneurship, addressing motivations, challenges, and benefits.
- Illustrates the existing confronts and prospects in separate sectors, providing insights into industry-specific appropriate practices for sustainable development.
- Investigates the transformative stimulus of green innovation on entrepreneurial ventures and its broader consequences for environmental sustainability.
- Significantly evaluates existing policies, assessing their impact on businesses and sustainable development goals (SDGs) while spotting areas for refinement and improvement.

- Finally, future research directions and lessons learned from the chapter are presented, equipping readers with perspectives essential to steer the complex terrain of sustainable entrepreneurship in the advanced world.

1.2. Chapter Organization

Section 2 presents an analysis of sustainable business models. Section 3 portrays the identified role of Corporate Social Responsibility (CSR) in shaping sustainability in developing technological societies. Section 4 illustrates the integration of sustainable practices across diverse industries and their associated benefits. Section 5 investigates the impact of green innovation and eco-friendly technologies. Section 6 analyzes existent policies, assessing their impact on businesses and sustainable development. Finally, Section 7 presents the prospects, insights obtained from the chapter, and the conclusion.

2. ANALYZING SUSTAINABLE BUSINESS MODELS

In exploring sustainable service versions that focus on both ecological preservation and social health, it ends up being obvious that these cutting-edge techniques expand past simple company duty; they envelop a basic reimagining of business frameworks and worths as demonstrated.

2.1. Circular Economy Model

This stands as a sign of sustainability, stressing source performance and decreasing waste. This model looks to get rid of the idea of "waste" deliberate items for recyclability and advertising the reuse of products. Businesses embracing this technique not only enhance a decrease in ecological influence but also furthermore locate financial pluses in expense financial savings with source optimization (Buturlina et al., 2021). The circular economy paradigm standard not only advertises sustainability within the boundaries of a business but also emits favorable effects throughout supply chains, urging an extra accountable and regenerative method for the organization to increase sustainable development, as illustrated in Figure 2.

Figure 2. Sustainable Development Approaches

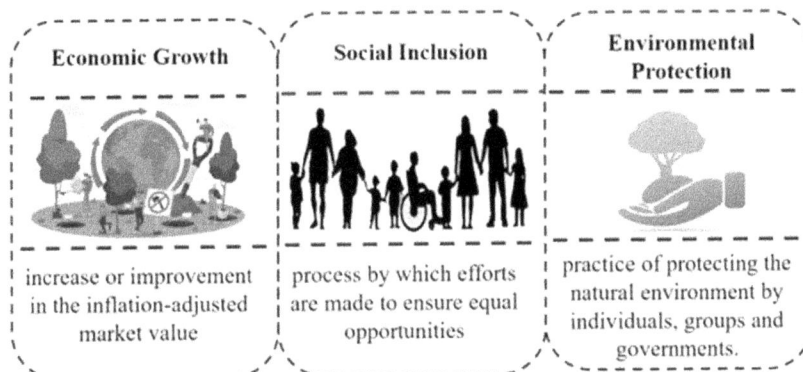

Economic Growth	Social Inclusion	Environmental Protection
increase or improvement in the inflation-adjusted market value	process by which efforts are made to ensure equal opportunities	practice of protecting the natural environment by individuals, groups and governments.

2.2. B Corporation (B Corp) Certification

A dedication identifies this certification version to conference strenuous social and ecological requirements. B Corps[4] goes through a thorough evaluation, considering their influence on employees, consumers, providers, area, and the atmosphere (Rahma et al., 2019). Accomplishing B Corp's qualification symbolizes a commitment to all-natural sustainability. Beyond the instant improvements to the firm, for example, enhanced credibility and accessibility to an expanding market of aware customers, the wider effect depends on motivating a change in the company landscape (Ho et al., 2022). B Corps acts as leaders, establishing criteria for liable company methods and motivating a standard change towards a much more eco-friendly and fairer international economic situation.

2.3. Social Entrepreneurship

In the context of the organization, social entrepreneurship describes a vibrant organization version that deals with social issues while all at once preserving economic safety and security. These companies include social influence right into their main objective, and they regularly take advantage of market-driven options to effectively cause favorable modification (Fu et al., 2022). Social business owners are an archetype of how organizations can be a favorable force in the globe because they integrate the search for revenue with the search for social suitability. The influence is not restricted to private organizations; instead, it has stimulated a wave of mindful industrialism that recognizes the interconnectedness of the success of organizations and the wellness of culture (Ghobakhloo et al., 2022).

2.4. Impact Investing and Triple Bottom Line (TBL) Model

Along with economic worries, the TBL[5] model in design includes dimensions that determine the social and ecological effect of financial investments. The capitalists that utilize this method assess firms not simply based on their earnings but additionally on the advantages they make to both individuals and the atmosphere (Zakari et al., 2022). Financiers cause a change in the goals of firms by putting a focus on three-way profits, which include earnings, individuals, and the world. By giving monetary rewards to services, this design motivates sustainable growth by urging them to straighten their approaches with social and ecological objectives (Nunkoo et al., 2023). This, subsequently, enhances favorable results and affects a larger recalibration of company worth from a bigger viewpoint.

2.5. Employee Ownership and Cooperative Models

With the redistribution of possession and decision-making authority inside a company, worker possession, and participating versions put a focus on the improvement of social health. Producing a feeling of possession, interaction, and shared success amongst workers can be achieved with the application of devices like Employee Stock Ownership Plans (ESOPs) and cooperatives (M. M. L. Lim et al., 2018). These devices enable staff members to end up being stakeholders in the firm. This idea motivates economic equal rights, employee joy, and area advancement past the range of private firms (Bishoge et al., 2019). It functions as a presentation of the advanced possibility of business frameworks that are worth not just for success but also for the general well-being of individuals, which contributes to the success of the company.

Figure 3. Sustainable Development Controls

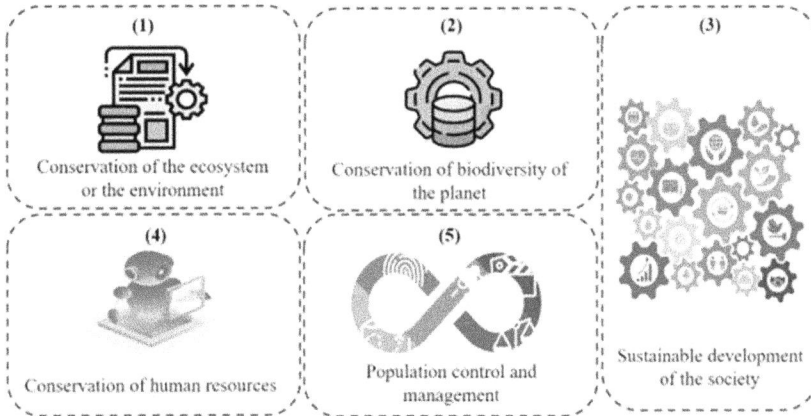

2.6. Cradle to Cradle (C2C) Design Framework

This C2C[6] has to do with seeing rubbish as an infinite source and making the best point from the get-go. It has to do with making neighborhood and item advancement features similar to a healthy and balanced eco-friendly system where all sources are made use of properly and in an intermittent method (Shulla et al., 2020). Likewise, it is rooted in the concepts of waste removal and the development of items with continual life processes. By taking into consideration the whole life process of an item, from product sourcing to disposal, businesses embracing this design decrease the ecological effect and advertise the development of products that can be constantly reused or upcycled, as demonstrated in Figure 3 (Bogers et al., 2022). The C2C design cultivates a reimagining of producing procedures, affecting whole markets to welcome sustainable style techniques and add to the growth of a round economic situation.

3. THE ROLE OF CORPORATE SOCIAL RESPONSIBILITY

This section presents some roles of CSR in developing ecologically friendly societies and integrating environmental, ethical, and social considerations into business operations in the quest to attain substantial, sustainable development.

3.1. Environmental Stewardship

CSR efforts add to ecological preservation and sustainability. Firms take part in environmentally friendly methods, power effectiveness, waste decrease, and sustainable sourcing of resources. The duty of CSR in ecological stewardship is to guarantee that services run in a fashion that is environmentally accountable and sustainable (Niemets et al., 2021). Firms take advantage of decreased ecological threats, boost source effectiveness, and boost brand name online reputation as eco-mindful entities. Ecological stewardship with CSR adds to mitigating environment adjustment, shielding communities, and promoting much more sustainable use of natural deposits.

3.2. Social Equity and Inclusion

CSR cultivates social equity by attending to concerns such as variety, incorporation, and reasonable labor methods. Firms that focus on CSR jobs in the direction of producing comprehensive work environments, making sure reasonable earnings, and valuing civil rights. CSR plays an important duty in developing reasonable and simple workplaces, cultivating variety, and supporting civil rights (Leal Filho et al., 2023). Organizations gain boosted worker complete satisfaction, improved company society, and a favorable public image by focusing on social equity. Social equity campaigns add to constructing extra comprehensive cultures, minimizing revenue inequality, and promoting a society of regard and justness (Visseren-Hamakers, 2020).

3.3. Community Engagement and Development

CSR efforts entail services in area growth jobs. Firms sustain neighborhood areas with education and learning, health care, facilities growth, and various other efforts. The duty is to be involved with regional areas, comprehend their demands, and add to their social and financial wellness. Businesses acquire neighborhood assistance, enhance relationships with neighborhood stakeholders, and have a favorable effect on their social permit to run (Leal Filho et al., 2018). Area interaction with CSR increases sustainable growth by attending to regional obstacles and constructing durable and equipped neighborhoods.

3.4. Ethical Business Practices

CSR stresses honest actions and honesty in service procedures. Businesses devote themselves to clear and accountable methods, consisting of fair trade, anti-corruption procedures, and moral supply chain monitoring. CSR makes sure that services run morally and with stability, thinking about the effect of their activities on numerous stakeholders (Mukhuty et al., 2022). Moral service techniques improve brand name track record, construct count on with customers, and add to a favorable company photo. Moral service methods through CSR cultivate a society of stability, increase the reasonable worldwide profession, and protect against unfavorable social and ecological influences (Spaiser et al., 2017).

3.5. Stakeholder Engagement and Communication

CSR also involves involving different stakeholders, consisting of clients, staff members, financiers, and the bigger area. Via clear interaction concerning CSR campaigns, companies construct trust funds and trustworthiness. The duty is to develop, depend on, and collect responses and line up organization approaches with social assumptions with reliable stakeholder involvement (Hummels & Argyrou, 2021). Corporate acquires stakeholder commitment, boosted partnerships, and a favorable assumption of company obligation. Development entities are illustrated in Figure 4. Stakeholder interaction via CSR ensures that companies consider varied viewpoints, resulting in even more sustainable and socially liable decision-making (Giangrande et al., 2019).

Figure 4. Sustainable Development Circle

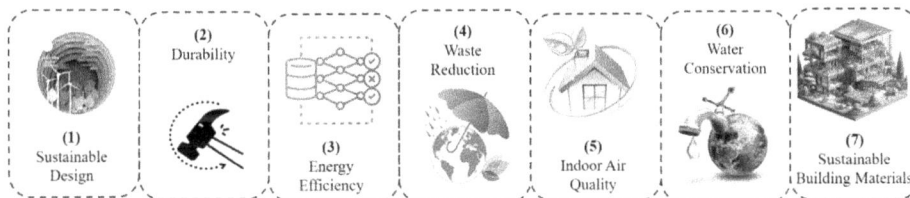

3.6. Innovation for Social and Environmental Solutions

CSR motivates companies to introduce ways to deal with social and ecological obstacles. Businesses purchase research and development to produce services and products that have a favorable influence on culture. CSR drives businesses to buy research and development for services that add to sustainability (Xu et al., 2023). Advancement via CSR can bring about brand-new income streams, market distinction, and favorable ecological and social effects. CSR-driven development cultivates technical improvements, dealing with international difficulties and adding to a much more sustainable and durable future.

3.7. Risk Management and Resilience

CSR systems run the risk of monitoring by recognizing and dealing with social and ecological threats. Proactively resolving problems such as environmental adjustment, civil rights infractions, or supply chain susceptibilities boosts a firm's durability to outside shocks and regulative adjustments, therefore making sure of long-sustainable sustainability (C. K. Lim et al., 2022). CSR makes certain that organizations proactively handle dangers connected with environmental modification, supply chain susceptibility, and various other social and ecological aspects. Stiffens take advantage of raised strength, decreased monetary threats, and improved flexibility to alter market problems (Fei et al., 2021). CSR-driven danger administration adds to sustainable service sustainability, decreasing adverse influence on both the firm and culture.

4. SUSTAINABLE PRACTICES ACROSS DIVERSE INDUSTRIES INTEGRATION

This combination includes the organized consolidation of sustainable concepts and methods right into every element of market procedures, going beyond sectorial limits, as illustrated.

4.1. Environmental Management and Resource Efficiency

The execution of sustainable techniques requires organizations to embrace eco-liability methods in their procedures to be taken into consideration. The decrease in waste, the application of cleaner commercial modern technology, and the reduction of source intake all consisted of this (Shulla et al., 2021). As an example, the production markets might adhere to the concepts of a round economic situation to make the best use of the usage of sources (Weiland et al., 2021). At the same time, the transport industry might check out innovations that are fuel-efficient and alternate power resources. Via the prioritization of source performance, sectors make a payment to the conservation of the atmosphere and its long-sustainable presence.

4.2. Supply Chain Sustainability

Ecologically accountable company methods are strongly implanted in supply chain administration methods throughout a wide variety of sectors. For the objective of guaranteeing moral sourcing, reasonable labor criteria, and ecological obligation, this assimilation demands an extensive analysis of the whole supply chain (Dhaoui, 2022). To deal with issues such as logging, employee exploitation, and carbon discharges, markets are pursuing attaining visibility and liability in their supply chains. By accepting sustainable supply chain approaches, sectors not only minimize the threats to their credibility but likewise add to the global initiatives that are being made to advertise liable company tasks (Ferguson et al., 2021).

4.3. Industry-Specific Sustainability Initiatives

In a considerable method, sustainable ideas are integrated right into the monitoring of supply chains in a wide range of various companies. This assimilation asks for an extensive examination of the full supply chain to ensure honest sourcing, reasonable labor criteria, and ecological obligation (Morton et al., 2017). A complete examination is called for to achieve these objectives. Industries are pursuing developing visibility and obligation concerning their supply chains to deal with issues such as logging, labor exploitation, and carbon exhausts. These steps are being taken to address these concerns. Industries do not just complement worldwide campaigns to advertise accountable means of carrying out service (Stawicka, 2021). Hitherto, they additionally lower the threats to their track records by carrying out sustainable supply chain methods. This is because these markets reduced the dangers to their track records.

4.4. Cross-Industry Collaboration and Knowledge Sharing

Identifying that sustainability difficulties are typically interconnected, sectors take part in cross-sector cooperation and understanding sharing. This entails collaborations with non-governmental organizations[7] (NGOs), governmental bodies, and various other stakeholders to trade ideal techniques, line up requirements, and jointly address sustainability difficulties (Achim et al., 2023). By leveraging varied experiences and experiences, sectors improve their capability to create cutting-edge options and browse the intricacies of sustainable service techniques. Cross-industry partnership increases the rate of favorable adjustment and promotes an extra alternative strategy for sustainability (Hák et al., 2016). This all-natural method includes environmental management, accountable source usage, sustainable supply chain methods, industry-specific campaigns, and cross-sector cooperation.

4.5. Consumer Education and Market Transformation

Customer education and learning and market change are dual vital parts that need to be included right into the procedure of taking on sustainable methods throughout a selection of companies. Significantly, companies are placing even more of their focus on spreading out understanding concerning eco-friendly items and treatments, given that they understand the effect that client choices have (Ruggerio, 2021). Services instruct clients regarding the ecological and social repercussions of their choices via numerous advertising methods, consisting of labeling, instructional initiatives, and advertising projects. As a result, this leads to a boost in the popularity of eco-friendly products and inspires services to change their product or services (Mohamad Taghvaee et al., 2023). The unification of sustainable methods is feedback to the ever-changing assumptions of customers, which eventually leads to the modification of markets towards alternatives that are much more liable and eco delicate.

5. THE IMPACT OF GREEN INNOVATION AND ECO-FRIENDLY TECHNOLOGIES

The effect of eco-friendly advancement and environment-friendly modern technologies expands many past technical improvements, penetrating different elements of culture, the economic climate, and the setting.

5.1. Environmental Conservation and Resource Efficiency

Eco-friendly technology and eco-friendly modern technology offer a substantial payment to the conservation of the setting by decreasing the environmental impact that is left by human tasks. Their effect is incredible (Kota et al., 2021). Resources of renewable resources, home appliances that are power reliable, and farming methods that are ecologically liable are instances of innovations that can aid in lessening source usage, air pollution, and exhaust of greenhouse gases. Furthermore, the quantity of electrical energy that is made use of is lowered because of these modern technologies (Kopnina, 2020). Due to this impact, ecological concerns such as environmental adjustment, damage to the environment, and the deficiency of natural deposits are quickly attended to, which contributes to the growth of a world that is much more sustainable and resistant.

5.2. Economic Growth and Occupation Creation

The introduction of eco-friendly innovation and eco-friendly advancements brings about the advancement of brand-new sectors and the development of brand-new work possibilities, which consequently boosts the development of the economic situation (Lyaskovskaya & Khudyakova, 2021). Development fads are being observed in a variety of sectors, consisting of renewable resources, power effectiveness, and eco-friendly production, as the demand for sustainable options remains to enhance throughout the globe (van Zanten & van Tulder, 2021). The shift to an eco-friendly economic climate not only enhances financial efficiency but also urges advancement and entrepreneurialism, which positions federal governments and ventures at the center of the motion toward sustainable advancement.

5.3. Health and Well-Being

Developments that get along to the setting have a huge impact on the wellness of individuals. Lowering contamination of airborne and water can be achieved with the execution of eco-friendly modern technology, for example, renewable resource resources and transport that is eco-accountable (van Vuuren et al., 2022). Therefore, this leads to an improvement in the high quality of the air and improves the ecological communities. The application of these innovations can cause a variety of results, consisting of the enhancement of public health, the decrease of prices related to health care, and the improvement of basic health (Maka & Alabid, 2022). On top of that, sustainable farming methods advertise far better food systems, which, because of their favorable impact, have a positive influence not just on nourishment but also on food safety, increasing several ecological inputs, as in Figure 5.

Figure 5. Sustainable Development Contributors

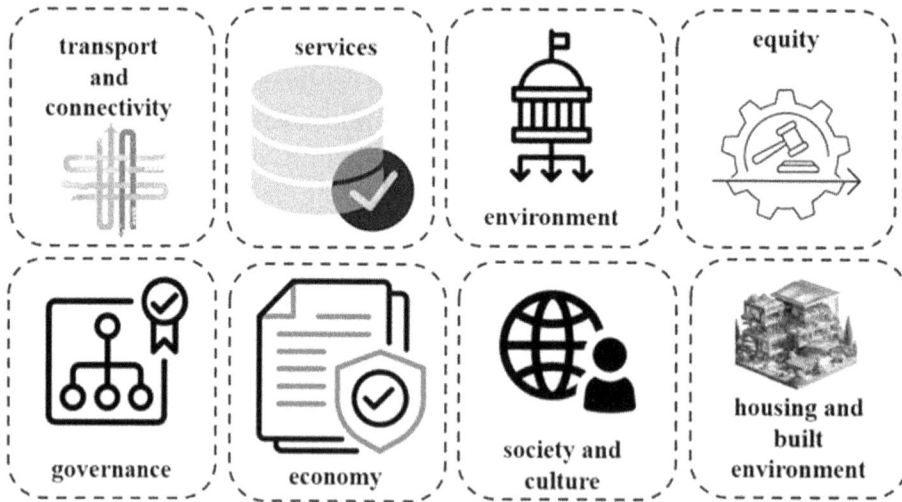

5.4. Climate Change Mitigation and Adaptation

Environment-friendly technology plays a variety of vital functions in the fight against environmental adjustment, one of the most essential of which is the stipulation of different services to habits that make considerable use of carbon (Ogryzek, 2023). To maintain the decline of greenhouse gas discharges, the application of sustainable land-use techniques, carbon capture and storage space modern technology, and renewable resource modern technologies are all required. Furthermore, environment-friendly innovation makes it less complex to execute adjustment methods, which subsequently assist areas much better in handling the repercussions of environmental modification (Nousheen et al., 2020). This impact is necessary to construct an international reaction to the difficulties presented by an altering environment and to achieve the objective of developing environmental durability.

5.5. Global Competitiveness and Corporate Responsibility

Taking on environment-friendly technology and environment-friendly modern technologies improves the worldwide competition of companies and countries. In an age where sustainability is a vital vehicle driver of customer selections and capitalist choices, businesses that focus on environment-friendly techniques are more likely to draw in consumers and capitalists (Patel et al., 2021). Business obligation campaigns that include eco-friendly technology do not just add to favorable brand name photos but likewise show a dedication to dealing with international obstacles. This effect is critical for organizations intending to grow in a socially and eco-mindful market (Apostu & Gigauri, 2023). As these innovations continue to advance, their favorable influences are anticipated to play a progressively crucial role in shaping a much more sustainable and unified future for our earth.

6. EVALUATING THE EFFECTIVENESS OF POLICIES

While effective plans result in a favorable effect on sustainability, continuous assessment, and modifications are critical to address obstacles and guarantee long-sustainable efficiency.

6.1. Renewable Energy Policies

The adoption of renewable energy laws, such as the Feed-in Tariff[8] (FiT) mechanism, has shown to be highly successful in expediting the transition to environmentally friendly resources. For example, the implementation of FiT in Germany led to a rise in the capacity of renewable energy sources, a significant reduction in carbon emissions, and a stable investment environment for clean energy technology (Khan et al., 2023; Sinakou et al., 2018). These effects resulted directly from the installation of FiT. Spain's achievement in the energy industry is comparable to that of other countries, demonstrating the positive impact of well-designed regulations on global advancements.

6.2. Carbon Pricing Mechanisms

It has been demonstrated that cap-and-trade systems, which are a type of carbon pricing, are effective in lowering greenhouse gas emissions. One example of such a system is the European Union Emissions Trading System[9] (EUETS) (Zwolińska et al., 2022). The implementation of such regulations results in the creation of economic incentives for firms to adopt cleaner technologies. These rules restrict the total amount of emissions and permit the trade of permits (Pan et al., 2023). A notable example of the potential of market-based techniques in mitigating climate change is the EUETS, which has made a substantial contribution to the reduction of emissions across all industries.

6.3. Plastic Waste Management Policies

Restrictions and levies on single-use plastics are two instances of plans that have been carried out in different areas of the globe with the objective of minimizing the amount of rubbish that is created by plastics. These plans have shown differing levels of success (Sharpley, 2020). Effective applications, such as the restrictions on plastic bags that have been enforced in the East African countries of Rwanda and Kenya, highlight the favorable impact that rigorous procedures have on the establishment of cleaner environments (Prieto-Jiménez et al., 2021). These restrictions have been applied in their corresponding nations. It is important to stress that the efficiency of such plans is dependent upon a variety of variables, consisting of the schedule of practical choices, public understanding projects, and serious enforcement (Rasoolimanesh et al., 2023).

6.4. Sustainable Agriculture and Building Energy Efficiency Policies

Plans advertising sustainable farming, such as aids for natural farming or agroecological techniques, have revealed guarantees in boosting ecological stewardship and food system durability (Holden et al., 2017). The Common Agricultural Plan[10] (CAP) of the European Union, including agri-environmental actions, works as an effective version, cultivating dirt wellness and biodiversity and lowering dependence on dangerous chemicals. Rigid power performance criteria in structure construction, exhibited by the Golden State's Title 24 criteria, have confirmed reliability in decreasing power intake and carbon exhausts (Guarini et al., 2022; Shafik, 2023). These plans drive developments in building methods, reduce power expenses for customers, and add to total sustainability objectives. The success of Title 24 emphasizes the capacity for policy-driven improvements in structure power effectiveness (Gupta & Vegelin, 2016).

6.5. Circular Economy Legislation and Sustainability Reporting Requirements

Regulations advertising a round economic climate, stressing recycling, waste decrease, and item life expansion, have been critical in improving usage patterns. The Extended Producer Responsibility (EPR) structure in the European Union works as an archetype, promoting accountable item layout and source performance (Al-Jayyousi et al., 2022; Shafik, 2024a). Such plans add to sustainable techniques, decrease ecological effects, and urge an extra round and accountable strategy to source usage. Obligatory company sustainability coverage demands engaging businesses to divulge ecological and social influences and boost openness and responsibility (Shi et al., 2019). The Global Reporting Initiative[11] (GRI) requirements, for instance, show exactly how standard coverage can drive favorable ecological and social effects. These demands motivate companies to embrace sustainable techniques, interact with their payments efficiently, and foster stakeholder count and involvement (Shafik, 2024b).

7. FUTURE RESEARCH DIRECTIONS, LESSONS LEARNED, AND THE CONCLUSION

As we draw the chapter conclusion, some future research directions are illustrated, and lessons from the chapter and conclusion are presented within this section.

7.1. Future Research Directions

By focusing on a research study in these instructions, scholars and policymakers can add to a much deeper understanding of the intricacies bordering sustainable growth, making it possible for the style of even more reliable approaches and plans for a durable and fair future.

7.1.1. Integrated Assessment Models for Sustainable Development

The advancement of highly sophisticated Integrated Assessment Models[12] (IAMs) that consider the elaborate partnership that exists between ecological, social, and financial problems should be the key emphasis of research in the future (Agbedahin, 2019). To supply a complete understanding of the harmonies and compromises associated with sustainable growth efforts, these versions must provide the needed info. The consolidation of vibrant and multidimensional variables will certainly enhance the precision of estimates, which will certainly make it possible for policymakers to make enlightened choices that strike an equilibrium between the conservation of the atmosphere, the promotion of social justice, and the growth of the economic climate (Subramaniam et al., 2023; Shafik, 2024b).

7.1.2. Technological Innovation and Sustainable Solutions

It is recommended that research activities center on the confluence of technology and sustainable development, with a particular emphasis on the development and implementation of innovative solutions (Sever & Tok, 2023). This category encompasses the most recent advancements in some fields, including but not limited to renewable energy, circular economy technology, sustainable agriculture approaches, and environmentally friendly materials (Degai & Petrov, 2021; Shafik, 2024c). Conducting research into the impacts that evolving technologies, such as biotechnology and artificial intelligence, have on society and the environment will be crucial for the goal of directing the creation of a sustainable future. This research will be necessary to guide the development of a sustainable future (Shafik, 2024d).

7.1.3. Social and Behavioral Dimensions of Sustainability

In the future, research ought to put a higher focus on getting a much deeper understanding of the social and behavioral facets that influence sustainable administration methods. The examination of customer actions, the expedition of social perspectives towards sustainability, and the examination of the duty that education and learning play in the development of ecologically mindful individuals are all covered in this (Bali Swain & Yang-Wallentin, 2020). The establishment of plans and programs that reverberate with a variety of neighborhoods will certainly be implemented because of the exam of efficient interaction methods and behavior treatments. This will certainly aid in sustaining and fostering a sustainable way of living (Shafik, 2024e).

7.1.4. Global Governance and Policy Integration

Within the context of sustainable development, research ought to concentrate on enhancing global governance frameworks to solve difficulties that are not limited by national boundaries. The refinement of existing policies and the development of new initiatives will be guided by the findings of an investigation of the success of international agreements, such as the Paris Agreement[13] and the SDGs established by the United Nations (Mensah, 2019). A greater emphasis must be placed on the enhancement of policy coherence across all sectors and levels of governance to develop a more integrated and efficient approach to sustainability on a global scale.

7.1.5. Resilience and Adaptation Strategies in the Face of Climate Change

The immediate demand for resistant approaches and flexible actions to handle the results of environmental adjustment on sustainable growth ought to be the emphasis of research study that will certainly be performed in the future (Castro & Lopes, 2022; Shafik & kalinaki, 2023). The research study of the climate-resilient framework, community-based adjustment programs, and the consolidation of environmental factors to consider right into a selection of industries are all consisted of in this. It will certainly be important to establish positive approaches to construct strength to alleviate the unfavorable impacts of environmental adjustment and ensure the sustainability of neighborhoods throughout the globe (Fonseca et al., 2020). This will certainly be completed by obtaining an understanding of the susceptibility that is characteristic of different places. Moreover, the examination of the duty that nature-based remedies and ecological community solutions play in environment adjustment techniques could offer helpful understandings that can be made use of in the building and construction of cultures that are both resistant and sustainable (Shafik & Azriur, 2024; Sampedro, 2021).

7.2. Lessons Learned From the Chapter

The lessons gained from the phase on sustainable development incorporate crucial understandings that can assist both academic understanding and useful applications.

- Sustainable growth demands an alternative strategy that identifies the inter-connectedness of ecological preservation, social equity, and financial success. Plans and efforts must focus on the vibrant connections between these elements to attain long-term and well-balanced results.
- From renewable resource options to round economic situation techniques, welcoming technical innovations is essential for reducing ecological influences and advertising sustainable techniques throughout varied markets.
- The requirement for advanced IAMs emerges, stressing the significance of detailed designs that represent the diverse measurements of sustainable advancement. IAMs use a device for policymakers to analyze the elaborate interaction of ecological, social, and financial variables in decision-making.
- Attaining sustainable advancement objectives calls for efficient global participation, plan comprehensibility, and the constant improvement of administration structures to deal with facility, interconnected difficulties.
- The relevance of including varied stakeholders, consisting of federal governments, services, neighborhoods, and non-governmental companies, to guarantee that techniques are comprehensive, depictive, and straightened with common objectives.
- Sustainable advance techniques need to integrate steps to resolve the effects of environmental adjustment, stressing the value of climate-resilient facilities, community-based adjustment, and nature-based services.

7.3. Conclusion

The expedition of sustainable growth in this phase lights up the elaborate equilibrium needed amongst ecological, social, and financial factors to consider. The insight found highlights the essential duty of advancement and innovation in driving sustainability throughout varied markets. IAMs have become important devices for policymakers, highlighting the demand for detailed structures that represent the diverse measurements of sustainable advancement. Difficulties in international administration and plan combination ask for ongoing improvement and partnership. The phase stresses the relevance of behavior and social measurements, advising a social change in the direction of sustainability via education, learning, and stakeholder interaction. As environment modification presents powerful difficulties, the essentials for flexibility and durability become clear. The continual examination and model of plans are crucial for browsing the vibrant landscape of sustainable advancement, leading us in the direction of a future where ecological stewardship, social equity, and financial success sympathetically exist together.

REFERENCES

Achim, M. V., Văidean, V. L., Sabau, A. I., & Safta, I. L. (2023). The impact of the quality of corporate governance on sustainable development: An analysis based on development level. *Economic Research-Ekonomska Istrazivanja*, 36(1). Advance online publication. 10.1080/1331677X.2022.2080745

Agbedahin, A. V. (2019). Sustainable development, Education for Sustainable Development, and the 2030 Agenda for Sustainable Development: Emergence, efficacy, eminence, and future. *Sustainable Development (Bradford)*, 27(4), 669–680. Advance online publication. 10.1002/sd.1931

Al-Jayyousi, O., Tok, E., Saniff, S. M., Wan Hasan, W. N., Janahi, N. A., & Yesuf, A. J. (2022). Re-Thinking Sustainable Development within Islamic Worldviews: A Systematic Literature Review. *Sustainability (Basel)*, 14(12), 7300. Advance online publication. 10.3390/su14127300

Apostu, S. A., & Gigauri, I. (2023). Sustainable development and entrepreneurship in emerging countries: Are sustainable development and entrepreneurship reciprocally reinforcing? *Journal of Entrepreneurship. Management and Innovation*, 19(1), 41–77. Advance online publication. 10.7341/20231912

Azrour, M., Dargaoui, S., Mabrouki, J., Guezzaz, A., Benkirane, S., Shafik, W., & Ahmad, S. (2024). A Survey of Machine and Deep Learning Applications in the Assessment of Water Quality. In *Technical and Technological Solutions Towards a Sustainable Society and Circular Economy* (pp. 471–483). Springer Nature Switzerland. 10.1007/978-3-031-56292-1_38

Bali Swain, R., & Yang-Wallentin, F. (2020). Achieving sustainable development goals: Predicaments and strategies. *International Journal of Sustainable Development and World Ecology*, 27(2), 96–106. Advance online publication. 10.1080/13504509.2019.1692316

Bishoge, O. K., Zhang, L., & Mushi, W. G. (2019). The Potential Renewable Energy for Sustainable Development in Tanzania: A Review. In *Clean Technologies* (Vol. 1, Issue 1). https://doi.org/10.3390/cleantechnol1010006

Bogers, M., Biermann, F., Kalfagianni, A., Kim, R. E., Treep, J., & de Vos, M. G. (2022). The impact of the Sustainable Development Goals on a network of 276 international organizations. *Global Environmental Change*, 76, 102567. Advance online publication. 10.1016/j.gloenvcha.2022.102567

Bolton, M. (2021). Public sector understanding of sustainable development and the sustainable development goals: A case study of Victoria, Australia. *Current Research in Environmental Sustainability*, 3, 100056. Advance online publication. 10.1016/j.crsust.2021.100056

Buturlina, O., Dovhal, S., Hryhorov, H., Lysokolenko, T., & Palahuta, V. (2021). Stem education in Ukraine in the context of sustainable development. *European Journal of Sustainable Development*, 10(1), 323. Advance online publication. 10.14207/ejsd.2021.v10n1p323

Castro, C., & Lopes, C. (2022). Digital Government and Sustainable Development. *Journal of the Knowledge Economy*, 13(2), 880–903. Advance online publication. 10.1007/s13132-021-00749-2

Chauhan, C., Kaur, P., Arrawatia, R., Ractham, P., & Dhir, A. (2022). Supply chain collaboration and sustainable development goals (SDGs). Teamwork makes achieving SDGs dream work. *Journal of Business Research*, 147, 290–307. Advance online publication. 10.1016/j.jbusres.2022.03.044

Clark, W. C., Van Kerkhoff, L., Lebel, L., & Gallopin, G. C. (2016). Crafting usable knowledge for sustainable development. In *Proceedings of the National Academy of Sciences of the United States of America* (Vol. 113, Issue 17). 10.1073/pnas.1601266113

Danilov, Y. A. (2022). Coalitions for Sustainable Finance and Sustainable Development. *Herald of the Russian Academy of Sciences*, 92(S2), S91–S99. Advance online publication. 10.1134/S1019331622080032

Degai, T. S., & Petrov, A. N. (2021). Rethinking Arctic sustainable development agenda through indigenizing UN sustainable development goals. *International Journal of Sustainable Development and World Ecology*, 28(6), 518–523. Advance online publication. 10.1080/13504509.2020.1868608

Dhaoui, I. (2022). E-Government for Sustainable Development: Evidence from MENA Countries. *Journal of the Knowledge Economy*, 13(3), 2070–2099. Advance online publication. 10.1007/s13132-021-00791-0

Duvnjak, B., & Kohont, A. (2021). The role of sustainable hrm in sustainable development. *Sustainability (Basel)*, 13(19), 10668. Advance online publication. 10.3390/su131910668

Fei, W., Opoku, A., Agyekum, K., Oppon, J. A., Ahmed, V., Chen, C., & Lok, K. L. (2021). The critical role of the construction industry in achieving the sustainable development goals (Sdgs): Delivering projects for the common good. *Sustainability (Basel)*, 13(16), 9112. Advance online publication. 10.3390/su13169112

Ferguson, T., Roofe, C., & Cook, L. D. (2021). Teachers' perspectives on sustainable development: The implications for education for sustainable development. *Environmental Education Research*, 27(9), 1–17. Advance online publication. 10.1080/13504622.2021.1921113

Fonseca, L. M., Domingues, J. P., & Dima, A. M. (2020). Mapping the sustainable development goals relationships. *Sustainability (Basel)*, 12(8), 3359. Advance online publication. 10.3390/su12083359

Fu, B., Meadows, M. E., & Zhao, W. (2022). Geography in the Anthropocene: Transforming our world for sustainable development. In *Geography and Sustainability* (Vol. 3, Issue 1). 10.1016/j.geosus.2021.12.004

Ghobakhloo, M., Iranmanesh, M., Mubarak, M. F., Mubarik, M., Rejeb, A., & Nilashi, M. (2022). Identifying industry 5.0 contributions to sustainable development: A strategy roadmap for delivering sustainability values. *Sustainable Production and Consumption*, 33, 716–737. Advance online publication. 10.1016/j.spc.2022.08.003

Giangrande, N., White, R. M., East, M., Jackson, R., Clarke, T., Coste, M. S., & Penha-Lopes, G. (2019). A competency framework to assess and activate education for sustainable development: Addressing the UN sustainable development goals 4.7 challenge. *Sustainability (Basel)*, 11(10), 2832. Advance online publication. 10.3390/su11102832

Glavič, P. (2020). Identifying key issues of education for sustainable development. *Sustainability (Basel)*, 12(16), 6500. Advance online publication. 10.3390/su12166500

Guarini, E., Mori, E., & Zuffada, E. (2022). Localizing the Sustainable Development Goals: A managerial perspective. *Journal of Public Budgeting, Accounting & Financial Management*, 34(5), 583–601. Advance online publication. 10.1108/JPBAFM-02-2021-0031

Gupta, J., & Vegelin, C. (2016). Sustainable development goals and inclusive development. *International Environmental Agreement: Politics, Law and Economics*, 16(3), 433–448. Advance online publication. 10.1007/s10784-016-9323-z

Hák, T., Janoušková, S., & Moldan, B. (2016). Sustainable Development Goals: A need for relevant indicators. *Ecological Indicators*, 60, 565–573. Advance online publication. 10.1016/j.ecolind.2015.08.003

Ho, S. J., Hsu, Y. S., Lai, C. H., Chen, F. H., & Yang, M. H. (2022). Applying Game-Based Experiential Learning to Comprehensive Sustainable Development-Based Education. *Sustainability (Basel)*, 14(3), 1172. Advance online publication. 10.3390/su14031172

Holden, E., Linnerud, K., & Banister, D. (2017). The Imperatives of Sustainable Development. *Sustainable Development (Bradford)*, 25(3), 213–226. Advance online publication. 10.1002/sd.1647

Hummels, H., & Argyrou, A. (2021). Planetary demands: Redefining sustainable development and sustainable entrepreneurship. *Journal of Cleaner Production*, 278, 123804. Advance online publication. 10.1016/j.jclepro.2020.123804

Jilcha, K., & Kitaw, D. (2017). Industrial occupational safety and health innovation for sustainable development. *Engineering Science and Technology, an International Journal, 20*(1). 10.1016/j.jestch.2016.10.011

Khan, I. S., Ahmad, M. O., & Majava, J. (2021). Industry 4.0 and sustainable development: A systematic mapping of triple bottom line, Circular Economy and Sustainable Business Models perspectives. In *Journal of Cleaner Production* (Vol. 297). 10.1016/j.jclepro.2021.126655

Khan, I. S., Ahmad, M. O., & Majava, J. (2023). Industry 4.0 innovations and their implications: An evaluation from sustainable development perspective. *Journal of Cleaner Production*, 405, 137006. Advance online publication. 10.1016/j.jclepro.2023.137006

Kopnina, H. (2020). Education for the future? Critical evaluation of education for sustainable development goals. *The Journal of Environmental Education*, 51(4), 280–291. Advance online publication. 10.1080/00958964.2019.1710444

Kota, H. B., Singh, G., Mir, M., Smark, C., & Kumar, B. (2021). Sustainable development goals and businesses. *Australasian Accounting, Business and Finance Journal, 15*(5 Special Issue). 10.14453/aabfj.v15i5.1

Leal Filho, W., Azeiteiro, U., Alves, F., Pace, P., Mifsud, M., Brandli, L., Caeiro, S. S., & Disterheft, A. (2018). Reinvigorating the sustainable development research agenda: The role of the sustainable development goals (SDG). *International Journal of Sustainable Development and World Ecology*, 25(2), 131–142. Advance online publication. 10.1080/13504509.2017.1342103

Leal Filho, W., Yang, P., Eustachio, J. H. P. P., Azul, A. M., Gellers, J. C., Gielczyk, A., Dinis, M. A. P., & Kozlova, V. (2023). Deploying digitalisation and artificial intelligence in sustainable development research. *Environment, Development and Sustainability*, 25(6), 4957–4988. Advance online publication. 10.1007/s10668-022-02252-335313685

Lee, J. W. (2020). Green finance and sustainable development goals: The case of China. *Journal of Asian Finance. Economics and Business*, 7(7), 577–586. Advance online publication. 10.13106/jafeb.2020.vol7.no7.577

Liengpunsakul, S. (2021). Artificial Intelligence and Sustainable Development in China. *Chinese Economy*, 54(4), 235–248. Advance online publication. 10.1080/10971475.2020.1857062

Lim, C. K., Haufiku, M. S., Tan, K. L., Farid Ahmed, M., & Ng, T. F. (2022). Systematic Review of Education Sustainable Development in Higher Education Institutions. *Sustainability (Basel)*, 14(20), 13241. Advance online publication. 10.3390/su142013241

Lim, M. M. L., Søgaard Jørgensen, P., & Wyborn, C. A. (2018). Reframing the sustainable development goals to achieve sustainable development in the anthropocene—A systems approach. *Ecology and Society*, 23(3), art22. Advance online publication. 10.5751/ES-10182-230322

Lyaskovskaya, E., & Khudyakova, T. (2021). Sharing economy: For or against sustainable development. *Sustainability (Basel)*, 13(19), 11056. Advance online publication. 10.3390/su131911056

Maka, A. O. M., & Alabid, J. M. (2022). Solar energy technology and its roles in sustainable development. *Clean Energy*, 6(3), 476–483. Advance online publication. 10.1093/ce/zkac023

Mensah, J. (2019). Sustainable development: Meaning, history, principles, pillars, and implications for human action: Literature review. *Cogent Social Sciences*, 5(1), 1653531. Advance online publication. 10.1080/23311886.2019.1653531

Mohamad Taghvaee, V., Assari Arani, A., Nodehi, M., Khodaparast Shirazi, J., Agheli, L., Neshat Ghojogh, H. M., Salehnia, N., Mirzaee, A., Taheri, S., Mohammadi Saber, R., Faramarzi, H., Alvandi, R., & Ahmadi Rahbarian, H. (2023). Sustainable development goals: Transportation, health and public policy. *Review of Economics and Political Science*, 8(2), 134–161. Advance online publication. 10.1108/REPS-12-2019-0168

Morton, S., Pencheon, D., & Squires, N. (2017). Sustainable Development Goals (SDGs), and their implementation. In *British Medical Bulletin* (Vol. 124, Issue 1). 10.1093/bmb/ldx031

Mukhuty, S., Upadhyay, A., & Rothwell, H. (2022). Strategic sustainable development of Industry 4.0 through the lens of social responsibility: The role of human resource practices. *Business Strategy and the Environment*, 31(5), 2068–2081. Advance online publication. 10.1002/bse.3008

Niemets, K., Kravchenko, K., Kandyba, Y., Kobylin, P., & Morar, C. (2021). World cities in terms of the sustainable development concept. In *Geography and Sustainability* (Vol. 2, Issue 4). 10.1016/j.geosus.2021.12.003

Nousheen, A., Yousuf Zai, S. A., Waseem, M., & Khan, S. A. (2020). Education for sustainable development (ESD): Effects of sustainability education on pre-service teachers' attitude towards sustainable development (SD). *Journal of Cleaner Production*, 250, 119537. Advance online publication. 10.1016/j.jclepro.2019.119537

Nunkoo, R., Sharma, A., Rana, N. P., Dwivedi, Y. K., & Sunnassee, V. A. (2023). Advancing sustainable development goals through interdisciplinarity in sustainable tourism research. *Journal of Sustainable Tourism*, 31(3), 735–759. Advance online publication. 10.1080/09669582.2021.2004416

Ogryzek, M. (2023). The Sustainable Development Paradigm. *Geomatics and Environmental Engineering*, 17(1), 5–18. Advance online publication. 10.7494/geom.2023.17.1.5

Pan, X., Shao, T., Zheng, X., Zhang, Y., Ma, X., & Zhang, Q. (2023). Energy and sustainable development nexus: A review. In *Energy Strategy Reviews* (Vol. 47). https://doi.org/10.1016/j.esr.2023.101078

Patel, V., Pauli, N., Biggs, E., Barbour, L., & Boruff, B. (2021). Why bees are critical for achieving sustainable development. *Ambio*, 50(1), 49–59. Advance online publication. 10.1007/s13280-020-01333-932314266

Prieto-Jiménez, E., López-Catalán, L., López-Catalán, B., & Domínguez-Fernández, G. (2021). Sustainable development goals and education: A bibliometric mapping analysis. *Sustainability (Basel)*, 13(4), 2126. Advance online publication. 10.3390/su13042126

Rahma, H., Fauzi, A., Juanda, B., & Widjojanto, B. (2019). Development of a composite measure of regional sustainable development in Indonesia. *Sustainability (Basel)*, 11(20), 5861. Advance online publication. 10.3390/su11205861

Rasoolimanesh, S. M., Ramakrishna, S., Hall, C. M., Esfandiar, K., & Seyfi, S. (2023). A systematic scoping review of sustainable tourism indicators in relation to the sustainable development goals. *Journal of Sustainable Tourism*, 31(7), 1497–1517. Advance online publication. 10.1080/09669582.2020.1775621

Ruggerio, C. A. (2021). Sustainability and sustainable development: A review of principles and definitions. In *Science of the Total Environment* (Vol. 786). 10.1016/j.scitotenv.2021.147481

Sampedro, R. (2021). The Sustainable Development Goals (SDG). *Carreteras*, 4(232), 38–46. Advance online publication. 10.1201/9781003080220-8

Scheyvens, R., Carr, A., Movono, A., Hughes, E., Higgins-Desbiolles, F., & Mika, J. P. (2021). Indigenous tourism and the sustainable development goals. *Annals of Tourism Research*, 90, 103260. Advance online publication. 10.1016/j.annals.2021.103260

Sever, S. D., & Tok, M. E. (2023). Education for Sustainable Development in Qatar. In *Gulf Studies* (Vol. 9). 10.1007/978-981-19-7398-7_17

Shafik, W. (2023). IoT-Based Energy Harvesting and Future Research Trends in Wireless Sensor Networks. *Handbook of Research on Network-Enabled IoT Applications for Smart City Services,* 282-306. 10.4018/979-8-3693-0744-1.ch016

Shafik, W. (2024a). Artificial Intelligence Models to Prevent Forest Fires. In *AI and IoT for Proactive Disaster Management* (pp. 78–106). IGI Global. 10.4018/979-8-3693-3896-4.ch005

Shafik, W. (2024b). Industry 4.0 Technologies' Opportunities and Challenges for Realising Net-Zero Economy. *Net Zero Economy, Corporate Social Responsibility and Sustainable Value Creation: Exploring Strategies, Drivers, and Challenges,* 19-41. 10.1007/978-3-031-55779-8_2

Shafik, W. (2024c). Industry Revolution 4.0 and Beyond: Abilities and Perils for Sustainable Zero Net Economy Development. In *Powering Industry 5.0 and Sustainable Development Through Innovation* (pp. 292-316). IGI Global. 10.4018/979-8-3693-3550-5.ch020

Shafik, W. (2024d). Shaping the Next Generation Smart City Ecosystem: An Investigation on the Requirements, Applications, Architecture, Security and Privacy, and Open Research Questions. In Smart Cities: Innovations, Challenges and Future Perspectives (pp. 3-52). Cham: Springer Nature Switzerland. 10.1007/978-3-031-59846-3_1

Shafik, W. (2024e). Toward a More Ethical Future of Artificial Intelligence and Data Science. In *The Ethical Frontier of AI and Data Analysis* (pp. 362–388). IGI Global. 10.4018/979-8-3693-2964-1.ch022

Shafik, W., & Azrour, M. (2024). Building a Greener World: Harnessing the Power of IoT and Smart Devices for Sustainable Environment. In Mabrouki, J., & Mourade, A. (Eds.), *Technical and Technological Solutions Towards a Sustainable Society and Circular Economy. World Sustainability Series.* Springer, 10.1007/978-3-031-56292-1_3

Shafik, W., & Kalinaki, K. (2023). Smart City Ecosystem: An Exploration of Requirements, Architecture, Applications, Security, and Emerging Motivations. In *Handbook of Research on Network-Enabled IoT Applications for Smart City Services* (pp. 75-98). IGI Global. 10.4018/979-8-3693-0744-1.ch005

Sharpley, R. (2020). Tourism, sustainable development and the theoretical divide: 20 years on. *Journal of Sustainable Tourism*, 28(11), 1932–1946. Advance online publication. 10.1080/09669582.2020.1779732

Shi, L., Han, L., Yang, F., & Gao, L. (2019). The Evolution of Sustainable Development Theory: Types, Goals, and Research Prospects. *Sustainability (Basel)*, 11(24), 7158. Advance online publication. 10.3390/su11247158

Shulla, K., Filho, W. L., Lardjane, S., Sommer, J. H., & Borgemeister, C. (2020). Sustainable development education in the context of the 2030 Agenda for sustainable development. *International Journal of Sustainable Development and World Ecology*, 27(5), 458–468. Advance online publication. 10.1080/13504509.2020.1721378

Shulla, K., Voigt, B. F., Cibian, S., Scandone, G., Martinez, E., Nelkovski, F., & Salehi, P. (2021). Effects of COVID-19 on the Sustainable Development Goals (SDGs). *Discover Sustainability*, 2(1), 15. Advance online publication. 10.1007/s43621-021-00026-x35425922

Sinakou, E., Boeve-de Pauw, J., Goossens, M., & Van Petegem, P. (2018). Academics in the field of Education for Sustainable Development: Their conceptions of sustainable development. *Journal of Cleaner Production*, 184, 321–332. Advance online publication. 10.1016/j.jclepro.2018.02.279

Spaiser, V., Ranganathan, S., Swain, R. B., & Sumpter, D. J. T. (2017). The sustainable development oxymoron: Quantifying and modelling the incompatibility of sustainable development goals. *International Journal of Sustainable Development and World Ecology*, 24(6), 457–470. Advance online publication. 10.1080/13504509.2016.1235624

Stawicka, E. (2021). Sustainable development in the digital age of entrepreneurship. *Sustainability (Basel)*, 13(8), 4429. Advance online publication. 10.3390/su13084429

Subramaniam, N., Akbar, S., Situ, H., Ji, S., & Parikh, N. (2023). Sustainable development goal reporting: Contrasting effects of institutional and organisational factors. *Journal of Cleaner Production*, 411, 137339. Advance online publication. 10.1016/j.jclepro.2023.137339

van Vuuren, D. P., Zimm, C., Busch, S., Kriegler, E., Leininger, J., Messner, D., Nakicenovic, N., Rockstrom, J., Riahi, K., Sperling, F., Bosetti, V., Cornell, S., Gaffney, O., Lucas, P. L., Popp, A., Ruhe, C., von Schiller, A., Schmidt, J. O., & Soergel, B. (2022). Defining a sustainable development target space for 2030 and 2050. In *One Earth* (Vol. 5, Issue 2). 10.1016/j.oneear.2022.01.003

van Zanten, J. A., & van Tulder, R. (2021). Improving companies' impacts on sustainable development: A nexus approach to the SDGS. *Business Strategy and the Environment*, 30(8), 3703–3720. Advance online publication. 10.1002/bse.2835

Visseren-Hamakers, I. J. (2020). The 18th Sustainable Development Goal. In *Earth System Governance* (Vol. 3). 10.1016/j.esg.2020.100047

Weiland, S., Hickmann, T., Lederer, M., Marquardt, J., & Schwindenhammer, S. (2021). The 2030 agenda for sustainable development: Transformative change through the sustainable development goals? In *Politics and Governance* (Vol. 9, Issue 1). 10.17645/pag.v9i1.4191

Xu, L., Ao, C., Liu, B., & Cai, Z. (2023). Ecotourism and sustainable development: a scientometric review of global research trends. In *Environment, Development and Sustainability* (Vol. 25, Issue 4). 10.1007/s10668-022-02190-0

Zakari, A., Khan, I., Tan, D., Alvarado, R., & Dagar, V. (2022). Energy efficiency and sustainable development goals (SDGs). *Energy*, 239, 122365. Advance online publication. 10.1016/j.energy.2021.122365

Zwolińska, K., Lorenc, S., & Pomykała, R. (2022). Sustainable Development in Education from Students' Perspective—Implementation of Sustainable Development in Curricula. *Sustainability (Basel)*, 14(6), 3398. Advance online publication. 10.3390/su14063398

ENDNOTES

[1] https://sdgs.un.org/goals
[2] https://en.wikipedia.org/wiki/Renewable_resource
[3] https://en.wikipedia.org/wiki/Corporate_social_responsibility
[4] https://www.bcorporation.net/en-us/certification/

5   https://www.ibm.com/topics/triple-bottom-line

6   https://c2ccertified.org/the-standard

7   https://popp.undp.org/taxonomy/term/6216

8   https://www.ofgem.gov.uk/environmental-and-social-schemes/feed-tariffs-fit

9   https://climate.ec.europa.eu/eu-action/eu-emissions-trading-system-eu-ets_en

10   https://agriculture.ec.europa.eu/common-agricultural-policy/cap-overview/cap-glance_en

11   https://www.globalreporting.org/

12   https://www.iamconsortium.org/what-are-iams/

13   https://unfccc.int/process-and-meetings/the-paris-agreement

Chapter 2
The Relevance of Sustainability in the 21st Century Is Paramount

Mohamad Knio

Lebanese International University, Lebanon

ABSTRACT

The chapter emphasizes the vital role of sustainability in the global landscape and businesses' role in driving sustainable practices. It advocates for a holistic approach, considering environmental, social, and governance factors, and highlights the benefits of transitioning to circular economies for a more environmentally friendly and economically viable future. Through case studies and insights, the chapter provides a comprehensive overview of sustainability's significance and actionable steps for organizations to embrace sustainable practices.

In the 21st century world, the significance of sustainability, sustainable development and all activities emanating around this concept is of principal importance. As such, this chapter discusses succinctly the *contextual framework* of sustainable development (briefly introduced in Section 1.1), while discussing, through the *critical review of the existing literature* the *main objective* of this research which is to both understand and explain the exact role of sustainability in a 21st century world. According to many experts the realm of sustainability (discussed in Section 1.2) discusses the *interaction of economics, environment and health realms* (Grynspan, 2012; Farnham, 2015; Al Sawi, 2018). These interplays discussed in various literature review researches need to be explored further in order to fully comprehend this relationship.

Geddes (1915) highlights the concept of *"thinking globally and acting locally"*. This is only to say that sustainability was not a new a concept, if a century ago, already focused and thought of these actions that would prove essential to preserving

DOI: 10.4018/979-8-3693-5405-6.ch002

Copyright © 2024, IGI Global. Copying or distributing in print or electronic forms without written permission of IGI Global is prohibited.

ressources for future generations uses. While in the late 1990s, the *triple bottom line concept* (Elkington, 1999) is explored (Section 1.3), the relationship that this plays in sustainable development an in the development of smart cities need to be discussed as well. Pradhan et al., (2017) and Mathers & Deonandan (2018) present an important point linked with the *relationship between sustainability, governance, society and businesses, and their interactions* (Section 1.4). In brief, for sustainability to be reached, exerts concur that terrorism, corruption, the lack of health among other impediments need to be overcome before considering attaining these sustainable development goals (Pradhan et al., 2017; Mathers & Deonandan, 2018). These points will be also objectively discussed in other sections as well.

The *impacts of governance and sustainability* are also explored in the current chapter (Section 1.5) and experts present evidence showing the link of these variables together, as well as their interplays (Pradhan et al., 2017; Mathers & Deonandan, 2018). While governance plays a role, the social responsibility also presents important contributions (Abdallah & Khattib, 2020). CSR also shows an important impact, and recent researches demonstrate clear *relationships between CSR and sustainability* (Wu, & Jin, 2022) as this chapter also presents (Section 1.6). The following two points that the chapter presents (Sections 1.7 and 1.8) shows the r*elationships between sustainable development and overall company benefits*, followed by several *examples of "successful enterprises" through explorative studies*.

The last part of this chapter (Section 1.9) is dedicated to presenting several relevant *case studies*, through discussing Nike, BMW, Nestlé, LG, IKEA, ING, among others, where the links between sustainability and governance proved to be successful (Ex. Khoury, 2022a).

1. INTRODUCTION TO SUSTAINABLE PRACTICES:

In today's global economic, political, and business context, sustainability is now recognized as a critical phrase for many decision makers throughout the world. A lot of companies have a responsibility to understand issues related to sustainability. However, this is owing to greater national and worldwide awareness, as well as the norms and regulations. However, many people's impressions of sustainability remain unclear. There are a number of ways to define sustainability, but among the most widely accepted is that offered by the United Nations. And it is the meaning of "*Sustainability meets the needs of the present without compromising the ability of future generations to meet their own needs*" (see: the 1987 Brundtland Report). There are numerous definitions for sustainability.

Sustainability is defined by Geddes (1915) as the actions that are done today with the current usage of resources that won't jeopardize the future uses of the same resources our descendants who will also need to use them. By this way, today's uses of our ressosurces should not compromise the uses of these resources by future generations who will also rely on them. This definition responds to the purpose of this research that needs to present the importance of the sustainable use of resources today for the possibility of future generations to also benefit from the. Khoury (2022a) discussed how through tourism education this could be beneficial, while s decade earlier Mr. Rebecca Grynspan presented in the UN headquarters in New York city (Grynspan, 2012), the 21st century definitions and societal expectations related to sustainability. Both researchers were presented inasmuch as sustainable tourism and education, several tangential variables that could be explored for a future study on sustainability and governance.

Yet, they all agree on one idea. And to do so, we must "avoid the depletion of our resources, in order to maintain a balanced ecosystem and preserve natural capital" (see: Bansard, & Schröder 2021). When considering sustainability, we must consider the interdependence of three elements. Environment, society, and the economy (cf. Asgari, & Reza, 2021). When we think of the environment, we consider the oxygen that we breathe, the water we conume, the soil in which we produce the food we eat, and the sources of energy we use (Craig, et al., 2010). When we think about society, we consider the interaction that occurs when people and groups decide in cities, towns, and villages (see: Youness, 2017). When we think about the economy, we are actually thinking about how to distribute scarce resources efficiently in response to our infinite ones (Farnhan, 2015). When we think about the economy, we know that there are limited resources, but the overarching economic goal is to generate profit, financial returns, and some type of value creation for the firm (see: Asgari, Reza, 2021; Joensuu, et al., 2020; Asgari, & Reza, 2021; Hailemariam, & Erdiaw-Kwasie, 2023; Heshmati, & Rashidghalam, 2021; Tan et al., 2023; Jha et al., 2024; Langergaard, & Krøjer. 2024). To comprehend sustainability, we must ask ourselves many questions. One refers to determining if we live in an unsustainable environment, and if so, what could the outcomes be (see: Youness, 2017). Are we living in an unsustainable world? What is the effect on our natural capital and the Earth's assets? Craig et al. (2010) discuss the importance of preserving natural resources, a point also explored by Grynspan (2012).

So, in order to address this or these questions, I'd want to discuss three things with you. For starters, it appears that natural resources are being overexploited in tandem with economic and demographic expansion. Second, it appears that there is some form of market failure. Market failure is an economic phrase because does not imply that nothing positive has occurred; rather, it suggests that the best possible results were not obtained. The final price of a product or service frequently includes private expenditures such as workers, supplies, direct expenses, and costs.

The third argument is that we see an acceleration in resource depletion, waste creation, and environmental contamination. And this might be related to a shorter product life cycle. Planned obsolescence is a word, however it might also be attributed to technical advancements and a changing lifestyle since the industrial revolution. So, to summarize, it appears that there is environmental devastation and deterioration. We can see waste, pollution, and the deterioration of the planet's resources. This is occurring at an alarming rate, and it is affecting the capital that we have (Craig et al., 2010).

Unsustainable waste collection systems can often and always play negative roles in sustainability and Tourism, especially in countries highly dependent on tourism, especially if the stakeholders were improperly educated about valorizing their touristic, or any ressource contributing to sustainable development if properly managed (Khoury, 2022a). Taking Naples in Italy, and Tripoli, Jbeil, Beirut, Saida, Tyre and other major touristic sites in Lebanon facing improper waste crises, touristic activities will be affected (see: Khoury, 2022a). Improper waste storage, and processing and disposal will ultimately lead to unsustainable or inequitable development, while major cultural and natural ressosures do offer to peoples a high sense of place. These points are important in terms of education and valorisation (Knio, 2020b; Khoury, 2022a).

2. NAVIGATING SUSTAINABILITY: UNDERSTANDING THE INTERPLAY OF ECONOMICS, ENVIRONMENT, AND HEALTH

Now I'd like to examine the topic of natural wealth and economics as previously said, sustainability and economics are inextricably linked. Economics is the study of how to best allocate of finite resources in response to our unlimited supply. Economics understands the scarcity of resources. In economics, we might discuss natural world, including materials, air, soil, water, and energy. Labor is another resource that is discussed in economics, along with technology and capital (see: Attaran, 2020). It is critical to recognize that economic actions over decades have exerted a significant influence on our sustainable resources. This idea most likely depicts an interconnectedness between economic decisions made in towns and cities, where economic decisions lead to production and consumption. Over time, production has polluted the air. Air pollution has caused climate change, which we describe in terms of its effects on our trees. What is happening with our forests? We ponder about soil erosion, wildlife habitats. We think about the species that live on our land, woods, and oceans (see: Craig et al., 2010). We ask about water contamination, all of the things I've described above are related to our environment. Overconsumption and overproduction have put pressure on our natural capital, leading many analysts, commentators, academics, and scientists to argue that in order to deal with natural capital degradation, the impact on our natural resources, as well as the effect on the environment, it is necessary to recognize how we deal with the economic decision of overconsumption and overproduction, thus, in order to know sustainability, it is important to examine the Environmental sustainability. And this refers to natural capital, which comprises, as previously said, air, water, soil, and energy. Sustainability in society as it relates to human interactions, Cities, household, wealth, poverty, education, health, Sustainability in economics, consumption, production, efficiency, and profitability. All of the connections described above may be reduced to three Ps, People, planet, and profit. When discussing the way, we manage sustainability in organizations, economies, cities, towns, and villages, as well as among individuals, we must consider several factors. To comprehend natural capital, we must first define the concerns that are considered while defining it. Natural capital refers to the quantity of resources available on Earth, including geology. Again, air, water, soil, and live beings that are around. It concerns the biological system and the ecology. A few of these assets are renewable while others are non-renewable and we may discuss sure plants, animals, air, water, soil, and minerals. The many aspects of natural capital work together to benefit society as a whole. Why is sustainability so important? It is significant because of the environmental quality that we must create for ourselves. We must breathe clean air, consuming pure water and healthy soil. All of these factors contribute to the quality of our surroundings. So, for economic growth, all of these factors must be considered. There will be greater supply as demand increases due to population growth (see: Craig, et al., 2010).

As we expand, we will need more resources, and sustainable solutions can help us use them more efficiently as it is critical for healthcare. Our environment and our health are inextricably linked because of the air, water, and soil. So we need to consider the link between sustainability and health care. Climate change is a major source of worry for global sustainability. We can detect critical indicators, such as greenhouse gas concentrations, which have hit new highs. Direct economic costs from disasters have risen over time, and climate disasters have killed people. Air pollution is an essential issue that we must consider. Worldwide bound is about outside air, this has led to negative health outcomes. Air pollution has been related to an increased risk of cancer, heart disease, strokes, and respiratory disorders. Poor air quality has an impact on both one's quality of life and capacity to work. Air pollution may have an influence on our natural environment and water shortages. Every day, approximately three billion liters of water are lost through the leaking system. According to projections, if no action is made to cut demand or expand water supply, most places would be unable to fulfill demand by 2050. Water is the wellspring of life, water restrictions literally cause vitamin deficiencies in some fish and birds and this is directly related to their demographic fall. Deep-water fishing harms marine life and contaminates animals and plants with illnesses. Plastic pollution, it is predicted that 311 million tons of plastic were manufactured in 2014, with the figure anticipated to treble over the following 20 years. Approximately 14% of plastic packaging is recovered for recycling. What happens to the plastic that is not collected for recycling? Oceans may have more plastic than fish in some regions and will undoubtedly have more plastic than fish by 2050 if we continue to waste plastic and dump it in the ocean. So the image you have with you summarizes all of the dimensions of climate change's social and economic consequences. We can tell that there is an influence on agriculture. And the impact on agriculture can be observed in several regions of the world, with people suffering from degradation, deforestation, and desertification in the places where they live, which is mostly caused by climate change. And this is what we mean by "impact on natural capital" (see" Craig et al., 2010). This impact, is important as both natural and cultural assets, that if properly valoriser, offer great potential for sustainable development and, through protecting human capital, like with the case of Valorizing Tyre the proper valorisation of Tyre's resources will benefit for tourism activities (Al Sawi, 2018). This point is important, as Grynspan (2012) discussed, since sustainability and sustainable development is beneficial for a country which, through focuisung on economic development will not compromise it environment, and harm the overall health of its population.

3. THE TRIPLE BOTTOM LINE: PEOPLE, PLANET, AND PROFIT IN SUSTAINABILITY EVALUATION

In this section, we will cover the three Ps: People, Planet, and Profit. There is something known as the triple bottom line, or the three P's. According to Slaper & Hall (2011) in their research article that appeared in the Indiana Business Review, sustainability has been a popular aim among corporations, non-profits, and government institutions during the last decade. However, determining the extent to which a business is sustainable or pursues sustainable growth may be challenging. According to an article by John Elkington (see: Elkington, 1999) on the Triple Bottom Line, he sought to assess sustainability during the mid-1990s by incorporating a new framework to analyze performance in corporate America. This accounting paradigm, known as the Triple Bottom Line (TBL), extended the standard measures of earnings or returns on investments and shareholder value to incorporate environmental and social elements (see: Gavin, 2019; Miller, 2020; El-Rifai, 2021; Feraday, 2022).

The TBL paradigm includes three elements of organizational performance: social, environmental, and financial (Elkington, 1999). This varies from the usual reporting framework in that it contains ecological, environmental, and social factors that might be difficult to quantify. The TBL dimensions are often known as the three Ps: people, planet, and profit. We'll refer to them as the three Ps. People, planet, and profits are crucial metrics for measuring sustainability goals. How do we evaluate the three Ps? There are social measures for people, environmental measures for the earth, and economic and financial measures for profit. If we take each item above and go further into it, we can see what will fall under social measurements. For example, social measures would contain things like social variables, which pertain to quality of life. It will assess education, equity, access to social services, health and wellbeing, and social capital. Social measurements will also consider items like the unemployment rate, gender equality in labor markets and income, and median family income. Relative poverty, proportion of people with postsecondary education or degrees or certificates, average commuting time between destinations, violent crime per capita, and health-adjusted life expectancy. All of them are part of the social measurements. So, after reading about environmental measures, what may be included in them? These points were also discussed by Grynspan (2012) to some extent.

Environmental measurements assess natural resources and reflect possible implications on their viability. It might include air and water quality, energy consumption, natural resources, solid and hazardous waste, and land use and cover, with long-term trends accessible for each environmental variable (Craig et al., 2010). That would assist us organize and frame our views on how we should deal with some of the difficulties surrounding CO_2 emissions, carbon footprints, sulfur issues, land use, soil nutrition, water quality, and so on (see: Craig et al., 2010). How about the economic and financial measures? In terms of economic and financial metrics, we consider economic variables that affect a company's bottom line, such as cash flow and profit. It might examine income and expenditures related to economic decisions. It might examine taxes, business, climate, employment, and business diversity considerations. We may provide particular examples such as revenue and expenses, productivity and effectiveness, size of organization and worth, business expansion, labor allocation by industry, proportion of companies in every sector, revenue contribution to GOP, and profit margins. Indices that incorporate the three P variables are known as the Real Progress Indicator, or GPI, and they comprise a variety of items related to 25 variables that include economic, social, and environmental concerns (see: Kubiszewski et al., 2013). This indicator seeks to determine if the environmental effect and social impact of financial manufacturing and consumer behavior in a country are either adverse or beneficial aspects in the general wellness and health of society. We can consider all of these factors. So, we can literally identify these three basic metrics, and each of these indicators has the ability to contribute to the construction of what we term the Genuine Progress Indicator Kubiszewski et al., 2013).

While one needs to focus on economic growth and concentrate on improving a country's industry, it is important to not overlook the environment and people's health (Craig et al., 2010). Grynpan (2012) and Kubiszewski et al. (2013) also raise these points as well.

4. NAVIGATING BETWEEN ESG AND SDGS: UNDERSTANDING THE INTERSECTION OF BUSINESS, SOCIETY, AND GOVERNANCE

Environmental, social, and governance (ESGs) are highly important concepts that are used in the business sector, academia, and policymaking, and can be explained through multilateral agreements between the public sector, businesses and educators, through a Helix Model (Marouni, 2021). Environment, social, and governance. This is a rather generic term. When we consider about ESGs, distinct features apply to each word. Environmental challenges include climate change, resource depletion, waste, pollution, and deforestation. When we think about the social, we're talking about human rights, modern-day slavery, child labor, working conditions, and employee relations. And when we think about governance, we are referring to the broader framework of how organizations make choices (Doni, & Johannsdottir, 2020; Sonko, & Sonko, 2023; Saini, & Shri, 2024). Mathers & Deonandan (2018) also raised similar issues in their study.

Things related to executive salaries, corruption, and bribes. Issues concerning board membership, inclusivity, and diversification. So ESGs are broad phrases. And, while we've identified a few situations that may be classified as ESGs, there may be others. We must distinguish between the terms environmental, social, and governance, as well as another word that is now popular: sustainable development goals (Saini, & Shri, 2024). And the United Nations has proposed 17 sustainable development objectives, known as SDGs, which we should aim to accomplish by 2030 (Youness, 2017). They look to be aims that will constitute the greatest strategy to create a better future for everyone. The United Nations' Sustainable Development Goals might be interpreted as a call to action by all governments. Poor, affluent, and middle-income people should work together to achieve prosperity while safeguarding the environment. The United Nations Sustainable Development Goals acknowledged that eradicating poverty must be combined with initiatives that promote economic growth and meet a variety of social needs, as well as combating climate change and striving to protect our seas and forests. As I previously stated, there are 17 goals, ranging from achieving zero poverty to promoting education, healthcare, and gender equality. Goals related to the environment and how we can care for our water, as well as a goal concerning peace and justice. So, there are 17 of these goals, and it's critical to understand them as a guideline, and as a framework of thought, in order to enable businesses to begin to think about what has to be accomplished. These 17 goals may be divided into five groups (Youness, 2017). There are specific goals that are related to individuals, such as eradicating poverty, ending hunger, and providing money for people based on their work and contributions to society. When we consider the globe, there is another category. There are specific goals that will help us attain literally, challenges pertaining to climate change, water, soil, and so forth. We have prosperity-related goals, such as how to accomplish economic growth, create jobs, and generate money, as well as what the difficulties are related to producing growth, creating income, creating employment, lowering unemployment, and maintaining stable pricing. There are also aims for peace, justice, and conflict prevention (see: Pradahan et al., 2017; Mathers & Deonandan, 2018)

All of this must be done in a collaborative atmosphere, with everyone participating. So, the 17 SDGs might be reduced to five categories, some of which will undoubtedly overlap with the categories indicated above. People, planet, prosperity, peace, and cooperation. There is frequently misunderstanding between the two words, ESG and SDG (Youness, 2017; Doni, & Johannsdottir, 2020; Sonko, & Sonko, 2023). ESGs literally refer to three things. The environmental, social, and governance. And they are generic. So we talk about the environment in broad terms (Doni, & Johannsdottir, 2020; Sonko, & Sonko, 2023; Saini, & Shri, 2024). We discuss society in general, and we consider government in generic terms. However, when we look at the SDGs, they become much more detailed. In other words, they are SDGs or sustainable development objectives related to the environment. There are SDGs that are relevant to society. And there are SDGs related to governance (see: Pradhan et al., 2017). So, literally, a shift from ESG to SDG and back. It's great since one is universal, while the other gets highly specialized. So, it is critical to recognize that ESG and SDGs are terms that are being considered and identified as goals to be met by many stakeholders in our society and economy, including consumers, academic institutions, businesses, policymakers, financial institutions and investors, non-profit organizations, and social impact enterprises (see: Asgari, & Reza, 2021). All of these stakeholders, all of these decision makers, who are making decisions that affect our environment, society, and economy, are considering these two terms: ESGs and SDGs (see: Pradahan et al., 2017; Mathers & Deonandan, 2018; Doni, & Johannsdottir, 2020; Sonko, & Sonko, 2023).

While the Helix approach (Marouni, 2021) could be useful, countries that have high indices of corruption, high civil unrest levels, high risks of political tensions, terrorism among other impediments to sustainability, the Helix Model can't apply.

That is why, through studying and investigating relevant literature it was noticed that the Helix Model cannot be applied in Lebanon, for reasons that were hinted out by Mathers & Deonandan (2018) among others.

5. ALIGNING ESG RATINGS WITH FINANCIAL SUSTAINABILITY: UNDERSTANDING THE IMPACT

It is critical to connect ESG ratings, which may be seen from a financial standpoint, with the whole notion of sustainability (see: Doni, & Johannsdottir, 2020; Sonko, & Sonko, 2023). Let us review what financial statements are in a corporation. Why is it important to comprehend a company's financial statements? Because if there is a corporate transformation, a cultural change, the introduction of a new idea, or the embrace of sustainability, it will be critical for us to determine the impact or impacts on organizations' financial situations. And we can comprehend the influence of the financial status of the company by looking at the financial accounts. We review the income, balance, and cash flow statements. These are the three most essential assertions we will consider. The income statements deal with the firm's economic viability and financial viability in terms of whether the company is making revenue. The income statements will inform us about the expenses--direct costs and indirect costs. The income statements will tell us about the profit margins. Income statements will tell us about the company's bottom line. Then we look at the balance sheet, which is a very essential statement that shows us what the corporation has and what it owes. A strong firm is typically reflected by a strong financial sheet, which literally characterizes a powerful corporation. What about the cash flow statements? Finance is about cash flow. And cash flow statements are literally about the cash inflows and outflows of the firm. What happens when we use sustainability models in the business? Do we minimize expenses, resulting in greater cash flow? Yassine et al. (2015) discussed these variables related to accounting in a clear way/

Do we boost revenue by discovering new prospects that will have an impact on our income statements? Do we make excellent and meaningful investments that effect the balance sheet? Financial statements document a company's total performance in terms of sales revenue, expenses, margins, profits, assets, liabilities, liquidity, growth, and investment decisions. And it is critical to assess the impact of sustainability on all of the financial items contained within the financial statements. We need to identify and pose the question, of course, how sustainability will affect liquidity ratios. How will sustainability affect our capacity as a firm to pay our short-term responsibilities to our suppliers? Sustainability should also be quantified using leverage ratios. And leverage ratios refer to debt. Leverage ratios compare our assets to the amount of debt we have incurred. Sustainability will have an influence on profit margins.

Returns on equity, assets, and net profit margins. Sustainability will have a direct influence on efficiency and asset-based ratios such as asset turnover, sales-to-net fixed assets, or PPE. Property, Plant, and Equipment. Sustainability will also have an influence on how the financial market perceives our organization. I'm referring to the market value ratios, which include the PE ratio and the market to book ratio. So all of these are critical financial indicators for the company's performance, and what we need to be able to monitor is what happens to these financial indicators when we implement sustainability (Harhman, 2015; Doni, & Johannsdottir, 2020; Sonko, & Sonko, 2023). How does using ESG ratings and embracing sustainability boost financial performance? According to an article in the SMP Global ranking, organizations who focus on ESG concerns have cut costs, boosted worker productivity, decreased risk potential, and established revenue-generating prospects (see: Doni, & Johannsdottir, 2020; Sonko, & Sonko, 2023).

All of these factors are financial. And what firms should seek for is a decrease in costs, an increase in productivity, a reduction in risk, and the production of income. And this analysis underlines that there is some evidence in the market that indicates that organizations' financial performance and position are improving. These are just a few of the ways that ESGs may improve business revenues and long-term sustainability. risks and seize opportunities that would not be captured in the absence of sustainability. This increases a company's creditworthiness. Accordingly, these ESG concerns may have a direct or indirect financial influence on the entity's performance and investment returns (see: Doni, & Johannsdottir, 2020; Sonko, & Sonko, 2023). For example, degradation of natural capital or the ecosystem may limit the future supply of raw materials, which would have an impact on businesses. And it is therefore critical to determine how environmental improvements and the influence on our natural capital would physically allow enterprises to have access to the raw materials they require to manufacture. Because a lack of access to raw materials will limit the commercial growth that companies seek for. Thus, the environment is the location where raw materials are generated. However, as previously said, the environment puts pressure on these basic commodities. There is strain on these resources, but if we adopt a sustainable strategy, this demand may be lessened. In certain industries, cost structures primarily reflect environmental costs, such as national raw material extraction, procurement, transportation, and energy usage, as well as social expenses such as labor. For example, in the pulp and paper industry, wood and transportation account for around 50% of total expenses, with the remaining consisting mostly of chemicals, energy, and labor. So, it is critical to identify and correlate the influence of ESG practices on company financial performance. And here I've given some of the points to consider while establishing the link between ESG and financial success (see: Doni, & Johannsdottir, 2020; Sonko, & Sonko, 2023).

ESG and financial success indeed show clear relationships (Farnham, 2015; Yassine et al., 2015; Youness, 2017). Taking countries with proper corporate governance mechanisms, where leaders as well as company CEOs are held accountable for their actions, decisions and don't rely on clientelist behaviours to opt out of their duties, show transparency in any (if not all their transaction) show the reliability and stability of the system. Such systems being sane for investors to conduct business transactions show, through presenting inviting investor conditions, welcome business activities and inasmuch as the activities remain the county will be in turn producing fairly well, having a good GDP, shoes high HDI values and present other indicators which will ultimately be beneficial to sustainable development (Mathers & Deonandan, 2018). Ideally, the case for all developed countries showing high HDI l;evels, all developing or underdeveloped cour=ties, not able to undergo sustainable development show, as a result low HDI values, and unfortunate don't present conditions favorable to sustainable development, which explain why in countries of low HDI, with corruption and other problems, the low GDP (per capita) or other measures of economic or facial activity show poor financial activity values (see: Farnham, 2015), low HDI, as linked to unsustainable development, inequitable conditions, no governance, among other issues preventing sustainable development (e.g. Mathers & Deonandan, 2018)..

6. ADVANCING GLOBAL SUSTAINABILITY: A COLLECTIVE RESPONSIBILITY

Global sustainability is about raising awareness about the environmental and economic difficulties that our society faces. This issue should not be addressed on a local level. When we consider the problems of our climate, poverty, waste, and so on, we should not consider them solely on a local or national level; all countries in the world must contribute to the preservation of our planet and its natural resources. What is the significance of global sustainability? Countries in general, and firms in particular, in the key industries, have some understanding of what global sustainability entails. The world's population is rapidly expanding. This is a worldwide sustainability concern. Nonrenewable natural resources are in limited supply. It is a component of the global sustainability issue. Prices for nonrenewable resources are under pressure, which will have an impact on economies and enterprises. This is part of global sustainability. Good examples of sustainability projects include solar energy, which uses the sun's electromagnetic radiation to generate power and heat. Another example of a sustainable endeavor is wind energy. Wind turbines are effective power generation technologies. Crop rotation in agriculture is the process of planting various crops to promote soil fertility and prevent industrial farming.

Water-efficient fixtures include no-flow taps, showerheads, and irrigation systems, among others. Green areas such as parks, marshes, lakes, forests, and other ecosystems are examples of sustainability initiatives. From a global sustainability viewpoint, as well as a policymaking or political standpoint, the Paris Agreement is one of the most important accords related to global sustainability objectives. The Paris Agreement placed a strong emphasis on the need for sustainability. This was the first time that all 195 countries embarked on an ambitious initiative to address climate change. It asserts that the earth should warm by no more than two degrees Celsius, with an optimal value of 1.5°C (see: Craig., et al., 2010).

According to the 2015 agreement, each member nation must use its best measures through the use of NDCs, or Nationally Determined Contributions, and boost its efforts to decrease GHGs, or greenhouse gas emissions, each year. Of sure, we needed something like that since there are signs of unsustainability (Craig., et al., 2010). What are the reasons for the unsustainability that we see? One explanation is overconsumption, another is overproduction, and the third is overtrade, all of which are economic considerations. So, as I previously stated, we are discussing consumption, production, and transportation while focusing on economics. As a result, if we have established that our economic actions as households, corporations, and governments have resulted in the kind of changes we are currently seeing in terms of sustainability, we require an economic response. When we think about sustainable consumption, do we consider economic alternatives that encourage sustainable consumption? The answer is yes. It is about using things, services, materials, energy, and resources with the least possible impact on the environment and society. A sustainable lifestyle should reduce environmental effect while providing a better living for people, households, and communities (see: Craig., et al., 2010).

Then there is the question of sustainable production. This is about creating and producing goods and services in a non-polluting manner, preserving energy and natural resources, increasing efficiency and productivity, and being economically and financially viable as a corporation. Achieving sustainable manufacturing. How do we do this? Well, choosing materials and resources from sustainable sources, including recycled items. We might also consider knowing the company and supplier chain. We need to explore producing locally and domestically in order to cut shipping expenses both environmentally and monetarily. However, we must also continue to educate and innovate in the field of sustainable design. Decisions on sustainability are business decisions. It's both an economic and political decision. Economic decision makers not only create sustainability difficulties, but they also solve them and propose sustainable solutions. As a result, we must highlight the relationships that exist on a global scale between various decision makers in government, industry, and society. And we shouldn't think about these issues from a local perspective (see: Geddes, 1915).

Geddes (1915) postulated the "*think global and act local slogan*". If we think of the world since the Mid-19th Century to modern times, in the wake of the 21st Century, we realize that many actions caused by mankind on local levels highly affected the globe. Not to mention World War I, World War II, and all successive conflicts that shaped the world in the past century and a half, so many things changed with the Industrial Revolution. Now, with Geddes's slogan in mind, how we act locally will definitely impact the globe. Take the US two Atom bombs dropped on Hiroshima and Nagasaki on 1945, causing Japan's capitulation during World War II, this unprecedented act that shook the globs in the Mid-20th Century changed military strategy and warfare tactics ever since the Atom bomb was introduced how through one bomb instantly silenced hundreds of thousands of people. But now look at the Nuclear Fallouts, still after nearly 80 years, nuclear fallout and radioactivity risks still are present in this part of the world. So, yes CSR is a must to show hoe people should act in a social and responsible way in order to avoid that one action like the A bombs dropped in Japan by the US Army would do unprecedented and irreversible damage. So, here people, through CSR need to think how their responsible actions will affect the world for the immediate future, the short term, and for the mid and long terms as well (Wu, & Jin, 2022)

7. EMBRACING SUSTAINABILITY: BENEFITS AND IMPERATIVES FOR ORGANIZATIONS

Embracing sustainability is a crucial part for all organizations, enterprises, and academic institutions. According to an article published by ING, a Dutch bank, transitioning to a more sustainable operating model can enhance a company's reputation, growth objectives, and finance (see: Al-Yafei, et al. 2021). They contend that companies, like humans, have complicated motivations. Many people really wish to discuss ethical concerns and interact with a broader variety of stakeholders. They recognize that power comes with responsibility. According to the report, one essential factor to consider is that companies are aware of the need to solve environmental, social, and governance challenges, which will have various advantages for them. So what are the benefits of embracing sustainability? According to the article, meeting public expectations, avoiding negative news, growing the firm, attracting and encouraging people, rewarding excellent behavior, and adhering to rules. We may examine each and every element listed in the report (cf. Al-Yafei, et al. 2021).

The *first issue* is matching popular expectations. There is a widespread conviction among consumers and businesses that the notion of sustainability is vital, and as a result, consumers and businesses must adopt a plan, a policy, to satisfy public expectations. One recent illustration of how public pressure might influence change is plastic litter. Plastic contamination occurs in several sites around the world's seas, while this situation has been worsening for years, a World Economic Forum and Ellen MacArthur Foundation analysis says that if present trends continue, there will be more plastic in the oceans than fish by 2050.In response, big global firms such as L'Oreal, Mars, Coca-Cola, Unilever, and Nestlé have stated plans to use 100% reusable, recyclable, or compostable packaging by 2025 (cf. Kotler & Keller, 2009; Miah, et al., 2015). The *second issue* concerns avoiding negative news. It has been revealed in the studies that firms are keen to keep the public onside, which basically requires that companies change their plans. Several large consumers, such Coca-Cola, Procter & Gamble, and Unilever, have established marketing strategies to demonstrate their commitment to the environment and society, and they do not participate in news stories that have a negative influence on demand for their products (Kotler & Keller, 2009). We discuss that many firms like the major corporations that recently got negative publicity since October 8 2023 need to reconsider their social responsibility (see:. Wu, & Jin, 2022). The issues recently appearing as Taboo, and eventually need to be reconsidered, as the line between politically correct and plain defamatory is quite thin, these major firms need to pay extreme caution inasmuch as the Near East's complex history o ensure what image it leaves in the consumer's minds. Other arguments need to be formulated as well, but in an objective way.

The t*hird issue* is growing the business, according to this research or this article, there are significant commercial benefits to embracing sustainability. It may be a strong tool for increasing efficiency. BASF, a German chemical company, uses a Verbund system to maximize resource efficiency and provide value to its operations. In terms of energy, it has encouraged BASF to use surplus heat from industrial processes in other facilities, for example, BASF saved around 19.2 million mega-watts of energy in 2017, providing them an overall competitive edge. Of course, the policy had a good environmental impact. The energy saved was comparable to 3.9 million metric tons of CO_2 emissions (cf. Craig et al., 2010). The *fourth issue*, which included in the study, is recruiting and motivating personnel. Organizations with strong corporate social performance are more appealing to employers, which should directly benefit the company's long-term profitability. The opinion is rein-forced by the report that was made by, or the analysis and discussion, and the article published by lNG pertaining to the experience, according to several persons cited in the report. It is considered that the sustainability perspective is critical to attracting employees to the organization. It has been stated that Millennials, in particular, do not want to work for firms that promote pollution or have low ethical standards. They worry about social and environmental concerns. The essay claims that it is a true topic in job interviews and how people choose who they want to work for. ATS tracking systems revolutionizing the field of HR and CV screening and access to several technology and AI breakthroughs can be beneficial in several sectors of operations and may eventually be beneficial in terms of sustainable development (Knio, 2020a).

The *fifth issue* concerns incentives for excellent conduct (cf. Abdallah & Khattib, 2020). Ethical investing is become a lucrative business. More than 1700 investment managers have signed up to the United Nations Principles for Responsible Investment, representing about $70 trillion in assets under administration (see: Abdallah & Khattib, 2020). A progressive approach addressing ESG concerns has been identified. It is also worth noting that consulting firms have emphasized the relevance of this positive behavior in terms of business performance. Well-governed enterprises with minimal or positive social and environmental consequences have lower capital costs and, as a result, produce greater value. The *sixth issue* is to comply with regulations. While many corporations are taking a proactive approach to sustainability, government pressure and regulation may also be viewed as a key driver of change (Wu & Tham, 2023). Many multinational firms, including Apple, Adidas, and Volvo, as well as hundreds of government officials, investors, and other leaders, have joined the We are still in campaign, which advocates for climate action to fulfill the Paris Agreement's goals (e.g. Abdallah & Khattib, 2020).

We decided to introduce briefly the legal implications pertaining to sustainability and to proper and ethical ways to do business, as this is essential to have access to effective sustainable development, while in counties with high terrorism and corruption Indeces among other impediments, sustainability will not be reached (Abdallah & Khattib, 2020).

8. UNDERSTANDING SUSTAINABLE ENTERPRISES: AN EXPLORATION

So, when we think about sustainable business and the difficulties surrounding it, what kinds of things should we consider? So, we may argue that sustainable enterprises are green. Their businesses strive to have the least harmful influence on the environment and society while also creating beneficial benefits on the local, regional, national, and global environments. On the community, society, and economics. A sustainable business aims to meet the three Ps, which we mentioned (see: section 1.3). Many businesses are actively implementing sustainability goals and practices into their strategy and operations (Youness, 2017). These firms meet sustainability goals by conserving energy, producing green goods, and keeping and inspiring staff, all of which contribute to company value creation through growth and return on capital (see: Pradhan et al., 2017; Youness, 2017). Can we provide some examples of sustainable practices? Well, yes! One part of sustainable practice is to reduce energy use and choose alternate energy sources. Reducing waste in all aspects, from resource acquisition to operations and production to distribution, just to mention a few. Knio (2020b) and Khoury (2022a) somehow also raised these issues.

Reducing trash is one example of sustainable methods. Managing reputation via accounting, sustainability practices, and analyzing the types of sustainability strategies that firms use (cf. Craig et al., 2010). Minimizing water consumption in operations, minimizing pollutants and CO_2 emissions from operations, doing R&D for sustainable goods, and incorporating climate change into risk management. Using sustainable products to reach new markets (see: Craig et al., 2010). All of these are examples of sustainable practice. So, when we consider the business case for sustainability, what can we conclude? We can think of at least five items. First of all, opportunity. The green technology and sustainability market is likely to be over \$8.7 billion, with a cumulative growth rate of around 27.1 percent (see: Farham, 2015; Yassine et al., 2015; Attaran, 2020; GRI Medium, 2020). Cost reduction is defined as a drop in operations costs through additions to what we term COGS and cost of goods sold processes, and ultimately, the concept of cost reduction means that we want to lower both our COGS and our operating expenditures (Farham, 2015; Yassine et al., 2015). And there are several chances to lower our operating costs. Innovative skills emerge when we strive for new ideas to preserve competitiveness and convert ourselves, corporations/companies, and countries into sustainable organizations, businesses, or even governments. Brand value and reputation are where you get worldwide recognition and new commercial prospects. Value for stakeholders 93% of the world's top 250 firms currently report on sustainability (GRI Medium, 2020). Increased demand from a diverse set of stakeholders, including shareholders, employees, society, governments, and media, they all require these things. We can really provide some instances of sustainable activities to help illustrate the issues. We can consider, for example, reducing the use of plastic packaging in supermarkets and focusing on alternative packaging options. Food that is offered in bulk and does not always require plastic containers. There are a variety of things that we might think about in terms of sustainable alternatives, refilling systems, and delivering information to clients (Coelho, et al., 2020).

All of these elements are essential components of a sustainable practice. So, when we think about sustainability practices, we must identify the main factors that will contribute to the business case for sustainability in order to gain corporate buy-in. The aim here is for businesses to identify, define, analyze, and assess the opportunity component of sustainability. Companies should consider cost-cutting measures. Define, analyses, and measure it. Innovative capabilities and how we cope with them adds value to the brand and reputation. Furthermore, there is benefit for the stakeholders and those engaged. That is a very crucial point to make when dealing with sustainability challenges. Companies should be involved (Feraday, 2022).

9. CASE STUDIES

The following 6 case studies present examples about what the current chapter is discussing regarding the SDGS and the ESGs, and their various relationships. But, we need to reestimate this in terms of the involvement of some of those firms with respect to the Gaza War.

9.1. Nike

Let us start with Nike (cf. Valjakka, 2013). Nike, as we all know, is a corporation that makes sporting goods. This fantastic organization is a perfect example of sustainable innovation and environmental effect. Nike produces a variety of items, including yarn, soles, and basketball courts, by converting plastic bottles, manufacturing debris, and old products into new materials. 75% of all Nike shoes and clothing now include recycled materials. Nike asserts that, in addition to reusing, some of its most famous goods are manufactured in a sustainable manner. In fact, Air is one of Nike's most environmentally friendly technologies. Nike debuted the Air unit in 1979. Today, the technology comprises of pressurized air nitrogen inside a durable yet flexible bag known as the Nike Air Sole unit, which fits in the center under the heel and front of shoes to create the illusion of walking or running on air. Nike actually highlights the five Air sustainability facts, which are about a dyeing technique for Air soles that recycles 99% of recoverable coloring water. All Air soles innovations created after 2008 include at least 50% recycled produced waste. Nike's Air manufacturing innovation facilities now remove more than 95% of production waste from landfills, which is a significant achievement. The new Nike Max 2017 Air Sole has one of the biggest, tallest, and most noticeable cushioning systems to date, providing plenty of comfort to those who wear them. So Nike is a very important case study in terms of sustainability (Valjakka, 2013). We need to reestimate this in terms of its involvement with the Gaza War.

9.2. IKEA

IKEA is another notable example of a company that is regarded to be sustainable or is aiming toward greater sustainability (Alänge, et al., 2016). Is IKEA selling green furniture? According to them, the answer is yes in more ways than one. They say they're dedicated to using more renewable and sustainable furniture materials, such as sustainably sourced cotton and better plastics. They also employ sustainable timber sources, such as bamboo, to create more environmentally friendly furniture. In addition, IKEA claims that it offers inexpensive, sustainable furniture and energy-saving products that help consumers live more sustainably at home.

They want customers to learn more about some of their sustainable products, such as the kitchen and cabinet fronts made from reused plastic bottles, or some of the eco-friendly products that they produce, such as bamboo furniture and accessories. IKEA claims that they are devoted to decreasing wasteful consumption by packing a lunch, keeping vegetables fresher for longer, and greening the morning with UTZ-certified teas and coffees that enable smallholder farmers to pursue sustainable agricultural practices. So these are all instances of what IKEA claims to be doing to contribute to a more sustainable production process (Alänge, et al., 2016).

9.3. ING

Another notable example of sustainability comes from lNG, a Dutch bank (see: https://www.ing.com, the ING;s official website for more information). In general, we've noticed a new trend forming in the banking industry as more financial institutions seek to include sustainability into their business plans. In the Dow Jones Sustainability Index yearly assessment, LNG seems to have the highest score in the diversified financials category. LNG has regularly scored highly on the index. They claim that they want more firms in their portfolio that are doing sustainable things. Why? They say that it is good business. They understand that resource efficient organizations generate 33% greater returns than their less resource efficient competitors, exhibit high levels of innovation and entrepreneurship, and are cognizant of the economic imperatives resulting from resource restrictions. So, in general, we can conclude that the banking industry is quite interested in sustainable firms. When it comes to analyzing the strength of a balance sheet, sustainable enterprises most likely have more and stronger indicators. Companies with a robust financial sheet are typically more bankable. Companies are really working hard to build and strengthen their balance sheets so that they may obtain financing. On the other side, banks are also searching for these types of businesses. So we're seeing a literal confluence of firms wanting to be more sustainable and banks prepared to support their progress and growth.

9.4. Nestlé

Nestlé is another notable example of a sustainable corporation. Nestlé got the industry's highest score in all three areas of economic, environmental, and social sustainability, with an overall score of about 92 out of 100. The index recognizes the company's efforts to integrate human rights into supplier management strategies, as well as its leadership in health and nutrition. The index awarded Nestlé an environmental score of 100, recognizing the company's dedication to making its goods and operations as ecologically and socially beneficial as possible (see: Nestlé, 2017)

Nestlé has teamed with local farmers to establish Switzerland's largest agriculture biogas plant, which generates green energy from bovine dung, as well as its Heinz bottled water business and the Swiss electricity grid. In exchange, farmers receive more ecologically friendly manure, and Nestlé assists them in caring for the local environment through initiatives like this one, which helped earn a firm a score of 98 out of 100 in the Dow Jones Sustainable Index social aspects for corporate citizenship and charity. So, Nestlé is a really significant case to study about and learn from their path toward being a sustainable firm (ex. Nestlé, 2017). We need to reestimate this in terms of its involvement with the Gaza War.

9.5. BMW

Another key example of sustainability comes from the automotive sector, namely the automobile manufacturing company (see: BMW Group, 2020). Also, consider the BMW situation. According to the Dow Jones Sustainability Index, BMW is the industry leader in terms of environmental and social performance. Over the previous year, the company's efficiency gains have resulted in a 3.3% reduction in average fleet CO_2 emissions per km. According to the ranking, in addition to its excellent environmental performance, BMW is one of the world's most appealing employers. It provides a variety of educational and training possibilities for employees (see: Craig et al., 2010). The corporation has also shown a strong commitment to human rights. BMW, a conventional automobile manufacturer, is making significant progress toward sustainability, as can be seen throughout the automotive sector. Of fact, several of these firms are beginning to produce electric vehicles. Electric automobiles, as we all know, are ecologically beneficial. So all of these are actual instances of where the automotive industry is going in terms of sustainability, and they are certainly an excellent example to study, investigate, and analyze as we move forward in the sustainability sector (BMW GRouyp, 2020).

9.6. LG

Another wonderful example of sustainability comes from LG, a consumer products company. LG has established an objective named "Greener 2020 Goals" that includes a 40% reduction in greenhouse gas emissions and a 15% growth in green in new business (see: Jun, & Minseok. 2021). According to the Dow Jones Sustainability Index, LG has successfully reduced overall greenhouse gas emissions by 353,000 tons over the years. LG lowered packing weight and logistics expenses by following green packaging rules. LG contributed 91% of its social investment budget in community activities, utilizing the company's technical ability to create accessibility apps for public use. So, as a firm in the consumer product market, it is critical to identify the kind of actions that a company like LG has been doing, learn from them, and literally observe where they will go next in the consumer product sector. Because we know that consumer items generate a lot of garbage. And if the corporations that make these consumer items can help reduce trash, that would be fantastic for sustainability (Jun, & Minseok, 2021).

REFERENCES:

Abdallah, F., & Khattib, K. (2020). Introduction to Business Law (2nd ed.). Academic Press.

Al-Sawi, M. (2018). The Effective Valorization of Resources for the Economic Development of Tyre. *MBA Thesis presented to the Lebanese International University.*

Al-Yafei, H., Aseel, S., Kucukvar, M., Onat, N. C., Al-Sulaiti, A., & Al-Hajri, A. (2021). *A systematic review for sustainability of global liquified natural gas industry: A 10-year update* (Vol. 38). Energy Strategy Reviews.

Alänge, S., Clancy, G., & Marmgren, M. (2016). Naturalizing sustainability in product development: A comparative analysis of IKEA and SCA. *Journal of Cleaner Production*, 135, 1009–1022. 10.1016/j.jclepro.2016.06.148

Asgari, A., & Reza, A. (2021). How circular economy transforms business models in a transition towards circular ecosystem: The barriers and incentives. *Sustainable Production and Consumption*, 28, 566–579. 10.1016/j.spc.2021.06.020

Attaran, M. (2020). Digital technology enablers and their implications for supply chain management. In *Supply Chain Forum. International Journal (Toronto, Ont.)*, 21(3), 158–172.

Bansard, J., & Schröder, M. (2021). The Sustainable Use of Natural Resources: The Governance Challenge. Retrieved from: https://www.iisd.org/articles/deep-dive/sustainable-use-natural-resources-governance-challenge

Coelho, P. M., Corona, B., Ten Klooster, R., & Worrell, E. (2020). *Sustainability of reusable packaging–Current situation and trends. Resources, Conservation & Recycling, (6).*

Doni, F., & Johannsdottir, L. (2020). *Environmental social and governance (ESG) ratings*. Climate Action. 10.1007/978-3-319-95885-9_36

El-Rifai, A. (2021). "What is Sutainability"? In *The Sustainable 'Triple Bottom Line' Approach*. Retrieved June 26, 2024, from: https://cose-eu.org/2021/05/02/the-sustainable-triple-bottom-line-approach

Elkington, J. (1999). *Cannibals with forks: the triple bottom line of 21st century business*. Capstone.

Farnhan, P. (2015). *Economics for Managers* (Global Edition). Pearson.

Feraday, S. (2022). 5 Sustainability Challenges and How to Overcome Them. Retrieved from: https://www.apriori.com/blog/five-sustainability-challenges-and-how-to-overcome-them

Gavin, M. (2019). How to create social change: 4 business strategies. Retrieved April 14, 2021, from https://online.hbs.edu/blog/post/how-can-business-drive-social-change

Geddes, P. (1915). *Cities in Evolution: An Introduction to the Town Planning Movement and to the Study of Civics*. University of Michigan Library.

Group, B. M. W. (2020). BMW Group named sector leader in Dow Jones Sustainability Indices 2020. https://www.press.bmwgroup.com/global/article/detail/T0321071EN/bmw-group-named-sector-leader-in-dow-jones-sustainability-indices-2020?language=en

Grynspan, R. (2012). The Role of Natural Resources in promoting Sustainable Development. *Presented on the occasion of the Opening of the 67th UN General Assembly side event on the Role of Natural Resources in Promoting Sustainable Development*. Retrieved from: http://www.ar.undp.org

Hailemariam, A., & Erdiaw-Kwasie, M. O. (2023). Towards a circular economy: Implications for emission reduction and environmental sustainability. *Business Strategy and the Environment*, 32(4), 1951–1965. 10.1002/bse.3229

Heshmati, A., & Rashidghalam, M. (2021). Assessment of the urban circular economy in Sweden. *Journal of Cleaner Production*, 310, 127475. 10.1016/j.jclepro.2021.127475

Jha, S., Nanda, S., Acharya, B., & Dalai, A. K. (2024). Introduction to sustainability science in addressing energy security and achieving sustainable development goals. In *Biomass to Bioenergy* (pp. 1–14). Woodhead Publishing. 10.1016/B978-0-443-15377-8.00001-1

Joensuu, T., Edelman, H., & Saari, A. (2020). Circular economy practices in the built environment. *Journal of Cleaner Production*, 276, 276. 10.1016/j.jclepro.2020.124215

Jun, H, & Minseok K. (2021). From stakeholder communication to engagement for the sustainable development goals (SDGs): A case study of LG electronics. *Sustainability,13*(15), 8624.

Khoury, G. (2022a). Estimating the Influence of Obsolete Curricula on the Effective Tourism Education. *Abstract presented at the 5th International Conference on Multi-Disciplinary Research Studies and Education.*

Knio, M. S. (2020a). The effect of e-commerce richness on consumer behaviour. *Abstract presented at the İstanbul Aydın Üniversitesi Conference.*

Knio, M. S. (2020b). Estimating the impact of the effective valorization of cultural and natural resources for the economic growth of Beirut. *Abstract presented at the İstanbul Aydın Üniversitesi Conference.*

Kotler, P., & Keller, K. (2009). *Marketing Management.* Pearson Education.

Kubiszewski, I., Costanza, R., Franco, C., Lawn, P., Talberth, J., Jackson, T., & Aylmer, C. (2013). Beyond GDP: Measuring and achieving global genuine progress. *Ecological Economics*, 93, 57–68. 10.1016/j.ecolecon.2013.04.019

Langergaard, L. L., & Krøjer, J. (2024). Social Sustainability in Unsustainable Times: Introduction of One Book and Many Problems. In *Social Sustainability in Unsustainable Society: Concepts, Critiques and Counter-Narratives* (pp. 1–13). Springer International Publishing.

Mathers, A. & Deonandan, R. (2018). Are the Sustainable Development Goals Realistic and Effective: A Qualitative Analysis of Key Informant Opinions. *OIDA International Journal of Sustainable Development,* 11(3).

Medium, G. R. I. (2020). The business value of sustainability reporting. Retrieved from: https://globalreportinginitiative.medium.com/the-business-value-of-sustainability-reporting-a7a29992a074

Miah, J. H., Griffiths, A., McNeill, R., Poonaji, I., Martin, R., Morse, S., & Sadhukhan, J. (2015). Creating an environmentally sustainable food factory: A case study of the Lighthouse project at Nestlé. *Procedia CIRP*, 26, 229–234. 10.1016/j.procir.2014.07.030

Miller, K. (2020). The Triple Bottom Line: What it is & why it's important. Retrieved April 14, 2021, from https://online.hbs.edu/blog/post/what-is-the-triple-bottom-line

Nestlé. (2017). The Circular Economy: These are the world's most sustainable companies. Retrieved from: https://www.corporate.nestle.ca/en/stories/world-most-sustainable-companies-henniez

Pradahan, P., Costa, L., Rybski, D., Lucht, W., & Kropp, J. P. (2017). *A Systematic Study of Sustainable Development Goal (SDG) Interactions.* AGU Publications.

Saini, N., & Shri, C. (2024). Environmental, social, and governance reporting adoption factors for sustainable development at the country level. *Environment, Development and Sustainability*, 1–40.

Slaper, T., & Hall, T. J. (2011). The Triple Bottom Line: What is it and how does it work. *Indiana Business Review*, 86(1), 4–8.

Sonko, K. N., & Sonko, M. (2023). *Demystifying Environmental, Social and Governance (ESG)*. Palgrave Studies in Impact Finance. 10.1007/978-3-031-35867-8

Tan, J., Tan, F. J., & Ramakrishna, S. (2022). Transitioning to a circular economy: A systematic review of its drivers and barriers. *Sustainability (Basel)*, 14(3), 1757. 10.3390/su14031757

Valjakka, M. (2013). CSR and Company Reputation-Case study of Nike. PhD thesis, University of Wolverhampton.

Wu, L., & Jin, S. (2022). Corporate Social Responsibility and Sustainability: From a Corporate Governance Perspective. *Sustainability (Basel)*, 14(22), 1–15. 10.3390/su142215457

Wu, Y., & Tham, J. (2023). The impact of environmental regulation, Environment, Social and Government Performance, and technological innovation on enterprise resilience under a green recovery. *Heliyon*, 9(10), e20278. 10.1016/j.heliyon.2023. e2027837767495

Yassine, D. (2015). Principles of Accounting II. Academic Press.

Youness, H. (2017). Trends of Business (1st ed.). Academic Press.

Chapter 3
Socioeconomic Gaps and Foster Inclusive Growth:
Sustainable Tourism Initiatives

Mohammad Badruddoza Talukder
https://orcid.org/0000-0001-7788-2732
International University of Business Agriculture and Technology, Bangladesh

Musfiqur Rahoman Khan
Daffodil Institute of IT, Bangladesh

Sanjeev Kumar
https://orcid.org/0000-0002-7375-7341
Lovely Professional University, India

ABSTRACT

Sustainable tourism initiatives can help address socioeconomic disparities and promote inclusive growth. These initiatives prioritize social tourism, sustainable consumption, and responsible business practices. By doing so, resource entities can benefit local communities, preserve cultural and natural resources, and contribute to sustainable development. The study involved a literature review, conceptual framework development, research design, data collection, analysis, policy implications, and conclusion. The study considers economic, social, and environmental impacts. However, unplanned tourism growth can have negative consequences, highlighting the need for sustainable tourism strategies. Ongoing monitoring and participation of all stakeholders are crucial to achieve sustainable tourism. Sustainable tourism practices can attract environmentally conscious tourists and contribute to economic growth. The values address socioeconomic gaps, promoting inclusive growth, stakeholder engagement, policy-led changes, a balanced approach, ongoing monitoring, and strategic collaborations.

DOI: 10.4018/979-8-3693-5405-6.ch003

Copyright © 2024, IGI Global. Copying or distributing in print or electronic forms without written permission of IGI Global is prohibited.

INTRODUCTION

Sustainable tourism initiatives hold immense potential in bridging socioeconomic gaps and fostering inclusive growth. As one of the world's fastest-growing industries, tourism significantly contributes to foreign exchange and employment, particularly in developing countries. As defined by the World Tourism Organization, sustainable tourism encompasses its current and future economic, social, and environmental impacts, catering to visitors' needs, the industry, the environment, and host communities Mendes (Mendes et al., 2024; Talukder et al., 2024). In a significant move, the United Nations declared 2017 the International Year of Sustainable Tourism for Development, underscoring its global recognition and importance in promoting sustainable development and achieving the Sustainable Development Goals (SDGs), mainly SDG target 8.9. This target aims to create jobs and promote local culture and products through sustainable tourism by 2030.

Sustainable tourism development and economic growth are strongly correlated. A comprehensive review and analysis of sustainable tourism development and economic growth reveal that sustainable tourism practices, such as eco-friendly infrastructure and employee training, offer long-term benefits that far outweigh their initial costs (Sahu et al., 2024). These practices attract environmentally conscious tourists and contribute to economic growth, dispelling concerns about potential negative financial impacts during the transition to sustainability. However, sustainable tourism development faces challenges, such as regional imbalances, overcoming opposition to change, and creating awareness and collective commitment to sustainability. In addressing these challenges, stakeholder engagement is crucial. This includes the tourism industry and local communities, governments, and non-governmental organizations (Mehrotra et al., 2024). Strategic collaborations and policy-led changes are also essential for promoting sustainable tourism practices.

Inclusive economic sustainability is another critical aspect of sustainable tourism initiatives. Economic sustainability involves reducing indignities and empowering the poor, institutionalizing social norms, raising participation in production and consumption processes, reducing social conflict over resources, and limiting poverty resulting from the actions of others or the exploitation of the resource base by strong economic role monopolies. Sustainable tourism initiatives can significantly address socioeconomic gaps and foster inclusive growth by promoting sustainable development, creating jobs, and supporting local culture and products. However, sustainable tourism development requires addressing challenges such as regional imbalances, overcoming opposition to change, and creating awareness and collective commitment to sustainability (Dossou et al., 2023). As academic researchers, policymakers, and industry professionals, your engagement in stakeholder discussions, strategic collaborations, and policy-led changes is essential for promoting sustainable tourism practices and achieving inclusive economic sustainability.

LITERATURE REVIEW

Sustainable tourism initiatives are essential for addressing socioeconomic gaps and fostering inclusive growth. A systematic literature review of sustainability assessments in tourism reveals a range of approaches used to assess sustainability, including economic, social, and environmental dimensions. Sustainable tourism practices, such as investments in environmentally friendly infrastructure and employee training, can have long-term benefits that surpass initial costs, attracting environmentally conscious tourists and contributing to economic growth(Chen & Wu, 2024). However, challenges such as regional imbalances, overcoming opposition to change, and creating awareness and collective commitment to sustainability must be addressed. Inclusive economic sustainability is a critical aspect of sustainable tourism initiatives, involving reducing indignities and empowering people with low incomes, institutionalizing social norms, raising participation in production and consumption processes, and promoting relational and human well-being for future generations. The drivers and outcomes of global inequality and exclusion, such as historical inequalities or injustices, perverse growth, and consumption-based development models, impact sustainable tourism development (Moldovan & Moldovan, 2024). Sustainable tourism-led inclusive growth is an opportune moment to consider how the tourism industry may benefit more can be distributed. Strategic collaborations, policy-led changes, and proactive governmental initiatives are essential for promoting sustainable tourism practices and achieving inclusive economic sustainability. The onus is on governments to create a friendly environment for businesses to embrace and support sustainable practices and on companies to embed sustainability into their operations. However, sustainable tourism initiatives are crucial for addressing socioeconomic gaps and fostering inclusive growth. Sustainable tourism practices, such as eco-friendly infrastructure and employee training, can have long-term benefits that surpass initial costs, attracting environmentally conscious tourists and contributing to economic growth. Challenges such as regional imbalances, overcoming opposition to change, and creating awareness and collective commitment to sustainability must be addressed (Korov et al., 2024). Inclusive economic sustainability, reducing indignities and empowering people experiencing poverty, institutionalizing social norms, raising participation in production and consumption processes, and promoting relational and human well-being for future generations are critical aspects of sustainable tourism initiatives (Talukder et al., 2024) . Strategic collaborations, policy-led changes, and proactive governmental initiatives are essential for promoting sustainable tourism practices and achieving inclusive economic sustainability.

Understanding Inclusive Growth in Tourism Development

Tourism development has been recognized as a significant contributor to economic growth, job creation, and poverty reduction, particularly in developing countries. However, the benefits of tourism development are only sometimes evenly distributed, and there is a need to ensure that tourism contributes to inclusive growth. Inclusive growth in tourism development refers to a process that allows all individuals and groups, regardless of their social or economic status, to participate in and benefit from tourism activities (Tran, 2024). This includes marginalized and vulnerable groups who may not have had access to these opportunities.

Sustainable tourism initiatives, such as installing solar panels in hotels to reduce energy consumption and waste management programs to minimize environmental impact, can be crucial in promoting inclusive growth in tourism development. These practices have long-term benefits that surpass initial costs, attracting environmentally conscious tourists and contributing to economic growth. They also spread economic benefits more widely within local communities, improve the sustainability of destinations, and enhance the profile of destinations as preferred tourism destinations.

The Sustainable and Inclusive Tourism Development Project in Himachal Pradesh, India, stands as a beacon of success, demonstrating the potential of sustainable tourism initiatives to promote inclusive growth in tourism development. The project's impact is profound: the tourism economy in the five districts (Hamirpur, Kangra, Kullu, Mandi, and Shimla) is projected to completely recover from the pandemic downturn and return to a steady growth trajectory. This is achieved through sustainable and resilient tourism interventions that help spread tourism's social and economic benefits more widely (Gayathri Puwanendram et al., 2023). The project's outcomes are remarkable - a vibrant tourism economy, improved sustainability of destinations, resilience to seasonality, effectiveness in spreading economic benefits, and an enhanced profile as a preferred tourism destination.

The project's outcomes are achieved through interventions directed at three levels:

(i) At site-specific locations, tourist amenities that create a new tourism experience and positively impact local employment
(ii) district-level projects that provide benefits through improved connectivity, more vital industry ecosystems, community initiatives, and public sector destination management capacity
(iii) state-level initiatives aim to enhance institutional capacity and improve sector governance and gender-responsive sector management.

The importance of inclusive growth in tourism development extends beyond social justice. It is a crucial factor for the long-term sustainability of the tourism industry. Non-inclusive tourism can lead to detrimental outcomes such as social conflicts, environmental degradation, and economic losses (Dessai, 2023). Therefore, it is imperative to identify the barriers to tourism-driven inclusive growth and develop policies and strategies that effectively address these constraints.

In conclusion, sustainable tourism initiatives are not just a solution but a significant contribution to addressing socioeconomic gaps and fostering inclusive growth in tourism development. These initiatives, which include eco-friendly infrastructure and employee training, offer long-term benefits that far outweigh their initial costs. They attract environmentally conscious tourists, contribute to economic growth, spread economic benefits within local communities, improve destinations' sustainability, and enhance destinations' profile as preferred tourism destinations (Gupta et al., 2024). Inclusive growth in tourism development is not only a matter of social justice but also a prerequisite for the long-term sustainability of the tourism industry.

Socioeconomic Impacts of Tourism

The socioeconomic impacts of tourism on sustainable tourism initiatives are a significant area of study. Sustainable tourism practices contribute positively to social and economic development by generating employment opportunities, supporting local businesses, and promoting cultural preservation (Kumar et al., 2023). The tourism industry can create jobs, contribute to poverty alleviation, and improve residents' overall quality of life by providing better access to education, healthcare, and improved living conditions.

Sustainable tourism initiatives prioritize community involvement and benefits, ensuring that tourism revenues directly contribute to community development projects, education, and healthcare. These initiatives also encourage the preservation of local cultures and traditions, fostering pride among residents in their heritage and promoting cultural exchange between visitors and locals (Talukder et al., 2024).

To maximize the positive impact of sustainable tourism on local economic opportunities, it's crucial to prioritize community involvement, foster inclusive growth, and continually assess and adapt strategies based on the needs and aspirations of the local population. Sustainable tourism operations prioritize sourcing goods and services locally, supporting local businesses, reducing the carbon footprint associated with transportation, and contributing to the overall economic resilience of the destination (Mohammad et al., 2021).

However, sustainable tourism initiatives must minimize negative socioeconomic impacts and avoid harm. This can be achieved through community engagement and participation, community involvement in decision-making, and impact assessments to ensure that tourism activities align with the values and priorities of local communities.

Sustainable tourism initiatives have significant socioeconomic impacts on destinations, local communities, and the tourism industry itself. By prioritizing community involvement, fostering inclusive growth, and minimizing negative socioeconomic impacts, sustainable tourism practices can contribute positively to social and economic development while preserving cultural heritage and promoting environmental conservation (Makhdoomi & Khaki, 2023).

Figure 1. Socio-Economic Impacts of Tourism

Source: Authors compilation

Community-Based Tourism Models for Inclusive Growth

Community-based tourism (CBT) is a sustainable tourism support strategy emphasizing community welfare and empowerment.

CBT can contribute to inclusive growth through broad stakeholder engagement and sustainable development principles.

Long-term strategies and policies that promote quality employment, skills development, entrepreneurship, innovation, practical investment, and integrated regional development are crucial for achieving sustainable and inclusive tourism growth (Talukder et al., 2024).

Governments should strive to Create well-thought-out, cohesive tourism policy solutions that consider local communities and specific nations' unique needs.

CBT models are viable for promoting inclusive growth in sustainable tourism initiatives, emphasizing local community involvement and empowerment.

The Penta-Helix development strategy, involving collaboration between academics, businesses, government, media, and local communities, is a potential approach for implementing CBT (Talukder et al., 2024).

Effective whole-of-government policy responses to tourism should consider the cross-cutting, multi-level, and fragmented nature of tourism policy development, external factors, the global shift to a resource-efficient economy, and the transformation of tourism services linked with emerging technologies.

Tourism can contribute to more inclusive growth by providing employment and economic development opportunities in urban and rural areas, promoting social integration, raising awareness of cultural and environmental values, and helping finance, protect, and manage protected areas (Talukder et al., 2024).

Community-based tourism and best practices with the Sustainable Development Goals can support sustainable development and local communities.

Sustainable Tourism Policies and Strategies for Inclusive Growth

Sustainable tourism policies and strategies for inclusive growth aim to promote economic, social, and environmental sustainability while ensuring that the benefits of tourism are equitably distributed among all stakeholders, including local communities, women, youth, and vulnerable groups. The following are key points to consider in developing sustainable tourism policies and strategies for inclusive growth:

1. The cornerstone of tourism development is broad stakeholder engagement. This inclusive approach not only encourages social cohesion and more equitable growth but also recognizes the invaluable role of each stakeholder in creating jobs and possibilities for economic development in both rural and urban areas.

2. With its unique ability to raise awareness of cultural and environmental values, tourism can be a powerful tool. It can help finance the protection and management of protected areas and the preservation of biological diversity, inspiring a sense of responsibility and stewardship among all stakeholders (Bellato & Cheer, 2021).

3. Effective whole-of-government policy responses to tourism involve coordinated efforts from all relevant government departments and agencies. This approach should consider the cross-cutting, multi-level, and fragmented nature of tourism policy development, external factors, the global shift to a resource-efficient economy, and the transformation of tourism services linked with emerging technologies and digitalization.

4. Achieving sustainable and inclusive tourist growth requires long-term plans and policies prioritizing quality employment and job creation, skill development, entrepreneurship, innovation, efficient investment, and integrated regional development (Khusainova et al., 2024).

5. as critical players, governments have a crucial role in creating more cohesive and integrated tourist policy responses. By considering the unique needs of various nations and local populations, they can lead the way in providing consumers with access to high-quality, reliable, and safe tourism experiences, increasing productivity in the tourism sector, protecting and enhancing natural and cultural resources, improving competitiveness, and promoting inclusive growth and development within and across countries.

6. Tourism policies should consider the trade-offs and complementarities with related policy areas. For instance, while tourism can boost economic growth, it may also pressure the environment (Mohammad et al., 2021). Therefore, policies should be designed to identify win-win solutions that deliver stability for the industry and promote economic growth, quality jobs, and prosperity for countries and regions.

7. Tourism development and the creation of added value based on identified comparative advantages and diverse, high-quality tourism offerings such as adventure tourism, cultural tourism, ecotourism, and sustainable management of natural and cultural resources should be encouraged.

8. Tourism can be used as an engine for inclusive growth by creating quality jobs, business and regional development opportunities, and promoting decent work and social inclusion. This can be achieved through initiatives such as capacity building, community involvement, and the promotion of local entrepreneurship.

Figure 2. Sustainable Tourism Policies and Strategies for Inclusive Growth

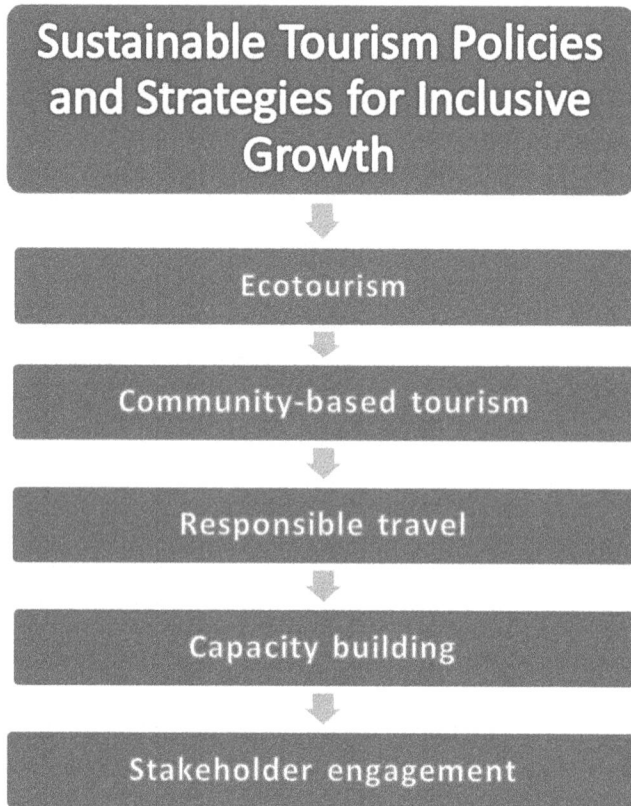

Source: Authors compilation

Leveraging Cultural Heritage for Socioeconomic Development in Tourism

Cultural heritage is vital in promoting socio-economic development in tourism through sustainable initiatives. Capitalizing on cultural heritage, travel, and tourism can contribute to sustainable development and inclusive growth by involving local communities in restoring, preserving, promoting, and capitalizing on tangible and intangible cultural assets. This active involvement fosters sustainable and inclusive growth, ensuring that benefits are distributed widely among community members. Cultural heritage tourism is a fast-growing sector that attracts high-yield tourists, who tend to stay longer and spend more money, contributing significantly to the local economy (Cheng et al., 2023). These tourists often visit historic sites, museums, and cultural attractions, enhancing their travel experiences and supporting local businesses. The economic benefits of cultural heritage tourism extend beyond direct spending, creating indirect benefits that further boost the local economy. In tough economic times, well-planned cultural heritage tourism projects can still yield significant economic and social benefits, even amidst financial constraints. Communities can leverage their cultural assets to attract visitors, promote local attractions, and capitalize on the unique heritage of their region. By focusing on community building, collaborative participation, and the preservation of cultural heritage, communities can maximize the potential of cultural tourism for socioeconomic development, even during challenging economic conditions. Cultural heritage for inclusive growth seeks to pioneer ways of creating inclusive and sustainable growth, enabling local communities to benefit from this growth and actively participate in the sharing and protecting their heritage. By investing in cultural heritage, communities can enhance social inclusion, develop intercultural dialogue, shape their identity, improve the environment, and stimulate tourism development (Stanikzai et al., 2024). This investment in heritage can generate social benefits and economic growth, reinforcing the connection between cultural heritage and inclusive growth for overall societal development.

Partnerships and Collaborations for Inclusive Tourism Development

Partnerships and collaborations are essential for inclusive tourism development and sustainable tourism initiatives. For instance, the partnership between the local government, private sector organizations, and non-governmental organizations has significantly improved tourism infrastructure and services, benefiting tourists and local communities. Multi-stakeholder partnerships have been recognized as an effective way to support tourism development by promoting collaboration between stakeholders, including local communities, government agencies, private sector organizations, and non-governmental organizations.

Inclusive tourism requires stakeholder collaboration to ensure that the benefits of tourism are shared equitably among all members of society, including marginalized and vulnerable groups (Iftikhar et al., 2024). Partnerships can help to promote inclusive tourism by emphasizing the development of accessible tourism, which caters to the diverse needs of people with disabilities and other accessibility requirements. Partnerships can also help build a shared vision for sustainable tourism development, essential for ensuring that tourism benefits local communities and preserves cultural and natural heritage. The process typically involves a series of consultations and collaborative decision-making, where regional stakeholders contribute their unique perspectives and expertise (Monroy-Rodríguez & Caro-Carretero, 2023). By involving local stakeholders in designing, planning, and implementing sustainable tourism models, partnerships can help ensure that tourism is inclusive, attractive, and competitive while providing economic benefits for operators, residents, and destinations.

Certifications, labels, and ethical codes play a crucial role in promoting quality products, responsible services, transparent businesses, and competitive destinations that contribute to the local well-being of residents. These tools provide a framework for companies to adhere to specific standards and practices, ensuring that their operations are environmentally friendly, socially responsible, and economically viable (Kargabayeva et al., 2023). Simplified standards, charters, and protocols can facilitate implementation for small and medium-sized enterprises (SMEs) and local businesses, making it easier for them to adopt and maintain sustainable practices. Partnerships can also help improve tourism's social and environmental performance by promoting accessibility, affordability, and inclusion for all visitors, including those with disabilities or differences. Tourism should contribute to the local well-being of residents, and thematic certification schemes, ethical codes, and eco-labels can significantly promote responsible and sustainable tourism practices.

Capacity Building and Skills Development for Local Communities in Tourism

Community capacity building (CCB) is not a solitary endeavor but a collaborative, ongoing, influential process that forms the backbone of community and tourism development. It is about increasing the personal and collective resources of individuals and communities, empowering them to respond to challenges and seize opportunities (Wang et al., 2023). Capacity building occurs at multiple levels, including individual, organizational, and community, and is sometimes described as 'the glue that binds' between all levels. Community capacity building is essential to the Stronger Communities Strategy for tourism development programs. It is about increasing the personal and collective resources of individuals and communities to help them develop the skills and capacities they need to respond to challenges and seize opportunities that come their way.

Capacity building is about community empowerment, helping individuals, organizations, and communities to find unused and undeveloped skills, resources, and geographic advantages that enable them to reconsider their strengths and opportunities (Arka, 2024). Tourism developers play a crucial role in this process by investing in community training and CCB, thereby contributing to long-term community development. Community capacity building enhances strengths and increases the confidence needed for tourism development. The success of tourism development requires that all stakeholders, including local government, NGOs, and community members, understand that investments in community capacities are necessary for tourism development processes to operate. Where there is sufficient community capacity to support tourism development processes, these processes will also generate community development. Without community development, the capacity to undertake tourism programs is limited (Managi et al., 2024).

Community capacity in tourism development is not just about the capacity of the people in communities to participate in tourism activities but about their integral role in shaping and driving these activities. Tourism developers often invest in community training and CCB to contribute to long-term community development, recognizing the value and importance of community participation. Capacity building is necessary for community development and participatory processes at the community level. Community capacity is widely used among those concerned about community development or involved in social work and social service delivery. In the context of tourism development, community capacity can be seen as the ability of the community to participate in and benefit from tourism activities (Melo et al., 2024). This capacity is built through various initiatives, such as training programs and infrastructure development, which in turn contribute to the community's overall development.

Measuring and Evaluating the Socioeconomic Impact of Tourism Initiatives

Quantitative assessment methodologies can be used to examine the socioeconomic impact of tourism in a region, as demonstrated in a study examining the social opportunities and costs of national and regional tourism.

The study of the socioeconomic impacts of tourism can benefit from a mixed-methods approach, combining organization statistics, participant studies, and trash audits to assess the progression of the Triple Bottom Line (TBL).

The need to standardize the social assessment of tourism packages following a Life Cycle Assessment approach has been identified, with a study taking steps towards this goal (Ahmed et al., 2023).

The role of local development initiatives in tourism and their impacts can be assessed using input-output matrices and survey-based vectors of tourist expenditure, calculating both direct and indirect effects using accounting multipliers.

The potential return on investment and the generation of future income resulting from tourism development initiatives can be estimated, providing valuable insights for policymakers, local communities, and tourism stakeholders.

Strategic planning, community engagement, and sustainable practices are essential in optimizing the benefits and addressing potential challenges associated with local development initiatives and tourism.

The economic impacts of tourism can be studied using a modified vision of the I-O model known as SAM, which incorporates links with other agents that cause further effects through the distribution of institutional income.

The SAM model is especially justified in economies with high unemployment figures and idle industrial capacity, serving as a central fulcrum for developing an economic growth model (Vashkevich & Barykin, 2023).

Research has been conducted in developing countries, such as Korea and Brazil, using the SAM model to evaluate the economic impacts of tourism.

The economic impacts of tourism can also be studied at the regional level, with examples of research conducted in Spain focusing on the Extremadura economy, the Catalan region, and Andalusia.

The update of economic impact matrices is less recurrent, with the last available for the Andalusian region being the MCSAN-10, published in 2016.

The effects of tourism taxation can be studied using the applied CGE model, which relaxes the SAM model assumptions about supply and demand and explicitly adjusts all prices, quantities, revenues, and equilibrium conditions.

Overcoming Barriers to Inclusive Growth in Sustainable Tourism

Sustainable tourism, when built upon broad stakeholder engagement and sustainable development principles, can contribute to more inclusive growth by providing employment and economic development opportunities in both urban and rural areas and promoting social integration. However, there are several barriers to achieving inclusive growth in sustainable tourism, including:

1. Complexity of tourism policy development: Tourism policy development is often complex due to its cross-cutting, multi-level, fragmented nature, competing policy priorities, and budgetary constraints.
2. External factors: Tourism is affected by external factors such as macroeconomic conditions, exchange rates, safety and security, and natural disasters (Talukder et al., 2024).
3. Global shift to a resource-efficient economy: The global shift to a resource-efficient economy poses challenges for tourism, which needs to adapt to new technologies and digitalization.

4. Lack of evidence-based sustainable planning: Effective planning with a sustainable long-term vision is vital for long-term economic and social development, visitor satisfaction, improved business success, social integration, and the protection of environmental assets. However, transitioning to a long-term sustainable approach to tourism planning via monitoring impacts requires efficient resourcing of Local Authorities.

5. Challenges facing the growth and development of ecotourism: Ecotourism focuses on minimizing tourism impact through responsible travel, conservation, and education. However, with the increased commodification of the natural world and exposure of these regions to humans, there are risks (Mohammad et al., 2021). Countries have reduced risks and increased benefits through ecotourism, including in marine areas, but challenges remain to be addressed.

6. Constraints deriving from the country's geographic, political, and socioeconomic realities: Applying the Tourism-Driven Inclusive Growth Diagnostic (T-DIGD) framework in North Macedonia identified several constraints deriving from the country's geographic, political, and socioeconomic realities that hinder the tourism sector's ability to contribute to inclusive growth.

To overcome these barriers, sustainable and inclusive growth policies should focus on promoting quality employment and job creation, skills development, entrepreneurship, innovation, adequate investment, and integrated regional development. Governments should strive to develop further integrated and coherent tourism policy responses that reflect the circumstances of individual countries and local communities in pursuit of shared goals to provide consumers with access to high-quality, reliable, and safe tourism experiences, increase productivity in the tourism sector, protect and enhance natural and cultural resources, improve competitiveness, and promote inclusive growth and development within and across countries (Gemar et al., 2023). Effective whole-of-government policy responses should consider the cross-cutting, multi-level, and fragmented nature of tourism policy development, external factors, the global shift to a resource-efficient economy, and the transformation of tourism services linked with emerging technologies and digitalization of the economy. They should also consider the trade-offs and complementarities with related policy areas, including transport, environment, culture, security, education, agriculture, new technologies, digital transformation, and broader economic policy, to identify win-win solutions that deliver stability for industry and promote economic growth, quality jobs, and prosperity for countries and regions (Sumardani & Wiramatika, 2023). Inclusive tourism strategies and community-based tourism models are essential for sustainable tourism development. These strategies involve designing community-based inclusive tourism programs, sustainable tourism planning for environmental and cultural heritage sites, destination visions, and government and private sector investment planning. Capacity building and skills development for local communities in tourism are also crucial for community development success (Talukder, Kabir, et al., 2024). Community capacity building emphasizes a collaborative, ongoing, influential process based on the relationships between people for development processes. It is necessary for community development and participatory processes at the community level.

Measuring and evaluating the socioeconomic impact of tourism initiatives is essential for understanding tourism development's benefits and challenges and informing policy decisions. Quantitative assessment methodologies, mixed-methods approach, and standardized social assessment of tourism packages following a Life Cycle Assessment approach can be used to assess the socioeconomic impact of tourism in a region (Talukder et al., 2024).

Case Studies of Successful Inclusive Tourism Projects

Inclusive tourism development is a crucial aspect of sustainable tourism, aiming to ensure that tourism benefits are accessible to all members of society, including marginalized and vulnerable groups. Tourism policies for sustainable and inclusive growth can contribute to more inclusive growth by providing employment and economic development opportunities in urban and rural areas and promoting social integration. One example of successful inclusive tourism development is the case of Ukraine, where the formation of principles of socioeconomic development of inclusive tourism as a multifunctional system has been initiated. This includes implementing seven principles of social rehabilitation of people with inclusion, which have been used to identify factors that contribute to the adaptation of persons with disabilities through inclusive tourism and factors that limit or influence the possibility of organizing inclusive tourism (Gigauri et al., 2024). This approach allows for a methodologly informative segment of developing an inclusive environment and a procedure for assessing the project's social and economic risks. Another successful example is implementing the Tourism-Driven Inclusive Growth Diagnostic (T-DIGD) framework in North Macedonia. This diagnostic framework can identify possible binding constraints to tourism-driven inclusive growth out of a large selection of potential factors, thereby contributing to systematically and transparently prioritizing policies to formulate a context-specific development strategy in the presence of limited resources (Mazza, 2023).

Barriers to evidence-based sustainable planning for inclusive tourism can be addressed through a political economy approach, which considers the attitudes towards sustainable tourism in local government and the role of residents' perceptions. Sustainable tourism implementation in urban areas like London can also serve as a successful case study for inclusive tourism development. Inclusive tourism development can also be fostered through sustainable development indicators for tourism destinations, as outlined in the UNWTO guidebook. These indicators can help monitor sustainable management in local tourist destinations, assess sustainable tourism development, and identify barriers to stakeholder involvement in sustainable rural tourism development (Peterson et al., 2020).

Overall, successful inclusive tourism projects can contribute to socioeconomic gaps and foster inclusive growth by promoting accessibility, social integration, and economic development opportunities for marginalized and vulnerable groups. These projects can be achieved by implementing diagnostic frameworks, evidence-based sustainable planning, and sustainable tourism indicators.

Sustainable Tourism Marketing Strategies for Inclusive Growth

Sustainable tourism marketing strategies for inclusive growth offer a shift from traditional marketing metrics to a holistic approach. This approach, which prioritizes protecting and managing natural and cultural assets, increased time spent in destinations, and responsible travel, ensures the preservation of our environment and cultural heritage and leads to a more equitable distribution of tourism benefits (Kusumah, 2023). By integrating sustainable development objectives with tourism marketing practices, these strategies foster a collaborative environment among stakeholders, including residents, thereby promoting a more sustainable and inclusive tourism industry.

Montenegro serves as a prime example of a successful sustainable tourism marketing strategy. The country has created synergies that enhance further sustainable development through a commitment to sustainability and collaborative network marketing. A key aspect of their plan is carefully selecting potential investors demonstrating commitment to sustainability principles. This approach has allowed Montenegro to attract significant financial investments in sustainable eco-resorts, eco-villages, and arts centers. These investments have incentivized communities to create a vibrant 'sustainable tourism identity' and sustainable place branding strategy (Talukder et al., 2024).

Another successful strategy is the development of a Sustainable Tourism Plan or a Destination Stewardship Plan, which can help ensure that a destination is ready for sustainable growth by building up infrastructure, supply chains, stakeholders, and resources. This approach involves setting new key performance indicators (KPIs) for destination measurements of success, such as quality of protection of natural and cultural assets, increased time spent in the destination, and responsible travel.

Inclusive and sustainable tourism marketing strategies emphasize empowering local communities and stakeholders (Hariyadi et al., 2024). Their active involvement is not just beneficial but crucial, ensuring that they reap the benefits of tourism and have a voice in decision-making processes. This empowerment is achieved by designing familiarization trips that showcase responsible and sustainable travel experiences, such as slow travel, longer stays, cultural experiences, off-season travel, and responsible tourism practices.

In summary, successful sustainable tourism marketing strategies for inclusive growth involve:

- A holistic approach that prioritizes the protection and management of natural and cultural assets.
- Increased time spent in destinations.
- Responsible travel.

These strategies underscore the importance of collaboration among stakeholders, including residents, and engagement with local communities and stakeholders (Strelnikova et al., 2023). This collective effort is a necessity and a shared responsibility, ensuring that tourism benefits are distributed equitably and that sustainable development objectives are seamlessly integrated with tourism marketing practices.

Figure 3. Sustainable Tourism Marketing Strategies for Inclusive Growth

Source: Authors compilation

Sustainable Tourism Education and Awareness for Community Empowerment

Sustainable tourism education and awareness are crucial in community empowerment for sustainable development. The following points are essential for a book chapter on this topic:

1. **The Crucial Role of Community Empowerment in Sustainable Tourism Development**: Community empowerment is not just a factor but the cornerstone of sustainable tourism development (Bole, 2024). It allows nearby towns to participate in tourism decision-making and development processes, ensuring equitable sharing of tourism benefits and integrating sustainable development objectives with tourism practices.

2. **Tourism Education and Training Programs**: Tourism education and training programs are essential for the community's awareness of tourism impacts and agreement to sustainable tourism development (STD). These programs can help communities understand the importance of protecting natural and cultural resources, managing tourism development, and ensuring sustainable livelihoods for local people.

3. **Community Support for Tourism**: Community support for tourism is crucial for the success of sustainable tourism initiatives. For instance, in [specific location], community-based tourism (CBT) has supported sustainable tourism in traditional villages by strengthening people's abilities in tourism decision-making and encouraging creative and innovative activities related to tourism (Ojha, 2022).

4. **Sustainable Ecotourism and Community Empowerment**: Sustainable ecotourism can contribute to community empowerment by maintaining ecological integrity and diversity, meeting basic human needs, and improving local people's welfare. Techniques and strategies in ecotourism development should be based on ecosystem properties, which are [specific definition of ecosystem properties], and management units, which are [particular management definition units, and integrated development of terrestrial and aquatic ecosystems (Kavitha & Ravi, 2024).

5. **The Vital Role of Youth in Sustainable Tourism Villages**: Youth involvement is not just beneficial but crucial for optimizing sustainable tourism villages. By engaging young people in tourism activities, communities can ensure the continuity of sustainable tourism practices and the preservation of cultural and natural resources for future generations, thereby securing the long-term sustainability of these villages.

6. **Challenges and Opportunities for Community Empowerment in Sustainable Tourism**: Despite the potential benefits of community empowerment in sustainable tourism, there are also challenges. These include the need for capacity building, awareness-raising, and the involvement of various stakeholders (Dwipayanti et al., 2022). To tackle these obstacles, one must thoroughly comprehend the local context, community needs, and the potential impacts of tourism development on regional communities.

Sustainable Food and Agriculture Initiatives in Tourism: Supporting Local Economies

Local food systems in tourism support sustainable practices and economic development by strengthening regional identity and supporting local economies.

Shorter food supply chains promote sustainability by reducing food miles, lowering CO_2 emissions, creating rural job opportunities, and preserving local heritage (Del Soldato & Massari, 2024).

Local food systems contribute to sustainable rural livelihoods, retain money in regional economies, and revitalize communities, especially in developing countries where tourism often excludes local farmers from supply chains.

Consumers play a crucial role in supporting local economies by choosing establishments prioritizing local produce. Their choices create a positive economic impact by directly supporting local farmers and businesses, thereby contributing to the sustainability and economic development of the local community (Noroozi, 2023).

Larger hospitality businesses are key players in local economic development. By engaging with local suppliers, fostering mutually beneficial relationships, and promoting local food stories and traditions, they contribute significantly to the growth and sustainability of regional economies, making them an integral part of the local food system.

Government policies and programs are increasingly supporting local food initiatives. This support enhances product quality, backs local farmers, and promotes sustainability in food systems, providing a reassuring and confident environment for the growth of local food systems (Martínez Rodríguez & Moreno, 2023).

RECOMMENDATIONS

To foster inclusive growth in sustainable tourism initiatives, consider the following recommendations, each of which holds the potential to transform the industry and create a brighter, more sustainable future:

1. **Rethink tourism success**: Shift the focus from traditional economic indicators to a more holistic approach that includes social and environmental sustainability.
2. **Adopt an integrated policy-industry-community approach**: We invite you to collaborate with local communities, businesses, and policymakers to create sustainable tourism strategies that benefit all stakeholders, recognizing the invaluable role each of you plays in this process.
3. **Mainstream sustainable policies and practices**: Incorporate sustainability into tourism policies, business models, and community development plans.
4. **Develop sustainable tourism business models**: We are confident that by encouraging businesses to adopt sustainable practices and strategies, we can support local economies and protect the environment, demonstrating that sustainability is not just a goal but a viable and beneficial business model.
5. **Implement better management measures**: Develop and implement effective monitoring and evaluation systems to track the effects of eco-friendly travel programs on regional economies and the environment.
6. **Create an enabling environment for tourism development**: Support the development of sustainable tourism infrastructure, training programs, and financial mechanisms that empower local communities and businesses.
7. **Inclusive supply chain**: Foster local economic development by involving local communities in the supply chain of tourism businesses, creating new opportunities for local entrepreneurs and small businesses.
8. **Inclusive concessions**: Develop tourism concessions that support local communities and protect the environment, ensuring that all parties in the tourism industry enjoy the advantages.

CONCLUSION AND FUTURE PROSPECTS

In conclusion, sustainable tourism initiatives are pivotal in bridging socioeconomic disparities and nurturing inclusive growth within communities. The tourism sector can drive economic advancement, safeguard natural resources, and promote social equality by adopting sustainable practices. The COVID-19 epidemic has disrupted the world, but it also offers a chance to revitalize the tourism sector with a renewed emphasis on sustainability and equitable development.

Looking ahead, the future of sustainable tourism initiatives holds promise in the formulation of innovative business models that prioritize sustainability, the establishment of conducive environments for sustainable tourism development, the cultivation of inclusive supply chains, and the implementation of robust governance frameworks to facilitate strategic planning, collaboration, and effective management. Embracing marginalized segments, including local communities, informal enterprises, and small-scale ventures, is imperative for fostering comprehensive and sustainable growth within the sector.

Furthermore, sustainable tourism endeavors have the potential to make a significant contribution to achieving the Sustainable Development Goals (SDGs) by emphasizing quality over quantity, ensuring tourism activities align with the capacity of destinations and communities, and advocating for responsible tourism expansion. By embracing these principles, sustainable tourism initiatives can pave the way for a new era of tourism that aligns closely with the SDGs, fostering a conscientious and regenerative tourism sector that benefits both local communities and the environment.

REFERENCES

Ahmed, S., Shamsuzzoha, A. T. M., & Zarif Rahman, M. (2023). Developing Inclusive Tourism in Chittagong Hill Tracts (CHT): A Case Study on Sajek Valley, Bangladesh. *Asian Review of Social Sciences*, 12(2), 1–9. 10.51983/arss-2023.12.2.3510

Arka, S. (2024). The role of institutions and globalization towards inclusive and sustainable green development (inclusive green growth). *Jurnal Ekonomi Kuantitatif Terapan*, 17(1), 145. 10.24843/JEKT.2024.v17.i01.p10

Bellato, L., & Cheer, J. M. (2021). Inclusive and regenerative urban tourism: Capacity development perspectives. *International Journal of Tourism Cities*, 7(4), 943–961. 10.1108/IJTC-08-2020-0167

Bole, D. K. (2024). Sustainable Wine Tourism: Best Practices. In Martínez-Falcó, J., Marco-Lajara, B., Sánchez-García, E., & Millán-Tudela, L. A. (Eds.), *Wine Tourism and Sustainability* (pp. 95–122). Springer Nature Switzerland. 10.1007/978-3-031-48937-2_5

Chen, W., & Wu, M. (2024). Exploring the role of psychological ownership in tourists' shift toward sustainable behavior in cultural tourism. *Journal of Sustainable Tourism*, 1–20. 10.1080/09669582.2024.2341890

Cheng, Z., Wang, R., Li, Y., & Dai, J. (2023). Paving the Way for a Sustainable Society: Assessing the Inclusive Tourism Development in Transition China. *Journal of Environment & Development*, 32(4), 323–342. 10.1177/10704965231197672

Del Soldato, E., & Massari, S. (2024). Creativity and digital strategies to support food cultural heritage in Mediterranean rural areas. *EuroMed Journal of Business*, 19(1), 113–137. 10.1108/EMJB-05-2023-0152

Dessai, A. G. (2023). Sustainable Tourism. In *Environment, Resources and Sustainable Tourism* (pp. 187–228). Springer Nature Singapore. 10.1007/978-981-99-1843-0_7

Dossou, T. A. M., Asongu, S. A., Kambaye, E. N., Dossou, K. P., & Alinsato, A. S. (2023). Governance, tourism and inclusive growth in Africa. *International Social Science Journal*. 10.1111/issj.12476

Dwipayanti, N. M. U., Nastiti, A., Johnson, H., Loehr, J., Kowara, M., De Rozari, P., Vada, S., Hadwen, W., Nugraha, M. A. T., & Powell, B. (2022). Inclusive WASH and sustainable tourism in Labuan Bajo, Indonesia: Needs and opportunities. *Journal of Water, Sanitation, and Hygiene for Development : a Journal of the International Water Association*, 12(5), 417–431. 10.2166/washdev.2022.222

Gemar, G., Soler, I. P., & Moniche, L. (2023). Exploring the impacts of local development initiatives on tourism: A case study analysis. *Heliyon*, 9(9), e19924. 10.1016/j.heliyon.2023.e1992437809430

Gigauri, I., Popescu, C., & Palazzo, M. (2024). Sustainability initiatives in tourism and marketing of sustainable tourism destination. In *Contemporary Marketing and Consumer Behaviour in Sustainable Tourism* (1st ed., pp. 121–140). Routledge. 10.4324/9781003388593-9

Gupta, R., & Mohd Ear, M. (2024). *Sustainable Tourism Development: Balancing Economic Growth And Environmental Conservation*. 10.13140/RG.2.2.18018.34245

Hariyadi, B. R., Rokhman, A., Rosyadi, S., Yamin, M., & Runtiko, A. G. (2024). The Role of Community-Based Tourism in Sustainable Tourism Village In Indonesia. *Revista de Gestão Social e Ambiental*, 18(7), e05466. 10.24857/rgsa.v18n7-038

Iftikhar, H., Ullah, A., & Pinglu, C. (2024). *From Regional Integrated Development towards Sustainable Future: Evaluating the Belt and Road Initiative's Impact between Tourism, Fintech and Inclusive Green Growth*. 10.21203/rs.3.rs-3841996/v1

Kargabayeva, S. T., Tuleubayeva, M. K., Makenova, G. U., & Kirichok, O. V. (2023). International tourism as a tool for inclusive development of region. *Bulletin of "Turan"University*, 4(4), 293–307. 10.46914/1562-2959-2023-1-4-293-307

Kavitha, K., & Ravi, G. R. (2024). Culinary Heritage as a Sustainable Tourism Product: A Review. In Bhartiya, S., Bhatt, V., & Jimenez Ruiz, A. E. (Eds.), *Advances in Hospitality, Tourism, and the Services Industry* (pp. 60–76). IGI Global. 10.4018/979-8-3693-4135-3.ch004

Khusainova, I., Gasimova, A. A., Mammadova, I. I., Yekimov, S., Tahirzade, J. F., Khalilova, R. F., & Sobirov, B. (2024). Studying the principles of sustainable tourism development in Karabakh. *BIO Web of Conferences, 93*, 05003. 10.1051/bioconf/20249305003

Korov, T., Šostar, M., & Andrlić, B. (2024). The model of strategic management of a religious tourism destination in function of sustainable development. *International Journal of Professional Business Review*, 9(4), e04599. 10.26668/business-review/2024.v9i4.4599

Kumar, S., Talukder, M. B., Kabir, F., & Kaiser, F. (2023). Challenges and Sustainability of Green Finance in the Tourism Industry: Evidence From Bangladesh. In Taneja, S., Kumar, P., Grima, S., Ozen, E., & Sood, K. (Eds.), (pp. 97–111). Advances in Finance, Accounting, and Economics. IGI Global. 10.4018/979-8-3693-1388-6.ch006

Kusumah, E. P. (2023). Sustainable tourism concept: Tourist satisfaction and destination loyalty. *International Journal of Tourism Cities*. 10.1108/IJTC-04-2023-0074

Makhdoomi, A., & Khaki, A. A. (2023). Journey to Resilience: Sustainable Tourism and Community Participation in Jammu and Kashmir. *International Journal of Management and Development Studies*, 12(12), 41–48. 10.53983/ijmds.v12n12.005

Managi, S., Chen, S., Kumar, P., & Dasgupta, P. (2024). Sustainable matrix beyond GDP: Investment for inclusive growth. *Humanities & Social Sciences Communications*, 11(1), 185. 10.1057/s41599-024-02659-5

Martínez Rodríguez, M. C., & Moreno, C. N. (2023). Perspectives for Resilience, Social Inclusion, and Sustainable Tourism in Mexico. In Aguilar-Rivera, N., Borsari, B., De Brito, P. R. B., & Andrade Guerra, B. (Eds.), *SDGs in the Americas and Caribbean Region* (pp. 49–74). Springer International Publishing. 10.1007/978-3-031-16017-2_49

Mazza, B. (2023). A Theoretical Model of Strategic Communication for the Sustainable Development of Sport Tourism. *Sustainability (Basel)*, 15(9), 7039. 10.3390/su15097039

Mehrotra, D. S., Subramanian, D., Krishnan, Dr. S., Bharat, Dr. A., & Garg, Dr. Y. K. (Eds.). (2024). *Calibrating Urban Livability in the Global South*. B P International. 10.9734/bpi/mono/978-81-971889-1-6

Melo, R. H., Pambudi, M. R., & Niode, A. (2024). Socioeconomic status, lake knowledge, and community participation in the sustainable Lake Limboto management, Gorontalo Regency. *Journal of Water and Land Development*, 177–182. https://doi.org/10.24425/jwld.2024.149119

Mendes, H. J. D. A., Paiva, T. M. D. D., Felgueira, T. M. M., Alves, C. A., & Costa, A. A. (2024). The need for business models in accessible, inclusive and sustainable tourism. *International Journal of Professional Business Review*, 9(4), e04542. 10.26668/businessreview/2024.v9i4.4542

Mohammad, B. T., & Mokarram Hossain, M. (2021). Prospects of future tourism in Bangladesh: An evaluative study. *I-Manager's. Journal of Management*, 15(4), 31. 10.26634/jmgt.15.4.17495

Moldovan, L., & Moldovan, F. (2024). Inclusive Innovation and Inclusive Growth Tools for Eliminating the Gaps Created by Economic Growth. In L. Moldovan & A. Gligor (Eds.), *The 17th International Conference Interdisciplinarity in Engineering* (Vol. 926, pp. 542–551). Springer Nature Switzerland. 10.1007/978-3-031-54664-8_46

Monroy-Rodríguez, S., & Caro-Carretero, R. (2023). Congress tourism: Characteristics and application to sustainable tourism to facilitate collective action towards achieving the SDGs. *Cogent Business & Management*, 10(3), 2286663. 10.1080/23311975.2023.2286663

Noroozi, H. (2023). *Sustainable tourism development in iranian nomadic areas: Study of Socio-cultural, Economy, Environment and Political of Iranian Pastoral Nomads, and Development of Sustainable Tourism in Nomadic Areas of Iran.* 10.13140/RG.2.2.18025.47207

Ojha, A. K. (2022). Strategies for Sustainable Tourism Business Development: A Comprehensive Analysis. *Journal of Social Responsibility. Tourism and Hospitality*, 24(24), 25–30. 10.55529/jsrth.24.25.30

Peterson, R. R., DiPietro, R. B., & Harrill, R. (2020). In search of inclusive tourism in the Caribbean: Insights from Aruba. *Worldwide Hospitality and Tourism Themes*, 12(3), 225–243. 10.1108/WHATT-02-2020-0009

Puwanendram, G., Silva, S., & Ganeshan, K. (2023). *Sustainable Tourism for Development and Value Chain Analysis Analyzing the Potential and Prospects for Agritourism Development in Sri Lanka: An Inclusive and Integrated Approach with Tea Industry and Homestay Services.* 10.13140/RG.2.2.24204.49281

Sahu, V. K., Baral, S. K., & Singh, R. (2024). Financial Empowerment of Tribal Women: An Inquiry into Sustainable Economic Justice Initiatives and Pathways towards Inclusive Development. *Asian Journal of Economics. Business and Accounting*, 24(4), 182–194. 10.9734/ajeba/2024/v24i41272

Stanikzai, I. U., Seerat, D. A. H., & Humdard, W. U. (2024). Role of Sustainable Tourism in Preserving Cultural Heritage of Afghanistan: A Comprehensive Review. *Society & Sustainability*, 5(2), 30–38. 10.38157/ss.v5i2.594

Strelnikova, M., Ivanova, R., Skrobotova, O., Polyakova, I., & Shelopugina, N. (2023). Development of inclusive tourism as a means of achieving sustainable development. *Journal of Law and Sustainable Development*, 11(1), e0273. 10.37497/sdgs.v11i1.273

Sumardani, R., & Wiramatika, I. G. (2023). The Sustainable Tourism Implementation in Bonjeruk Tourism Village, Central Lombok. *Jurnal Manajemen Pelayanan Hotel*, 7(2), 846. 10.37484/jmph.070213

Talukder, M. B., & Das, I. R. (2024). The Technology Impacts and AI Solutions in Hospitality. *i-Manager's Journal on Artificial Intelligence &Machine Learning*, 2(1), 56–72. 10.26634/jaim.2.1.20291

Talukder, M. B., Das, I. R., & Kumar, S. (2024). Implementing Digital Marketing Channels on BTHM Admission: Evidence from Dhaka City. *IUBAT Review*, 7(1), 142–170. 10.3329/iubatr.v7i1.74361

Talukder, M. B., Hoque, M., & Das, I. R. (2024). Opportunities of Tourism and Hospitality Education in Bangladesh: Career Perspectives. i-manager's. *Journal of Management*, 18(3), 21–34. 10.26634/jmgt.18.3.20385

Talukder, M. B., Kabir, F., Kaiser, F., & Lina, F. Y. (2024). Digital Detox Movement in the Tourism Industry: Traveler Perspective. In Grima, S., Chaudhary, S., Sood, K., & Kumar, S. (Eds.), (pp. 91–110). Advances in Marketing, Customer Relationship Management, and E-Services. IGI Global. 10.4018/979-8-3693-1107-3.ch007

Talukder, M. B., & Kaiser, F. (2023). Economic Impact of River Tourism: Evidence of Bangladesh. *i-manager's. Journal of Management*, 18(2), 47–60. 10.26634/jmgt.18.2.20235

Talukder, M. B., & Kumar, S. (2024). The Development of ChatGPT and Its Implications for the Future of Customer Service in the Hospitality Industry. In Derbali, A. (Ed.), *Blockchain Applications for Smart Contract Technologies* (pp. 100–126). IGI Global. 10.4018/979-8-3693-1511-8.ch005

Talukder, M. B., Kumar, S., & Das, I. R. (2024). Mindful Consumers and New Marketing Strategies for the Restaurant Business: Evidence of Bangladesh. In Ramos, C., Costa, T., Severino, F., & Calisto, M. (Eds.), *Social Media Strategies for Tourism Interactivity* (pp. 240–260). IGI Global. 10.4018/979-8-3693-0960-5.ch010

Talukder, M. B., Kumar, S., Kaiser, F., & Mia, Md. N. (2024). Pilgrimage Creative Tourism: A Gateway to Sustainable Development Goals in Bangladesh. In M. Hamdan, M. Anshari, N. Ahmad, & E. Ali (Eds.), *Advances in Public Policy and Administration* (pp. 285–300). IGI Global. 10.4018/979-8-3693-1742-6.ch016

Talukder, M. B., Kumar, S., Kaiser, F., & Mia, M. N. (2024). Pilgrimage Creative Tourism: A Gateway to Sustainable Development Goals in Bangladesh. In Hamdan, M., Anshari, M., Ahmad, N., & Ali, E. (Eds.), *Global Trends in Governance and Policy Paradigms* (pp. 285–300). IGI Global. 10.4018/979-8-3693-1742-6.ch016

Talukder, M. B., & Muhsina, K. (2024). Prospect of Smart Tourism Destination in Bangladesh. In Correia, R., Martins, M., & Fontes, R. (Eds.), *AI Innovations for Travel and Tourism* (pp. 163–179). IGI Global. 10.4018/979-8-3693-2137-9.ch009

Tran, L. T. T. (2024). Metaverse-driven sustainable tourism: A horizon 2050 paper. *Tourism Review*. Advance online publication. 10.1108/TR-12-2023-0857

Vashkevich, N., & Barykin, S. (2023). Methodological Approaches Towards the Use of Inclusive Tourism as a Tool of Economic Development of Russian Federation. *Research of Economic and Financial Problems*, 4(4), 10–10. 10.31279/2782-6414-2023-4-7

Wang, M., Su, M. M., Gan, C., Peng, X., Wu, Z., & Voda, M. (2023). Does digital inclusive finance matter in sustainable tourism development at the county level? Evidence from the Wuling Mountain area in China. *Sustainable Development*. 10.1002/sd.2838

Chapter 4
Exploring the Role of Sustainable Tourism in Building Environmental and Social Resilience

Gaurav Bathla
https://orcid.org/0000-0002-6992-811X
CT University, India

Ashish Raina
https://orcid.org/0000-0001-5812-5920
CT University, India

Amit Kumar
https://orcid.org/0000-0002-6915-5495
Central University of Haryana, India

Ranjeeta Tripathi
Amity University, Lucknow, India

Dalwinder Kaur
Manipal GlobalNxt University, Malaysia

ABSTRACT

This chapter delves into the critical intersection between sustainable tourism and the cultivation of environmental and social resilience. In an era marked by escalating environmental challenges and social disparities, understanding the potential of sustainable tourism as a catalyst for positive change is paramount. Through an interdisciplinary lens, this chapter navigates the intricate dynamics at play, examin-

DOI: 10.4018/979-8-3693-5405-6.ch004

Copyright © 2024, IGI Global. Copying or distributing in print or electronic forms without written permission of IGI Global is prohibited.

ing how sustainable tourism practices can contribute to the preservation of natural ecosystems while simultaneously fostering community empowerment and social cohesion. From promoting biodiversity conservation and mitigating climate change impacts to enhancing livelihood opportunities and cultural preservation, the chapter unravels the intricate web of benefits that sustainable tourism offers. Moreover, it delves into the complexities of stakeholder engagement, policy formulation, and innovative strategies necessary for realizing the full potential of sustainable tourism in building resilient societies.

1. BACKGROUND

The present study examines the complex correlation that exists between the implementation of sustainable tourism practices and the bolstering of social and environmental resilience. In a time characterised by increasing environmental difficulties and socioeconomic unpredictability, it has become critical to prioritise the development of resilience. Sustainable tourism, characterised by its emphasis on maximising socio-economic benefits and minimising negative environmental and community impacts, presents itself as a potentially effective approach to enhance resilience. The objective of this chapter is to examine the diverse manners in which sustainable tourism endeavours enhance social welfare and environmental preservation, thus strengthening resilience on a local and global level. Through an analysis of case studies, policy frameworks, and theoretical perspectives, the objective of this research is to provide a comprehensive understanding of the ways in which sustainable tourism can act as a catalyst for enhancing resilience in the context of increasing socio-economic vulnerabilities and environmental degradation. By conducting an extensive examination, this chapter aims to offer valuable insights and suggestions to policymakers, stakeholders in the tourism sector, and local communities regarding how to effectively utilise sustainable tourism as a proactive approach to addressing the challenges of the twenty-first century.

Figure 1. Sustainable Tourism (Shu-Yuan Pan et al., 2018)

2. INTRODUCTION

Amidst increasing apprehensions regarding the consequences of climate change on society and the environment, the notion of sustainable tourism has surfaced as an essential pathway to promote resilience (Palinkas, 2020). Sustainable tourism comprises a range of practices that are designed to mitigate the adverse environmental effects associated with tourism, safeguard indigenous cultures, and foster fair socio-economic progress (Dolnicar, 2020). In an era when destinations across the globe contend with the simultaneous issues of environmental deterioration and social disparities, it is critical to comprehend the significance of sustainable tourism in fostering resilience. The purpose of this introduction is to examine the various complex aspects of sustainable tourism, investigating its capacity to improve social welfare and community resilience while minimizing environmental damage.

Sustainable tourism is a fundamental concept that encompasses a comprehensive approach to leisure and travel, placing emphasis on the empowerment of communities, environmental conservation, and cultural preservation. Sustainable tourism aims to achieve a harmonious coexistence of ecological preservation and economic expansion through the promotion of accountability in travel practices, including the reduction of carbon footprints, patronage of local enterprises, and reverence for indigenous cultures. Furthermore, sustainable tourism endeavors frequently prioritize community involvement and the enhancement of local capabilities, thereby enabling citizens to actively partake in deliberations pertaining to the advancement of tourism. By means of collaborative partnerships and inclusive methodologies, sustainable tourism possesses the capacity to enhance social cohesion, promote cultural interchange, and fortify community resilience in the face of external disruptions.

Moreover, the interconnection between resilience and sustainable tourism transcends mere environmental stewardship and encompasses more extensive socio-economic aspects. Tourism is a crucial source of revenue and employment in numerous locales, especially in rural and disadvantaged communities (Zeng, 2021). Through the advocacy of sustainable tourism practices, destinations have the ability to augment socio-economic resilience, decrease reliance on resource-intensive sectors, and diversify their economies in the midst of worldwide challenges such as natural disasters and economic recessions. Furthermore, sustainable tourism endeavors frequently place emphasis on allocating resources towards improvements in community healthcare, education, and infrastructure, thus making a substantial contribution to the general welfare and fortitude of the communities that serve as hosts. Through an examination of the interdependencies among economic resilience, social equity and environmental sustainability this chapter endeavors to emphasize the critical significance of sustainable tourism in promoting comprehensive resilience within the contexts of travel destinations.

Figure 2. Community Resilience (Badoc-Gonzales, 2022)

2.1 Understanding Sustainable Tourism

Tourism, a purely human-centric sector, contributes to the economic growth and revenue generation of a destination (Pulido-Fernández, 2020). Nevertheless, ecological degradation, social unrest, heritage loss, and similar factors have the potential to significantly affect the economy and ecology of a given location. Sustainable tourism follows a similar trajectory as a sector that strives to create job prospects for indigenous populations while guaranteeing minimal negative effects on the natural world and local communities. Put simply, sustainable tourism encompasses the consideration of potential or likely consequences of tourism on the current and future economic, environmental, and social fabric of a destination, as well as the implementation of strategies to preserve the area's biodiversity and cultural heritage. Sustainable tourism is predicated on achieving sustainable development objectives that benefit local communities, visitors, and the tourism industry (Štreimikienė, 2020). Sustainable tourism from a development perspective considers not just total economic benefits for the community, but also how these benefits are distributed and the social and cultural effects of ecotourism development on local people (Inbakaran & Jackson 2005). Improvement of the socio-economic condition of the local people is one of the major objectives of developing sustainable tourism, which can lead to sustainable development. Sustainable tourism strives to be not only a conservation mechanism and an economic development tool, but also a development process that seeks to remain harmonious with local cultural and social needs (Wood, 2002).

2.2 Aims and Objectives of Sustainable Tourism

In addition to the implementation of sustainable practices, the objective of sustainable tourism is to increase consumer satisfaction (Han, 2021). While global objectives for equitable growth are absent, sustainable tourism assumes a significant role. Below is a summary of specific objectives that are attainable:

- **Preserve and conserve the sanctity of a place**

This entails valuing the environmental integrity and sanctity and striving to mitigate all forms of pollution, such as those found in the air, water, and noise, between others.

- **Preserve the biodiversity**

It is imperative to implement measures that mitigate the potential adverse effects on the ecological equilibrium of the area, whether they pertain to the fauna or the natural environment.

- **Optimally utilize the available resources**

Utilizing non-renewable and renewable resources with maximum efficiency and effectiveness is essential (Ibrahim, 2021). Additionally, measures must be implemented to promote waste prevention and encourage both local residents and tourists to minimize misuse.

- **Increase employment**

A substantial expansion in employment opportunities results from the tourism industry's current success. An objective of environmentally friendly tourism is to create a plethora of employment avenues and opportunities (Hasan, 2021).

- **To create awareness**

Promoting knowledge and fostering consciousness regarding the beneficial effects of environmentally friendly tourism in safeguarding our natural and cultural heritage are critical endeavors. Additionally, it is critical to pledge and initiate your own dedication by implementing a variety of sustainable tourism practices.

2.3 The Impacts of Sustainable Tourism

- **Prioritizing Environmental Sustainability in the Tourism Industry:**

Strategies for a Greener Future

i.   Ensuring environmental health takes precedence in a world that is contending with the challenges posed by global warming (Hodambia, 2020). Sustainability of the environment will be critical for the long-term viability of tourism enterprises, as the industry exports one of the five highest-value commodities in more than 150 countries. This involves the efficient use of resources to fulfil the requirements of the current generation while preserving the environment for future generations.

ii. **Conservation and preservation of natural resources:** By preserving and safeguarding resources of nature, tourism can aid in the protection of valuable habitats and biodiversity.

iii. **Responsible tourism practices, respecting wildlife and ecosystems:** Promoting conscientious conduct among visitors, including maintaining a safe distance when observing wildlife and adhering to disturbance reduction guidelines, contributes to the preservation and reverence of the natural environment.

iv. **Collaboration and stakeholder engagement, supporting local communities:** By fostering partnerships with local communities, the tourism industry can contribute to their economic growth and guarantee that its positive impacts are distributed to the indigenous populace. This cultivates a perception of proprietorship and promotes the conservation of cultural legacy.

v.   **Education:** A distinct opportunity exists to educate tourists regarding environmental health through the tourism industry (Dolnicar, 2020). Tourists have the capacity to become conservation advocates in their own neighbourhoods through the acts of raising consciousness and encouraging environmentally friendly behaviours.

3. SUSTAINABLE MANAGEMENT

Sustainable management is of utmost importance in the administration of the tourism sector, as it promotes economic expansion (Štreimikienė, 2020). It supports the implementation and strategic planning of sustainable tourism. A shift in management efficacy has the potential to impact the sustainability of the tourism industry.

The development of methods of management should be efficient; thus, they have to be produced in large quantities. In tourism, sustainability is an all-encompassing imperative due to its ability to foster equilibrium between economies and cultures (Li, 2022). Particularly in rural regions and neighbouring communities, the implementation of sustainable management practices can foster the expansion of tourism. This type of tourism has the potential to alleviate destitution, safeguard cultural liberties, and uphold social integrity. The optimistic nature of the sustainable management concept stems from the fact that it ensures individuals when residents of the area a responsible tourism experience.

Diverse opinions exist regarding the extent to which tourism failed to generate economic benefits due to a lack of strategy; therefore, management is necessary for the establishment of a proper infrastructure and the planning of tourism activities. It is among the most crucial locations to take into account when instituting sustainable tourism development. Local communities can be bolstered through the strategic incorporation of educational awareness campaigns, poverty reduction initiatives, and initiatives to preserve natural heritage. Sufficient community planning is imperative in order to surmount the obstacles that impede the integration of tourism advantages that can be obtained via sustainable administration of tourist destinations.

3.1 Principles of Sustainable Tourism Development

Protecting the environment and wildlife while supporting local communities are the pillars of sustainable tourism. Involving local communities in the transformation and formation of societies with diverse values and beliefs, as well as elevating the significance of these communities in the eyes of tourists, are a few of the numerous benefits that sustainable tourism provides for them. These communities have also articulated essential principles for the advancement of sustainable tourism. These principles encompass the following: advocating for the conservation and safety of valuable items on-site, reducing environmental impact, enhancing the local appeal of the tourism destination, stimulating economic development and job creation, encouraging site usage and its associated health benefits, and fostering communication regarding the site's values and services. These principles are also implemented in Finland by UNESCO in an effort to promote sustainable tourism development. Similarly, certain principles pertaining to the development of sustainable tourism have been delineated. These principles encompass intergenerational equity, which entails ensuring that ecological resources and activities are accessible to both current and future generations; intragenerational equity, which pertains to social welfare; and poverty alleviation, which concerns enhancing the welfare of local communities while ensuring that public participation is not limited to the advantage of the powerful. Environmental protection as an underlying principle signifies that economic development is not acceptable without environmental protection; and concluding with a prudent approach to risks and uncertainty, given that environmental impacts are unknown and subject to change with each passing second; thus, exercising caution when making decisions until the probable risks are ascertained. Therefore, in the scholarly literature, the authors have formulated a number of principles for safeguarding tourist destinations via sustainable tourism development.

As the notion of sustainable development gains traction across multiple domains, human decision-making has clarified that the efficacy of sustainable growth in the tourism industry is contingent upon the implementation of guiding principles that assist local governments in safeguarding tourist destinations and local communities. Ecological principles, financial principles, and social principles comprise the principles of sustainable tourism growth (Rauf, 2021). It was emphasized that merely establishing principles is insufficient for sustainable tourism development; rather, connecting these principles is crucial. For instance, the optimization of tourist infrastructure utilization while preserving natural resources can lead to the fulfilment of social principles, such as the creation of more employment opportunities for the local population. In a similar vein, it was clarified that the concept of sustainable development for the tourism industry was first presented in the 1960 Declaration of the United Nations Conference on the Human Environment. This document outlined 26 distinct principles that were deemed pertinent to the feasible growth in the tourism sector. Over time, various scholars expanded upon these principles in order to facilitate their adoption by the industry.

Furthermore, it was stated that the participation of local governments is necessary for the implementation of all principles put forth by authors or conferences in order to promote sustainable development within the tourism industry. The justification for this is to enable local governments to more efficiently implement the guiding principles and formulate policies and actions that align with their specific local requirements. Therefore, in order to attain sustainability development for the tourism industry, it is imperative that the local government enacts principles that benefit the local communities.

3.2 Social Resilience and Sustainable Tourism

Socio-Cultural Impacts of Tourism

A family residing in an urban environment, surrounded by state-of-the-art retail centers and other urban indulgences, may find the following destination more appealing? An analogous urban setting or a location characterized by distinct modes of existence and interactions between inhabitants and the natural world. It goes without saying that the probable destination will be a location characterized by diverse social and cultural contexts. Therefore, it can be deduced that the social and cultural environment of a destination serves as an incentive and attraction for potential visitors.

Currently, consider an alternative scenario. There are two available destination options that share a similar type of fundamental attraction. The distinction is attributable to the cultural and social milieu. One destination exhibits a social and cultural milieu that is amenable and accommodating towards the potential tourists' culture and society. Conversely, the social and cultural milieu of the other destination is antagonistic towards the culture and society of the potential tourists (Karoubi, 2021). Again, the likelihood that the tourist will visit the former is hardly debatable.

In conclusion, the aforementioned two situations demonstrate that a socio-cultural environment serves as an integral component of the overall tourism product, even when the primary attraction is not the environment itself. In a similar vein, we can assert that tourism facilitated the preservation and conservation of a destination's sociocultural environment when it served as the primary draw for tourists or was an essential component of the destination's overall tourism offering.

Similar to the correlation observed between the physical environment and the socio-cultural milieu, this relationship is symbiotic in nature.

Figure 3. Socio-Cultural Impacts of Tourism (TechnoFunc, 2023)

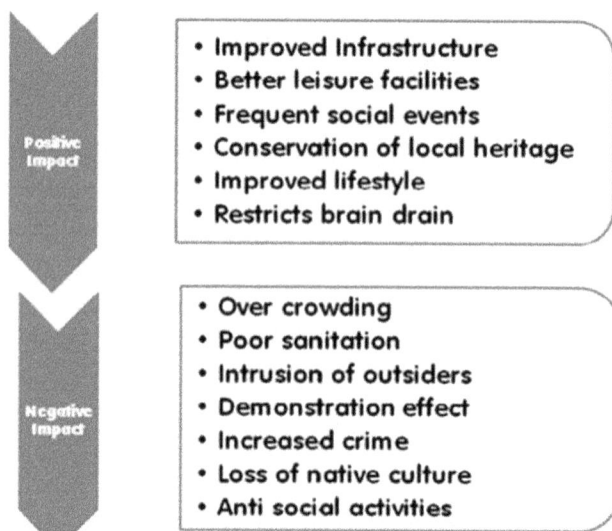

Positive Impact
- Improved Infrastructure
- Better leisure facilities
- Frequent social events
- Conservation of local heritage
- Improved lifestyle
- Restricts brain drain

Negative Impact
- Over crowding
- Poor sanitation
- Intrusion of outsiders
- Demonstration effect
- Increased crime
- Loss of native culture
- Anti social activities

The foundational tourism product, which is the attraction, or the additional tourism product in the form of advantageous socio-cultural conditions, is provided by the destination's socio-cultural environment. Tourism, in turn, offers the necessary preservation and conservation efforts. This creates a relationship of mutual benefit in which both entities contribute to the other's survival.

3.3 Tourism Impacts On Socio-Cultural Environment

Sociocultural impacts of tourism pertain to alterations in the way of life of the inhabitants of the host population, or the destination (Amoiradis, 2021). Additionally, it encompasses alterations in intellectual pursuits, artistic expressions, artifacts, customs, ceremonies and rituals, and moral and ethical principles, as well as modifications in the daily lives, value systems, and lifestyles of local inhabitants that result from tourism-related activities in the destination. A compilation of diverse socio-cultural impacts is as follows.

Table 1. Tourism Impacts on Socio-Cultural Environment

Positive Impacts	Negative Impacts
Social tourism, the all-inclusive character of new age tourism	Erosion of destination image
Promotion to social stability and peace	Commoditization of Culture
Enhanced understanding of social norms, practices and values	Demonstration effect
Social elevation and educational awareness	Socio-cultural conflicts
Improved social capital	Exploitation of local travel professionals
Rejuvenation of cultural symbols	Identity Crisis
International cultural relations and co-operation	Various kinds of abuses
Cultural values preservation	Loss of authenticity
Economic significance of cultural sites	Degradation of local customs
	Law and Order issues

The socio-cultural ramifications of tourism give rise to transformations in various aspects, including family dynamics, community structure, traditional lifestyle dynamics, and modes of expression. While negative impacts are not invariably the case, as demonstrated previously, positive impacts can also occur. Numerous variables affect the nature and magnitude of tourism's sociocultural effects, including the degree of cultural difference between the host and guest communities, the quantity and quality of their interactions, the average length of stay, and so forth.

3.4 Ecotourism and Environmental, Social, and Economic Impacts

When development safeguards future opportunities while satisfying the requirements of travellers and local residents, tourism can be made sustainable. Ecotourism provides educational opportunities, conservation efforts, and development benefits for local communities. Ecotourism is a form of tourism centered on natural resources that is environmentally sustainable. It emphasizes learning and witnessing about the local environment, including its landscape, flora, fauna, and habitats, in addition to cultural artefacts. Ecotourism is the economic integration of tourism and conservation for the advantage of local communities, with an emphasis on sustainability (Seervi, 2023).

Ecotourism is founded upon cultural and natural landscape values (Carvache-Franco, 2020). The values that contribute to a region include its historical significance, inhabitants, local handicrafts, microclimatic diseases water availability, natural beauty, vegetation, and wildlife, exterior features, geomorphologic structure, heritage appeals, architectural diversity, heritage music as well as folk dance, community festivals and pageants, and traditional agricultural structure.

Ecotourism functions to provide one or more environmentally sustainable alternatives to conventional economic activities such as mining, hunting, farming, and so forth, that utilize natural resources (Parakh, 2022). Ecotourism fosters an increased sense of environmental consciousness and admiration among natives and tourists through the provision of hands-on experiences with nature and conservation efforts.

The prevailing perception is that ecotourism protects natural areas, thus making a significant contribution to the preservation of biodiversity. It emphasizes learning and witnessing about the local environment, including its landscape, flora, fauna, and habitats, in addition to cultural artifacts. Concerning ecotourism planning, environmental conservation is the initial issue that arises.

Development of a destination for ecotourism must in no way occur without environmental planning. The presence of water resources within the tourism implementation facilitates benefits in terms of aesthetic appeal and practical application (Lu, 2020). The climatic characteristics of a given area have both direct and indirect effects on tourism, and are vital to its growth (Steiger, 2020). Plants that captivate observers through their dimensions, age, or aesthetic qualities constitute additional alluring aspects of ecotourism. In ecotourism, flowering flora are vital resources. Folklore, natural, and historical significance are significant ecotourism resources. Traditional commercial products, according to Soykan, are among the most influential factors influencing the growth of ecotourism in a given region. This is due to the fact that the entire production process, encompassing planting, harvesting, and processing, is influenced by cultural variations, with the majority of operations continuing to adhere to traditional methods.

Ecotourism possesses the capacity to significantly affect local communities, primarily attributable to Eco tourists' propensity for greater fascination with the local culture and environment in comparison to industrial tourists. Ecotourism destinations are consistently environmentally conscious due to the fact that ecotourism activities directly engage with a wide range of environmental phenomena (Jeong, 2021). These activities include but are not limited to observing birds, trekking, hiking, horseback riding, and elephant riding along forest nature trails; residing in natural caves; conducting research on flora and fauna; simple bush walking; fishing; and studying animal behavior and ecology. Ecotourism invariably encompasses a variety of natural activities (e.g., mountain climbing, trekking, observing wildlife in its natural habitat) but it may also integrate cultural experiences. Ecotourism serves as a significant educational element, providing opportunities for individuals to develop an appreciation for the local culture and environment, as well as engage in introspection while being awestruck by the splendor of their surroundings.

3.5 Interconnection Between Environmental and Social Resilience

Interconnection between environmental and social resilience encompasses a dynamic relationship where the well-being of communities and ecosystems are intertwined. Synergies and trade-offs are inherent in this relationship, where efforts to bolster environmental resilience can concurrently enhance social resilience, yet may also present trade-offs that necessitate careful consideration. For instance, initiatives such as afforestation not only contribute to ecosystem restoration but also provide economic opportunities and mitigate climate-related risks for vulnerable communities. However, trade-offs may arise when land allocation for afforestation competes with agricultural needs, potentially impacting food security. Understanding these synergies and trade-offs is crucial for crafting effective resilience strategies that optimize benefits while minimizing negative consequences.

Integrated approaches are vital for building resilience that addresses both environmental and social dimensions holistically (Li, 2020). By recognizing the interconnectedness of ecological systems and human societies, integrated approaches leverage diverse strategies to enhance adaptive capacity and mitigate vulnerabilities. For instance, ecosystem-based adaptation combines nature-based solutions with social interventions to address climate change impacts while promoting sustainable livelihoods and community well-being. Similarly, integrating green infrastructure with urban planning not only enhances environmental resilience against natural hazards but also improves social cohesion and quality of life for urban residents.

Stakeholder collaboration plays a pivotal role in fostering resilience by harnessing collective expertise, resources, and perspectives. Engaging diverse stakeholders, including governments, local communities, NGOs, academia, and private sectors, fosters inclusive decision-making processes that reflect the needs and priorities of all stakeholders. Collaboration facilitates knowledge exchange, innovation, and mutual support, thereby enhancing the effectiveness and sustainability of resilience-building efforts. For instance, participatory approaches that involve local communities in ecosystem management empower them as stewards of their natural resources while fostering social cohesion and ownership of resilience initiatives.

Interdisciplinary resilience building efforts offer valuable lessons derived from integrating diverse knowledge domains, methodologies, and perspectives. By transcending disciplinary boundaries, interdisciplinary approaches foster holistic understanding of complex socio-environmental systems and enable innovative solutions that address interconnected challenges. Lessons learned highlight the importance of co-designing and co-implementing resilience strategies with interdisciplinary teams to ensure contextual relevance, effectiveness, and sustainability. Moreover, interdisciplinary collaboration fosters adaptive learning, enabling continuous refinement and improvement of resilience strategies in response to changing environmental and social dynamics.

The interconnection between environmental and social resilience underscores the need for synergistic approaches that integrate diverse perspectives, foster stakeholder collaboration, and draw lessons from interdisciplinary efforts. By recognizing the inherent linkages between ecological health and human well-being, resilience-building endeavors can effectively navigate trade-offs, enhance adaptive capacity, and promote sustainable development pathways that benefit both people and the planet.

3.6 Policy and Governance for Sustainable Tourism Resilience

A. Role of Governments and Regulatory Bodies:

1. **Policy Formulation and Implementation**:

Governments play a crucial role in crafting policies that promote sustainable tourism practices (Štreimikienė, 2020). These policies encompass a wide range of areas, including environmental protection, cultural preservation, and community engagement. Regulatory bodies oversee the enforcement of these policies to ensure compliance within the industry.

2. **Capacity Building**:

Authorities promote capacity building initiatives with the aim of augmenting industry stakeholders' comprehension and application of sustainable tourism practices. This encompasses the provision of educational resources, seminars, and training programs with the objective of cultivating responsible tourism conduct.

3. **Monitoring and Evaluation**:

The responsibility of overseeing the effects of tourism operations on the natural world, neighbourhoods, and places of cultural significance falls upon regulatory bodies. By means of thorough evaluation procedures, governmental bodies are able to discern domains that require enhancement and subsequently modify policies in a manner that fosters resilience in the tourism industry.

B. Policy Instruments Supporting Sustainable Tourism:

1. **Incentive Mechanisms**:

Governments can incentivize sustainable practices within the tourism industry by offering tax breaks, subsidies, or grants to businesses that adopt environmentally friendly and socially responsible initiatives (21. Dolnicar, 2020). These incentives serve as powerful motivators for industry stakeholders to prioritize sustainability.

2. **Regulatory Frameworks**:

Establishing clear regulatory frameworks is essential for guiding sustainable tourism development. This includes zoning regulations, land-use planning, and building codes that safeguard natural habitats, biodiversity, and cultural integrity while managing visitor flows and infrastructure development.

3. **Certification Programs**:

Governments can support certification programs, such as eco-tourism certifications or sustainable tourism labels, to distinguish businesses that adhere to specific sustainability standards. These programs provide consumers with transparent information and encourage responsible tourism choices.

C. Public-Private Partnerships for Resilience Building:

1. **Collaborative Planning and Management**:

Public-private partnerships (PPPs) bring together government agencies, private sector entities, NGOs, and local communities to collaboratively plan and manage tourism destinations (Matteis, 2021). By leveraging diverse expertise and resources, PPPs can develop holistic strategies for enhancing resilience and sustainability.

2. Investment and Financing:

PPPs facilitate investment and financing mechanisms for sustainable tourism projects (Anggoro, 2022). This includes mobilizing private sector capital for infrastructure development, conservation initiatives, and community-based tourism enterprises, thereby fostering economic growth while preserving natural and cultural assets.

3. Stakeholder Engagement:

PPPs promote stakeholder engagement and participatory decision-making processes, ensuring that the interests of all relevant parties are considered in tourism development plans (Azazz, 2021). By fostering inclusivity and dialogue, PPPs build consensus and ownership, leading to more resilient and sustainable outcomes.

D. Global and Regional Initiatives Promoting Sustainable Tourism:

1. International Cooperation:

On sustainable tourism practices, worldwide and regional initiatives, such as the United Nations World Tourism Organization (UN WTO and regional tourism associations, promote international cooperation and the transmission of knowledge. These initiatives furnish forums for member states to exchange exemplary methodologies, carry out scholarly investigations, and cultivate discourse on policy matters.

2. Sustainable Development Goals (SDGs):

The SDGs provide a universal framework for promoting sustainable tourism development worldwide. Governments and international organizations align their efforts with specific SDGs, such as Goal 8 (Decent Work and Economic Growth) and Goal 12 (Responsible Consumption and Production), to integrate sustainability principles into tourism policies and practices.

3. Capacity Building and Technical Assistance:

Global and regional initiatives offer capacity building programs and technical assistance to support sustainable tourism development in developing countries and vulnerable regions (Iftikhar, 2022). By enhancing institutional capacity, promoting knowledge transfer, and facilitating access to funding, these initiatives empower governments and local stakeholders to build resilience within their tourism sectors.

3.8 Opportunities of Sustainable Tourism to the Local Communities

Sustainable has become a core element of both business as well as governmental agendas concerning hospitality, specifically the tourism sector, according to a growing number of reports and discussions. In fact, the tourism sector has been dubbed the "new industrial sector." In areas where sustainability is essential. The justification for this is that a sustainable tourism industry can offer numerous advantages to the surrounding communities. The potential benefits encompass elevated socioeconomic status, employment prospects, regional economic well-being, and stakeholder empowerment in the context of tourism strategy and implementation. Stakeholder empowerment has the potential to foster cooperation and alliance between service providers and local communities (Bajracharya, 2020). For example, the implementation of sustainable practices in the tourism industry can foster community collaboration and facilitate the efficient utilization of land and resources. Furthermore, it has been stated that locals also have the opportunity to promote the principles of their communities. It holds utmost significance within indigenous cultures. Sustainability in indigenous tourism, for instance, assists locals in these regions in promoting their cultures and distinctiveness. Additionally, tourism generates employment opportunities for a substantial number of locals. By doing so, the tourism industry can contribute to the long-term economic sustainability of the local community. Sustainable tourism promotes the empowerment of local communities, the elimination of a culture characterized by deprivation and isolation, the resolution of succession issues through the provision of rights to the desired individuals, the resolution of internal disputes, an appreciation for diverse traditions, and the facilitation of global community engagement among local populations. Social media marketing assists tourists and visitors in promoting local cultures and, at times, in raising consciousness about the social requirements of these cultures through the use of intermediaries. Therefore, sustainable tourism has the potential to offer a multitude of prospects for the local communities, some of which may even be passed down to future generations; this is, in essence, sustainability.

Several empirical studies commissioned by the United Nations for sustainable tourism development indicate that the tourism industry is among the most unsustainable; thus, it is critical to find possibilities for the community at large to contribute to sustainability. The advancement of sustainability within the tourism industry can solely be accomplished by emphasizing the tremendous economic growth prospects for the local community. Sustainable practices within the tourism industry have the potential to contribute to various positive outcomes for local communities, including but not limited to safety and security, economic expansion, and the mitigation of climate change risks. Furthermore, it has been stated that the tourism sector is one of the greatest industries globally, making a substantial contribution to the economic well-being of nations. Therefore, by implementing sustainable practices in the tourism industry's development, planning, and management, numerous opportunities may arise, including a surge in tourism. As per strategic management, the local populace can be assisted in adopting novel approaches to progress. Innovative endeavors can manifest in unique ways when executed with forethought, cooperation, and knowledge acquisition. Thus, through effective management, collaboration, and strategic planning, sustainable tourism can generate a variety of distinct possibilities for the local communities.

3.9 Challenges of Sustainable Tourism to the Local Communities

While sustainable tourism presents a multitude of prospects for the local communities, it also engenders a myriad of obstacles. The objective of sustainable tourism is to preserve and restore visitor destinations for future generations, as stated (Qiu, 2021). Nevertheless, the concept of environmentally friendly tourism in rural regions is inextricably linked to the fashion industry, necessitating a transformation of these areas into recreational spaces.

This transition gives rise to the difficulties of eradicating the authentic nature of rural regions, disrupting their cultural contexts, and heightening anxiety. The justification for this is that individuals residing in rural regions are not adequately prepared to employ innovative approaches to attract tourists. Consequently, this ignorance empowers intermediaries to exploit the tourism industry solely for their own financial gain, rather than for the betterment of the local community. Consequently, this situation gives rise to difficulties for the local populace.

Additionally, it is suggested that sustainable tourism necessitates the active participation of knowledgeable members of the local community. Not every nation can seize this opportunity; on the contrary, it presents them with a multitude of challenges. Tourist discontent, decreased tourism, employment decline, inadequate training, linguistic barriers, substandard service, and lack of integrity are some of these obstacles. Furthermore, it has been asserted that while sustainable tourism does generate employment opportunities for the local populace, it fails to ameliorate their economic circumstances as these individuals continue to endure inadequate compensation, inadequate work security, and safety and security concerns. Responsible tourism, while potentially generating prospects for local communities, concurrently exacerbates predicaments for impoverished individuals in dire need of urgent resolutions.

It has been shown that environmentally friendly tourism can present unique challenges for the criticisms of the local community. Sustainable tourism is deemed a fallacy by the author due to the hypocritical nature of its promotion, which, in spite of its advantages being extended to developed and well-educated nations, excludes emerging nations as well as communities from its advantages. According to the author, sustainable tourism promotes an inequitable distribution of benefits for some nations while posing a problem for others; thus, it is merely an inconsistent expression of Western hegemony. Additionally, the point of view of Hoffman was clarified, as he stated that tourism-related climate change debates no longer exist in the globe. Nevertheless, discussions pertaining to culture, values, worldviews, and ideology that are pertinent to the neighborhoods and tourist regions will ensue.

It describes the challenges that environmentally friendly tourism can present to local communities in relation to their traditions, numbers, and ideologies. Sustainable tourism is undeniably a commendable phenomenon; nevertheless, its implementation must be approached with an awareness of the obstacles it may impose on local communities.

4. FUTURE DIRECTIONS

Possible Trends in Sustainable Tourism's Future

With an eye toward the future, a number of nascent trends and advancements are influencing the terrain of sustainable tourism. These trends are indicative of the increasing consciousness and dedication to sustainable practices within the travel and industry sectors (Loureiro, 2021).

1. **Ecotourism and Nature-Based Experiences:** An increasing number of individuals are interested in nature-based experiences and ecotourism, in which they can fully engage with nature while also contributing to conservation initiatives. This phenomenon underscores the significance of safeguarding and conserving natural resources while promoting a more profound comprehension and admiration for the ecosystems of the globe.
2. **Cultural Heritage Tourism:** The objective of cultural heritage tourism is the celebration and preservation of a destination's distinctive culture (29. Zhang, 2020). Authentic experiences that facilitate connections with regional customs,

crafts, music, art, and cuisine practices are gaining increasing attention from travelers. It promotes the safeguarding and rejuvenation of cultural heritage, thereby aiding in the preservation of distinct identities and traditions.

3. **Sustainable Accommodation:** As the hospitality industry evolves, more sustainable lodging options are becoming available. Lodges, resorts, and hotels that prioritize the environment are adopting energy-efficient measures, including the utilization of renewable energy sources, waste reduction, and sustainable construction and design approaches. Such lodgings are being actively sought after by travelers in accordance with their values.

4. **Technology and Innovation:** Innovation and technology are propelling the development of sustainable tourism practices. Technology is significantly contributing to the sustainability of the tourism industry through the implementation of innovative and environmentally friendly innovations in transportation and infrastructure, as well as digital platforms that link tourists with nearby neighborhoods and sustainable businesses.

5. **Community-Based Tourism:** Tourism based on community models are experiencing a surge in popularity as they enable local communities to actively engage and derive advantages from tourism. These initiatives promote cultural preservation and genuine interactions between tourists and residents while making sure the economic benefits remain within the community through communal ownership and control of tourism activities.

6. **Responsible Travel Education and Awareness:** Increasing importance is being placed on educating tourists about the consequences of their decisions and responsible travel practices. Tourism groups and destinations are allocating resources towards awareness campaigns, disseminating information regarding sustainable travel alternatives, and promoting conscientious conduct in an effort to mitigate adverse effects on local communities and the environment.

7. **Circular Economy Initiatives:** In the tourism industry, the idea of the circular economy, which seeks to mitigate waste and optimize the use of resources, is gaining traction. Hotel, restaurant, and tour operator adoption of sustainable food systems, promotion of composting and recycling, and reduction of single-use plastics are among the initiatives currently occurring.

The tourism sector may further develop towards a more environmentally friendly future by wholeheartedly adopting these developments and trends. Sustained research, active stakeholder collaboration, and a steadfast dedication to ethical behavior will be indispensable for safeguarding the environmental and cultural legacy of the world and assuring its sustainable operation for posterity.

5. DISCUSSION AND CONCLUSION

This study delves into the significance of sustainable tourism as a tool for enhancing both environmental conservation and social well-being. The paper begins by acknowledging the increasing recognition of tourism's potential to either contribute positively or exacerbate existing environmental and social challenges. It emphasizes the need for a paradigm shift towards sustainable tourism practices, highlighting its capacity to foster resilience in communities and ecosystems.

One key aspect discussed is the environmental dimension of sustainable tourism. The paper elucidates how sustainable tourism practices can mitigate negative environmental impacts, such as habitat destruction, pollution, and overexploitation of natural resources. By promoting responsible tourism activities like wildlife conservation, energy efficiency, waste management, and sustainable transportation, destinations can reduce their ecological footprint while safeguarding biodiversity and ecosystem health.

Moreover, the paper underscores the crucial role of sustainable tourism in bolstering social resilience. It examines how tourism can serve as a catalyst for community empowerment, cultural preservation, and inclusive economic development. Sustainable tourism initiatives often prioritize local community engagement, equitable distribution of benefits, and the protection of indigenous cultures, thereby fostering social cohesion and resilience against external shocks.

Furthermore, the paper highlights the interconnectedness between environmental and social resilience in the context of tourism development. It elucidates how healthy ecosystems and vibrant communities are mutually reinforcing, creating a positive feedback loop that enhances overall resilience. Sustainable tourism practices that prioritize ecosystem conservation and community well-being can lead to long-term resilience against environmental degradation, economic downturns, and other socio-economic challenges.

This research advocates for a holistic approach to tourism development that integrates environmental sustainability and social equity. By embracing sustainable tourism principles, destinations can not only mitigate environmental degradation and enhance social well-being but also build resilience to future shocks and uncertainties. The paper calls for collaborative efforts among governments, businesses, local communities, and tourists to mainstream sustainability in tourism practices and maximize its potential as a driver of resilience.

REFERENCES

Amoiradis, C., Velissariou, E., & Stankova, M. (2021). Tourism as a Socio-Cultural Phenomenon: A Critical Analysis. Social Sciences eJournal. .10.31014/aior.1991.04.02.271

Anggoro, D., Ramadhan, H., & Ngindana, R. (2022). *Public Private Partnership in Tourism: Build Up a Digitalization Financial Management Model.* Policy & Governance Review., 10.30589/pgr.v6i3.510

Azazz, A., Elshaer, I., & Ghanem, M. (2021). Developing a Measurement Scale of Opposition in Tourism Public-Private Partnerships Projects. *Sustainability (Basel)*, 13(9), 5053. 10.3390/su13095053

Badoc-Gonzales, B. P., Mandigma, M. B. S., & Tan, J. J. (2022). SME Resilience as a Catalyst for Tourism Destinations: A Literature Review. *Journal of Global Entrepreneurship Research*, 12(1), 23–44. 10.1007/s40497-022-00309-1

Bajracharya, B., & Hastings, P. (2020). Stakeholder engagement for disaster management in master-planned communities. *Australian Journal of Emergency Management*, 35, 41–47.

Carvache-Franco, M., Pérez-Orozco, A., Carvache-Franco, O., Víquez-Paniagua, A., & Carvache-Franco, W. (2020). The perceived value in ecotourism related to satisfaction and loyalty: A study from Costa Rica., 24, 229-243. .10.5937/gp24-25082

Dolnicar, S. (2020). Designing for more environmentally friendly tourism. Annals of Tourism Research. https://doi.org/10.31235/osf.io/s76mj

Elmo, G., Arcese, G., Valeri, M., Poponi, S., & Pacchera, F. (2020). Sustainability in Tourism as an Innovation Driver: An Analysis of Family Business Reality. *Sustainability (Basel)*, 12(15), 6149. Advance online publication. 10.3390/su12156149

Han, H. (2021). Consumer behavior and environmental sustainability in tourism and hospitality: A review of theories, concepts, and latest research. *Journal of Sustainable Tourism*, 29(7), 1021–1042. 10.1080/09669582.2021.1903019

Hasan, A. (2021). *Green Tourism*. Media Wisata. 10.36276/mws.v12i1.195

Hodambia, M., & Dandala, S. (2020). Impact of Global Warming on Public Health. *Impact of Global Warming on Public Health.*, 1(2), 65–70. 10.48173/jwh.v1i2.35

Ibrahim, R., & Ajide, K. (2021). Nonrenewable and renewable energy consumption, trade openness, and environmental quality in G-7 countries: The conditional role of technological progress. *Environmental Science and Pollution Research International*, 28(33), 45212–45229. 10.1007/s11356-021-13926-233860425

Iftikhar, H., Chen, P., Ullah, S., & Ullah, A. (2022). Impact of tourism on sustainable development in BRI countries: The moderating role of institutional quality. *PLoS One*, 17(4), e0263745. Advance online publication. 10.1371/journal. pone.026374535436304

Inbakaran, R., & Jackson, M. (2005). Understanding Resort Visitors through Segmentation. *Tourism and Hospitality Research*, 6(1), 53–71. 10.1057/palgrave.thr.6040044

Jeong, E., Lee, T., Brown, A., Choi, S., & Son, M. (2021). Does a National Park Enhance the Environment-Friendliness of Tourists as an Ecotourism Destination? *International Journal of Environmental Research and Public Health*, 18(16), 8321. Advance online publication. 10.3390/ijerph1816832134444073

Karoubi, M., & Ferdowsi, S. (2021). Impact of Perceived Social Apathy on Tourists' Behavioral Intentions. *Leisure Studies*, 40(5), 628–644. 10.1080/02614367.2021.1888308

Li, T., Dong, Y., & Liu, Z. (2020). A review of social-ecological system resilience: Mechanism, assessment and management. *The Science of the Total Environment*, 723, 138113. 10.1016/j.scitotenv.2020.13811332224405

Li, X., Abbas, J., Wang, D., Baig, N., & Zhang, R. (2022). From Cultural Tourism to Social Entrepreneurship: Role of Social Value Creation for Environmental Sustainability. *Frontiers in Psychology*, 13, 925768. Advance online publication. 10.3389/fpsyg.2022.92576835911048

Loureiro, S., & Nascimento, J. (2021). Shaping a View on the Influence of Technologies on Sustainable Tourism. *Sustainability (Basel)*, 13(22), 12691. Advance online publication. 10.3390/su132212691

Lu, Y., Chen, M., & Xue, J. (2020). Water Culture in the Development of National Cultural Tourism under the New Ecological Environment. *Journal of Coastal Research*, 104(sp1), 746–750. 10.2112/JCR-SI104-130.1

Matteis, F., Notaristefano, G., & Bianchi, P. (2021). Public—Private Partnership Governance for Accessible Tourism in Marine Protected Areas (MPAs). *Sustainability (Basel)*, 13(15), 8455. Advance online publication. 10.3390/su13158455

Palinkas, L., & Wong, M. (2020). Global climate change and mental health. *Current Opinion in Psychology*, 32, 12–16. 10.1016/j.copsyc.2019.06.02331349129

Parakh, N. (2022). Understanding the importance of ecotourism by supporting eco-design principles. *International Journal for Research in Applied Science and Engineering Technology*, 10(6), 4865–4872. Advance online publication. 10.22214/ijraset.2022.45085

Pulido-Fernández, J., & Cárdenas-García, P. (2020). Analyzing the Bidirectional Relationship between Tourism Growth and Economic Development. *Journal of Travel Research*, 60(3), 583–602. 10.1177/0047287520922316

Qiu, M., Sha, J., & Scott, N. (2021). Restoration of Visitors through Nature-Based Tourism: A Systematic Review, Conceptual Framework, and Future Research Directions. *International Journal of Environmental Research and Public Health*, 18(5), 2299. Advance online publication. 10.3390/ijerph1805229933652652

Rauf, J. (2021). Sustainable Tourism. 10.4135/9781483368924.n438

Seervi, D. (2023). *Ecotourism and Sustainable Development*. International Journal For Multidisciplinary Research. 10.36948/ijfmr.2023.v05i05.7049

Shu-Yuan Pan, M., Gao, M., Kim, H., Shah, K. J., Pei, S.-L., & Chiang, P.-C. (2018). Advances and challenges in sustainable tourism toward a green economy. *The Science of the Total Environment*, 635, 452–469. 10.1016/j.scitotenv.2018.04.13429677671

Steiger, R., Posch, E., Tappeiner, G., & Walde, J. (2020). The impact of climate change on demand of ski tourism - a simulation study based on stated preferences. *Ecological Economics*, 170, 106589. 10.1016/j.ecolecon.2019.106589

Štreimikienė, D., Švagždienė, B., Jasinskas, E., & Simanavicius, A. (2020). Sustainable tourism development and competitiveness: The systematic literature review. *Sustainable Development (Bradford)*, 29(1), 259–271. 10.1002/sd.2133

TechnoFunc - Social & Cultural Impact of Tourism. (n.d.). https://www.technofunc.com/index.php/domain-knowledge/travel-and-tourism-domain/item/social-cultural-impact

Wood.Hey, P. (1990). Truth and Beauty in hand space-Trends in landscape and Leisure. *Land Space Australia*, 12(1), 43–47.

Zeng, Z., & Wang, X. (2021). Spatial Effects of Domestic Tourism on Urban-Rural Income Inequality. *Sustainability (Basel)*, 13(16), 9394. Advance online publication. 10.3390/su13169394

Zhang, G., Chen, X., Law, R., & Zhang, M. (2020). Sustainability of Heritage Tourism: A Structural Perspective from Cultural Identity and Consumption Intention. *Sustainability (Basel)*, 12(21), 9199. 10.3390/su12219199

Chapter 5
Community–Based Tourism Development in Gurez Valley:
A Planning Perspective

Hafizullah Dar
https://orcid.org/0000-0003-2388-9474
Lovely Professional University, India

Mudasir Ahmad Dar
Indira Gandhi National Open University, India

ABSTRACT

This study examined diverse tourism potentials and possibilities of community-based tourism development (CBTD) in Gurez valley. Desk research approach was adopted in which various theories and cases, apart from the other sources, were reviewed to accomplish the study purpose. The results, based on natural, socio-cultural, symbiotic, and event-based tourism resources, paved a way to design community-based tourism (CBT) model for Gurez valley. The hexagonal CBT model constitutes 1) involvement of local people, 2) training local people, 3) developing cooperative ownership, 4) developing local products, 5) creating partnership, and 6) product marketing. Applications of this model will help tourism planners and decision-makers in developing the community-based tourism and encouraging the local community to participate in CBT activities. Its applications will have direct positive impacts on the local economy, tourism resources, tourist experience, business, infrastructure, jobs, and other related aspects in the area.

DOI: 10.4018/979-8-3693-5405-6.ch005

Copyright © 2024, IGI Global. Copying or distributing in print or electronic forms without written permission of IGI Global is prohibited.

INTRODUCTION

Tourism comes in major businesses in the world with millions of human resources and trillions of income in dollars. All the same, efforts are made to use tourism as an instrument in uplifting the poor communities in backward areas by developing tourism (UNWTO, 2020). Utilizing untapped tourism resources, developing tourist attractions, designing tourist circuits, standing infrastructure, framing local markets, creating jobs for local people, and generating income are taken into account when it comes to working on community development through tourism under Community Based Tourism Development (CBTD) concept (Polnyotee & Thadaniti, 2015; Witchayakawin, et al., 2020).

This study aims to understand the feasibility of Community Based Tourism Development (CBTD) and modeling of community-based tourism in Gurez valley in northern Kashmir. Gurez Valley is a beautiful mountainous tourist adobe with rich natural and cultural heritage (Dar, 2018). It is pivotal to have Community Based Tourism in such mountain areas for improving the rural economy, involvement, and empowerment of the local community, sustainability, and poverty reduction (Lama, 2014; Gupta et al, 2018). Monitoring the advantages of Community Based Tourism through research is very important (Giampiccoli & Saayman, 2018) and the support from the local community is crucial to make it a successful on ground (Polnyotee & Thadaniti, 2015).

Gurez Valley: Study Area

Gurez is the Himalayan Valley located at an altitude of 2400m AMSL in Jammu and Kashmir, a Union Territory (UT) in northern India, nearly 124 km from Srinagar (summer capital of UT). Gurez Valley is a border tourism destination (Dar, 2014) touching the Line of Control (LoC) that separates Indian administered Kashmir (IAK) from Pakistan occupied Kashmir (PoK). Gurez Valley remained the gateway to the legendary Silk Route transversely to central Asia in the past (Shaheen, et al., 2017).

Gurez is walled by sky touching, lofty and snow-capped mountains denote diversity in characteristics, appearances, elevation, ruggedness, glacial work, and landmarks that leave the Valley identical to a mesmerizing adobe on the earth. Besides, the fast-flowing and roaring Kishangana River pours through the Gurez valley in a temperate climate (Dar, 2018).

Local people of Gurez belong to the Dard tribe, originally from Gilgit valley (currently in Pakistan). They are quite similar to people living in the upper reaches of mountains in Kashmir in their dress, looks, and various other lifestyles. Despite difficult living in the Valley, Dards have raised themselves and changed their fate by the proper education and hard work in every field of the walk (Shaheen, et al., 2017; Atta, et al., 2018).

Gurez Valley is a 3 to 6 nights' destination to visit. This beautiful adobe takes about 7 to 8 hours from Srinagar to access it. This Srinagar-Gurez journey crosses Sumbal and Bandipora towns and gives breathtaking views of illustrious Manasbal Lake, Walur Lake, Razdan Pass, Shrine of Peer Bubo, and various other imperative tourist spots. Apart from a few seasonal hotels, tents and homestay are the common accommodation options in the Valley. Moreover, a few seasonal restaurants are serving local food during the day only in the Valley (Khan, 2019).

LITERATURE REVIEW

Community-Based Tourism (CBT)

The immersion in Community Based Tourism mends the way of life and inspires inordinate interchange in socio-cultural aspects among the local societies and tourists. Although Community Based Tourism was, by and large, assumed as ecotourism for the conservation of nature (Zapata et al., 2011); later on, the concept has been enlarged and the colossal amount of tourism products such as traditional presentations, and handcraft makings are offered to tourists (Lama, 2014). Therefore, the positive involvement of local communities is highly important in interacting with tourists and caring for the local natural and cultural heritage of the destination (Polnyotee & Thadaniti, 2015). The goodness of the local community, towards community-based tourism, ensures the continuous and balanced supply of tourism services to the tourists (Sita & Nor, 2012). Besides, CBT allows local people to adopt a sustainable approach in local resource planning and consumption for conservation and long-lasting benefits (Dangi & Jamal, 2016; Dar, 2024). Therefore, community-based tourism constitutes the apt set of managerial practices in managing tourism resources and interacting with the diverse segments of people (Sita & Nor, 2012). Similarly, Goodwin and Santilli (2009) have defined Community Based Tourism as *"a means of development whereby social, environmental and economic needs of local communities are met through the offering of a tourism product"*. In Community Based Tourism, usually, lodges and homestay services are widely offered by the local people to visitors which make local community decision-maker and manager of local resources for their sustainable benefits (Sita and Nor, 2015).

Community-based tourism (CTB) has deep relations with the cultural heritage of the indigenous people. CBT allows tourists to visit indigenous communities to experience their cultural diversity such as dress, food, belief systems, rituals, traditions, customs, lifestyle, art, architecture, and so on (Polnyotee & Thadaniti, 2015).

However, natural resources are major aspects of community-based tourism and CBT product. Therefore, tourists can experience indigenous communities as well as the natural setting of the destination under community-based tourism. Tourists compare diverse cultures, have strong bonds and attachments with local communities, and spend quality time with them, gain knowledge, enable local people to earn and utilize tourism resources properly. These tourist activities are a complete set of tourism products (Dunn, 2007). Hence community-based tourism paves way for the local communities to establish their small-scale self-managed businesses.

Understanding the concept of community-based tourism through different perspectives is very important. *Indigenous leadership, sustainability, and cultural immersion* features give a better understanding of the Community-Based Tourism concept (Han, et al., 2019; Mayaka et al, 2019).

Indigenous Leadership: Indigenous communities manage Community-Based Tourism themselves, which explains the community takes accountability for tourist accommodation, food, local sightseen, cultural activities, and other travel activities (Witchayakawin, et al., 2020). Local communities are taking various socio-cultural, environmental, and economic advantages from community-based tourism and they also make CBT an alternate to those travel firms which usually ignore indigenous communities and the natural environment they use (Okazaki, 2008; Hung, et. al., 2019).

Sustainability: Local communities accommodate guests as per the occupancy to maintain the standards of sustainability and protection of tourism resources from excessive pressure due to over-tourism (Witchayakawin, et al., 2020). Food is generally grown locally with sustainable practices for communities and to serve an adoptable number of guests while keeping in mind the future supply from local resources. Besides, community-based tourism sustains and revives the indigenous cultures from diminution in the present swiftly altering world (Polnyotee & Thadaniti, 2015).

Cultural Immersion: Community-based tourism allows tourists to explore the cultural diversity of rural areas and causes social interactions among guests and hosts (Han, et al., 2019; Hung, et. al., 2019). Traditional accommodation, attire, cuisine, feasts, rituals, and various other cultural activities lay down a strong base for improved knowledge of other cultures, social norms, and diverse belief sets through Community Based Tourism (Mayaka et al, 2019; Arintoko, et al, 2020).

Community-Based Tourism is getting its momentum at present. Tourists are choosing it for many reasons. They are showing their gratitude towards the destination and local communities for every belonging aspect to make their travel cherished. Tourists see, touch, hear, taste, and do things in community-based tourism they might not ever have done before in life (Sita & Nor, 2015). CBT leaves a deeper bond among guests, hosts, and places. Direct interactions happen amongst CBT stakeholders for knowledge exchange/gain and which impact the lives of every individual involved in the process (Thadaniti, 2015). Hence, community-based tourism is one of the greatest means of empathy and awareness of other cultures which narrates itself that how CBT shapes human lives and ensures the diverse benefits of tourism to local communities in sustainable manners (UNWTO, 2020).

Community-Based Tourism Development Strategies

Community-Based Tourism Development strategies have been studied by various researchers differently (Arintoko, et al, 2020; Giampiccoli, and Saayman, 2018; Mtapuri, and Giampiccoli, 2016; Polnyotee and Thadaniti, 2015; Peredo, and Chrisman, 2006). However, Mintzberg (2009) has given a set of strategies (figure 1) for the sustainable development of CBT.

Figure 1. Community-Based Tourism Development Strategies

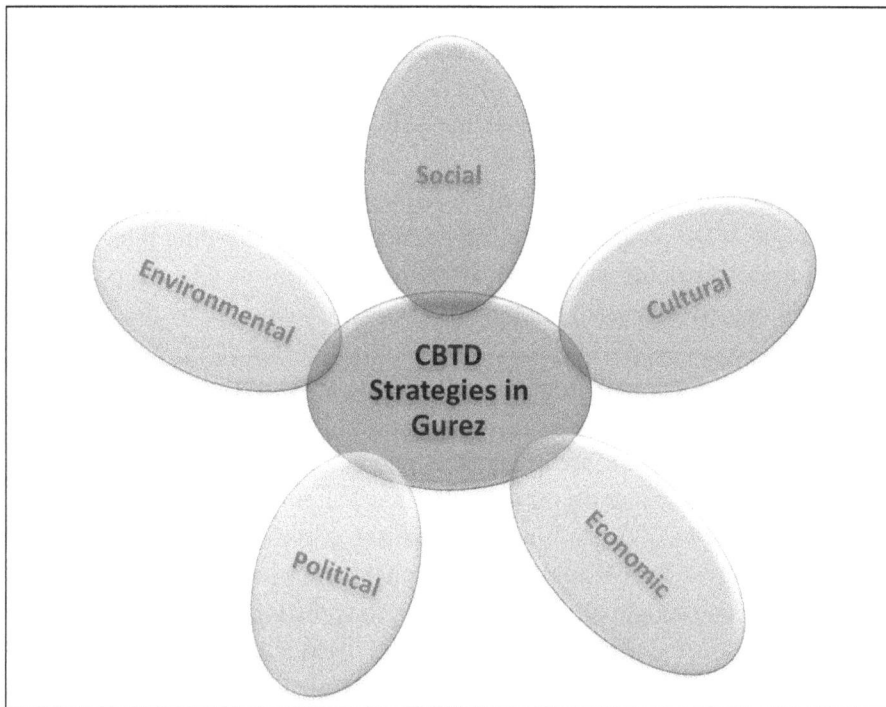

Source: *Mintzberg (2009)*

Many tourist destinations fall on the international boundaries of India in Kashmir (Dar, 2014); Kozak and Buhalis (2019) and Sofield (2006) stressed that the political relations with the neighboring country should be friendly for destination peace. On the other hand, Polnyotee and Thadaniti (2015) studied that government empowers local people, who are involved, in CBTD decision making for their goodwill. Besides, local people are enabled by local agencies to manage and protect their local natural resources for employability, survival, and identity.

Border Tourism and Border
Communities: An Overview

Juma and Vidra (2019) researched that while developing and protecting the local environment, eco-friendly approaches (like waste management, green products etc. are must to be adopted. Giampiccoli and Saayman (2018) concluded that it is pertinent to educate the local people and other stakeholders about the importance of eco-friendly approaches in environmental conservation and destination beautification. The destination carrying capacity is vital to understand for bearable tourist arrival at a particular destination and destination planning stage (Juma and Vidra, 2019).

Social development strategies in CBTD emphases on healthy wellbeing, quality of life, local culture, customs, festivals, rituals, traditions, safety, security, destination quality, people to people access, public safety campaigns, creation of green zones, and community parks (Han, et. al., 2019; Najaz, et al, 2022). It is important to promote the pride of the people of the local community by exhibiting their locality as a safer, beautiful, hygienic, and tourist-friendly destination by all aspects. Arintoko, et al, (2020) opined the horizontal linkage should be supported by the fair division of roles among local people in collaboration with other concerned stakeholders and agencies (like professionals, tourists, politicians, employers, activists, and other beneficiaries). However, considering Polnyotee and Thadaniti's (2015) observation, it is crucial too to create a sense of oneness among local people for protecting their social norms to aid community-based tourism development in the areas.

Displaying (by locals), learning (by tourists), and accepting (by tourists) are three fundamental aspects of cultural development at any tourist destination (Bagus, et al., 2019). This triangle allows any culture to spread its wings and make roots stronger. According to Polnyotee and Thadaniti (2015), it is also important to foster community gratitude and involvement in cultural altercation besides developing and out-spreading the prospects for tourism stakeholders to involve in activities that endorse sustainable cultural blend in the locality. Giampiccoli and Saayman (2018) specified the thought by saying that cultural expressions come from residents hence local people of the destination have to express the cultural originality which would further aid in cross-cultural relationships for community development and individuality. Hence local festivals are crucial tools to market the cultural identity of the research area which displays the centuries-old cultural heritage of local people (Polnyotee & Thadaniti, 2015).

Past literature (Peredo & Chrisman, 2006) is witness that economic development at a destination is inevitable from the increase of per capita income of locals, growth in employment opportunities, improved living standards, the existence of small and large scale businesses, and other income-generating activities. Hence a multidimensional approach is needed in areas where CBTD is planned for economic development. Giampiccoli and Saayman (2018) pointed out that the approach should cover all tourism stakeholders at the destination for diverse economic activities where the interest of the local community is more focused on. To pave the way for economic development in desired areas, government and local authorities must frame policies for sustainable community tourism development where protection of tourism resources, growth in tourist arrivals, opportunities of small and medium scales businesses, employment creation, income opportunities, and other crucial aspects are highly emphasized (Polnyotee & Thadaniti, 2015). Private players should be invited to infrastructure development and jobs for locals. On the other hand, the local people are needed to be aware of community-based tourism development at the earliest. Peredo and Chrisman (2006) discussed that the local people need to be guided for small scale and medium scale businesses like restaurants, homestay accommodation, local transport, selling locally grown and produced products, and so on. Therefore, local jobs should be reinforced through the enlargement of employment activities that increase knowledge among the local community about job projections in the tourism sector and help them in identifying job opportunities in the hospitality industry (Polnyotee & Thadaniti, 2015).

Research Methodology

This research work is qualitative in nature aimed to ascertain the available community-based tourism resources which will help in designing a model for Community Based-Tourism Development in Gurez valley. Hence, desk research approach has been adopted to conduct this research work. Various dimensions of CBT development and CBT models were reviewed from the past literature (Table 1) to lay down a strong theoretical foundation of this study. Data were collected from various research papers, articles, theses, reports, books, and other published and unpublished sources.

The dimensions of the proposed model of CBTD for Gurez valley are widely discussed and stressed upon by the researchers. Their arguments give large space to the model parameters in this study. Content analysis approach helped to focus on a certain themes which were later considered as the main research model dimensions.

The nature of the proposed model will explain for the swarms of players exist in any genuine sustainable development resourcefulness in the study area and the model applications has tendency to maximize the benefits in the area.

Table 1. Matrix of Model Centered Community Based-Tourism Development Studies

S. No	Author(s) and Year	Research Title
1.	Hung, et. al. (2019)	Incorporating on-site activity involvement and sense of belonging into the Mehrabian-Russell model—The experiential value of cultural tourism.
2.	Giampiccoli and Saayman (2018).	Community-Based Tourism Development Model and Community Participation.
3.	Runyowa, D. (2017	Community-based tourism development in Victoria Falls, Kompisi Cultural Village: an entrepreneur's model
4.	Acharya and Halpenny, (2016).	Applying the Tourism Area Life Cycle and Small Tourism Enterprises' Growth Cycle Models to Explain Communities
5.	Choo, et. al. (2016).	An integrated model of festival revisit intentions: Theory of planned behavior and festival quality/satisfaction
6.	Mtapuri and Giampiccoli, (2016).	Towards a comprehensive model of community-based tourism development.
7.	Zhang and Xiao, (2014).	Destination development in China: towards an effective model of explanation
8.	Lama, R., (2014)	Community-Based Tourism Development: A Case Study of Sikkim.
9.	Mtapuri and Giampiccoli, (2013).	Interrogating the role of the state and non-state actors in community-based tourism ventures: toward a model for spreading the benefits to the wider community
10.	Okazaki, E. (2008)	A community-based tourism model: Its conception and use.

Community-Based Tourism Potential in Gurez Valley

Gurez is a captivating and fascinating Valley among the mighty Himalayan Mountains in Kashmir. Hence physiography of Gurez makes it an effective tourist place with diverse natural tourism resources (Dar, 2018a). It remained an imperative destination for adventurers and explorers before 1950. Besides the natural setting, the native tribes of Gurez live inimitable lifestyles proudly. The cultural identity of local people appeals and mesmerizes visitors in Gurez (Shaheen, et al., 2017). However, despite having huge tourism potentials, the fame of Gurez is not much higher at present due to certain reasons (Dar, 2014; Kumar & Dar, 2014). Therefore, Gurez, once prominent, is now one of the lesser-known destinations in Kashmir valley.

The people of Gurez are having a very attractive and unique cultural dress code. They wear long overcoat up to knees, locally known as *Pheran*, made of woolen material which is generally gathered from domestic sheep. Pheran has enough space to carry fire pot (locally known as *Kangri*) made of earthenware for generating heat and body warming in winters. Like males, females wear Pheran in different types and looks, caps are also dissimilar in colors, sizes, and designs for male and female (Kaul, 2014)

People of Gurez live in *Kutcha Makaan* (earthen house) and *Pucca Makaan* (concrete house). Kutcha makkan is the traditional dwelling style of local people in the area. It is made of wooden logs with muddy plaster on the walls. The wooden roof is supported by also large wooden beams. Tulail town has an important place in preserving such houses with all its traditional features. These houses are furnished with beautiful traditional *namdas*. Doors and Windows of rooms are reasonably small to uphold room temperature. These traditional houses have two floors, generally, the ground floor is meant for cattle (sheep, goats, horse, cow bull, mule, etc.) and the second floor is inhabited by the family members (Bamzai, 1994; Dewan, 2011). On the other hand, Pucca makkan is made of stones and concrete bricks with suitable windows and doors. *Pucca makaan* has a concrete base along with the rainwater system; unlike *kutcha makaan*, cattle sheds are built at a good distance from *Pucca makaan* (Kaul, 2014; Dar & Islam, 2018).

People of Gurez use a traditional instrument called *Chhaproo'*, a butter churner used to turn curd and cream into buttermilk and butter. It is a power-driven manual method in which a wooden pole is put in through the lid of the device into the bowl. Usage of *Chhaproo* needs well expertise. Shin *Chhaproo* is quite different from other *Chhaproos* used in other parts of the country (Dewan, 2011). This could give a unique experience to visitors in the Valley.

Local people of Gurez valley speak an endangered Shina language which is also spoken by the various people living in Pakistan occupied Kashmir, on the other side of the Line of Control (LoC). Shina language has been worst affected due to modernization. Today, Habba Khatoon Drama Club is working actively for its protection and spread (Kaul, 2014). Here, *Community Based Tourism* can be a crucial tool in the hands of local people and other bodies to safeguard this beautiful language of Gurez valley.

The Valley is almost entirely inhabited by the Muslims. People can marry some-one irrespective of distance. Unlike consanguineous marriages, child marriage, polygamy, and inter-religious marriages are forbidden in the Gurez (Dar, 2018a). Apart from the Islamic principles, marriages in Gurez are decorated and celebrated with various local traditions, rituals, rites, and other local cultural facets which can offer a long last experience to every visitor (Dewan, 2011).

People in Gurez are following Islam and they are largely Sunni Muslims. Before the existence of Islam in the Valley, people were following Hinduism (Dar, 2020). Seven companions (*Sadaats*) of Shah Hamdan (1372 AD) visited Gurez to spread the message of Allah. All of them are highly respected and followed by local people. Shrines of these saints are present in Gurez which are visited by local people widely and outsiders as well. Fakirpora, Chorwan, Bagtore, and Dangital, Tulail areas are known for these saints (Dewan, 2011). Thus, the religious atmosphere is another tool to strengthen community-based tourism in the area (Dar, 2014).

The rich cultural heritage of Gurez is showcased in its very popular two days Gurez Festival every summer of the year. The festival is organized by the Department of Tourism, Jammu, and Kashmir aiming for the promotion of tourism potentials of Gurez worldwide. More stress, in the festivals, is given on adventure, leisure, and cultural tourism aspects of the area (Dar, 2018). Usually, the festival remains full of attractive cultural programs and adventure activities to entertain and recreate the participants and visitors in Gurez. The festival could be the spirit of community-based tourism in the Valley while displaying the lifestyle of local people and natural beauty. Local people such as artists, students, businesspersons, and other groups are actively participating in this festival for its noble cause (Atta, et al., 2018; Khan, 2019).

Gurez is known for world-famous trout and many other varieties of fishes which are largely found in the acclaimed Kishanganga River. Rainbow trout fish is the best variety for industrial supply and production because this variety is quite easy to feed and handle for water quality and temperature requirements. Thus, the fisheries world is another positive aspect of Gurez to help its Community-Based Tourism Development plan by pulling the attention of fish lovers for angling and best proteins (Dar, 2018a).

Habba Khatoon peak is a very popular and beautiful pyramid-shaped mountain in Gurez. This peak is named after the well-known Kashmiri poetess Habba Khatoon, initially named *Zoon*. She was very intelligent and keen on poetry and singing. This beautiful lady was ill-treated by her mother-in-law due to which she got a divorce and later married Emperor Yousuf Shah Chak. She was in deep love with the emperor. When Emperor Yousuf Shah Chak was imprisoned by Emperor Akbar, Habba Khatoon used to wander near this mountain peak in search of her love. This is how the peak is named after her. She was mourning the death of Emperor Yousuf Shah Chak for twenty years till her last breath by wandering the banks of River Jhelum and was entombed in Athawajan, Srinagar (Dewan, 2011; Dar, 2014).

Water bodies, such as rivers, lakes, seas, springs etc. have been mesmerizing tourist attractions. Likewise, Gurez houses the very beautifully Kishanganga River to appeal to tourists for their long-lasting memories. Kishanganga River originates from Krishansar Lake near Sonamarg and flows downhill through Badoab village (Dar, 2014). It meets the Jhelum River in Muzafarabad in PoK. Out of 245 km of total length, Kishanganga River covers merely 50 km in Indian administered Gurez valley. This crucial river could be used as one of the fundamental pillars of Community Based Tourism Development in Gurez valley (Khan, 2019).

The food habits of people in Gurez are highly influenced by its geo-climatic aspects. They are generally non-vegetarian and rice is their main food. They eat meat, such as beef, muttan, chicken, eggs et al, twice or thrice a week, depends on their economic conditions. Rajma, pea, cabbage, potatoes, tomato, turnip, reddish, carrot, et al, are widely consumed in vegetables by the local people in the Valley. Besides, they eat some wild leafy vegetables as well in summer times, which are also dried up for consumption in winter. People in Gurez are also habitual of walnut and wild almond eating which are profusely available in the Valley (Bamzai, 1994; Kaul, 2014).

Archaeological Survey of India (ASI) has discovered hundreds of Kharoshthi, Hebrew, Brahmi, and Tibetan inscriptions in the *Chilas* area, along the Silk Route, of Gurez valley which reveal the origin of Kashmiri people and subsistence of Buddhism in around 1st to 6th centuries AD in the area. Kanzilwan is an important ASI site where the last Buddhist council is believed to have been held. Besides, the ruins of Sharada University and Dawar (capital of Dards') are other significant ASI sites in Gurez. As the Valley is historically crucial for many reasons, more archeological research is continuing in Gurez (Kaul, 2014). Hence ASI sites could be used for Community Based Tourism Development purposes in the area.

Kishanganga Hydroelectric Plant (KHP) could be included in the Community Based Tourism Development framework as it remains in the minds of visitors in Gurez. 330 MW and 37-meter reservoir KHP is basically around 6 km towards the North of Bandipora which also submerges some parts of Gurez valley. A 24 km long water tunnel is also a part of this plant. This project remained disputed for several years as Pakistan sued for violation of the Indus Water Treaty (IWT) because of this power project by India. The Hague's Permanent Court of Arbitration halted the construction of the dam in October 2011, later in February 2013, the court ruled in favor of India with certain conditions.

The geophysical setting of Gurez makes it one of the thrilling adventure destinations in the Himalayas. It is surrounded by massive mountain peaks significant for trekking, mountaineering, camping, and rock-climbing. Gurez serves as a base camp of Kishensar Lake and Gangabal Lake for trekking expeditions. The trekking routes from Gurez and Tilel lead up to Sonamarg and Gangabal to its east and Drass,

Zanskar, and Dahanu to its north. Besides, the Kishanganga River is appropriate for white water rafting, canoeing, kayaking, swimming, and many other water sports activities in Gurez valley (Khan, 2019; Dar, 2018; Dar, 2014).

Community-Based Tourism Development Model for Gurez Valley

Community-based tourism is difficult without the involvement and participation of the local community (Polnyotee & Thadaniti, 2015). They should be ready for change. In the change, they have to teach tourists some socio-cultural things, such as agricultural activities, cooking, dance, some words of the local language, etc. in Gurez (Dar, 2018b). Planners have to get connect with the local people of Gurez valley to support and guide them so that to get participation from local people for tourism product creation (Peredo & Chrisman, 2006).

Once the local people of Gurez agreed to participate in CBTD, the second thing comes to train them in tourism activities (Fig. 2). Because educating and developing basic skills among local people is imperative before they participate in tourism activities (Dangi & Jamal, 2016; Gohori & van der Merwe, 2024). They can be trained through various workshops for different roles and job positions. Training and development of the local community will help them to understand and accept the tourism culture and they will be able to know that what to expect from tourism. Generating basic professionalism among local people will take time depending on people how they react towards tourism development and their involvement in tourism activities (Sita & Nor, 2015; Tristanti, et al., 2024). Generally, age and gender are not any bars in training the local community because people from any age group, irrespective of their gender, are interested in serving tourists (Witchayakawin, et al., 2020). Trainees from the local community should be 18 years and above to avoid issues like child labor as per the law of the land.

One of the imperative aspects of community-based tourism development is a sense of responsibility among local people or a sense of ownership (Hung, et. al., 2019; Romero–Medina, et al., 2024). Therefore, planners must create oneness, leadership, and ownership sagacity among the people of Gurez for successful community-based tourism development in the region. It is needed to bring the local community to a stage where they would contribute towards the local tourism after training and take care of local tourism resources in sustainable manners (Hung, et. al., 2019; Suksmawati, et al., 2024). They should form self-regulating unions of local community members to make decisions for better tourism in the region (Polnyotee & Thadaniti, 2015). This will ensure a fair-minded sustainable community-based tourism development in Gurez and benefits from tourism to maximum local people. Empowering the local community in decision making will also help in creating a sense of ownership among the local people of Gurez valley and this will have a profound impact on sustainable tourism development in the region (Witchayakawin, et al., 2020; Na thongkaew, et al., 2024).

Figure 2. Community-Based Tourism Development Model

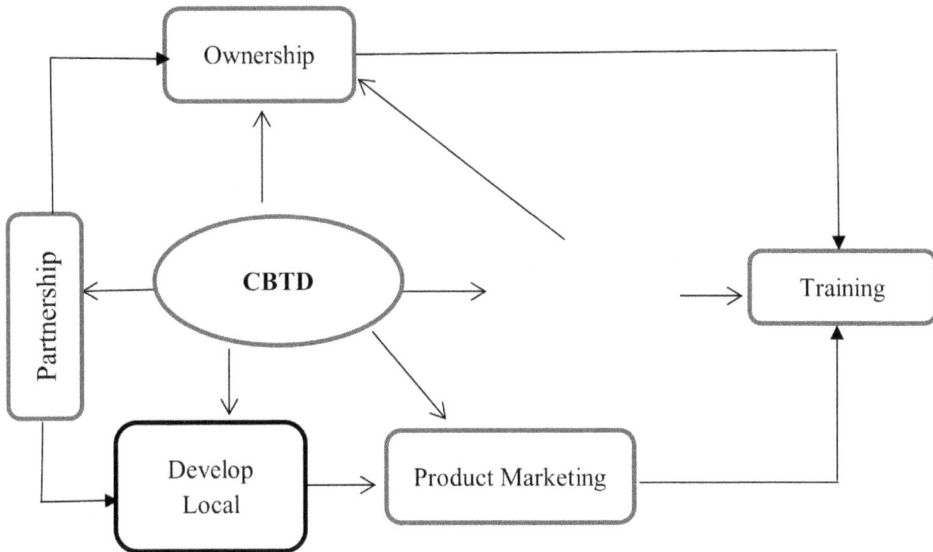

Source:*Designed by Author*

Community-based tourism development creates a favorable atmosphere in which various service providers from respective areas come closer for partnerships to get diverse benefits from the tourism business (Polnyotee & Thadaniti, 2015; Suksmawati, et al., 2024). Therefore, creating partnerships among local businesses in Gurez is pivotal for the success of community-based tourism development and this will have a significant impact on tourism planning in the region as well. This partnership should be among local hoteliers, homestay owners, lodges, tour operators, restaurants, handicraft traders, and other beneficiaries (Sita & Nor, 2015; Na thongkaew, et al., 2024). The partnership among local businesses is exceptionally essential for fashioning the forthcoming proof tourism industry in Gurez and such partnerships among local tourism businesses are one the goals of United Nations Sustainable Development Goals (Polnyotee & Thadaniti, 2015). Having sound integrations among these local tourism businesses will create an effective business environment in the region with effective impacts.

Local products are a major dimension of community-based tourism, in other words, community-based tourism revolves around the locally grown and developed products in the designed areas (Han, et. al., 2019; Ditta-Apichai, et al., 2024).

Consequently, it is imperative to develop community products in Gurez to make community-based tourism strong and visible in the region. Planners can guide local people in creating community products after having a clear understanding of local natural, cultural, symbiotic, event-based, and site-based tourism resources (Mintzberg, 2009; Acharya & Halpenny., 2016; Ngo, et al., 2024). Local excursions and other tourist activities are undertaken by tourists should provide them an understanding of the local community and tourism resources in Gurez valley. While developing local community-based tourism products, it is essential to include interactive components of tourism products (Polnyotee & Thadaniti, 2015; Hung, et. al., 2019; Ditta-Apichai, et al., 2024). Tourists like to observe the process of traditional dish preparation, tea making, agricultural activities, raising cattle, performing local dances, fetching water, and various other things that local people do (Giampiccoli, & Saayman, 2018). It is a fact that what is conventional for the local people is an inimitable experience for the tourist. Well trained local tourist guides would be strategic here as they would guide tourists perfectly in their local areas as no one knows their community and area better than them (Arintoko, et al, 2020; Ngo, et al., 2024).

For making sustainable community-based tourism development projects successful in Gurez, after creating a partnership atmosphere among the businesses, planners must promote local tourism products to tourists (Polnyotee & Thadaniti, 2015; Runyowa, 2017; Lee, et at., 2024). The marketing of community-based tourism products will have a positive impact on the project and surely attract a sound number of tourists in the region (Witchayakawin, et al., 2020). For marketing respective tourism products, various marketing approaches could be used in this process (Sugandini, et al., 2018; Kozak & Buhalis, 2019; Lee, et at., 2024). Offering FAM tours to writers, electronic and print media agencies, tour operators, and other concerned agencies; discussing tourism potentials at local, national, and international level; promoting Gurez in various trade fairs; celebrating local socio-cultural and commercial events; inviting filmmakers, liaising with tourism actors, developing attractive and informative websites, and other appropriate marketing approaches social media platforms such as Facebook, Instagram, travel blogs, Twitter, YouTube, travel applications (Sugandini, et. al., 2018), and so on are also useful tools in promoting community-based tourism of Gurez. Community-based tourism planners should design an effective and appropriate marketing mix to promote the region among tourists. While marketing the local community-based tourism product of Gurez, it is essential to highlight and provide local cultural heritage insights and surroundings which will have more impact on the tourist mind and experience (Acharya & Halpenny, 2016; Kozak & Buhalis, 2019).

Challenges in implementing the Community-Based Tourism Development Model in Gurez

The implementation of the proposed Community-Based Tourism (CBT) development model in Gurez Valley, Kashmir, is not as easy as in other places around the world due to available infrastructure, geo-political reasons, economic issues, regulator frameworks and several others. The implementation process will have to have faces several challenges, such as:

Limited Infrastructure: Poor road connectivity and limited current transport options hinder access to Gurez valley. Besides, insufficient and substandard accommodation facilities in the Valley may not meet tourist expectations.

Political and Security Apprehensions: Being an international border between India and Pakistan, the area is often in surveillance to control the infiltration from Pakistan due to which the ongoing political tensions and security concerns can deter tourists and investors (Najar, et al, 2022). This atmosphere has created negative perceptions of safety in Gurez which may affect tourist inflow.

Community Commitment: The lack of awareness about tourism benefits and inadequate training among local people can hamper effective participation of the people. Moreover, balancing tourism development with the safeguarding of local culture and traditions entails careful management.

Economic Challenges: The limited access to financial resources and investment for developing tourism infrastructure is one of the grave challenges in Gurez and risk of over-dependence on tourism, which can be volatile and seasonal is another concern in the region.

Regulatory and Policy Issues: The composite regulatory frameworks and bureaucratic bottlenecks can slow down project implementation in Gurez valley. To make it happen, strong governmental policies and support is needed to foster CBT initiatives in the beautiful Gurez valley.

To overcome the aforementioned challenges, improving roads and accommodation sector through government and private investment, enhancing safety measures and promoting a positive regional image, educating locals on tourism benefits and providing hospitality trainings, facilitating access to microloans for local entrepreneurs, implementing eco-friendly practices and waste management systems, simplifying regulations and offer government incentives, and use of digital platforms to promote Gurez's unique cultural and natural attractions are imperative to be worked on to implement the model successfully in the region:

CONCLUSION AND FUTURE RESEARCH

This research work underlined the feasibility of the community-based tourism development in Gurez valley, a Himalayan tourist destination in north India. An effective diversity of lesser-known cultural, natural, symbiotic, and event-based tourism resources have been studied in Gurez valley which paved the way for designing an applicable community based-tourism development model in the region. The proposed model would be an effective tool for tourism planners and decision-makers. The CBTD model includes the following six stages: *Involvement of Local People, Training Local People, Developing Cooperative Ownership, Developing Local Products, Creating Partnership and Product Marketing.*

After applying this model, the local people will contribute significantly to Community Based-Tourism Development process in Gurez valley. Their interest will increase in CBT activities by empowering them in the decision-making process and maintaining the originality of their cultural heritage. This CBTD model will open the doors of employment, business, income, conservation of tourism resources, needed guest-host relationship, infrastructural development, and various other related things in the area. Moreover, tourists will get unique travel experiences in Gurez they are looking for and more importantly this will achieve the UNWTO *Sustainable Development Goals* such as 8th and 16th (UNWTO SDP - 2030 Agenda) in the region. This study paves the way for further research on residents' willingness and participation in tourism activities, guest and host relationships, and travel perception of tourists in Gurez valley.

REFERENCES

Acharya, B. P., & Halpenny, E. A. (2016). Applying the Tourism Area Life Cycle and Small Tourism Enterprises' Growth Cycle Models to Explain Communities' Sustainability. 2016 *Conference. 4, University of Massachusetts* – Amherst, ScholarWorks@UMass Amherst.

Arintoko, A., Ahmad, A. A., Gunawan, D. S., & Supadi, S. (2020). Communitybased Tourism Village Development Strategies: A Case of Borobudur Tourism Village Area, Indonesia. *Geo Journal of Tourism and Geosites*, 29(2), 398–413. 10.30892/gtg.29202-477

Atta. (2018). Socio-economic Profile of Shina Community Subsisting on NTFPs in Gurez Valley of Kashmir. *International Journal of Advance Research in Science and Engineering.*

Bagus, . (2019). Community Based Tourism as Sustainable Tourism Support. *Russian Journal of Agricultural and Socio-Economic Sciences*, 94(10), 70–78. 10.18551/rjoas.2019-10.09

Bamzai, P. N. K. (1994). *Cultural and Political History of Kashmir* (Vol. 1). M. D. Publishers Private Limited.

Choo, H., Ahn, K., & Petrick, J. F. (2016). An integrated model of festival revisit intentions: Theory of planned behavior and festival quality/satisfaction. *International Journal of Contemporary Hospitality Management*, 28, 818–838. 10.1108/IJCHM-09-2014-0448

Dangi, T., & Jamal, T. (2016). An Integrated Approach to Sustainable Community-Based Tourism. *Sustainability (Basel)*, 8(5), 475. 10.3390/su8050475

Dar, H. (2014). The potential of Tourism in border destinations: A study of Jammu and Kashmir. *African Journal of Hospitality, Tourism and Leisure*, 4(2).

Dar, H. (2018a). Tourists satisfaction of tourism services in Kashmir valley. PhD thesis submitted in *Kurukshetra University Kurukshetra University.*

Dar, H. (2018b). Satisfaction of domestic tourists visiting Gulmarg in Jammu and Kashmir, India. *International Journal on Recent Trends in Business and Tourism*, 2(1), 16–22.

Dar, H. (2020). Hindu religious motivations in Kashmir valley. *International Journal of Religious Tourism and Pilgrimage*, 8(3), 2.

Dar, H. (2024). Sustainable Measures Deterring Ethical and Decent Dilemmas in Tourism. In *Managing Tourism and Hospitality Sectors for Sustainable Global Transformation* (pp. 219–229). IGI Global. 10.4018/979-8-3693-6260-0.ch016

Dar, H. & Islam, N., (2018). Tourism Development in Kashmir: The Policy Perspective. *International Research Journal of Management Science & Technology*.

Dewan, P. (2011). *The people and culture of Jammu-Kashmir-Ladakh*. Manas Publication.

Ditta-Apichai, M., Sroypetch, S., & Caldicott, R. W. (2024). A critique of community-based tourism development: The comparative case of Betong and Pho Tak Districts, Thailand. *Community Development (Columbus, Ohio)*, 55(1), 67–84. 10.1080/15575330.2022.2144921

Dunn, S. (2007). Toward empowerment: Women and community-based tourism in Thailand. Master Thesis, *University of Oregon*, The Faculty of Graduate Studies USA.

Giampiccoli, A., & Saayman, M. (2018). Community-Based Tourism Development Model and Community Participation. African Journal of Hospitality, Tourism and Leisure, 7(4).

Gohori, O., & van der Merwe, P. (2024). Barriers to community participation in Zimbabwe's community-based tourism projects. *Tourism Recreation Research*, 49(1), 91–104. 10.1080/02508281.2021.1989654

Goodwin, H., & Santilli, R. (2009). Community-Based Tourism: a success? *ICRT* Occasional Paper 11, 1-37.

Gupta. (2018). Community Based Tourism Development amid Complex Mountain Issues: A Strategic Analysis of Chakrata Region of Uttarakhand. *International Journal of Hospitality& Tourism Systems,* 12.

Han, H., Eom, T., Ansi, A., Ryu, H. B., & Kim, W. (2019). Community-Based Tourism as a Sustainable Direction in Destination Development: An Empirical Examination of Visitor Behaviors. *Sustainability (Basel)*, 11(10), 2864. 10.3390/su11102864

Hung, K.-P., Peng, N., & Chen, A. (2019). Incorporating on-site activity involvement and sense of belonging into the Mehrabian-Russell model—The experiential value of cultural tourism. *Tourism Management Perspectives*, 30, 43–52. 10.1016/j.tmp.2019.02.003

Jong, A. (2019). How to develop community-based tourism? Blog. Retrieved on 30/11/2020 from: https://fairsayari.com/blog/how-to-develop-community-based tourism#:~:text=Community%2Dbased%20tourism%20is%20a,their%20culture%20 and%20daily%20lives.&text=These%20types%20of%20activities%20create,its%20 beliefs%20 and%20social%20norms

Juma, L. O., & Khademi-Vidra, A. (2019). Community-Based Tourism and Sustainable Development of Rural Regions in Kenya; Perceptions of the Citizenry. *Sustainability (Basel)*, 11(17), 4733. 10.3390/su11174733

Kaul, A. K. (2014). *Studies in geography of Jammu and Kashmir*. Rawat Publications.

Khan. (2019). Gurez Valley: The Most Comprehensive Travel Guide. Retrieved on 26/11/2020 from: https://vargiskhan.com/log/gurez-valley/

Kozak, M., & Buhalis, D. (2019). Cross–border tourism destination marketing: Prerequisites and critical success factors. *Journal of Destination Marketing & Management*, 14, 1–9. 10.1016/j.jdmm.2019.100392

Kumar, R. B., & Dar, H. (2014). Developmental shift of tourism in Kashmir. *Abhinav International Monthly Refereed Journal of Research in Management & Technology, 3*(11).

Lama, R. (2014). Community Based Tourism Development: A Case Study of Sikkim. *PhD thesis submitted,* Department of Tourism and Hotel Management Kurukshetra University, Kuruksetra.

Lee, S., Lee, N., Lee, T. J., & Hyun, S. S. (2024). The influence of social support from intermediary organizations on innovativeness and subjective happiness in community-based tourism. *Journal of Sustainable Tourism*, 32(4), 795–817. 10.1080/09669582.2023.2175836

Mayaka, M., Croy, W. G., & Cox, J. W. (2019). A dimensional approach to community-based tourism: Recognising and differentiating form and context. *Annals of Tourism Research*, 74, 177–190. 10.1016/j.annals.2018.12.002

Mintzberg, H. (2009, July– August). Rebuilding Companies as Communities. *Harvard Business Review*.

Mtapuri, O., & Giampiccoli, A. (2013). Interrogating the role of the state and non-state actors in community-based tourism ventures: Toward a model for spreading the benefits to the wider community. *The South African Geographical Journal*, 95(1), 1–15. 10.1080/03736245.2013.805078

Mtapuri, O., & Giampiccoli, A. (2016). Towards a comprehensive model of community-based tourism development. *The South African Geographical Journal*, 98(1), 154–168. 10.1080/03736245.2014.977813

Na Thongkaew, B., Ruksapol, A., & Brewer, P. (2024). The Role of Local Networks in Supportive Mechanisms Model for Sustainable Community-based Tourism Administration. *Tourism Planning & Development*, 1-23.

Najar, P. A., Dar, H., Singh, P., & Najar, A. H. (2022). Anti-Social Factors Influence the Decision Making of Tourists: A Study of Kashmir. *International Journal of Cyber Warfare & Terrorism*, 12(1), 1–14. 10.4018/IJCWT.315590

Ngo, T. H., Tournois, N., Dinh, T. L. T., Chu, M. T., & Phan, C. S. (2024). Sustainable Community-Based Tourism Development: Capacity Building for Community; The Case Study in Cam Kim, Hoi An, Vietnam. *Journal of Sustainability Research*, 6(2).

Okazaki, E. (2008). A community-based tourism model: Its conception and use. *Journal of Sustainable Tourism*, 16(5), 511–529. 10.1080/09669580802159594

Peredo, A. M., & Chrisman, J. J. (2006). Toward a Theory of Community-Based Enterprise. *Academy of Management Review*, 31(2), 309–328. 10.5465/amr.2006.20208683

Polnyotee, M., & Thadaniti, S. (2015). Community-Based Tourism: A Strategy for Sustainable Tourism Development of Patong Beach, Phuket Island, Thailand. *Asian Social Science*, 11(27), 90. Advance online publication. 10.5539/ass.v11n27p90

Romero–Medina, N., Flores–Tipán, E., Carvache-Franco, M., Carvache-Franco, O., Carvache-Franco, W., & González-Núñez, R. (2024). Organizational design for strengthening community-based tourism: Empowering stakeholders for self-organization and networking. *PLoS One*, 19(1), e0294849. 10.1371/journal.pone.029484938261593

Runyowa, D. (2017). Community-based tourism development in Victoria Falls, Kompisi Cultural Village: An entrepreneur's model. *African Journal of Hospitality, Tourism and Leisure*, 6(2), 1–7.

Shaheen, . (2017). Disadvantaged Mountain Farmers of Gurez Valley in Kashmir: Issues of Livelihood, Vulnerability, Externality and Sustainability. *Indian Journal of Agricultural Economics*, 72(3).

Sita, S. E. D., & Nor, N. A. M. (2015). Degree of Contact and Local Perceptions of Tourism Impacts: A Case Study of Homestay Programme in Sarawak. *Procedia: Social and Behavioral Sciences*, 211, 903–910. 10.1016/j.sbspro.2015.11.119

Sita & Nor. (2012). Community-Based Tourism (CBT): Local Community Perceptions toward Social & Cultural Impacts. Proceedings of the Tourism and Hospitality International Conference. Retrieved on 26/11/2020 from: https://www.researchgate.net/publication/275953671_Communitybased_Tourism_CBT_Local_Community_Perceptions_toward_Social_and_Cultural_Impacts

Sofield, T. (2006). Border Tourism and Border Communities: An Overview. *Tourism Geographies*, 8(2), 102–121. 10.1080/14616680600585489

Sugandini, D., Effendi, M. I., Aribowo, A. S., & Utami, Y. S. (2018). Marketing strategy on community based tourism in special region of Yogyakarta. *Journal of Environmental Management and Tourism*, 9(4), 733–774. 10.14505//jemt.v9.4(28).06

Suksmawati, H., Nuryananda, P. F., & Rahmatin, L. S. (2024). Local Community Awareness in Inclusive Tourism Development in Tegaren Village, Trenggalek. *Nusantara Science and Technology Proceedings*, 52-58.

Tristanti, T., Nurhaeni, I. D. A., Mulyanto, M., & Sakuntalawati, R. D. (2024). Model of Women's Empowerment in the Economic Aspects of the Tourism Field Through Community-Based Education in Gunungkidul. *International Journal of Religion*, 5(1), 702–710. 10.61707/vnck6s02

UNWTO. (2020). Tourism and Poverty Alleviation. Project report, *World Tourism Organization*. https://www.e-unwto.org/doi/pdf/10.18111/9789284405497

Witchayakawin. (2020). Factors on Development of Community-Based Tourism (CBT) in Phitsanulok Province of Thailand. *Journal of Critical Reviews*.

Zapata, , Hall, C. M., Lindo, P., & Vanderschaeghe, M. (2011). Can community-based tourism contribute to development and poverty alleviation? Lessons from Nicaragua. *Current Issues in Tourism*, 14(8), 725–749. 10.1080/13683500.2011.559200

Zhang, C., & Xiao, H. (2014). Destination development in China: Towards an effective model of explanation. *Journal of Sustainable Tourism*, 22(2), 214–233. 10.1080/09669582.2013.839692

Chapter 6
A Netnographic Analysis of Tourists' Experiences in the Rural Tourism Village of India

Vaibhav Bhatt
https://orcid.org/0000-0003-2859-7913
Central University of Tamil Nadu, India

Pramendra Singh
https://orcid.org/0000-0002-9142-265X
Lovely Professional University, India

Shivam Bhartiya
https://orcid.org/0000-0001-5532-2283
Jain University, India

Shreeansh Mishra
https://orcid.org/0009-0004-8847-6587
Central University of Tamil Nadu, India

Akhilesh Kumar Singh
https://orcid.org/0000-0002-5429-6607
Sikkim University, India

ABSTRACT

The study aims to investigate the experiences of the tourists at Raghurajpur and employed netnographic study approach to extract the tourists' experience from TripAdvisor website. Raghurajpur in Indian state of Odisha is a popular rural

DOI: 10.4018/979-8-3693-5405-6.ch006

Copyright © 2024, IGI Global. Copying or distributing in print or electronic forms without written permission of IGI Global is prohibited.

tourism destination known for its different kinds of traditional art forms including paintings, engravings, and craft making. On thematic analysis of the data, the study came out with identification of four components of tourists' experience at Raghurajpur, namely travel motives, positive experience, negative experience, and concern for art and artisans. The study explains the reasons to visit Raghurajpur and sheds light on other aspects of tourists' experiences. This will help the stakeholders better understand the nature and status of Raghurajpur village so that they can take corrective actions to serve the exact needs of the tourists along with preserving its rich culture, heritage, and art.

INTRODUCTION

The research article attempts to study the experiences of tourists in the rural tourism village of Raghurajpur as presented by the tourists' in their online reviews about the village on TripAdvisor website. Raghurajpur is a small village in the Puri district of the Indian state Odisha. It is also known as artisans or crafts village as the village is home of skilful artisans who specialise in traditional crafts such as patta paintings, tusser paintings, palm leaf engravings, papier mache toys and masks and cow dung toys. The village is situated at a distance of 14 km from the Hindu pilgrimage town of Puri on the southern bank of river Bhargavi. The temple town of Puri is well connected with the road and rail services from all the prominent cities of India. Nearest airport is Bhubaneshwar airport which is at a distance of 67 km from the village of Raghurajpur. The village was recognised as a Heritage Village in 2000 by the Government of India (Behera, S.K. et al., 2021).

The Indian state of Odisha is a destination rich in culture and heritage (Panigrahi, 2005; Mahapatra, 2011). The cultural and heritage attractions available in the state for rural tourists include indigenous tribes, unique art forms, ethnic cuisine and handicrafts. Considering the potential of Raghurajpur village in terms of availability of unique rural tourism attractions, the village was identified by the Ministry of Tourism of Govt. of Odisha and developed as a rural tourism destination. The focus was on improving infrastructure and provide skill development and training to the local artisans (Mohanty et.al., 2018). This study adopts netnographic method to critically examine the tourists' online reviews extracted from the TripAdvisor website to have an understanding of their experiences after visiting the rural tourism village of Raghurajpur. The structure of the article includes introduction to the research problem followed by the review of the related literature discussing the previous studies on the subject. The latter part of the article elaborates the methodology applied in the research study followed by presenting the findings and concluding with the implications of the study for the destination, tourism stakeholders and the limitations and the scope for further research.

LITERATURE REVIEW

The question arises, why tourists travel to other destinations? Tourists seek pleasure and a different kind of experience in a novel setting with differentiated activities other than their usual ones. Therefore, it becomes important to pay more attention on the kind of experience tourists are expecting and are provided the same. A better understanding of tourist experiences provides better opportunity to the industry to serve them better (Zhang & Walsh, 2021). In tourism, tourist experience is seen as the interaction of one's physical, mental, emotional, intellectual and spiritual being with an event or special place (Noy, 2007; Pine & Gilmore, 1998). This tourist experience is different from their usual day to day experience (Cohen, 2004). The tourist experience can be viewed as on-site experience and past travel experience. The on-site tourist experience is the interaction between tourist and attractions or events during the visitation process (Stamboulis & Skayannis, 2003) and past travel experience is something worth memorising (Larsen, 2007).

Tourism researchers have explained tourist experience in multiple ways considering different aspects in mind. Most of these explanations have revolved around site or place experience, however the tourist experience starts evolving before the visit, develops during the visit and consolidates after the visit in the form of memory (Clawson & Knetsch, 1966). In tourism and hospitality industry, tourist experience plays pivotal role (Pizam, 2010). All activities of tourism businesses revolve around enhancing this experience for tourists. Businesses and destinations try to enhance engagement with tourists and hence bring unique positive experience to differentiate themselves and their services (Cetin & Bilgihan, 2016). The destinations should try to provide the kind of experience which tourists had expected from the destinations (Barnes, Mattsson, & Sørensen, 2014).

An experience becomes memorable when it is remembered & recalled later on too (Kim, Ritchie, & Tung, 2010). And on the basis of these experiences tourists post their emotions & feelings on social media which we may refer to as user generated content (UGC). UGC is helpful for the tourism businesses because on the basis of this, they get to know market needs, demand and other information (Bigne et. al., 2020). UGC also helps other tourists in influencing their travel related decisions (Kim, Mattila, & Baloglu, 2011; Mauri & Minazzi, 2013) and their expectations too (Narangajavana, Callarisa, Moliner, Rodríguez, & Sánchez, 2019). And the content posted on social media also contributes in creating destination image (Bigne, Ruiz, & Currás-Pérez, 2019). Therefore, in order to get competitive advantage over others, the destinations need to provide superior experiences to the tourists (Dwyer & Kim, 2003).

The experience of the tourists which they share as UGC on social or other online media has been a point of interest for tourism and hospitality researchers. Many researchers have studied what impact UGC may have on tourism businesses, how it can drive or diminish sales, where it can be useful for the businesses and destinations in improving their competitiveness. Some notable researchers have carried out related researches for online hotel bookings and its sales (Zhao, Wang, Guo, & Law, 2015; Zhu & Zhang, 2010), guest satisfaction (Xiang, Schwartz, Gerdes, & Uysal, 2015), tourists and destination satisfaction (Narangajavana et al., 2019) and destination imagery (Bigne et al., 2019).

On the basis of these studies, the tourist experience could well be understood. Tourism experience is not a commodity with predefined features rather it includes integrated clues and perceptions gathered from interaction with the destination (Smith, 1994). And this experience is different for different tourists, which they build it themselves by incorporating different elements of the destination (Swarbrooke, 2001). Therefore, it is very imperative for the tourism industry and destinations to understand the importance of tourist experience and its role in deciding the future of the tourist destinations.

The paper tries to bring forward the experience of the visitors in rural setting, especially in this case of the experience at rural tourism village Raghurajpur of Indian state Odisha. Tourists' experience varies at different destinations as per the characteristics of the destinations and relevant expectations from it. Different types of tourism provide different kind of opportunities and experiences to the visitors which result in different experiences for them. Rural tourism is one of the types of tourism dependent on rural setting, rural livelihood and traditions.

Many researchers have tried to define Rural Tourism, but none of them have been able to come up with a universally accepted definition (Pearce 1989; Bramwell 1994; Seaton et al. 1994). World Tourism Organisation defined rural tourism as a concept that "gives to visitors a personalized contact, a taste of physical and human environment of countryside and as far as possible, allows them to participate in the activities, traditions and lifestyles of local people" (Aref and Gill, 2009). The Responsible Travel Handbook (2006) defined rural tourism as "Rural tourism provides travellers with an opportunity for recreational experiences involving visits to non-urban settings for the purpose of participating in or observing activities, events, or attractions that are a fundamental part of rural communities and environments. These are not necessarily agricultural in nature." As per Oppermann (1997), rural tourism can be defined as "tourism in a nonurban territory where human activity is going on and primarily agriculture". Rural tourism encompasses a wide range of activities, including not only those associated with agricultural tourism, but also those related to the natural environment. These activities include nature holidays, eco-tourism, adventurous activities, walking and climbing, horseback riding, fishing and hunting, health and sporting activities, arts and heritage, education and ethnic tourism. (OECD 1994: 9).

METHODOLOGY

The researchers applied netnographic approach in this study, also known as "ethnography in internet" (Kozinets, 2002), and is the best method to investigate tourist experiences and feelings shared online (Rageh et al., 2013). It has its roots in ethnography; a research methodology that focuses on studying a culture-sharing group (Kulavuz-Onal & Vasquez, 2013) to identify common beliefs, values and behaviours amongst members. Kozinets (2002) defined netnography as a 'new qualitative research methodology that adapts ethnographic research techniques to study the cultures and communities that are emerging through computer mediated communications' (p.62). It utilizes publicly available information in online forums to determine and comprehend the requirements of relevant online consumer populations (Kozinets, 2002; Mkono, 2013). Social networking sites are ideal online platforms for the implementation of netnography approaches as they combine the following: web-page; private email; blog; forums; and chat room access (Kozinets, 2010). The use of netnography is also on the rise in tourism studies, as tourists share their experiences and photos of the places they visit on travel websites and blogs, as well as on social media. Netnography is also faster, easier and cheaper to use than offline methods (Rokka, 2010; Le et al., 2019; Mkono, 2014; Markwell, 2014; Rageh, 2013; Wu & Pearce, 2014).

In this study, 130 online reviews posted by tourists between 2018 to 2022 for rural tourism village of Raghurajpur were downloaded from the Trip Advisor website (https://www.tripadvisor.in/Attraction_Review-g503703-d3806619-ReviewsRaghurajpur_Artist_Village-Puri_Puri_District_Odisha.html) and examined. In order to study the experience of tourists' with regard to Raghurajpur as a rural tourism attraction, Braun and Clarke's (2013) methodology was adopted in the study to analyse the TripAdvisor website's online reviews. Following were the objectives of the study:

1. To determine the tourists' experiences of Raghurajpur in India as a rural tourism attraction.
2. To ascertain the reasons for tourists' visiting Raghurajpur as per the online reviews

As part of the methodology, the researchers initially reviewed the data gathered from TripAdvisor multiple times to enhance their comprehension of the reviews related to Raghurajpur village. Subsequently, the data was categorized into distinct segments that elucidated the tourists' experiences. The identified relevant data was then subjected to further scrutiny and analysis. The fourth phase entailed grouping the data, which had been segmented in the previous step, into primary themes that illuminated the tourists' experiences and travel behaviors. The final stage of this methodology revolved around analyzing the predominant themes derived from the data. Within the findings section, representative comments are provided within quotation marks to exemplify the various themes and offer insight into how visitors perceived their experiences (Woyo & Amadhila, 2018). Grammatical and typographical mistakes have not been edited to prevent the chance of distorting the tourists' reviews. (Mkono, 2012).

FINDINGS

Demographic Details of Reviewers

Figure 1. Gender Distribution of the Reviewers

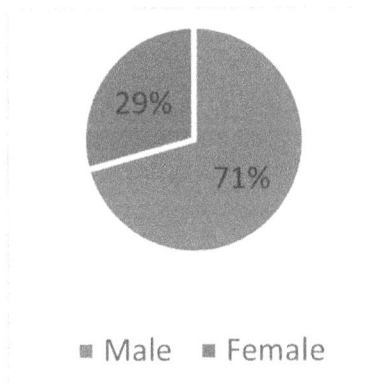

Figure 2. Year-Wise Distribution of Reviewers

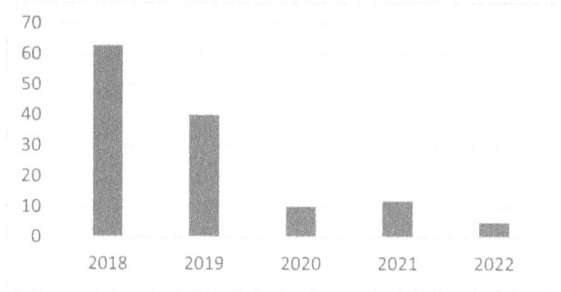

The reviews posted on TripAdvisor reflect the experience of visitors regarding their interaction with the destination and its different components. 71% reviews were posted by males and 29% reviews were posted by female (Figure 1). Majority of the reviews were posted in the year 2018 and 2019 while the least number of reviews were in 2022 (Figure 2). Of the total 130 reviewers, 119 were Indians and 11 were foreign tourists (02 each from USA, Canada and UK, and 01 each from Netherlands, Oman, Israel, Qatar and Singapore). All the reviews were posted in English.

This section of the research paper showcases the actual experiences of the tourists as per their reviews in the Trip Advisor website. The online reviews are depicted by means of short quotations to give a better understanding. The detailed analysis of reviews resulted in the emergence of four main components regarding the tourists' experiences in the rural tourism village of Raghurajpur. These components were:

1. Travel Motivations
2. Positive Experiences
3. Negative Experiences
4. Concern for the Art and Artisans

Figure 3. Conceptual Framework

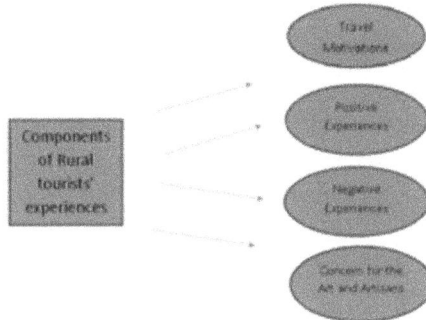

Figure 4. Travel Motivations

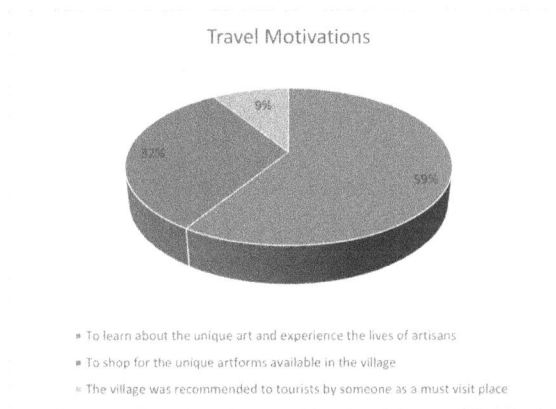

1. Travel Motivations

The first component of the tourists' experiences was to explore the various motives of tourists for visiting the rural tourism village of Raghurajpur. On analysing the reviews, it was found that following were the major motives for the people to travel:

a. To learn about the unique art and experience the lives of artisans (59%)
b. To shop for the unique artforms available in the village (32%)
c. The village was recommended to tourists by someone as a must visit place (9%)

a. To Learn About the Unique Art and Experience the Lives of the Artisans

The following reviews depict the primary motivations for visiting Raghurajpur (please note that the reviews have been unaltered to prevent any distortion of meaning)

*"This is a fantastic art & craft Heritage Village, which tries to preserve local handicrafts especially Pattachitra, with all mythological themes, and palm leaf etching painting etc . A must visit for art afficinados ...lots of orginal art works you can pick up for your home ..please do not bargain with the local artisans .."***(Review 13)**

*"Pattachitra is a general term for traditional, cloth-based scroll painting of Odisha and Raghurajpur is home to it. A small village 15-20 kms out of Puri, coming to limelight for is Pattachitras. Traditional families hereditarily engaged in painting intricate details as well as mythological narratives and folktales in cloth scrolls. A value for the money for Art lovers"***(Review 17)**

*"A different experience in the routine sightseeing around Puri. One would love the variety of art & craft things that are made & being sold in the village. Many things of different price range is available. Was mesmerized by the intricate details of the paintings. Worth visiting"***(Review 19)**

*"We stopped by on our way back to Bhubaneswar . The place can be reached through narrow lanes from the Bhubaneswar highway. It is an excellent place to visit because at one place one gets to see the Pattachitra making on Tussar, Palm Leaves and other materials and also get an opportunity to buy these at a reasonable cost . One can watch the artists making the Pattachitras in their small rooms by single strokes of their .000 brushes. It is experience to savor. There are other articles too which are made there"***(Review 31)**

*"A living museum village - mesmerizing experience, worth a visit. A living museum is what we can describe this village where 140 families live close to each other and are advancing the art form of Pattachitra, Taal Patra etc. Very talented family members specializing in painting, dancing, and other forms of fine art. The residents are very nice, peaceful, knowledgeable"***(Review 46)**

*"Excellent place to visit and enjoy the place. Spent a whole afternoon by roaming around the Raghurajpur Heritage village. This is must visit place. Right from entering the village, the artists at every house was welcoming to visit their house and see their specialty. Even they were giving demonstrations of how they make the "Pata chitra" and "Palm Leaf art". Great heritage to know about"***(Review 116)**

b. To Shop for the Unique Artforms Available in the Village

The following reviews depict the primary motivations for visiting Raghurajpur (please note that the reviews have been unaltered to prevent any distortion of meaning):

"Exellent crafts village. Worth a visit. Raghurajpur Village is worth a visit for the engraving on palm leaves and painting . excellent crafts manship and worth buying for the home and collection"(**Review 44**)

"A Hamlet of Incredible Artists and Centuries old Art. We interacted with few artisans and most of us could not resist to buy some mementos for ourselves and to give as gifts"(**Review 45**)

"Was happy to visit the place and meet the artists. Bargaining is necessary as the prices quoted are on the high"(**Review 47**)

"Village of traditional artists. The place has an immense talent.. The artists over there have won many national-level awards.. The road to this place is very narrow.. Govt should do someting about it.. You should visit and get art pieces from there as this will motivate the artists and keep the tradition alive"(**Review 49**)

"Beautiful village beautiful people worth visiting. You can visit all the houses and see how they are making Pattachitra paintings on cloth,canvases etc they also teach on request and can buy directly from the artists at a cheaper rate compared to show rooms"(**Review 55**)

"know the art. We spent time with award-winning Pattachitra artist's family. They took us through in detail on various painting methods and a whole collection of their beautiful paintings. In the end, we knew how to differentiate between quality paintings and run off the mill paintings"(**Review 68**)

c. The Village Was Recommended to Tourists by Someone as a Must Visit Place

The following reviews depict the primary motivations for visiting Raghurajpur (please note that the reviews have been unaltered to prevent any distortion of meaning)

"Delightful artist village outside Puri, We went for a visit as my friend had heard about this village"(**Review 27**)

"Exquisite paintings. We were told by our relatives before start of the trip to Puri that we should visit this village also"(**Review 33**)

"artist village. Visited one of the shops through a contact. Found the work carried out by Artisans to be very unique. To encourage them and as appreciation to the work they do, did not bargin and bought few items"(**Review 111**)

The above motivations elucidate the reasons for the tourists to visit the destination at the first place. In sync with the travel motivations conceptualised by Pine and Gilmore (1998,2002), the motivations will give the policy planners a clear understanding of strategies to be devised to not only market the destination to the right clientele but it would also help them in accentuating the tourist experience.

Figure 5. Word Cloud of the Rural Tourists' Experiences

2. Positive Experiences

The online reviews from the TripAdvisor website depicted what tourists felt after visiting the rural tourism village of Raghurajpur. They used the following words to describe their experience in the village i.e.,"Superb / Excellent / Mesmerizing / Satisfying / Amazing experience", "Must visit / Worth visiting", "Beautiful / Good / Great / Nice / Unique / Excellent place", "Value for money", "Famous / Excellent crafts / art village", "Excellent / Delightful artist village", "Wonderful / Incredible artists", "Exquisite paintings / Excellent / Great / Amazing art work" (see Table 1). The usage of these words in the online reviews indicated that the experience of the tourists was positive and they were satisfied with their visit.

Table 1. Positive Experiences

Experience Description	Frequency (%)
Superb / Excellent / Mesmerizing / Satisfying / Amazing experience	12 (9)
Must visit / Worth visiting	32 (25)
Beautiful / Good / Great / Nice / Unique / Excellent place	8 (6)
Value for money	3 (2)
Famous / Excellent crafts / art village	6 (5)

continued on following page

Table 1. Continued

Experience Description	Frequency (%)
Excellent / Delightful artist village	**7 (5)**
Wonderful / Incredible artists	**5 (4)**
Exquisite paintings / Excellent / Great / Amazing art work	**8 (6)**

Following are some of the reviews that highlight the positive experiences with regard to Raghurajpur as a rural tourism attraction:

*"A Street of Artist Families. Really feast for your eyes to see the drawing and art work done by the families of this village"***(Review 1)**

*"Superb experience. Everyone must visit this place"***(Review 4)**

*"invaluable Art, people are so talented and they have done well to preserve their traditional art forms.unique and exclusive articles"***(Review 5)**

*"amazing living museum"***(Review 8)**

*"Must visit place for all travellers"***(Review 10)**

*"This is a fantastic art & craft Heritage Village"***(Review 13)**

*"Definitely worth many visits!!! Highly recommended for the quality art work"***(Review 22)**

*"Wonderful artists and their paintings"***(Review 29)**

*"Exquisite paintings"***(Review 33)**

*"A living museum village - mesmerizing experience, worth a visit"***(Review 46)**

*"Beautiful village beautiful people worth visiting"***(Review 55)**

*"Worth spending time and money here"***(Review 68)**

*"Creative Artisans and must visit place"***(Review 80)**

*"Mesmerising art work on palm-leaf and canvas"***(Review 130)**

3. Negative Experiences

Tourist experiences can be both positive as well as negative in a destination (Locher et.al., 2005; Pine and Gilmore, 1998) and the detailed analysis of the tourists' online reviews projected some negative experiences too. The prominent challenge faced by the tourists was the problem of bargaining which was highlighted in lot of negative tourism online reviews. High pricing of the art forms left a lot of tourists dissatisfied with their experience. Also, the local people on some occasions pestered the tourists to purchase the art forms which also left a negative impression on the minds of tourists thereby spoiling their experience. The tourism policy planners and the stakeholders need to overcome these challenges in order to provide a holistic satisfying experience to the tourists.

Following are some of the reviews that highlight the negative experiences with regard to Raghurajpur as a rural tourism attraction:

"Did not have a great feel of this place as hard bargaining required" **(Review 7)**

"Seeing you as tourists they demand a high price, so do not forget to bargain" **(Review 58)**

"We were really disappointed of the whole trip" **(Review 79)**

"Not a happy visit (despite paying double the price on few items)" **(Review 81)**

"The place needs to be made more tourist-friendly and interesting, and less jostling" **(Review 95)**

"Please check the product before buying that is it a real painting or screen prints. So you may be cheated by them" **(Review 97)**

"Super disappointed with their approach and wouldn't recommend this trip for anyone expecting a leisurely wander around" **(Review 126)**

"Slightly difficult to find as its a couple of kms off the main road" **(Review 129)**

4. Concern for Art and Artisans

Apart from the positive and negative reviews, the detailed analysis of tourists' online reviews also brought forward a commonly recurring theme in the extracted online reviews i.e., concern for the art and the local artisans.

Following are some of the reviews that highlight the concern for art and artisan experiences with regard to Raghurajpur as a rural tourism attraction:

"Wonderful artists and their paintings. But saddened to see the condition of artists. Not much source of income despite extremely talented artists. Hope we contribute to their upliftment by buying some paintings. A sample of their art. Painting done on the walls" **(Review 29)**

"A village struggling to keep alive the traditional art of pattachitra. Full family of every house is engaged in this. Great art, vivid color combinations. All the houses are devastated by Fani, lacs lost in damage. Odisha Government's initiative is missing to develop this village as a tourist attraction" **(Review 54)**

"Visit the village and they are more than eager to show their art. My suggestion would be not to buy from one place. Instead buy from different houses and encourage their art. They need both the money and the encouragement would be not to buy from one place. Instead buy from different houses and encourage their art. They need both the money and the encouragement" **(Review 70)**

*"The only problem is that every one is asking us to come and see their work and seeing their poor condition and their talent we bought two painting from different place. I think those who can afford must buy at least one painting to encourage their heritage art from dying"***(Review 100)**

*"Please try to visit in this village. They are so talented. They are famous for " potochitro" and that is not easy to paint!! Please try to buy something from them . They are very needy bt talented people!!"***(Review 107)**

DISCUSSION AND IMPLICATIONS

The objective of the research was to analyse the experiences of the tourists who visited the rural tourism village of Raghurajpur in Odisha as per the tourists' online review data extracted from the TripAdvisor website. The researchers employed netnographic approach in studying the 130 tourists' online reviews.

The researchers found four themes in tourists' experience data extracted from the TripAdvisor website i.e., travel motivations, positive experiences, negative experiences and concern for art and artisans. Majority of the tourists had travelled to the destination to learn about the unique art and to experience the lives of the artisans, followed by visiting to shop for the unique artforms available in the village. Also, some tourists had visited the destination as it was recommended by someone to them as a must visit place.

Majority of the tourists had a good time in the village which was confirmed by the large number of positive experiences online reviews in the TripAdvisor website. "Superb / Excellent / Mesmerizing / Satisfying / Amazing experience", "Must visit / Worth visiting", "Beautiful / Good / Great / Nice / Unique / Excellent place", "Value for money", "Famous / Excellent crafts / art village", "Excellent / Delightful artist village", "Wonderful / Incredible artists", "Exquisite paintings / Excellent / Great / Amazing art work", were the frequently occurring words in the online reviews of the tourists' who had positive experience in the village and they also recommended the readers to visit the place. Tourists' negative experiences highlighted the problem of bargaining to buy the art forms in the village. A large number of reviews suggested that the prices of the art forms were quoted usually high and in order to get them for actual price then bargaining was required. This also created problem for people who were not good or didn't like bargaining. The accessibility of the village was also a concern for some tourists. Some tourists shared the instances of getting cheated by the cab driver who took them to the village which made the experience very disappointing. Few tourists also highlighted the social and economic problems faced by the local people and artisans of the village and urged the tourists visiting the destination to buy few artforms in order to help the local people economically and to also encourage their art. They also requested the government to work for the upliftment of the talented local people.

The word cloud in Figure 5 illustrates the terms commonly used in online reviews to describe the tourists' experiences. These terms include "paintings", "place", "art", "village", "visit" and "artists". This indicates that the vast majority of tourists visiting a rural tourism village used these terms explicitly in their reviews, thus confirming that the tourists' experience was primarily related to paintings, art, and artists.

CONCLUSION

Raghurajpur is a small tourist village located in the rural area of Indian state Odisha. It is well known as a craft village or artisan village for its splendid art forms including variety of paintings, engravings and toy making. This village has also been recognized as heritage village by the government of India in 2000. It gives visitors opportunity to engage in artistic and recreational activities surrounded by countryside environment. The art, craft, recreation, traditions of the village make it an ideal destination for rural tourism. Rural tourism has been much studied about by many researchers and still attracting the attention of future researchers too. It has been now developed as a niche tourism product. One of the most important variables for any destination to be successful and competitive is tourist experience at the destination with its services, activities and opportunities provided to the tourists for recreation. Tourists' experience has been a core area for the destinations to look at for their performance. Like other destinations, rural tourism destinations too hugely dependent for their development on tourists' experience. TripAdvisor is one of the digital platforms that provides opportunities to the tourists to reflect their tourism experiences with the destination elements. The tourists have liberty to post their tour and destination related experiences on TripAdvisor. These reviews reflect the image of the destination and tourists' experience with it.

The present study used Netnography method to extract the reviews of the visitors from TripAdvisor website and analyze these reviews. Netnography is a qualitative research methodology tool which is used to investigate the tourists' experiences and reviews shared online. A total of 130 reviews were shared between the period of 2018 and 2022 and include 119 responses from Indians and 11 responses from foreign tourists. The detailed analysis of these reviews resulted in forming four main components of tourists' experiences namely – travel motivations, positive experiences, negative experiences and concern for the art & artisans. On further analysis of the reviews, it was found that the motives for visiting Raghurajpur were to learn more about the art, experience artisans' lives, shop for unique art work and also because it was recommended by others to the tourists. Majority of the tourists had very good experience with their stay at Raghurapur while few had bad experience as well that too mainly because of high prices of the artefacts and bargaining requirement. The tourists also had concern for the art and artisans due to negligence of the government, lack of opportunities which are reflected in their reviews. Overall, the rural tourism village Raghurajpur has been an artisans' paradise which also has become a major tourist attraction and tourists had good experience with the destination and its artistic creativity.

Limitations and Scope for Future Studies

The study used netnographic approach in finding out the experiences of tourists at Raghurajpur village through their reviews on TripAdvisor website. The limitation of the study is that it extracted the tourists' reviews only from TripAdvisor website and not any other sources including primary data sources. Future studies can be conducted for the same or similar rural tourism destinations considering comprehensive approach for data collection and analysis.

REFERENCES

Aref, F., & Gill, S. S. (2009). Rural tourism development though rural cooperatives. *Nature and Science*, 7(10), 68–73.

Barnes, S. J., Mattsson, J., & Sørensen, F. (2014). Destination brand experience and visitor behavior: Testing a scale in the tourism context. *Annals of Tourism Research*, 48, 121–139. 10.1016/j.annals.2014.06.002

Behera, S. K., Gautam, P., & Lenka, S. K. (2021). *Purchasing behavior of tourists toward prominent souvenirs of Odisha*. Vilakshan-XIMB Journal of Management. 10.1108/XJM-10-2020-0165

Bigne, E., Ruiz, C., & Curras-Perez, R. (2019). Destination appeal through digitalized comments. *Journal of Business Research*, 101, 447–453. 10.1016/j.jbusres.2019.01.020

Bigné, E., Zanfardini, M., & Andreu, L. (2020). How online reviews of destination responsibility influence tourists' evaluations: An exploratory study of mountain tourism. *Journal of Sustainable Tourism*, 28(5), 686–704. 10.1080/09669582.2019.1699565

Bramwell, B. (1994). Rural tourism and sustainable rural tourism. *Journal of Sustainable Tourism*, 2(1-2), 1–6. 10.1080/09669589409510679

Braun, V., & Clarke, V. (2013). *Successful qualitative research: A practical guide for beginners*. Sage.

Cetin, G., & Bilgihan, A. (2016). Components of cultural tourists' experiences in destinations. *Current Issues in Tourism*, 19(2), 137–154. 10.1080/13683500.2014.994595

Clawson, M., & Knetsch, J. L. (1966). *Economics of outdoor recreation*. Johns Hopkins Press.

Cohen, E. (2004). *Contemporary tourism: Diversity and change*. Elsevier.

Dwyer, L., & Kim, C. (2003). Destination competitiveness: Determinants and indicators. *Current Issues in Tourism*, 6(5), 369–414. 10.1080/13683500308667962

Kim, E. E. K., Mattila, A. S., & Baloglu, S. (2011). Effects of gender and expertise on consumers' motivation to read online hotel reviews. *Cornell Hospitality Quarterly*, 52(4), 399–406. 10.1177/1938965510394357

Kim, J. H., Ritchie, J. R. B., & Tung, V. W. S. (2010). The effect of memorable experience on behavioral intentions in tourism: A structural equation modeling approach. *Tourism Analysis*, 15(6), 637–648. 10.3727/108354210X12904412049776

Kozinets, R. V. (2002). The field behind the screen: Using netnography for marketing research in online communities. *JMR, Journal of Marketing Research*, 39(1), 61–72. 10.1509/jmkr.39.1.61.18935

Kozinets, R. V. (2010). Netnography: The marketer's secret weapon. *White paper*, 1-13.

Kulavuz-Onal, D., & Vásquez, C. (2013). Reconceptualising fieldwork in a netnography of an online community of English language teachers. *Ethnography and Education*, 8(2), 224–238. 10.1080/17457823.2013.792511

Larsen, S. (2007). Aspects of a psychology of the tourist experience. *Scandinavian Journal of Hospitality and Tourism*, 7(1), 7–18. 10.1080/15022250701226014

Le, T. H., Arcodia, C., Novais, M. A., & Kralj, A. (2019). What we know and do not know about authenticity in dining experiences: A systematic literature review. *Tourism Management*, 74, 258–275. 10.1016/j.tourman.2019.02.012

Locher, J. L., Yoels, W. C., Maurer, D., & van Ells, J. (2005). Comfort foods: An exploratory journey into the social and emotional significance of food. *Food & Foodways*, 13(4), 273–297. 10.1080/07409710500334509

Mahapatra, B. (2011). *Ethnic Dances and Music of Western Orissa: An Anthropological Study Towards Promoting Ecotourism*. Concept Publishing Company.

Mauri, A. G., & Minazzi, R. (2013). Web reviews influence on expectations and purchasing intentions of hotel potential customers. *International Journal of Hospitality Management*, 34, 99–107. 10.1016/j.ijhm.2013.02.012

Mkono, M. (2012). Netnographic tourist research: The internet as a virtual fieldwork site. *Tourism Analysis*, 17(4), 553–555. 10.3727/108354212X13473157390966

Mkono, M. (2013). Using net-based ethnography (Netnography) to understand the staging and marketing of "authentic African" dining experiences to tourists at Victoria Falls. *Journal of Hospitality & Tourism Research (Washington, D.C.)*, 37(2), 184–198. 10.1177/1096348011425502

Mkono, M., & Markwell, K. (2014). The application of netnography in tourism studies. *Annals of Tourism Research*, 48, 289–291. 10.1016/j.annals.2014.07.005

Mohanty, P., Chandran, A., & Mathew, R. (2018). Branding Odisha as a rural tourism destination: An alternate approach. *International Journal of Creative Research Thoughts*, 6. Advance online publication. 10.5281/zenodo.1164173

Narangajavana Kaosiri, Y., Callarisa Fiol, L. J., Moliner Tena, M. A., Rodríguez Artola, R. M., & Sanchez Garcia, J. (2019). User-generated content sources in social media: A new approach to explore tourist satisfaction. *Journal of Travel Research*, 58(2), 253–265. 10.1177/0047287517746014

Noy, C. (2007). The poetics of tourist experience: An autoethnography of a family trip to Eilat. *Journal of Tourism and Cultural Change*, 5(3), 141–157. 10.2167/jtcc085.0

Oppermann, M. (1997). First-time and repeat visitors to New Zealand. *Tourism Management*, 18(3), 177–181. 10.1016/S0261-5177(96)00119-7

Organization for Economic Cooperation and Development (OECD). (1994). *Tourism Strategies and Rural Development*.

Panigrahi, N. (2005). Development of eco-tourism in tribal regions of Orissa: potential and recommendations. *CEWCES Research Papers*, 9.

Pearce, D. (1989). *Tourism Development* (2nd ed.). Longman Scientific and Technical with John Wiley and Sons.

Pine, B. J., & Gilmore, H. J. (1998). *The experience economy: Work is theatre & every business a stage*. Harvard Business School Press., 10.4337/9781781004227.00007

Pine, B. J., & Gilmore, J. H. (2002, June). Differentiating Hospitality Operations via Experiences. *The Cornell Hotel and Restaurant Administration Quarterly*, 43(3), 87–96. 10.1016/S0010-8804(02)80022-2

Pizam, A. (2010). Creating memorable experiences. *International Journal of Hospitality Management, 29*(3), 343. 10.1016/j.ijhm.2010.04.003

Rageh, A., Melewar, T. C., & Woodside, A. (2013). Using netnography research method to reveal the underlying dimensions of the customer/tourist experience. *Qualitative Market Research*, 16(2), 126–149. Advance online publication. 10.1108/13522751311317558

Responsible Travel Handbook (2006).

Rokka, J. (2010). Netnographic inquiry and new translocal sites of the social. *International Journal of Consumer Studies*, 34(4), 381–387. 10.1111/j.1470-6431.2010.00877.x

Seaton, A. V., Jenkins, L. L., Wood, R. C., Picke, P. U. C., Bennett, M. M., & MacLellan, L. R. (1994). *Tourism the State of Art*. John Wiley and Sons Ltd.

Smith, S. L. (1994). The tourism product. *Annals of Tourism Research*, 21(3), 582–595. 10.1016/0160-7383(94)90121-X

Stamboulis, Y., & Skayannis, P. (2003). Innovation strategies and technology for experience-based tourism. *Tourism Management*, 24(1), 35–43. 10.1016/S0261-5177(02)00047-X

Swarbrooke, J. (2001). Key challenges for visitor attraction managers in the UK. *Journal of Retail & Leisure Property*, 1(4), 318–336. 10.1057/palgrave.rlp.5090130

Woyo, E., & Amadhila, E. (2018). Desert tourists experiences in Namibia: A netnographic approach. *African Journal of Hospitality, Tourism and Leisure*, 7(3), 1–13.

Wu, M.-Y., & Pearce, P. L. (2014). Chinese recreational vehicle users in Australia: A netnographic study of tourist motivation. *Tourism Management*, 43, 22–35. 10.1016/j.tourman.2014.01.010

Xiang, Z., Schwartz, Z., Gerdes, J. H.Jr, & Uysal, M. (2015). What can big data and text analytics tell us about hotel guest experience and satisfaction? *International Journal of Hospitality Management*, 44, 120–130. 10.1016/j.ijhm.2014.10.013

Zhang, J., & Walsh, J. (2021). Tourist experience, tourist motivation and destination loyalty for historic and cultural tourists. *Pertanika Journal of Social Science & Humanities*, 28(4), 3277–3296. 10.47836/pjssh.28.4.43

Zhao, X. R., Wang, L., Guo, X., & Law, R. (2015). The influence of online reviews to online hotel booking intentions. *International Journal of Contemporary Hospitality Management*, 27(6), 1343–1364. Advance online publication. 10.1108/IJCHM-12-2013-0542

Zhu, F., & Zhang, X. (2010). Impact of online consumer reviews on sales: The moderating role of product and consumer characteristics. *Journal of Marketing*, 74(2), 133–148. 10.1509/jm.74.2.133

Chapter 7
Evaluation of Tourism Infrastructure Around the Ancient Marvels of Mahabalipuram and Pattadakal

Sreshtaa S. Kumar
https://orcid.org/0000-0002-5859-4644
Christ University, India

Suja John
Christ University, India

ABSTRACT

India is rich in culture and well-known for its mythological knowledge. It has plenty of architectural marvels recognized by UNESCO and maintained by the Archaeological Survey of India (ASI). For this chapter, two of the cultural UNESCO sites, Mahabalipuram and Pattadakal, have been taken as the scope of the chapter. The introduction section talks about the history of the monuments and provides a brief overview of the tourism infrastructure. The following section, evaluation of tourism infrastructure, aims to analyze Mahabalipuram and Pattadakal's tourism infrastructure using four parameters: transportation and connectivity, accommodation, gastronomical facilities, and tourist amenities. An observational study of the sites was conducted between December 2023 and January 2024. This is followed by the recommendations provided by the authors to improve the tourism infrastructure in these sites and, finally, the chapter's conclusion and future scope for researchers.

DOI: 10.4018/979-8-3693-5405-6.ch007

Copyright © 2024, IGI Global. Copying or distributing in print or electronic forms without written permission of IGI Global is prohibited.

1. INTRODUCTION

India is rich in its cultural heritage and mythology. It has 42 world heritage sites, out of which 34 are cultural sites (UNESCO, 2024). The study's scope is two cultural sites: Mahabalipuram in Tamil Nadu and Pattadakal in Karnataka. These are well-known for their unique architecture which attracts tourists worldwide. Tourism infrastructure marks the foundation of a site or venue. Without proper amenities, a site does not get adequate recognition. As defined by Panasiuk, 2007 and cited by Som et al., 2020 and Rani et al., 2017, tourism infrastructure is a range of devices and institutions constituting material and the organizational basis for tourism development. Panasiuk has classified tourism infrastructure into four components: 1. Typically touristic infrastructure comprises accommodation facilities; 2. Para tourist infrastructure, which addresses the transportation facilities; 3. Gastronomy facilities, and 4. Services in the range of active leisure address recreational activities such as skiing, golfing, etc.

In today's world, the growth of tourism infrastructure at any site or place has become a priority for governments as this will help positively shape the destination's image and bring in more business and tourists. (Lanzara & Minerva, 2018) Tourism infrastructure has a vital role in the tourist's overall experience and impression regarding a specific destination. (Jovanovic & Ilic, 2016). The quality of tourism infrastructure is affected by the satisfaction of tourists in a destination. (Sugiama, Oktavia, & Karlina, 2022) Satisfaction is essential to maintain tourist relationships, thereby increasing the chances of tourists revisiting the same destination again and in enhancing the development of a tourist site (Bazneshin et al., 2015). As defined by Vaselikh, tourism infrastructure is a combination of material objects, which are the carriers of various tangible and intangible properties that ensure the highest possible quantitative and qualitative implementation of the tourists' objectives in certain spatial-temporal parameters. (Velichkina, 2014)

The following sections will delve into the evaluation of the tourism infrastructure at Mahabalipuram and Pattadakal, highlighting areas that could be improved. The chapter includes the following sections: evaluation of the current tourism infrastructure, the methodology adopted, recommendations for improvement in both these places, and a conclusion.

Mahabalipuram

The Group of Monuments at Mahabalipuram, a UNESCO-defined site, was established by the Pallavan king, Narasimhavarman I (ca. 630–670), in the 7th Century AD. The place, also known as Mammallapuram, was named after his other name, Mammalla, meaning a wrestler. (Francis, 2024) Mahabalipuram, known by many names, including the Seven Pagodas, by early mariners in the 16th Century AD: Mamallapattana, Mavalipuram, Mavalivaram, Mavellipore, and Mauvellipooram, holds a significant place in history. It is situated on the Coromandel Coast of the Bay of Bengal, in close proximity to Chennai, Tamil Nadu.

Mahabalipuram is renowned for monolithic temples, which are sculpted out of a single boulder or rock. The Pancha Rathas (five chariots) is a fine example of monolithic architecture. This is a group of five monolithic temples, each built on a raised platform, resembling chariots, adorned by carvings of Hindu Gods and Goddesses on the walls. Mahabalipuram also has rock-cut cave temples, structural temples, and bas-relief sculptures carved on the hillsides. Arjuna's Penance, which is a bas-relief, with its intricate description of the river Ganga's descent to the earth carved on the face of the hill, is another hallmark of Mahabalipuram. (UNESCO, 2024) The rock-cut temples with panels showing the battle between the Hindu Goddess Durga and the demon Mahishasura and the panel showing Krishna lifting the Govardhana Mountain to save the cowherds of Mathura from flood beautifully capture the movements and the moods in these stories. The iconic shore temple is the oldest structural temple in South India. During the 2004 Tsunami, evidence of the submerged six pagodas were found. The Shore Temple is the only remaining pagoda of Mahabalipuram, made out of granite (Babu, 2024). Numerous other monolith temples, rock-cut caves, etc., are strewn all over the seaside town of Mahabalipuram, which can be a tourist delight.

Pattadakal

The Group of Monuments at Pattadakal (as called by UNESCO), also known as Pattadakallu, Raktapura (meaning city of red), and Kisuvolal or Kichuvolal (meaning valley of soil), is one of the Chalukyan group of monuments built during the 7th and 8th Century AD. It was one of the three capitals of the Chalukyan Dynasty, located in the district of Bagalkot, Karnataka.

Pattadakal used to be the place of coronation for kings from all dynasties. Inscriptions with the coronated king's names were available in the Sangameshvara temple in Pattadakal. (Annigeri, 1961) Kings from various dynasties ruled this Chalukyan capital from 543 to 757 AD. (Kaligotla, 2019) All the temples had beautiful carvings depicting tales from Hindu mythologies, such as tales from the Ramayana, Mahabharata, stories of Lord Krishna, and many more. (Suebsantiwongse, 2023)

This is a group of ten monuments, out of which eight: Lokeshwara (now known as Virupaksha), Trailokeswara (now known as Mallikarjuna), Kashivishveswara, Vijayeswara (now known as Sangameshwara), Chandrashekara, Galaganatha, Jambulingeswara, Kadasiddheswara. are east-facing temples located in the complex, on the banks of the Malaprabha River. The other two monuments, the Jain Narayana

Temple and the Papanatha Temple, are outside the complex. The Jain temple alone has been constructed during the reign of the Rashtrakutas (Filliozat, 2015). These monuments are 1300 years old, each made out of red sandstone. The Malaprabha River, when in spate, tends to flood the group of monuments; the last time it flooded the complex was in 2019. (DHNS, 2019)

Four of the temples, Virupaksha, Mallikarjuna, Chandrashekara, and Sangamesh-wara, are built in the Dravidian (South Indian) style; four of them, Kashivishveswara temple, Galaganatha temple, Jambulingeswara temple and Kadasiddeswara temple have Nagara (North Indian) influence, Jain Narayana temple is built in Jain style, as the name suggests. The Papanatha temple has a hybrid of all the influences.

Each of these temples had Goddess Ganga on the left-hand side of the manda-pa entrance and Goddess Yamuna on the right side of the mandapa entrance. The North Indian temples could be recognized by the Shuka naasika (shuka – parrot, naasika - nose) or sukanasa shape in the gopuram. There were two temples built by Chalukya king Vikramaditya II, one for each of his two wives: Mallikarjuna temple, built for his first wife, Lokamahadevi & Virupaksha temple, built for his second wife, Trilokyamahadevi. These temples were built to honor the king's victory over the Pallava kingdom in Kanchipuram.

An ancient quarry named Motara Maradi, from which the sandstones were exca-vated for the temples' construction was found 3 kilometers northwest of the temples of Pattadakal (Menon, 2020). Motara Maradi, as quoted by Menon, "is a rocky spur jutting out from the main sandstone ranges which bound the northern limit of the valley." These temples are mainly dedicated to Shiva and represent various schools of architecture of ancient times. The author met Mr. Veeranna Akki, a 65-year-old tourist guide appointed by the government at Pattadakal, who explained the place's history and grandeur and guided us through the site's beautiful architecture.

2. EVALUATION OF TOURIST INFRASTRUCTURE

This section will compare the infrastructure in Mahabalipuram and Pattadakal on key parameters:

2.1. Connectivity and Transportation

Transport is a fundamental component of the tourism industry and a key ingredi-ent to tourism development. As stated by Kaul, 1985 and cited by (Prideaux, 2000), "Transport plays an important role in the successful creation and development of new attractions as well as the healthy growth of existing ones. The provision of suitable transport has transformed dead centres of tourist interest into active and prosperous places that attract multitudes of people."

Tourists are dependent on various modes of transportation available at the tourist sites. They have the freedom to choose whichever service they wish. This, in return, plays a vital role in influencing the tourist's satisfaction with the site. (Virkar & Mallya, 2018) During the 6th Century, Mahabalipuram was a famous seaport where trade occurred between countries such as Portugal and Rome. (Vora & Sundaresh, 2003) Sea transport was the only way for sailors to travel and trade back then. However, with the evolution of time and the development of roads, tourists have begun traveling more conveniently by air and road.

Mahabalipuram is 60 km away from Chennai by road. The nearest airport, which is situated in Meenambakkam, is located 61 km away from the site. The closest railway station is situated in Chengalpattu, which is 23 km away from the town of Mahabalipuram. There are two entrances to Mahabalipuram: one is through Kovalam on the East Coast Road (ECR), and the other is an inner entrance through Thiruporur. These roads are well-laid. One could commute from Chennai by a public bus or by a cab. An entry fee of Rs 75/- is charged for everyone entering the town from either route.

People can catch Metropolitan Transport Corporation (MTC) buses, either local or deluxe buses, from Koyambedu, Ashok Nagar, Guindy, or Thiruvanmiyur bus stands and get down at Mahabalipuram. Proper navigation boards are available leading to the town. The Government of Tamil Nadu has maintained the roads leading to the town well. Table 1 shows the bus routes from various parts of Chennai to Mahabalipuram. The fare charges for the deluxe bus are Rs 65/-, and the local buses charge Rs 80/- to Rs 90/-. Autorickshaws are available to commute from the ECR bus stand to the town.

Table 1. Bus Routes from Various Parts of Chennai to Mahabalipuram

	Bus Number	Type	Boarding Bus stand	Ending Bus stand	Number of buses running per day
1.	515	Local	Tambaram	Mahabalipuram	44
2.	568	Deluxe bus	Koyambedu	East Coast Road (a kilometre by auto to Mahabalipuram)	03
3.	588	Deluxe bus	Adyar OT	Mahabalipuram	15
4.	589	Deluxe bus	Velachery	Mahabalipuram	04
5.	599	Deluxe bus	T. Nagar	Mahabalipuram	24

Source: primary.

Buggies, known as EcoDrive, are available around the Shore temple, especially for senior citizens and pregnant ladies to go around. There are parking facilities arranged by the Tamil Nadu Tourism Development Corporation (TTDC) for two-wheelers, cars, tempo, mini-bus, and buses. The parking charges were Rs 10 (two-wheelers), 30 (cars), 50 (tempo and mini-bus) and 100 (bus) respectively.

Pattadakal is 444 km away from Bangalore, located in the Bagalkote district in Karnataka. To commute to Pattadakal, the nearest town is Badami. Tourists traveling by train can get down at Gadag or Hubbali railway stations, which are 71km and 120km away from Badami. The nearest airport is situated in Hubbali, 2 hours (120 km) from Badami. The road from the Banashankari Temple, Badami, to Pattadakal was muddy and initially narrow but adequately laid, but towards Nageshwar temple, the road was more comfortable to travel on. To witness the grandeur of the Chalukyan architecture, one can plan a trip to Badami-Pattadakal-Aihole, spacing it out to 3 days. According to Annigeri, another well-laid route originates from the Badami Railway Station towards Pattadakal; the closest railway station situated 6 km away (Annigeri, 1961). However, since the road winds through isolated agricultural land, it may not be entirely safe for tourists traveling alone.

Local Karnataka Sarige buses travel from Pattadakal to Badami in 30 to 45 minutes. They charge Rs 30/-. This is the only direct route available to commute to Pattadakal directly. Many North Western Karnataka Road Transport Corporation (NWKTDC) buses are available from the Badami bus stand to commute to places like Bagalkote, Ilkal, Hubbali, Aminagad, etc. According to a report by the Directorate of Urban Land Transport (DULT), Urban Development Department of Bangalore in 2016, the following inferences related to the bus stop enroute to Badami were made:

1. Only five buses, in scheduled route 19/21/22, are available from the Badami-Gudur route. This stops at Nandikeshwar temple and Pattadakal in between (as shown in Table 2).
2. There are government schools available on the way, whose staff and teachers are dependent on these buses to commute daily.
3. Bus shelters were absent on this route. Even if they were present, they were not utilized due to their ill design.
4. Safety of the passengers was a significant concern.
5. The absence of basic infrastructural facilities, such as passenger information systems and information kiosks at bus stands/stops, leads to people feeling unsafe. (DULT, 2016)

Table 2. Bus Routes from Badami to Gudur, Enroute Pattadakal

	Route Number	Type	Boarding Bus stand	Bus stops	Ending Bus stand	Number of buses running per day
1.	19/21/22	Local	Badami	Pattadakal	Gudur (Andhra Pradesh)	05
2.	11	Local	Badami	Pattadakal, Aihole	Gudur (Andhra Pradesh)	01

Source: (NWKRTC Report, 2024)

As per a study by Neal & Gursoy, it was deduced that many tourists prefer public transport to travel while visiting a site, influencing the tourists' experience. Tourists visiting Mahabalipuram and Pattadakal prefer traveling to these sites by share autos or available buses. Parking facilities were available for vehicles away from the monument complex in Pattadakal, but it was for free, unlike in Mahabalipuram.

2.2. Tourist Accommodation

Nutsugbodo (2016) defined accommodation as "an indispensable element in developing and promoting tourism in any destination. The scope and quality of available accommodation facilities can mirror the extent of tourism development at the destination and persuade visitors to choose that destination." Akyeampong (2007) defined tourist accommodation as an establishment that offers its facilities and services to individuals or groups. Tourist accommodation typically refers to a broad range of contemporary hotels, resorts, motels, and alternative establishments such as private cottages/commercial homes, homestays, bed and breakfasts, guesthouses, hostels, and service apartments (Shah & Trupp, 2021).

Accommodation of good quality, aesthetics, and location helps tourists form a long-lasting impression of their destination. In India, a proverb is followed in the hospitality industry, "Atithi Devo Bhava," which means, Guest is God. Hence, care is taken that the guests come back as repeat visitors to the accommodations. Accommodations also enable people to have good family time with their children and parents (Siwek, et al, 2022).

The first thing a tourist looks for while planning to visit a destination is accommodation, which is accessible, safe, hygienic, and economical. They come with an expectation of "being home away from home"; otherwise, they seek alternative options (Khadaroo & Seetanah, 2007). Privacy is another factor that tourists look for in an accommodation so that they do not feel disturbed. Courteousness and politeness of staff are other factors that decide whether tourists will revisit their place of stay or not. (Shah & Trupp, 2021)

They use search engines to research their preferred accommodations to fulfill this criterion. The reviews these search engines provide are crucial in deciding where a tourist wants to stay. (Pjero & Gjermëni, 2020) This leads to tourists being satisfied and enhancing the destination's image. Some tourists prefer having recreational facilities, such as table tennis, swimming pool, spa, gym, etc. Having recreational facilities in the accommodation helps tourists relax during their trip (Mandić et al., 2018). Apart from recreational facilities, tourists can use facilities such as conference rooms, banquet halls, etc, to conduct meetings and host parties.

According to Burkart & Medlik (1984), tourist accommodation is classified into four categories, namely: 1) service accommodation, which includes hotels, apartments, guest houses, and boarding houses; 2) Self-catering accommodation, the accommodation that requires its consumers to provide their own meals, such as camping, caravans, rented flats, and houses; 3) House of friends and relatives, in this case, accommodation does not need any cost because it has been provided by a friend, relative or family in the destination area; and 4) Other accommodations, including hostels, youth hostels, boats, etc. (Simarmata, et al. 2016) Those tourists who do not want to stay in hotels can opt for alternative accommodations, such as guest houses, service apartments and commercial homes that provide paid lodging to tourists on a short-term basis, to get the local touch. Factors such as personal space, safety and security, value for money, convenience, and a homely atmosphere influence a tourist to choose the accommodation of their preference. (Gunasekaran & Anandkumar, 2012)

Availability of safe, hygienic and economical places for staying close to the historical sites can improve the tourist influx as well as enhance the image of a tourist destination. Mahabalipuram has many budget and premium hotels in close proximity to the group of monuments. There are many hotels, resorts, and lodges in and around Mahabalipuram where tourists can choose to stay based on their affordability.

Table 3 shows the list of star hotels available at Mahabalipuram. The 1-star, 2-star and 3-star rated properties include lodges, guest houses, villas, and beach houses and have been categorized as 'top-reviewed hotels of Mahabalipuram' by the search engine booking.com, whereas the properties rated as 4-star and 5-star are luxury hotels.

Table 3. List of Star-Rated Accommodations Available at Mahabalipuram

	Name of the Hotel	Category
1	Radisson Blu Temple Bay Mamallapuram	5*
2	Sheraton Grand Chennai Resort	5*
3	Kaldan Samudhra Palace	5*
4	InterContinental Chennai Mahabalipuram Resort, an IHG Hotel	5*
5	Taj Fisherman's Cove Resort & Spa, Chennai	5*
6	Welcomhotel by ITC Hotels, Kences Palm Beach, Mamallapuram	5*

continued on following page

Table 3. Continued

	Name of the Hotel	Category
7	Four Points by Sheraton Mahabalipuram Resort & Convention Center	4*
8	Grande Bay Resort and Spa Mamallapuram	4*
9	Chariot Hotel	4*
10	Coral beach resort	4*
11	Redhomex The Moon Villa	4*
12	Esthell Village Resort	4*
13	Manna Villa	4*
14	Ivy Villa	4*
15	Lotus Villa	4*
16	Blue Moon Guest House	3*
17	See Breeze Beach Resort	3*
18	Hotel Sri Murugan Guest House	3*
19	Thiru Pavilion Retreat	3*
20	Sangam Inn & Banquets	3*
21	Hotel Mamalla Heritage	3*
22	Hotel Mahabs	3*
23	Hotel Bay Treasure	3*
24	Ruthran Guest House	3*
25	Aura East Bay	3*
26	Meya Beach Walk Hotel	2*
27	Sri Murugan Beach Paradise Hotel	2*
28	Srinivasa Residency	2*
29	Hotel Ramakrishna	2*
30	NH Gardens Villa Mahabalipuram By Lexstays	2*
31	Siva Residency	1*
32	Flagship M M Park Inn	1*

Source: Booking.com

There were no youth hostels or hostels found in the town, as there are enough facilities for hostels and youth hostels in Chennai. One can stay at a PG in Adyar, Thiruvanmiyur, ECR, etc. There were no self-catering accommodations available. The area had more service-related accommodations as it catered to tourists from foreign countries.

However, during the annual Indian Dance Festival, the 4-star and 5-star hotels ran at total capacity and could not accommodate all the guests, based on interviews of staff at the hotels.

There are no places for tourist accommodation close to the Pattadakal group of monuments. One has to book accommodation at Badami, which is 30 minutes away by car and is the nearest accommodation option. Table 4 shows the best accommodation options available at Badami. From the table, we can infer that few options are available for tourists to stay while visiting Pattadakal. There are no luxury or premium hotels in the vicinity; only 3-star- and 4-star hotels with decent amenities and facilities were available.

Table 4. List of Accommodations Available at Badami, Karnataka

S.No	Name of the Hotel	Category
1	Hotel Mayura Chalukya KSTDC	3*
2	Hotel Badami Court	3*
3	Hotel Anand Deluxe	3*
4	Hotel Mookambika Deluxe	3*
5	Badami Heritage Resort	4*
6	Clarks Inn Badami	4*
7	Krishna Heritage	4*
8	Kanthi Resort, Bagalkot	4*

Source: TripAdvisor.

2.3. Gastronomical Facilities

Gastronomy is defined as the art of making food. In the tourism context, gastronomic tourism has been defined by the UNWTO as *"a type of tourism activity which is characterized by the visitor's experience linked with food and related products and activities while traveling"*. Gastronomy and tourism go hand-in-glove with each other. One develops their gastronomic experiences by trying local foods and cuisines, considering other features, such as the food price and the destination's overall environment, and receiving high customer service. (Ullah, et al., 2022)

The saying aptly goes, *"A way to a man's heart is through his stomach."* Good food creates a good impression. When looking for a place to stay, local food availability is essential in helping tourists decide where to stay. This helps in spreading the word about the destination's popularity. (Shah & Trupp, 2021) While staying in their accommodation, good food and hygiene must be present. This is one of the parameters that increase the ratings of the place of

the accommodation. Tourists search for cuisines unique to that destination to savor the authenticity the destination has to provide and boost the economy. (Shunali & Arora, 2014) For instance, in Chennai, tourists prefer to have idly and dosa, with a variety of chutneys for breakfast, as it is the staple food of Tamil Nadu. In Karnataka, tourists prefer having special dishes like Bisibela bath and Udupi meals for lunch. A destination's cuisine enhances a tourist's experience and allows them to immerse themselves completely in the culture.

Mahabalipuram is well endowed with gastronomical facilities in all ranges. For authentic South Indian food, one could eat at the famous franchise, Adyar Ananda Bhavan, also known as A2B. To eat food at a 5-star restaurant, one could eat at Lattitude 49 and Radisson Blu Temple Bay. People can eat North Indian, Chinese, and German cuisines, too. In Chennai, food streets are available in various locations, allowing tourists to experience various Indian cuisines, apart from South Indian. As per information taken from TripAdvisor, 2024, it was found that there were 60 famous gastronomical facilities available for tourists to choose from. They have been tabulated below in Table 5.

Table 5. List of Gastronomical Facilities Available at Mahabalipuram

Fine-Dining	Budget Eateries	Mid-Range
The Reef	Babu's Café	Petals - Multi Cuisine Restaurant
C Salt	Eagle's Nest	WelcomCafe Riva
The Melting Pot	Mamalla Bhavan	Fish and French Fries
The Wharf	Samovar	Searock Restaurant
Kokommo tiki shack	Grains Multi-Cuisine Restaurant	Le Yogi
Waters Edge	Dany's Barbeque and Kitchen	Hotel Guru
Pelican Deck	Bhakaya Seafood Restaurant	Gecko Restaurant
Tao of Peng	Local flavours by Wok to Dhaba	The New Café
Lattitude 49	Crocodile Café	Eli's Kitchen
The Pisces, GRT Temple Bay	Gazebo Lodge and Restaurant	Freshly 'n' Hot Café
	Food Express	Nautilus
	Si Mangia	Buddha Cafe Restaurant
		Joe's café
		Motel Mamalla
		Johnny's Corner Sea Food Restaurant
		The Golden Palate
		Ideal Garden Restaurant
		Adyar Ananda Bhavan
		Bambino Beach Restaurant
		Masala Café

continued on following page

Table 5. Continued

Fine-Dining	Budget Eateries	Mid-Range
		Wok to Dhaba
		Namaste Restaurant and German bakery
		Santana Beach Restaurant
		Idlers' Farm Shop and Café
		Delhi Dhaba
		Nightmare Restaurant
		Chettinadu Virundhu
		Sandy Bottom Cafe
		Moonrakers
		Luna Magica
		Seashore Restaurant
		18th Century Café
		Courtallam Border Parotta
		Golden Sun
		Village Inn
		Vinodhara
		Sri Ananda Bhavan
		Neelam Café & Restaurant

Source: (TripAdvisor, 2024)

From the list of restaurants mentioned in Table 5, the following observations were made:

- The fine-dining restaurants had a star rating of 4 & 5. These were preferred by guests who preferred high-budgeted hotels for stay. Some of these restaurants were located inside hotels with high reputations.
- The mid-range and cheap eats restaurants were all stand-alone, ranging from 3-star to 5-star. Some were located on highways, and some were in the town.
- These eateries had various cuisines, ranging from Continental, German to Indian. Some of them were cafes, too.
- There were two separate vegetarian restaurants, such as Motel Mamalla and Sri Ananda Bhavan
- Moonrakers is a well-rated mid-range restaurant that transports tourists back to Goa when they step foot there.
- There are many small stalls and street vendors selling juices, snacks, etc, to tourists around the monuments.

The author observed a few small stalls and street vendors around the Pattadakal group of monuments, but there were no hotels or restaurants nearby where tourists could get a complete meal or refresh themselves. The nearest restaurant was 15 km away from the Group of Monuments. It is an area that needs further development. At least a few restaurants selling local cuisine can be set up close to the site so tourists can eat and refresh themselves. To have a proper meal, one must go to hotels located at Badami, which is 15km from Pattadakal. Table 6 consists of a list of hotels available at Badami for tourists to eat.

Table 6. List of Eateries Available at Badami, the Nearest Place from Pattadakal by 15 km.

	Name of the Establishment	Type	Star Rating
1.	Hotel Pink Palace Badami	Restaurant	5*
2.	Hotel Brahmi	Restaurant	5*
3.	Sri Veerabhadreshwar lingayat khanavali	Local restaurant	4*
4.	Hotel Paradise Family Restaurant	Restaurant (for budget- friendly guests)	4*
5.	Basaveshwar Kanavali	Restaurant with PG	4*
6.	Banashri Hotel & Shubashree Bar	Hotel & Bar	4*
7.	Hotel Bharat	Restaurant	4*
8.	Pakwan Hotel	Restaurant	4*
9.	Geeta Darshini	South Indian Restaurant	4*
10.	Hotel Food Plaza	Dhaba	4*
11.	Golden Caves Restaurant	Restaurant	3*
12.	The Bridge Restaurant	Restaurant (located inside Clarks Inn Badami Hotel)	3*

2.4. Tourist Amenities

Amenities are those services required by tourists to facilitate their travel. These are primarily developed for the residents but utilized by tourists, too. (Sharma & Bains, 2021) When tourists visit a destination, the basic amenities they expect are adequate and well-equipped public restrooms, drinking water facilities, dustbins, medical shops, hospitals or clinics (in case of emergency), ATMs to withdraw cash, security personnel (police), signboards to navigate to the venue properly, information desks having brochures, etc. Tourists enjoy some man-made amenities, too, such as dance and music festivals. These dance festivals are being used to attract tourists to the destination. (Georgoula & Terkenli, 2017) This section will highlight the amenities available during the dance festivals in Mahabalipuram and Pattadakal, respectively. Having souvenir shops in a destination enables the local people to earn their livelihood, which helps increase business and bring in a rise in the destination's economy. (Marcouiller, Kim, & Deller, 2004) The quality of amenities in a destination increases tourists' satisfaction. (Sugiama et al., 2022) Enhancing amenities on the sites assists with their local development. (Yun, 2014)

To enter all the places in Mahabalipuram, we had to pay an entry fee of Rs 40, according to the Archaeological Survey of India (ASI). Tourists could use a standard ticket to visit the rest of the monuments. All the monuments had adequate drinking water and toilet facilities available for tourists. Inside the shore temple complex, close to 50 shops lead up to an open beach area surrounding the shore temple. The shops had products ranging from souvenirs and clothes to refreshments such as potato spring rolls, water, and juices. There were shops that sold products made of shells. While conversing with one of the souvenir shop owners, Ms Ganga, she told the author that during the dance festival, the crowd to Mahabalipuram increases every year, which is the peak season. For shop owners like them, they experience a boom in their businesses due to tourists buying products from them. Some tourists took a dip in the beach and enjoyed the view of the temple simultaneously. However, a help desk that can answer tourist queries or guide them was absent. There were no medical facilities around the venue. One would have to come out of town and onto East Coast Road to find a medical facility. There was a help desk available only at the ticket counter. Crowd management was adequately done.

To draw attention to the site's grandeur, the state government and the Ministry of Tourism organize the Indian dance festival Mamallapuram every year, which domestic and international tourists attend. The dance festival in Mahabalipuram lasts 21 days, starting from the last week of December and concluding in the third week of January. Each day, the cultural programs begin at 6 pm and last up to 8.30 pm. Police personnel and an ambulance were present during the dance festival.

In Pattadakal, we had to pay an entry fee of Rs 40 to enter the monument complex, according to the Archaeological Survey of India (ASI). There was a lack of crowd management at the ticket counter. There were limited toilets and drinking water facilities available at the monuments. Some refreshment stalls selling sugarcane and lemon juices were available outside the monument complex, but there were not enough souvenir shops. No help desk kiosk was available either. Pattadakal organizes the Chalukya dance festival every year in January, inviting domestic and international tourists. On enquiring with the locals, we discovered that the state government had not organized the festival for the last four years due to political reasons.

Table 7. Summarizes the List of Amenities that were Available or not Available During these Dance Festivals

Name of the Amenity	Indian Dance Festival, Mamallapuram	Chalukya Festival, Pattadakal
Public Restrooms	Available. The ASI separately arranged restrooms for the Physically challenged people. There were some pay-and-use restrooms available in the town.	Available. Only two, arranged by the ASI, were available. Restrooms for the physically challenged were not available.
Drinking Water	Available	Available
Dustbins	Available	Available
Parking Facility	Available	Available
ATM	Available – 3 booths	Not Available. Banks and ATMs were found on the way to Badami.
Helpdesks / Kiosks	Not Available	Not Available
Tourist Guides (employed by the Government)	Available	Available
Ticket counter	Available	Available
Bus stands	Available	Available but not properly maintained
Ambulance	Available only during the dance festival	Not available
Police Personnel	Available only during the dance festival	Not available
Signboards	Available	Available
Fueling stations	Available	Available
Medical Shops	Not Available	Not available
Hospitals	Not Available	Not available
Dance Festival posters	Available	Not available
Souvenir shops	Available	Minimally available
Refreshment stalls (eg: juice stalls)	Available	Available

3. METHODOLOGY

The chapter adopts an observational study and some secondary data from search engines for information regarding accommodation and gastronomical facilities. The author has visited these two sites and observed the destinations from December 2023 to January 2024. The dance festivals of these sites were used as a tool to conduct a study regarding the availability of essential tourism infrastructural amenities for tourists.

4. RECOMMENDATIONS

The recommendations for improvement in each category of tourism infrastructure have been listed below under each sub-title by the author.

4.1. Connectivity and Transportation

Access to Mahabalipuram is good, as the road from Chennai is well-laid and relatively safe. It is also well connected by public buses and cabs. The government can improve connectivity by providing special buses, especially for tourists, from the Chennai airport and Chengalpattu railway station to Mahabalipuram at two hourly intervals throughout the day. The number of EcoDrives, which are pollution-free, should be increased to run on the main roads leading from the Shore temple to the rest of the monuments in the complex, such as Arjuna's Penance, Krishna's Butterball, Mahishasura Mardini cave, etc. The MTC buses from Chennai to Mahabalipuram can be increased during the Mahabalipuram dance festival in December and January when the tourist influx is higher.

However, Pattadakal is far from the nearest airport, Hubbali. The government of Karnataka can consider constructing a smaller airport at Badami to help visitors. The connecting road between Badami and Pattadakal can be made safer by constructing security kiosks at regular intervals as they pass through isolated areas. The Karnataka Government must improve the infrastructural facilities at the bus stops en route to Badami and Pattadakal so that people, especially school children and teachers, feel safe waiting at the bus stands at late hours. More KTDC-operated buses, which ply every two hours from Badami to Pattadakal, can also be considered. The Karnataka Tourism Ministry can provide electrical buggies in Pattadakal for tourist use, as the TTDC has done in Mahabalipuram.

4.2. Tourist Accommodation

Mahabalipuram has enough tourist accommodation for traditional foreign and domestic tourists. There are both luxury and budget accommodations available to suit all budgets. However, additional rooms are required during busy seasons, such as during the Indian dance festival at Mammallapuram. The tourism ministry can increase the number of rooms in TTDC to accommodate guests during peak season. With the traveling habits of the youth requiring alternative accommodations such as outdoor campsites, homestays, bed and breakfast accommodations, youth hostels, etc., the tourism ministry can consider providing these accommodation facilities closer to the Mahabalipuram group of monuments. Varied options for stay will increase the site's attractiveness for the younger generation, which will drive the tourist inflow in the coming years.

Places for tourists to stay need to be constructed close to the Pattadakal group of monuments to increase their value as tourist destinations. The KSTDC has to take the initiative here and create a large eco-hotel or a guest house that merges with the surrounding farmland and does not disturb the serenity of the place. Alternatively, private hotel companies can be provided subsidies to set up hotels around the area, but the plan needs to be approved by the government to ensure that the hotels do not mar the landscape and are in tune with the surrounding environment. The number of such accommodations close the site should not be more than 5, to prevent the area from becoming another noisy tourist hub.

Options for stay in Badami need to be improved considerably. There are no luxury or premium hotels available, where international tourists and the more affluent domestic tourists can stay. The available 4-star hotels do not have facilities such as swimming pool, spa, gym etc, which makes tourists stay at a destination longer.

Besides luxury hotels, hostels and guest-houses need to be increased to cater to the younger tourists. The government can provide incentives to the local residents to start home-stays which can provide multiple benefits. One, it can increase the number of rooms available in the area. Two, it will allow tourists to savour local hospitality and cuisine which makes the entire experience more wholesome. Three, it will enable the locals to earn additional income.

4.3. Gastronomical Facilities

Mahabalipuram has ample gastronomical facilities to cater to all palettes. The tourism department can consider setting up a food court consisting of stalls for residents in nearby localities. Also, a food festival can be held annually, yet another event around which the destination can be promoted.

The Karnataka Tourism Development Corporation (KTDC) urgently needs one or two restaurants providing hygienic and healthy food to open establishments in Pattadakal. However, the government should be careful not to hand out too many licenses to prevent the area from getting cluttered. The KSTDC can open a restaurant, run by local cooks, showcasing the delicacies in the area to add to the rich experience of visiting the ancient monuments.

4.4. Tourist Amenities

Basic tourist amenities are available in Mahabalipuram. The availability of ambulances and police personnel should be made mandatory in these sites, even on regular days. Medical shops on both sites must be constructed. Tourist amenities at Pattadakal are minimal and need a thorough overhaul. The development of these amenities can help enhance the tourist in-flow and destination image. In Pattadakal, most tourist amenities, as mentioned in Table 7, must be made available for the tourists to have easy access and not depend solely on Badami for travel and accommodation.

5. CONCLUSION

The study concludes that developing tourism infrastructure in Pattadakal and Mahabalipuram is a work in progress. The stakeholders, both from private and government, must come together to properly shape the tourism infrastructure, especially in Pattadakal. Being a country rich in cultural heritage, it is essential for India to highlight their heritage sites as these act as tools for each state's destination marketing.

Despite both places being known for their grandeur, more infrastructural tourism facilities must be developed. The Ministry of Tourism of Tamil Nadu and Karnataka needs to focus on providing a pleasurable experience to tourists so that they return and also recommend the place to other tourists. Mahabalipuram and Pattadakal need more government-run buses for tourists and more government employees to manage helpdesks. However, it was noted that the basic tourist infrastructure is almost absent in close proximity to the Pattadakal group of monuments. The bus stands in Pattadakal must be made safer so the locals can wait during the late hours. These issues must be addressed quickly to showcase this grand legacy in the best light in the world.

Future researchers have some scope for conducting a study regarding the infrastructural improvement in other UNESCO sites, with inputs from this chapter. This chapter has covered four main domains of infrastructure: transportation, accommodation, gastronomical facilities, and tourist amenities. These domains can provide insights for readers to research the impact of the infrastructure on the tourist footfall during peak and off seasons. An analysis of the implications of the infrastructural improvement on the locals (especially their economic development) of the other states can be another area to explore. Researchers interested in studies related to cultural tourism, tourism infrastructure, event promotion, and event marketing shall find this chapter helpful.

REFERENCES

Ahmed, S. (2020). Pancha rathas, the five stone temples of the Mahabalipuram site: Opportunity to revive its lost garden heritage through ecotourism. *Paranoá*, 13(28), 1–27. 10.18830/issn.1679-0944.n28.2020.07

Ali, F., & Amin, M. (2014). The Influence of Physical Environment on Emotions, Customer Satisfaction and Behavioural Intentions in Chinese Resort Hotel Industry. *Journal for Global Business Advancement*, 7(3), 249–266. 10.1504/JGBA.2014.064109

Annigeri, A. M. (1961). *A Guide to the Pattadakal Temples*. Dharwar: Archaeological Survey of India.

Babu, M. (2024, January 12). *10 Must-See Tourist Attractions in and Around Mahabalipuram*. Retrieved from Wander Wisdom: https://wanderwisdom.com/travel-destinations/must-see- attractions-in-mahabalipuram

Bazneshin, S. D., Hosseini, S. B., & Azeri, A. R. K. (2015). The physical variables of tourist areas to increase the tourists' satisfaction regarding the sustainable tourism criteria: Case study of Rudsar Villages, Sefidab in Rahim Abad. *Procedia: Social and Behavioral Sciences*, 201, 128–135. 10.1016/j.sbspro.2015.08.141

Blazeska, D., Strezovski, Z., & Klimoska, A. (2018). The influence of tourist infrastructure on the tourist satisfaction in Ohrid. *UTMS Journal*, 85-93.

Chambers, W. (1869). *The Seven Pagodas on the Coromandel Coast*. Archaeological Survey of India.

Chavan, R. R., & Bhola, S. S. (2016). Assessment of Variables in Measuring Tourist Infrastructure. *Vishwakarma Business Review*, 105–115.

DHNS. (2019, August 11). *Heritage sites Hampi, Pattadakal besieged by water*. Retrieved from Deccan Herald: https://www.deccanherald.com/india/karnataka/heritage-sites-hampi- pattadakal-besieged-by-water-753728.html

DULT. (2016). *City Service Bus Evaluation - Badami*. Bengaluru: Urban Development Department. Filliozat, V. (2015). *Saiva Monument at Pattadakal*. Unpublished manuscript.

Francis, E. (2024). Pallavas (D. Potts, E. Harkness, J. Neelis, & R. McIntosh, Eds.). *The Encyclopedia of Ancient History*, 1-4.

Georgoula, V., & Terkenli, T. (2017). Tourism Impacts of International Arts Festivals in Greece. The Cases of the Kalamata Dance Festival and Drama Short Film Festival. *Innovative Approaches to Tourism and Leisure: Fourth International Conference IACuDiT, Athens 2017* (pp. 101-114). Athens: Springer International Publishing.

Gunasekaran, N., & Anandkumar, V. (2012). Factors of influence in choosing alternative accommodation: A study with reference to Pondicherry, a coastal heritage town. *Procedia: Social and Behavioral Sciences*, 62, 1127–1132. 10.1016/j.sbspro.2012.09.193

Jovanovic, S., & Ilic, I. (2016). Infrastructure as important determinant of tourism development in the countries of Southeast Europe. *Ecoforum Journal, 5*(1), 288-294.

Kaligotla, S. (2019). *A Temple without a Name: Deccan Architecture and the Canon for Sacred Indian Buildings. Canons and Values: Ancient to Modern.* Academia.

Khadaroo, J., & Seetanah, B. (2007). Transport infrastructure and tourism development. *Annals of Tourism Research*, 34(4), 1021–1032. 10.1016/j.annals.2007.05.010

Lanzara, G., & Minerva, G. A. (2018). Tourism, amenities, and welfare in an urban setting. *Journal of Regional Science*, 59(3), 452–479. 10.1111/jors.12440

Mandić, A., Mrnjavac, Ž., & Kordić, L. (2018). Tourism infrastructure, recreational facilities and tourism development. *Tourism and Hospitality Management*, 24(1), 41–62. 10.20867/thm.24.1.12

Marcouiller, D. W., Kim, K. K., & Deller, S. C. (2004). Natural amenities, tourism and income distribution. *Annals of Tourism Research*, 31(4), 1031–1050. 10.1016/j.annals.2004.04.003

Menon, S. M. (2020, September 26). *Megaliths of Pattadakal.* Retrieved from Deccan Herald: deccanherald.com/spectrum/megaliths-of-pattadakal-893182.html

MTC. (2024, April 15). *Bus route from Mahabalipuram to Thirupporur.* Retrieved from MTC Chennai: https://mtcbus.tn.gov.in/Home/bustimingsearch

Nair, B., & Sathiyabamavathy, K. (2020). Visitor perception and expectation of heritage tourism at Mahabalipuram monuments. *Strategies for promoting sustainable hospitality and tourism services*, 191-210.

Nutsugbodo, R. (2016). Tourist accommodation. *Tourism development in Ghana's Brong-Ahafo Region: Demand and supply dynamics*, 73-88.

NWKRTC. (2024, April 16). *Bus Time Table.* Retrieved from North Western Karnataka Road Transport Corporation: https://nwkrtc.karnataka.gov.in/info-3/Bus+Time+Table/en

Pjero, E., & Gjermëni, O. (2020). Tourist's satisfaction in terms of accommodation: A case study in Vlore, Albania. *Business Perspectives and Research*, 8(1), 67–80. 10.1177/2278533719860022

Prideaux, B. (2000). The Role of the Transport System in Destination Development. *Tourism (Zagreb)*, 53–63.

Rani, H., Afifuddin, M., & Akbar, H. (2017). Tourism infrastructure development prioritization in Sabang Island using analytic network process methods. *AIP Conference Proceedings*, 1-6.

Richards, G. (2000). Tourism and the World of Culture and Heritage. *Tourism Recreation Research*, 25(1), 9–17. 10.1080/02508281.2000.11014896

Shah, C., & Trupp, A. (2021). Trends in consumer behaviour and accommodation choice: perspectives from India. *Tourism in India*, 68-83.

Sharma, S., & Bains, H. (2021). Tourism System: Components, Elements and Models. In *S. o. (SOTHSM), BTMC-135: Concept and Impacts of Tourism* (pp. 81–96). IGNOU.

Shunali & Arora, M. (2014). Gastronomy Tourism and Destination Image Formation. *Indian Journal of Applied Hospitality & Tourism Research, 6*, 68-75.

Simarmata, J., Yuliantini, Y., & Keke, Y. (2016). The influence of travel agent, infrastructure and accommodation on tourist satisfaction. *International Conference on Tourism, Gastronomy, and Tourist Destination (ICTGTD 2016)* (pp. 281-283). Atlantis Press.

Sivaramamurthy, C. (2004). *Mahabalipuram*. Archaeological Survey of India.

Siwek, M., Kolasińska, A., Wrześniewski, K., & Zmuda Palka, M. (2022). Services and amenities offered by city hotels within family tourism as one of the factors guaranteeing satisfactory leisure time. *International Journal of Environmental Research and Public Health*, 19(14), 1–18. 10.3390/ijerph1914832135886167

Som, J., Chatterjee, S., & Suklabaidya, P. (2020). Stakeholders' Perspective on Tourism Infrastructure at Khajuraho Dance Festival. *Global Journal of Enterprise Information System*, 12(2), 82–90.

Suebsantiwongse, S. (2023). Frozen sentiments: The transformation of Kālidāsa's Drama to sacred art at the Cālukya Court. *Humanities, Arts and Social Sciences Studies*, 49-56.

Sugiama, A. G., Oktavia, H. C., & Karlina, M. (2022). The Effect of Tourism Infrastructure Asset Quality on Tourist Satisfaction: A Case on Forest Tourism in Tasikmalaya Regency. *International Journal of Applied Sciences in Tourism and Events*, 6(1), 65–71. 10.31940/ijaste.v6i1.65-71

TripAdvisor. (2024, April 18). *Restaurants in Mahabalipuram*. Retrieved from TripAdvisor: https://www.tripadvisor.in/FindRestaurants?geo=1162480&broadened=true

Ullah, N., Khan, J., Saeed, I., Zada, S., Xin, S., Kang, Z., & Hu, Y. (2022). Gastronomic Tourism and Tourist Motivation: Exploring Northern Areas of Pakistan. *International Journal of Environmental Research and Public Health*, 19(13), 1–17. 10.3390/ijerph1913773435805393

UNESCO. (2024, March 21). *UNESCO*. Retrieved from Group of Monuments at Mahabalipuram: https://whc.unesco.org/en/list/249

Unknown. (2024, April 15). *Chennai City Bus*. Retrieved from Chennai Bus Route & Timings (MTC): https://chennaicitybus.in/

Velichkina, A. V. (2014). The assessment of the regional tourism infrastructure development. Ehkonomicheskie i sotsialnye peremeny: fakty, tendentsii, prognoz, 239-250.

Verma, A., & Rajendran, G. (2017). The effect of historical nostalgia on tourists' destination loyalty intention: An empirical study of the world cultural heritage site – Mahabalipuram, India. *Asia Pacific Journal of Tourism Research*, 22(9), 977–990. 10.1080/10941665.2017.1357639

Virkar, A. R., & Mallya, P. D. (2018). A review of dimensions of tourism transport affecting tourist satisfaction. *Indian Journal of Commerce and Management Studies*, 9(1), 72–80. 10.18843/ijcms/v9i1/10

Vora & Sundaresh. (2003). Mahabalipuram: A Saga of Glory to Tribulations. *Migration & Diffusion, 4,* 67-80.

Yun, H. (2014). Spatial Relationships of Cultural Amenities in Rural Tourism Areas. *Tourism Planning & Development*, 11(4), 452–462. 10.1080/21568316.2014.894557

KEY TERMS AND DEFINITIONS

Accommodation: A place where tourists feel "home away from home". The basic expectations one has from their accommodation are good hygiene, good food, safety, security, and budget-friendly.

Alternative Accommodation: These are places of stay that provide a local and authentic touch rather than the usual hotel touch. They are cheap and affordable, e.g., guest houses, service apartments, etc.

Gastronomical Facilities: These are facilities that offer a variety of food options to travelers and, at the same time, allow them to create new experiences.

Kiosk: A stand-alone portal that provides information regarding travel and tourism facilities to tourists.

NWKTDC: North Western Karnataka Tourism Development Corporation. They are responsible for the tourism development in the North West Karnataka. Badami, Pattadakal, Hubbali, etc. are places that come under this sector.

Transportation: A facility that enables a tourist to travel from one place to another comfortably. This is an important component in the tourism industry.

Tourism Infrastructure: Tourism infrastructure are the resources necessary to develop tourist inflow and is the backbone of any destination.

Tourist Amenities: These are basic services and facilities which are essential in a destination for a tourist, such as restrooms, drinking water, sign boards, postal services, hospitals, medical stores, ATM, etc.

Chapter 8
Revitalizing Ancient Sites:
Sustainable Tourism Strategies for Preservation and Community Development

Pallavi Mohanan
https://orcid.org/0000-0002-4048-9870
Amity University, Noida, India

ABSTRACT

This chapter explores how Egypt, Greece, Mexico, and India use sustainable tourism to revive ancient sites and promote local communities. It looks at historical tourism trends, initiatives for preservation, and community involvement. Strategies include site management, education, and community partnerships. Economic benefits like revenue and jobs, waste management, and cultural impacts on indigenous groups are assessed. Challenges and lessons learned provide insights for sustainability. Comparative analysis shows diverse approaches to balancing tourism and heritage preservation. Responsible tourism is advocated for site protection and community empowerment.

INTRODUCTION

Ancient archaeological sites are crucial repositories of cultural heritage and major tourist attractions globally. These sites provide tangible connections to our past, offering insights into ancient civilizations, their beliefs, customs, and accomplishments. The appeal of exploring ancient ruins, temples, and artifacts attracts millions of tourists annually, making substantial contributions to local economies and facilitating global cultural exchange (Sonuç, 2020). Egypt, Greece, Mexico,

DOI: 10.4018/979-8-3693-5405-6.ch008

Copyright © 2024, IGI Global. Copying or distributing in print or electronic forms without written permission of IGI Global is prohibited.

and India are notable for their rich archaeological heritage, showcasing diverse civilizations and historical epochs that continue to fascinate visitors worldwide.

Egypt is famous for iconic ancient sites like the Pyramids of Giza, Luxor Temple, and the Sphinx, which hold significant places in human history (Hawass, 2015). These monumental structures, built millennia ago by the ancient Egyptians, symbolize their advanced architectural skills and spiritual beliefs. Egypt's archaeological treasures not only captivate tourists but also contribute significantly to the country's tourism sector, generating revenue for conservation efforts and local communities (Weaver, 2007).

Similarly, Greece possesses numerous ancient archaeological sites that echo the legacy of classical civilization. The Acropolis of Athens, Delphi, and Olympia are renowned sites that attract history enthusiasts, scholars, and tourists interested in experiencing the birthplace of democracy, philosophy, and the Olympic Games (Grima, 2017). Sustainable tourism initiatives at these sites prioritize preserving ancient monuments while promoting responsible visitor behavior and community engagement (Iliopoulou-Georgudaki, et all, 2017).

In the Americas, Mexico's archaeological marvels such as Chichen Itza, Teotihuacan, and Palenque offer insights into the rich heritage of pre-Columbian civilizations like the Maya and Aztecs (Gratacap, 1883). These sites showcase remarkable architectural achievements and highlight the cultural and religious practices of ancient Mesoamerican societies. Sustainable tourism practices in Mexico focus on conservation, education, and collaboration with indigenous communities to protect these invaluable cultural assets (McIntyre, 1993).

India's archaeological landscape is incredibly diverse, reflecting millennia of civilization and cultural interchange. From the iconic Taj Mahal to the ancient city of Varanasi and the temples of Khajuraho, India's archaeological sites span various historical periods and architectural styles (Yellowhom, 2000). Sustainable tourism initiatives in India stress heritage conservation, community involvement, and responsible tourism to safeguard these sites for future generations (Kaul & Gupta, 2009).

Therefore, ancient archaeological sites play a crucial role as cultural heritage and tourist attractions, preserving tangible remnants of human history while promoting sustainable tourism and contributing to local economies and cultural understanding (Spenceley & Rylance, 2019). Adopting sustainable tourism practices is essential for countries like Egypt, Greece, Mexico, and India to preserve and promote their rich archaeological heritage while benefiting local communities and future generations socio-economically.

METHODOLOGY

This chapter adopts a qualitative research approach, relying on secondary data sources to examine sustainable tourism strategies for revitalizing ancient sites while promoting community development. The research methodology involves a comprehensive literature review, case study analysis, and comparative evaluation of sustainable tourism practices in Egypt, Greece, Mexico, and India (Snyder, 2019). By employing a qualitative approach, this study aims to provide an in-depth understanding of the complexities and nuances associated with sustainable tourism initiatives at ancient archaeological sites (Mohajan, 2018).

The literature review process entailed a systematic examination of scholarly articles, books, and reports related to sustainable tourism, heritage preservation, and community development. Key databases such as Scopus, Web of Science, and Google Scholar were utilized to identify relevant literature (Xiao & Watson, 2019). The selection criteria focused on articles published in peer-reviewed journals, ensuring the credibility and reliability of the sources (Snyder, 2019).

Case study analysis formed a crucial component of the research methodology, allowing for a detailed exploration of sustainable tourism practices in specific contexts (Yin, 2018). The case studies of Egypt, Greece, Mexico, and India were purposefully selected based on their rich archaeological heritage and diverse approaches to sustainable tourism development (Crowe et al., 2011). By examining these case studies, the chapter aims to identify best practices, challenges, and lessons learned in revitalizing ancient sites through sustainable tourism (Mohajan, 2018).

Comparative analysis was employed to identify similarities, differences, and patterns across the selected case studies (Esser & Vliegenthart, 2017). This approach facilitated the identification of common themes, success factors, and areas for improvement in sustainable tourism initiatives at ancient sites (Yin, 2018). The comparative analysis also allowed for the generation of insights and recommendations that can be applied to other contexts facing similar challenges (Crowe et al., 2011).

The qualitative research approach adopted in this chapter aligns with the exploratory nature of the study, enabling a comprehensive understanding of the complex interplay between sustainable tourism, heritage preservation, and community development (Mohajan, 2018). By leveraging secondary data sources, case study analysis, and comparative evaluation, this chapter aims to contribute to the growing body of knowledge on sustainable tourism practices at ancient archaeological sites (Snyder, 2019).

Historical Context of Tourism Development

The historical development of tourism at ancient sites in countries like Egypt, Greece, Mexico, and India spans centuries, reflecting shifting societal attitudes, technological advancements, and economic progress (Edgell Sr, 2019; Dehejia, 2019). Early forms of tourism were often associated with religious pilgrimages, where travelers visited sacred sites for spiritual reasons (Collins-Kreiner & Wall, 2015). Over time, these sites gained broader appeal, attracting tourists interested in cultural heritage, archaeology, and history (Barkin, 2013). However, this evolution has also brought significant challenges, including environmental degradation, over-tourism, and the threat of looting, impacting the preservation and sustainability of ancient sites (Pechlaner, et all, 2019; Richards, 2007).

Tourism at ancient sites in Egypt has a long history dating back to antiquity (Murnane, 1995). The pyramids of Giza, temples of Luxor, and the Valley of the Kings have long fascinated travelers from around the world (Edgell Sr, 2019). Early tourism in Egypt was closely linked to religious pilgrimages, such as the journey to the temple of Amun at Karnak (Collins-Kreiner & Wall, 2015). These pilgrimages contributed to infrastructure development and services for travelers. However, with modern mass tourism, challenges emerged, including environmental degradation due to increased foot traffic, erosion of fragile structures, and pressure on local resources (Dehejia, 2019).

Similarly, Greece has been a significant destination for cultural tourism, with ancient sites like the Acropolis in Athens and the ruins of Delphi attracting visitors interested in ancient Greek civilization (Bora, 2018). Early tourism in Greece often centered on religious festivals and athletic competitions, drawing pilgrims and athletes from across the Mediterranean region (Pechlaner, et all, 2019). As tourism evolved, ancient sites became key attractions, leading to the development of touristic infrastructure and interpretation centers (Richards, 2007). However, the influx of tourists has posed challenges such as overcrowding, damage to archaeological remains, and the need for sustainable management practices to balance conservation and visitor experience (Edgell Sr, 2019).

In Mexico, ancient sites like Chichen Itza, Teotihuacan, and Palenque have played a central role in tourism development (Barkin, 2013). Early tourism in Mexico was intertwined with indigenous cultural practices and ceremonial pilgrimages to sacred sites (Collins-Kreiner & Wall, 2015). These pilgrimages contributed to the preservation of cultural heritage but also faced challenges such as looting of artifacts and damage to archaeological sites (Pechlaner, et all, 2019). With the growth of international tourism, ancient sites in Mexico experienced increased visitation, leading to concerns about over-tourism, environmental impact, and the need for responsible tourism practices to protect the country's cultural legacy (Murnane, 1995).

In India, ancient sites like the Taj Mahal, Qutub Minar, and Ajanta Ellora caves have attracted tourists interested in exploring the country's rich history and architectural heritage (Dehejia, 2019). Tourism in India has ancient roots, with historical sites often serving as centers of pilgrimage and cultural exchange (Bora, 2018). However, the transition to modern mass tourism has brought challenges such as pollution, encroachment, and inadequate conservation measures (Richards, 2007). Preservation efforts face complexities due to the diverse cultural and religious significance of ancient sites, requiring careful management and community engagement to ensure sustainable tourism practices (Edgell Sr, 2019).

The challenges faced by ancient sites in Egypt, Greece, Mexico, and India are diverse (Murnane, 1995). Environmental degradation, including erosion, pollution, and habitat destruction, threatens the integrity of archaeological remains and surrounding ecosystems (Pechlaner, et all, 2019). Over-tourism exacerbates these issues by putting pressure on infrastructure, causing overcrowding, and impacting local communities (Dehejia, 2019). Additionally, the illicit trade in cultural artifacts, fueled by looting and smuggling, poses a significant threat to the preservation of ancient sites and their historical significance (Richards, 2007).

To address these challenges, proactive measures are necessary, including sustainable tourism management plans, conservation initiatives, community engagement, and international cooperation (Bora, 2018). Efforts to limit visitor numbers, regulate access to sensitive areas, implement waste management strategies, and educate tourists about responsible behavior can help mitigate the negative impacts of tourism on ancient sites (Edgell Sr, 2019). Furthermore, fostering partnerships between stakeholders, including government agencies, local communities, heritage organizations, and tourism industry players, is essential for promoting sustainable tourism practices and safeguarding ancient sites for future generations (Murnane, 1995).

Sustainable Tourism Initiatives

Sustainable tourism initiatives at ancient sites are pivotal in conserving cultural heritage and promoting community development. For instance, the Giza Pyramids complex in Egypt showcases effective sustainable tourism practices through a blend of site management strategies, visitor education programs, and community involvement efforts. The Supreme Council of Antiquities oversees site management, implementing conservation measures to safeguard the pyramids and surrounding structures from environmental degradation due to tourism (Hassan, et all, 2024). These efforts include limiting visitor access to sensitive areas, enforcing guidelines for tour operators and guides, and utilizing advanced monitoring technologies to assess visitor impact.

Educational initiatives at the Giza Pyramids focus on promoting responsible tourism behavior and raising awareness about the site's historical significance. Interpretive signage, guided tours, and multimedia exhibits inform visitors about the pyramids' architectural wonders, historical context, and the importance of conservation (Shackley, 2009). Educational programs also emphasize sustainable tourism practices like waste reduction, water conservation, and respecting cultural norms.

Community engagement is integral to sustainable tourism at the Giza Pyramids, with collaborative projects benefiting local communities and involving them in heritage conservation. The Giza Community Development Foundation works with tourism authorities on community-based tourism projects such as handicraft workshops, cultural performances, and homestay experiences (Ali, et all 2020). These initiatives not only provide income for residents but also facilitate cultural exchange and understanding between tourists and locals.

Similarly, Greece's Acropolis of Athens serves as a model for sustainable tourism management and preservation. The Hellenic Ministry of Culture and Sports oversees site management, employing experts to ensure the Acropolis monuments' integrity (Gimouki, 2022). Measures like visitor capacity limits, timed entry tickets, and conservation zones protect the ancient structures from overcrowding and physical damage.

Visitor education at the Acropolis includes interpretive centers, guided tours, and multimedia presentations to educate visitors on the site's historical significance and conservation ethics (Eleftheriou, et all, 2020). Interactive exhibits and virtual reality experiences enhance the visit's educational value, promoting responsible behavior among tourists.

Community engagement at the Acropolis involves collaboration with local stakeholders, including residents and businesses. The Acropolis Restoration Service works with community groups on sustainable tourism initiatives that benefit the local economy and promote cultural heritage (Gimouki, 2022). Events such as traditional festivals and art exhibitions showcase local culture and encourage community participation.

In Mexico, Chichen Itza exemplifies innovative sustainable tourism and community development approaches. Managed by the National Institute of Anthropology and History, Chichen Itza implements conservation measures and sustainable transportation options to minimize ecological impact (Milman, 2015).

Visitor education includes interpretive signage, guided tours, and workshops highlighting the site's significance and conservation challenges (Ely, 2013). Eco-friendly practices are promoted among visitors to reduce environmental footprint.

Community engagement at Chichen Itza focuses on empowering local communities through tourism-related opportunities. Collaboration with indigenous groups and rural communities leads to sustainable tourism ventures, supporting community projects like education and infrastructure development (Ely, 2013).

In India, the Ajanta and Ellora Caves showcase sustainable tourism practices managed by the Archaeological Survey of India. Conservation strategies and visitor education efforts emphasize the caves' historical importance and conservation needs (Kumar, 2009).

Community engagement includes partnerships with local communities, offering experiences that showcase local culture and support community development (Mishra & Maitra, 2022). These examples demonstrate how integrated approaches to site management, visitor education, and community engagement contribute to sustainable tourism and the preservation of cultural heritage at ancient sites globally.

Economic Benefits for Local Communities

Sustainable tourism at historical sites brings substantial economic benefits to local communities, including revenue generation, job opportunities, and support for local businesses (Budeanu, 2005). The adoption of sustainable practices not only safeguards cultural heritage but also stimulates economic growth and community development (Imon, 2013). This section examines the economic advantages of sustainable tourism initiatives, highlighting the role of community-based tourism enterprises and collaborations with tour operators and heritage organizations.

One of the key economic advantages of sustainable tourism at historical sites is the generation of revenue. Tourism-related activities such as guided tours, cultural events, and souvenir sales contribute significantly to revenue generation, which can be reinvested in site conservation and community development projects (Sofield, 2003). For example, ticket sales at iconic archaeological sites like the Pyramids of Giza in Egypt or the Acropolis in Greece generate substantial income, often allocated to conservation efforts and infrastructure enhancements (Wahhab Ajeena, 2022). According to research by the World Tourism Organization (UNWTO), revenue from sustainable tourism at historical sites has exhibited consistent growth, providing a reliable income stream for local economies (Larson & Poudyal, 2012).

Furthermore, sustainable tourism initiatives at historical sites create employment opportunities for local residents, addressing unemployment issues and supporting livelihoods (Sofield, 2003). These jobs span various sectors, including tour guiding, hospitality, transportation, handicrafts, and cultural heritage conservation (Imon, 2013). For instance, in India, the promotion of community-based tourism initiatives around heritage sites such as the Taj Mahal has resulted in the creation of jobs for local guides, artisans, and hospitality personnel (Banik & Mukhopadhyay, 2020).

This not only boosts the local economy but also empowers communities by providing stable employment and income-generating avenues.

In addition to direct economic benefits, sustainable tourism stimulates the growth of local businesses by creating demand for goods and services (Wahhab Ajeena, 2022). Local entrepreneurs, including restaurants, hotels, craft shops, and transportation providers, benefit from increased tourist activity and spending (Larson & Poudyal, 2012). These businesses often collaborate with community-based tourism enterprises to offer authentic experiences and products, contributing to the overall tourism value chain (Sofield, 2003). Collaborations between tour operators and heritage organizations also play a vital role in promoting sustainable tourism and supporting local businesses (Imon, 2013). For example, partnerships between tour operators and local artisans facilitate the promotion and sale of authentic handicrafts, benefiting both parties and enhancing the tourist experience (Barkin & Bouchez, 2002).

Moreover, community-based tourism enterprises play a pivotal role in sustainable tourism development at historical sites (Budeanu, 2005). These enterprises, typically owned and operated by local communities or indigenous groups, promote cultural authenticity and community engagement in tourism activities (Wahhab Ajeena, 2022). Community-based initiatives focus on preserving traditional practices, promoting environmental conservation, and ensuring equitable distribution of tourism benefits among community members (Sofield, 2003). For instance, in Mexico, community-based cooperatives near archaeological sites like Chichen Itza offer guided tours, cultural workshops, and eco-friendly accommodations, creating a sustainable tourism model that benefits both visitors and locals (Barkin & Bouchez, 2002).

Sustainable tourism at historical sites generates significant economic benefits for local communities, including revenue generation, job creation, and business opportunities (Larson & Poudyal, 2012). The collaborative efforts of community-based tourism enterprises, tour operators, and heritage organizations are essential in promoting sustainable tourism practices and maximizing the socio-economic impact of tourism on communities (Imon, 2013). Through partnerships and investments in sustainable initiatives, historical sites can continue to drive economic growth, preserve cultural heritage, and enhance community well-being.

Environmental Conservation Efforts

Environmental conservation efforts are integral to sustainable tourism, aiming to mitigate its negative impact on delicate ecosystems. Effective waste management stands out as a crucial initiative in this realm. Tourism often results in heightened waste production, encompassing plastic pollution, littering, and waste from hospitality establishments. Numerous destinations have thus adopted comprehensive waste management strategies. For instance, in Greece, initiatives such as beach clean-up programs, recycling facilities, and public awareness campaigns have played a pivotal role in reducing marine debris and preserving coastal ecosystems (Ezeah, et all, 2015). Similarly, in India, national campaigns like the Swachh Bharat Mission have concentrated on waste segregation, recycling, and proper disposal, contributing significantly to cleaner and more sustainable tourist destinations (Ansari, et all, 2024).

Conservation projects are pivotal in safeguarding biodiversity and natural habitats from tourism-related impacts. Many nations have set up protected areas, national parks, and wildlife reserves to protect endangered species and fragile ecosystems. For example, Mexico's Sian Ka'an Biosphere Reserve, recognized as a UNESCO World Heritage Site, enforces stringent regulations on visitor activities to minimize disruptions to wildlife and habitats (Carrillo-Barrios-Gómez & Herrmann-Martinez, 2024). Likewise, in Egypt, conservation endeavors at sites like the Pyramids of Giza entail habitat restoration, reforestation, and sustainable land use practices to counter erosion and desertification stemming from tourism-related activities (Soliman, 2010).

Sustainable transportation also plays a pivotal role in environmental conservation within tourism. The transportation sector contributes significantly to carbon emissions and air pollution in tourist destinations. To address this, numerous countries are promoting eco-friendly transportation alternatives such as electric vehicles, bicycles, and public transit systems. In Greece, initiatives like the Athens Metro and electric buses in major tourist hubs reduce carbon emissions and congestion while offering convenient transportation for visitors (Profillidis, et all, 2018). Similarly, in India, eco-tourism initiatives in wildlife reserves and national parks often feature guided tours on foot, bicycle, or electric vehicles to minimize the ecological impact of tourism activities (Joshi, 2010).

Environmental conservation efforts tied to sustainable tourism practices are indispensable for preserving fragile ecosystems and mitigating tourism's negative repercussions. Embracing effective waste management, conservation projects, and sustainable transportation initiatives contributes to cleaner, healthier, and more resilient tourist destinations. By implementing these strategies and fostering responsible tourism practices, countries can strike a balance between tourism development and environmental preservation, ensuring the long-term sustainability of their natural resources and cultural heritage.

Socio-Cultural Impacts and Community Engagement

Assessing the socio-cultural impacts of tourism on local communities and indigenous groups is vital for understanding how tourism activities affect their economic, social, and cultural aspects (Alouthah, 2023). This evaluation also explores how communities participate in tourism planning and efforts to conserve cultural heritage, such as traditional crafts, festivals, and storytelling (Timothy, 2014). Within sustainable tourism frameworks, these factors are crucial for ensuring that tourism benefits local communities while preserving their cultural identity and heritage (Moscardo, 2018).

Tourism can have positive and negative socio-cultural effects on local communities and indigenous groups (Chauhan, 2023). Positively, it can bring economic opportunities, job creation, and infrastructure development, leading to improved living standards and socio-economic empowerment (Wibowo & Hariadi, 2022). However, rapid tourism growth may also lead to challenges like cultural commodification, the erosion of traditional practices, and social disruptions (Shiri, et all, 2022). Hence, a comprehensive assessment is necessary to develop strategies that maximize tourism's benefits while mitigating potential negative impacts (Chauhan, 2023).

Community involvement in tourism planning and decision-making is a key strategy for addressing socio-cultural impacts (Alouthah, 2023). Engaging local communities and indigenous groups in tourism policies, infrastructure projects, and visitor experiences ensures their inclusion and consideration of their needs (Timothy, 2014). This involvement may include participatory workshops, community consultations, and partnerships with local stakeholders (Moscardo, 2018), leading to tourism initiatives that respect and preserve local cultures, traditions, and values (Wibowo & Hariadi, 2022).

Preserving cultural heritage is crucial for sustainable tourism, particularly in reviving traditional crafts, festivals, and storytelling (Chauhan, 2023). These elements not only showcase local communities' unique identity but also provide authentic experiences for tourists (Shiri, et all, 2022). Preservation efforts often include heritage conservation programs, cultural events, artisan markets, and educational programs for tourists (Alouthah, 2023), contributing to both cultural heritage conservation and economic opportunities for local artisans and cultural practitioners (Timothy, 2014).

Reviving traditional crafts plays a significant role in sustaining local economies and preserving cultural heritage in many destinations (Moscardo, 2018). Local artisans pass down traditional knowledge and skills, serving as cultural ambassadors (Wibowo & Hariadi, 2022). Supporting local craft industries through tourism helps communities maintain their cultural heritage while creating income opportunities (Chauhan, 2023). Similarly, cultural festivals and events celebrate indigenous traditions, fostering cultural exchange and showcasing heritage to a broader audience (Shiri, et all, 2022).

Storytelling is also vital in cultural heritage preservation and tourism experiences (Alouthah, 2023). Through oral traditions, folklore, and myths, communities share their history and values with visitors, creating immersive experiences (Timothy,

2014). Storytelling programs enhance tourists' understanding of local cultures, promoting cross-cultural dialogue (Moscardo, 2018).

Evaluating the socio-cultural impacts of tourism on local communities and indigenous groups requires considering economic, social, and cultural dimensions (Wibowo & Hariadi, 2022). Involving communities in tourism planning, preserving cultural heritage, and promoting traditional crafts and storytelling contribute to sustainable tourism practices that benefit both tourists and local residents (Chauhan, 2023). These efforts support cultural diversity, empower communities, and promote responsible tourism (Shiri, et all, 2022).

Challenges and Lessons Learned

Implementing sustainable tourism initiatives encounters numerous challenges that necessitate careful deliberation and strategic planning. One major obstacle is finding a harmonious balance among tourism expansion, heritage conservation, and community welfare (Page, 2014). Over-tourism, characterized by excessive tourist numbers, stands out as a prominent issue that can lead to environmental degradation, erosion of local culture, and disruptions to indigenous communities (Tosun, 2000). For instance, iconic ancient sites like the Pyramids of Giza in Egypt or the Acropolis in Greece often grapple with overcrowding during peak tourist seasons, resulting in strain on infrastructure, environmental pollution, and deterioration of historical structures (Grimm, et all, 2018). To mitigate this challenge, destination management organizations have adopted strategies such as implementing visitor quotas, introducing timed entry tickets, and encouraging off-peak travel seasons to distribute tourist influx more evenly throughout the year (Hall & Page, 2009).

Preserving cultural heritage while catering to tourism demands presents another complex challenge. Ancient sites hold immense cultural significance, and their preservation is crucial for maintaining historical authenticity and cultural identity (Park, 2013). However, tourism activities can inadvertently contribute to heritage degradation through factors like foot traffic, souvenir sales, and unauthorized excavations (Richards, 2007). Lessons learned from these challenges stress the importance of integrating heritage conservation measures into tourism planning and development (Hoang, 2021). This includes implementing site-specific conservation plans, providing heritage interpretation training to local guides, and engaging communities in cultural heritage preservation to ensure sustainable tourism practices that protect historical assets (Jagić, 2017).

Community well-being is also a crucial aspect of sustainable tourism initiatives but can pose challenges related to socio-economic disparities, displacement, and loss of traditional livelihoods (Scheyvens, 2002). For example, rapid tourism growth in coastal regions of Mexico or India has led to conflicts over land usage, water resources, and access to economic opportunities for local populations (Noronha, 2010). Addressing these challenges necessitates a participatory approach involving local communities in decision-making processes, fostering inclusive economic growth through tourism, and supporting community-based tourism enterprises (Munt, 1998). Best practices include establishing mechanisms for community benefit-sharing, supporting small-scale tourism ventures, and investing in skills training and capacity-building programs that empower communities to actively participate in and benefit from tourism development (Macleod & Carrier, 2009).

Infrastructure development and environmental sustainability are fundamental components of sustainable tourism but present challenges in terms of resource management, waste disposal, and energy consumption (Sharpley & Telfer, 2014). Developing infrastructure that supports tourism activities while minimizing environmental impacts necessitates innovative solutions such as green building practices, renewable energy sources, and sustainable transportation options (Hall & Lew, 2009). Lessons learned underscore the importance of conducting comprehensive environmental impact assessments, implementing sustainable tourism certification programs, and fostering public-private partnerships to promote eco-friendly practices and reduce the ecological footprint of tourism operations (Eagles, et all, 2002).

Regulatory frameworks and governance structures play a crucial role in overcoming challenges and promoting sustainable tourism practices (Gössling, 2006). However, inconsistencies in regulations, weak enforcement mechanisms, and lack of coordination among stakeholders can impede effective implementation (Hall & Jenkins, 2004). Best practices involve establishing clear policies and guidelines for sustainable tourism, enhancing inter-agency cooperation, and fostering public-private partnerships for collaborative decision-making and resource management (Bramwell & Lane, 2011). Additionally, engaging with indigenous and local communities in governance processes ensures that their rights, cultural heritage, and traditional knowledge are respected and integrated into tourism strategies (Belkayali & Kesimoğlu, 2015).

Therefore, identifying and addressing challenges in implementing sustainable tourism initiatives are crucial for achieving a balance among tourism development, heritage preservation, and community well-being (Leiper, 1990). Lessons learned from these challenges emphasize the importance of strategic planning, collaboration among stakeholders, and adaptive management approaches that prioritize sustainability, inclusivity, and responsible tourism practices (He, 2019). By incorporating best practices and lessons learned into tourism planning and development processes, destinations can create meaningful experiences for visitors while safeguarding cultural heritage, promoting economic prosperity, and enhancing the quality of life for local communities.

Comparative Analysis

In the realm of sustainable tourism, Egypt, Greece, Mexico, and India have implemented diverse strategies influenced by their distinct cultural, historical, and economic circumstances. Despite their differences, these nations share common objectives of conserving heritage, promoting community development, and encouraging responsible tourism practices (Das, 2019).

Egypt has placed a strong emphasis on sustainable tourism to safeguard its extensive archaeological legacy, particularly focusing on renowned sites like the Pyramids of Giza and Luxor (Helmy, 2004). Efforts by the Egyptian government include policies to balance tourism growth with heritage preservation, such as zoning regulations to safeguard archaeological areas and endorsing sustainable tourism practices through certification programs (Rasethuntsa & Perks, 2022). Collaboration with international organizations, local communities, and private sector entities has been pivotal in achieving sustainable development goals (Díaz-Andreu, 2013), leading to increased visitor satisfaction, revenue generation, and improved heritage protection measures (Das, 2019).

Contrastingly, Greece has prioritized community engagement and heritage interpretation in its sustainable tourism strategy (Giampiccoli & Saayman, 2018). Policies underscore the active involvement of local communities in tourism planning and decision-making processes, promoting the development of community-based tourism initiatives around ancient landmarks like the Acropolis in Athens and the archaeological sites of Delphi and Olympia (Koutsouris, 2009). Collaborative efforts with heritage organizations, tour operators, and educational institutions have been instrumental in advocating responsible tourism practices and fostering cultural exchange (Helmy, 2004), resulting in enhanced heritage conservation, enriched visitor experiences, and economic benefits for local communities (Rasethuntsa & Perks, 2022).

Mexico's approach to sustainable tourism at ancient sites revolves around cultural heritage preservation and environmental stewardship (Díaz-Andreu, 2013). Policies concentrate on promoting sustainable tourism practices, such as visitor management, waste management systems, and restoration of archaeological structures (Giampiccoli & Saayman, 2018). Collaboration with indigenous communities, government bodies, and non-profit organizations is crucial to safeguarding cultural resources and supporting community development initiatives (Das, 2019), leading to improved site management, biodiversity conservation, and cultural revitalization efforts benefiting local populations (Koutsouris, 2009).

India's sustainable tourism strategy at ancient sites integrates heritage preservation with community empowerment and socio-economic progress (Rasethuntsa & Perks, 2022). Policies prioritize heritage conservation through protective measures, restoration projects, and heritage interpretation initiatives (Helmy, 2004). Collaborative efforts with local communities, tourism agencies, and heritage experts are aimed at promoting sustainable tourism practices and enhancing cultural awareness (Giampiccoli & Saayman, 2018), resulting in enhanced visitor experiences, economic opportunities for communities, and the preservation of intangible cultural heritage alongside tangible archaeological sites (Díaz-Andreu, 2013).

Therefore, Egypt, Greece, Mexico, and India have distinctive yet interconnected strategies for promoting sustainable tourism at ancient sites. Despite facing unique challenges and opportunities, their shared commitment to heritage preservation, community engagement, and responsible tourism practices highlights the significance of sustainable development in safeguarding cultural legacies for future generations (Das, 2019).

Practical Implications

The findings and insights presented in this chapter have significant practical implications for tourism managers, policymakers, and community stakeholders involved in revitalizing ancient sites through sustainable tourism. The case studies of Egypt, Greece, Mexico, and India demonstrate the importance of adopting a holistic approach that balances heritage preservation, community well-being, and environmental sustainability (Landorf, 2009).

Tourism managers can draw valuable lessons from the sustainable tourism initiatives discussed in this chapter. Implementing effective site management strategies, such as visitor caps, timed entry systems, and designated pathways, can help mitigate the negative impacts of tourism on ancient sites (Buckley, 2012). Moreover, investing in visitor education programs and interpretive facilities can enhance tourists' understanding and appreciation of the cultural and historical significance of these sites (Moscardo, 2014).

Policymakers play a crucial role in creating an enabling environment for sustainable tourism development at ancient sites. Developing comprehensive tourism policies that prioritize heritage conservation, community participation, and sustainable practices is essential (Hall, 2011). Governments should also provide financial incentives and support for community-based tourism initiatives, ensuring that local communities benefit from tourism activities (Zapata et al., 2011).

Community engagement and empowerment are key to the success of sustainable tourism initiatives at ancient sites. Tourism managers and policymakers should actively involve local communities in decision-making processes, capacity building, and tourism development (Okazaki, 2008). Encouraging community-based tourism enterprises, such as locally owned accommodations, guided tours, and handicraft businesses, can generate economic benefits and foster a sense of ownership among community members (Salazar, 2012).

Furthermore, collaboration and partnerships among stakeholders are essential for the effective implementation of sustainable tourism strategies. Tourism managers should foster collaborations with heritage conservation organizations, academic institutions, and local NGOs to leverage expertise, resources, and knowledge sharing (Aas et al., 2005). Establishing multi-stakeholder platforms can facilitate dialogue, coordination, and collective action towards sustainable tourism development (Waligo et al., 2013).

Monitoring and evaluation mechanisms should be put in place to assess the effectiveness of sustainable tourism initiatives and identify areas for improvement. Regular monitoring of visitor impacts, community well-being indicators, and environmental quality can inform adaptive management strategies (Agyeiwaah et al., 2017). Sharing best practices and lessons learned among destinations can contribute to the continuous improvement of sustainable tourism practices at ancient sites worldwide (Sautter & Leisen, 1999).

FUTURE DIRECTIONS AND RECOMMENDATIONS

Enhancing the sustainability of tourism at ancient sites necessitates a comprehensive strategy that incorporates digital advancements, alternative tourism approaches, and international partnerships to promote responsible tourism practices. These suggestions are crucial for safeguarding cultural heritage, mitigating environmental impact, and engaging local communities in tourism development.

One crucial step toward enhancing sustainability involves integrating digital technologies strategically into tourism management at ancient sites. Platforms like mobile apps, virtual reality (VR) tours, and interactive exhibits can enrich visitor experiences while minimizing physical presence. For instance, augmented reality (AR) apps can offer historical context and interactive maps, reducing the need for physical signage and interpretive panels. Moreover, online booking systems and digital payment solutions can streamline visitor flow and improve operational efficiency (Ali & Frew, 2014).

Simultaneously, adopting alternative tourism models can play a pivotal role in promoting sustainable practices. Initiatives like community-based tourism, homestay programs, and local tour guide cooperatives empower communities to benefit directly from tourism while preserving their heritage. Collaborating with indigenous communities to offer authentic cultural experiences fosters meaningful connections between visitors and locals, promoting cultural exchange (Simons & de Groot, 2015).

Furthermore, international collaborations are essential for sharing best practices and resources to support sustainable tourism. Projects involving governments, heritage organizations, academia, and the private sector facilitate knowledge exchange, capacity building, and funding opportunities. For example, joint research initiatives can explore innovative conservation techniques and sustainable infrastructure development tailored to each ancient site's unique challenges (Landorf, 2009).

Educating and engaging visitors in sustainable behaviors is also crucial. Visitor education programs, interpretive signage, and eco-friendly guidelines raise awareness about conservation and cultural sensitivity. Encouraging visitors to support local businesses and respect heritage sites' rules contributes to sustainable tourism (Avraham, 2021).

Investing in infrastructure upgrades and green technologies can further enhance environmental sustainability. Implementing renewable energy systems, water conservation measures, waste management solutions, and sustainable transportation options minimizes carbon footprints and preserves natural resources (Futures, n.d.).

Therefore, a holistic approach combining digital innovations, alternative tourism models, international partnerships, visitor education, and eco-friendly practices is essential for enhancing tourism sustainability at ancient sites, ensuring their preservation and contributing to sustainable development goals.

CONCLUSION

Sustainable tourism plays a crucial role in safeguarding ancient sites for future generations and fostering community resilience and economic development. Through an in-depth analysis of sustainable tourism initiatives at ancient archaeological sites in various countries, such as Egypt, Greece, Mexico, and India, several key insights emerge regarding the importance and advantages of sustainable tourism in heritage preservation and community well-being.

One significant finding is the positive impact of sustainable tourism on ancient site preservation. For example, in Egypt, the adoption of sustainable tourism practices at iconic sites like the Pyramids of Giza and the temples of Luxor has led to improved conservation efforts. Strategies such as controlled visitor access, heritage interpretation programs, and ecosystem restoration projects have played a vital role in mitigating environmental degradation and safeguarding the structural integrity of these historic landmarks (Mustafa, 2021).

Additionally, sustainable tourism initiatives have been instrumental in enhancing community resilience by creating economic opportunities and promoting cultural heritage preservation. In Greece, programs such as the UNESCO World Heritage Sites initiative have empowered local communities through training in heritage management, tour guiding, and hospitality services (Theodora, 2020). This has enabled residents near sites like the Acropolis in Athens or the archaeological sites of Delphi to diversify their income streams, improve their living standards, and enhance their resilience to economic fluctuations and external challenges.

Moreover, sustainable tourism practices have facilitated the transfer of cultural heritage knowledge and traditions to future generations. In Mexico, community-based tourism models at sites such as Chichen Itza and Teotihuacan have allowed indigenous communities to showcase their cultural heritage through traditional arts, crafts, and storytelling experiences (Holley-Kline & Papazian, 2020). This not only fosters a sense of cultural pride and identity among local populations but also contributes to the preservation of intangible cultural heritage for posterity.

Another critical observation from this study is the role of sustainable tourism in promoting environmental conservation and biodiversity protection. In India, initiatives like eco-friendly accommodations near heritage sites such as the Taj Mahal or Hampi have reduced the environmental impact of tourism activities (Babu, 2008). Furthermore, community-led conservation projects, including reforestation and wildlife conservation efforts around ancient sites, have contributed significantly to preserving natural ecosystems and promoting sustainable tourism practices.

Significantly, sustainable tourism has emerged as a driver of economic development in communities surrounding ancient sites. In Egypt, revenues generated from sustainable tourism initiatives have been reinvested in community development projects such as education, healthcare, and infrastructure enhancements (El Azazy, 2022). Similarly, in Greece, the growth of the tourism sector has spurred entrepreneurship and job creation, particularly in sectors like cultural heritage interpretation, sustainable agriculture, and handicraft production (Boukas, 2008).

In conclusion, the research findings emphasize the critical role of sustainable tourism in protecting ancient sites for future generations, enhancing community resilience, and fostering economic development. By embracing sustainable tourism practices, countries like Egypt, Greece, Mexico, and India showcase the potential to balance heritage preservation, socio-economic empowerment, and environmental stewardship. These insights highlight the transformative impact of sustainable tourism and its contribution to sustainable development and inclusive growth in heritage-rich regions globally.

REFERENCES

Aas, C., Ladkin, A., & Fletcher, J. (2005). Stakeholder collaboration and heritage management. *Annals of Tourism Research*, 32(1), 28–48. 10.1016/j.annals.2004.04.005

Agyeiwaah, E., McKercher, B., & Suntikul, W. (2017). Identifying core indicators of sustainable tourism: A path forward? *Tourism Management Perspectives*, 24, 26–33. 10.1016/j.tmp.2017.07.005

Ali, A., & Frew, A. J. (2014). Technology innovation and applications in sustainable destination development. *Information Technology & Tourism*, 14(4), 265–290. 10.1007/s40558-014-0015-7

Ali, D. F., Zein, M., & Heragi, M. (2020). The Grand Egyptian Museum and its Role in Achieving Sustainable Tourism in the Memphite Necropolis. International Journal of Heritage. *Tourism and Hospitality*, 14(3 (Special Issue)), 175–193.

Alouthah, D. (2023). Towards a Framework for the Socio-Spatial-Economic Regeneration of Historical Suqs (Doctoral dissertation, Effat University).

Ansari, A., Dutt, D., & Kumar, V. (2024). Catalyzing paradigm shifts in global waste Management: A case study of Saharanpur Smart city. *Waste Management Bulletin*, 2(1), 29–38. 10.1016/j.wmb.2023.12.003

Avraham, E. (2021). Recovery strategies and marketing campaigns for global destinations in response to the Covid-19 tourism crisis. *Asia Pacific Journal of Tourism Research*, 26(11), 1255–1269. 10.1080/10941665.2021.1918192

Babu, A. S. (2008). *Tourism Development in India: A case study*. APH publishing.

Banik, S., & Mukhopadhyay, M. (2020). Model-based strategic planning for the development of community based tourism: A case study of Ayodhya Hills in West Bengal, India. *GeoJournal*, 1–17.

Barkin, D. (2013). Strengthening domestic tourism in Mexico: challenges and opportunities. The Native Tourist, 30-54.

Barkin, D., & Bouchez, C. P. (2002). NGO–community collaboration for ecotourism: A strategy for sustainable regional development. *Current Issues in Tourism*, 5(3-4), 245–253. 10.1080/13683500208667921

Belkayali, N., & Kesimoğlu, M. D. (2015). The stakeholders' point of view about the impact of recreational and tourism activities on natural protected area: A case study from Kure Mountains National Park, Turkey. *Biotechnology, Biotechnological Equipment*, 29(6), 1092–1103. 10.1080/13102818.2015.1072054

Bora, A. (2018). Archaeology, cultural heritage and tourism from the past to the future: on the cultural heritage of a dynasty from the Hellenistic period.

Boukas, N. (2008). *Cultural tourism, young people and destination perception: A case study of Delphi, Greece*. University of Exeter.

Bramwell, B., & Lane, B. (2011). Critical research on the governance of tourism and sustainability. *Journal of Sustainable Tourism*, 19(4-5), 411–421. 10.1080/09669582.2011.580586

Buckley, R. (2012). Sustainable tourism: Research and reality. *Annals of Tourism Research*, 39(2), 528–546. 10.1016/j.annals.2012.02.003

Budeanu, A. (2005). Impacts and responsibilities for sustainable tourism: A tour operator's perspective. *Journal of Cleaner Production*, 13(2), 89–97. 10.1016/j.jclepro.2003.12.02432288344

Carrillo-Barrios-Gómez, E., & Herrmann-Martinez, H. (1989). Sian Ka'an: A new biosphere reserve model in Mexico. In Worldwide Conservation: Proceedings of the Symposium on Biosphere Reserves (p. 223). US Department of the Interior, National Park Service, Science Publications Office.

Chauhan, E. (2023). Role Of Community In Managing Cultural Heritage Tourism In Historical Quarters Of Delhi (Doctoral Dissertation, Brandenburg University Of Technology Cottbus).

Collins-Kreiner, N., & Wall, G. (2015). Tourism and religion: Spiritual journeys and their consequences. The changing world religion Map: Sacred places, identities, practices and politics, 689-707.

Das, S. (2019). Towards the Development of Sustainable Tourism in Sikkim, India: Issues and Challenges. *International Journal of Research in Social Sciences*, 9(2), 575–592.

Dehejia, V. (2019). The Future of India's Past: Conservation of Cultural Heritage. In *India Briefing, 1990* (pp. 131–157). Routledge. 10.4324/9780429033636-6

Díaz-Andreu, M. (2013). Ethics and archaeological tourism in Latin America. *International Journal of Historical Archaeology*, 17(2), 225–244. 10.1007/s10761-013-0218-1

Eagles, P. F., McCool, S. F., & Haynes, C. D. (2002). *Sustainable tourism in protected areas: Guidelines for planning and management (No. 8)*. Iucn.

Edgell, D. L.Sr. (2019). *Managing sustainable tourism: A legacy for the future*. Routledge.

El Azazy, S. A. (2022). Tourism development of the cultural heritage and archaeological sites within the national project for urban sustainable development in Egypt. *International Journal of Humanities and Education Development*, 4(2), 53–68. 10.22161/jhed.4.2.8

Eleftheriou, V., Lembidaki, E., & Kaimara, I. (2020). Forty-five Years in Engaging the Public with the Restoration of the Acropolis of Athens. Material Cultures in Public Engagement, 21.

Ely, P. A. (2013). Tourism Management Perspectives. *Tourism Management*, 8, 80–89.

Esser, F., & Steppat, D. (2017). News media use: International comparative research. The international encyclopedia of media effects, 1-17.

Ezeah, C., Fazakerley, J., & Byrne, T. (2015). Tourism waste management in the European Union: Lessons learned from four popular EU tourist destinations. *American Journal of Climate Change*, 4(5), 431–445. 10.4236/ajcc.2015.45035

Futures, T. Sustainable Tourism Futures.

Giampiccoli, A., & Saayman, M. (2018). Community-based tourism development model and community participation. *African Journal of Hospitality, Tourism and Leisure*, 7(4), 1–27.

Gimouki, E. (2022, November). Sustainable Tourism Development in Less Touristy Destinations; The Case of Epirus, Greece. In The International Conference on Cultural Sustainable Tourism (pp. 13-20). Cham: Springer Nature Switzerland.

Gössling, S. (2006). Tourism and water. In *Tourism and global environmental change* (pp. 180–194). Routledge. 10.4324/9780203011911-12

Gratacap, L. P. (1883). Ancient Mexican Civilization. The American Antiquarian And Oriental Journal, 5(3), 255.

Grima, R. (2017). Presenting archaeological sites to the public. Key concepts in public archaeology, 73-92.

Grimm, I. J., Alcântara, L., & Sampaio, C. A. C. (2018). Tourism under climate change scenarios: impacts, possibilities, and challenges. Revista Brasileira de Pesquisa em Turismo, 12, 1-22.

Hall, C. M. (2013). Policy learning and policy failure in sustainable tourism governance: From first-and second-order to third-order change? In *Tourism governance* (pp. 239–261). Routledge.

Hall, C. M., & Jenkins, J. (2004). Tourism and public policy. A companion to tourism, 523-540.

Hall, C. M., & Lew, A. A. (2009). *Understanding and managing tourism impacts: An integrated approach*. Routledge. 10.4324/9780203875872

Hall, C. M., & Page, S. J. (2009). Progress in tourism management: From the geography of tourism to geographies of tourism–A review. *Tourism Management*, 30(1), 3–16. 10.1016/j.tourman.2008.05.014

Hassan, T. H., Almakhayitah, M. Y., & Saleh, M. I. (2024). Sustainable Stewardship of Egypt's Iconic Heritage Sites: Balancing Heritage Preservation, Visitors' Well-Being, and Environmental Responsibility. *Heritage*, 7(2), 737–757. 10.3390/heritage7020036

Hawass, Z. (2015). *Magic of the Pyramids: My adventures in Archeology*. Leonardo Paolo Lovari.

He, Z. (2019). Increasing challenges for world heritage sites protection as a result of the development of sustainable tourism: a case of The Old Town of Lijiang, China (Master's thesis, Universitat Politècnica de Catalunya).

Helmy, E. (2004). Towards integration of sustainability into tourism planning in developing countries: Egypt as a case study. *Current Issues in Tourism*, 7(6), 478–501. 10.1080/1368350050408668199

Hoang, K. V. (2021). The benefits of preserving and promoting cultural heritage values for the sustainable development of the country. In *E3S Web of Conferences* (Vol. 234, p. 00076). EDP Sciences. 10.1051/e3sconf/202123400076

Holley-Kline, S., & Papazian, S. (2020). Heritage Trekking: Toward an Integrated Heritage Studies Methodology. *Journal of Field Archaeology*, 45(7), 527–541. 10.1080/00934690.2020.1807241

Huby, G., Avery, A., & Sheikh, A. (2011). The case study approach. *BMC Medical Research Methodology*, 11(1), 100. 10.1186/1471-2288-11-10021707982

Iliopoulou-Georgudaki, J., Theodoropoulos, C., Konstantinopoulos, P., & Georgoudaki, E. (2017). Sustainable tourism development including the enhancement of cultural heritage in the city of Nafpaktos–Western Greece. *International Journal of Sustainable Development and World Ecology*, 24(3), 224–235. 10.1080/13504509.2016.1201021

Imon, S. S. (2013). Issues of sustainable tourism at heritage sites in Asia. In *Asian Heritage Management* (pp. 253–268). Routledge.

Jagić, I. (2017). Natural and cultural heritage interpretation for the sustainable development of local communities. Models of valorisation of cultural heritage in sustainable tourism, 228.

Joshi, R. (2010). Eco-tourism as a viable option for wildlife conservation: Need for policy initiative in Rajaji National Park, North-West India. *Global Journal of Human Social Science Research*, 10(5), 19–30.

Kaul, H., & Gupta, S. (2009). Sustainable tourism in India. *Worldwide Hospitality and Tourism Themes*, 1(1), 12–18. 10.1108/17554210910949841

Koutsouris, A. (2009). Social learning and sustainable tourism development; local quality conventions in tourism: A Greek case study. *Journal of Sustainable Tourism*, 17(5), 567–581. 10.1080/09669580902855810

Kumar, R. B. (2009). Indian heritage tourism: Challenges of identification and preservation. *International Journal of Hospitality and Tourism Systems*, 2(1), 120.

Landorf, C. (2009). Managing for sustainable tourism: A review of six cultural World Heritage Sites. *Journal of Sustainable Tourism*, 17(1), 53–70. 10.1080/09669580802159719

Larson, L. R., & Poudyal, N. C. (2012). Developing sustainable tourism through adaptive resource management: A case study of Machu Picchu, Peru. *Journal of Sustainable Tourism*, 20(7), 917–938. 10.1080/09669582.2012.667217

Leiper, N. (1990). Tourist attraction systems. *Annals of Tourism Research*, 17(3), 367–384. 10.1016/0160-7383(90)90004-B

Macleod, D. V., & Carrier, J. G. (Eds.). (2009). *Tourism, power and culture: Anthropological insights*. Multilingual Matters. 10.21832/9781845411268

McIntyre, G. (1993). *Sustainable tourism development: guide for local planners*.

Milman, A. (2015). Preserving the cultural identity of a World Heritage Site: The impact of Chichen Itza's souvenir vendors. *International Journal of Culture, Tourism and Hospitality Research*, 9(3), 241–260. 10.1108/IJCTHR-06-2015-0067

Mishra, A., & Maitra, R. (2022). Sustainable Tourism At Lonar Lake. In *Maharashtra: A Geopark Approach*. Impact And Policy Research.

Mohajan, H. K. (2018). Qualitative research methodology in social sciences and related subjects. Journal of economic development, environment and people, 7(1), 23-48.

Moscardo, G. (2015). Tourism and sustainability: Challenges, conflict and core knowledge. Education for Sustainability in Tourism: A Handbook of Processes, Resources, and Strategies, 25-43.

Moscardo, G. (2018). Rethinking the role and practice of destination community involvement in tourism planning. In *Tourism policy and planning implementation* (pp. 36–52). Routledge. 10.4324/9781315162928-3

Munt, I. (1998). *Tourism and sustainability: new tourism in the third world.* Routledge.

Murnane, W. (1995). The History of Ancient Egypt: An Overview. *Civilizations of the Ancient Near East*, 2, 712–714.

Mustafa, M. H. (2021). Cultural heritage: A tourism product of Egypt under risk. *Journal of Environmental Management and Tourism*, 12(1(49)), 243–257. 10.14505/jemt.v12.1(49).21

Noronha, L. (2010). Tourism products, local host communities and ecosystems in Goa, India. Sustainable Production Consumption Systems: Knowledge, Engagement and Practice, 237-249.

Okazaki, E. (2008). A community-based tourism model: Its conception and use. *Journal of Sustainable Tourism*, 16(5), 511–529. 10.1080/09669580802159594

Page, S. J. (2014). *Tourism management*. Routledge. 10.4324/9781315768267

Park, H. Y. (2013). *Heritage tourism*. Routledge. 10.4324/9781315882093

Pechlaner, H., Innerhofer, E., & Erschbamer, G. (Eds.). (2019). *Overtourism: Tourism management and solutions*. Routledge.

Profillidis, V., Botzoris, G., & Galanis, A. (2018, May). Traffic noise reduction and sustainable transportation: A case survey in the cities of Athens and Thessaloniki, Greece. *In Conference on Sustainable Urban Mobility* (pp. 402-409). Cham: Springer International Publishing.

Rasethuntsa, B. C., & Perks, S. (2022). Travel and tourism policies and enabling conditions: An analysis of strategies in Mauritius and Egypt. *Turyzm (Łódz)*, 32(1), 159–183. 10.18778/0867-5856.32.1.08

Richards, G. (2007). *Cultural tourism: Global and local perspectives*. Psychology Press.

Salazar, N. B. (2017). Community-based cultural tourism: Issues, threats and opportunities. In *Tourism and Poverty Reduction* (pp. 131–144). Routledge.

Sautter, E. T., & Leisen, B. (1999). Managing stakeholders a tourism planning model. *Annals of Tourism Research*, 26(2), 312–328. 10.1016/S0160-7383(98)00097-8

Scheyvens, R. (2002). *Tourism for development: Empowering communities*. Pearson Education.

Shackley, M. (2009). *Visitor management*. Routledge. 10.4324/9780080520681

Sharpley, R., & Telfer, D. J. (Eds.). (2014). *Tourism and development: Concepts and issues*. Multilingual Matters. 10.21832/9781845414740

Shiri, A., Howard, D., & Farnel, S. (2022). Indigenous digital storytelling: Digital interfaces supporting cultural heritage preservation and access. *The International Information & Library Review*, 54(2), 93–114. 10.1080/10572317.2021.1946748

Simons, I., & de Groot, E. (2015). Power and empowerment in community-based tourism: Opening Pandora's box? *Tourism Review*, 70(1), 72–84. 10.1108/TR-06-2014-0035

Snyder, H. (2019). Literature review as a research methodology: An overview and guidelines. *Journal of Business Research*, 104, 333–339. 10.1016/j.jbusres.2019.07.039

Sofield, T. H. (Ed.). (2003). *Empowerment for sustainable tourism development*. Emerald Group Publishing.

Soliman, D. M. (2010). Managing visitors via demarketing in the Egyptian world heritage site: Giza pyramids. *Journal of Association of Arab Universities for Tourism and Hospitality*, 7(1), 15–20.

Sonuç, N. (2020). Culture, tourism and sustainability (cultural heritage and sustainable tourism, social sustainability of tourism, socio-cultural sustainability of tourism). In *Encyclopedia of sustainable management* (pp. 1–7). Springer International Publishing. 10.1007/978-3-030-02006-4_457-1

Spenceley, A., & Rylance, A. (2019). The contribution of tourism to achieving the United Nations Sustainable Development Goals. A research agenda for sustainable tourism, 107-125.

Theodora, Y. (2020). Cultural heritage as a means for local development in Mediterranean historic cities—The need for an urban policy. *Heritage*, 3(2), 152–175. 10.3390/heritage3020010

Timothy, D. J. (2014). Contemporary cultural heritage and tourism: Development issues and emerging trends. *Public Archaeology*, 13(1-3), 30–47. 10.1179/1465518714Z.00000000052

Tosun, C. (2000). Limits to community participation in the tourism development process in developing countries. *Tourism Management*, 21(6), 613–633. 10.1016/S0261-5177(00)00009-1

Wahhab Ajeena, D. (2022, May). Sustainable Tourism and Its Role in Preserving Archaeological Sites. In *International Symposium: New Metropolitan Perspectives* (pp. 2485–2495). Springer International Publishing. 10.1007/978-3-031-06825-6_237

Waligo, V. M., Clarke, J., & Hawkins, R. (2013). Implementing sustainable tourism: A multi-stakeholder involvement management framework. *Tourism Management*, 36, 342–353. 10.1016/j.tourman.2012.10.008

Weaver, D. (2007). *Sustainable tourism*. Routledge. 10.4324/9780080474526

Wibowo, J. M., & Hariadi, S. (2022). Indonesia sustainable tourism resilience in the COVID-19 pandemic era (Case study of five Indonesian super-priority destinations). Millennial Asia.

Xiao, Y., & Watson, M. (2019). Guidance on conducting a systematic literature review. *Journal of Planning Education and Research*, 39(1), 93–112. 10.1177/0739456X17723971

Yellowhom, E. (2000). Indians, archaeology and the changing world.

Yin, R. K. (2018). *Case study research and applications* (Vol. 6). Sage.

Zapata, M. J., Hall, C. M., Lindo, P., & Vanderschaeghe, M. (2013). Can community-based tourism contribute to development and poverty alleviation? Lessons from Nicaragua. In Tourism and the Millennium Development Goals (pp. 98-122). Routledge.

Chapter 9
Dive Into the Wreck of Peristera, Greece:
A Study of a Collaborative and Sustainable Tourism Development in the Blue Economy Framework

Erietta S. Kiachidou
https://orcid.org/0009-0003-2101-6351
University of the Aegean, Greece

Georgia C. Papadopoulou
https://orcid.org/0000-0002-9170-4278
University of the Aegean, Greece

ABSTRACT

The nexus of the soft tourism development model must serve the concepts of sustainability, resilience, and participation of the destination community. The chapter explores the case study of a diving tourism destination and how it responds to challenges for tourism development and environmental management, promoting natural resources conservation, cultural heritage, and inclusive community well-being. It provides the structural framework of the synergies that realize and the prospects that offered to realize a unique proposal, an expanded tourism product that increases the beneficial impact of tourism both locally and nationally.

DOI: 10.4018/979-8-3693-5405-6.ch009

Copyright © 2024, IGI Global. Copying or distributing in print or electronic forms without written permission of IGI Global is prohibited.

CHAPTER OBJECTIVES

The main objective of this chapter is to explore the possibilities of promoting a model of soft tourism development that combines social, economic and environmental aspects as best practice, prioritizing sustainability and resilience of the destination in times of intense challenges on the global stage. It focuses on the synergies that take place at local and international level and are achieved by moving away from exploitative practices and adopting diversified and inclusive alternative ways of developing tourism, while respecting the carrying capacity of the destination.

INTRODUCTION

1. Sustainable Diving Tourism

The development of diving tourism is a growing international trend that serves marine ecotourism initiatives and pursues objectives of restoration and sound management of the marine environment alongside community development objectives.

As a form of alternative tourism, it includes the coastal community promoting various other forms of soft tourism where synergies are the tool to address economic challenges in the marine environment with social and environmental priorities. The growing interest in the combination of travel experiences that a diving destination can offer is the driving force behind the continued evolution of the diving industry.

Diving tourism is being repositioned as adventure tourism, supporting active marine restoration and playing a critical role in raising awareness among visitors and residents alike for the protection of the marine environment (Kieran, 2021; Brylske et al, 2023).

The main challenge and priority on the international environmental agenda presented in the development of marine tourism is the conservation and sustainable management of marine reserves. The coupling of marine tourism and its development initiatives combines business activities with ecological restoration in marine ecotopes in ways that produce benefits for both the environment and the host community. Focusing on sustainable diving tourism, a model is being developed that integrates coastal management and the transition to practices prioritizing social and ecological restoration. It achieves improved environmental management as a visitor attraction, diversifying the tourism product, reducing seasonality, creating jobs and new income streams and enhancing the role of the community. Productive collaboration between different actors and departments with the government, international organizations and tourism businesses as well as Citizen Science leads to socio-economic benefits and consensual decision-making for sustainability (Ferretti et al., 2023).

2. Case Study: The Underwater Museum of Peristera, Greece

Greece's first underwater museum is located in the marine area of Allonissos on the island of Peristera in an underwater archaeological site where the oldest shipwreck on the planet from classical antiquity is located. It has been called the "Parthenon of underwater museums" because the shipwreck dates back to 425 B.C. It was discovered in 1980 near the western rocky coast of Peristera, at a depth of 25 meters (80 feet). It is located within Europe's largest Marine Protected Area (2,260 square kilometers), part of the EU Natura 2000 Network, in the National Marine Park of Alonissos - Northern Sporades and can be accessed by recreational divers accompanied by the diving centers of the area. Alternatively, those who wish to experience the wreck's exhibits without diving can visit the Public Information and Awareness Centre in Alonissos' Chora and, through cutting-edge 3D imaging applications for virtual diving, be informed and tour the wreck like real divers (Euronews, 2021).

The project was prepared in the framework of the funded cross-border cooperation project BLUEMED with 14 partners from five Mediterranean countries (Greece, Italy, Croatia, Cyprus, Cyprus, Spain), which supports the economic recovery of coastal and island regions in the Mediterranean. The aim is to enhance alternative tourism and sustainable development throughout the EU region. The Greek Ephorate of Maritime Antiquities also participated with funding from the Public Investment Programme and the project continued with funding from the Regional Operational Programme of Thessaly until 2023 (Hellenic Republic, Ministry of Culture, 2016).

Linking the local cultural heritage with smart tourism, the project has created jobs and established the region as a diving destination that respects the environmental management and sustainable development standards of "Blue Tourism" and the "European Green Deal" as it was presented in Brussels in October 2020 and has been highlighted by leading international media such as the New York Times, Lonely Planet, Daily Mail, Travel & Leisure and Deutsche Welle etc. (Hellenic Republic, Ministry of Culture, 2016; European Commission, 2017; BLUEMED, 2020).

During the 13th International Conference on Cultural Tourism that took place on 22-24 October 2020 in Croatia, organized by the European Cultural Tourism Network ETCN on "Development and promotion of heritage-based tourism", the project of the Peristera Underwater Museum won the first prize in the category "Innovation and digitization in sustainable cultural tourism towards smart destinations" (Archaeology Newsroom, 2020; Staikos, 2020).

Carrie Miller and Chris Taylor (2022) award-winning authors and divers in their book "A Diver's Guide to the World: Remarkable Dive Travel Destinations Above and Beneath the Surface" by National Geographic present Alonissos as the first in a series of 50 dive tourism destinations. They make special mention of the MPA and the Peristera shipwreck, marine life that divers can encounter, the 14 dive sites of interest and suggestions for alternative tourism in the region. They talk about the careful and calm management promoted by the host society and the specificity of the National Marine Park to preserve and protect archaeological and ecological treasures.

Finally, a huge international art project is underway on three Mediterranean islands, Alonissos (Greece), Ustica (Italy) and Gozo (Italy). The ART4SEA project by merging technology, art, creativity and marine sciences aims to contribute to the Decade of Ocean Science for Sustainable Development (2021 - 2030) with the ultimate goal of raising public awareness for greater respect for the marine environment on an individual and collective level. Twenty-four selected international artists are trained in sustainable practices in art, digital technologies and ocean conservation issues. In the summer of 2024 the eight of them will be hosted in Alonissos where they will be inspired by the natural environment, ancient maritime traditions and direct relationships with the local community to create digital and physical artworks with the aim that by 2025 the physical artworks will be integrated into the marine, natural and architectural landscapes of Alonissos, thus creating underwater and outdoor museums. The digital and digitized artworks will also be presented in a virtual exhibition accessible both online and in the metaverse. The ART4SEA consortium consists of seven cross-sectoral European partners from Greece, Italy, Malta, Spain, Italy and Albania who are distinguished for the knowledge, expertise and contemporary background needed to ensure the success of the project, as well as the sustainability of the proposed approach and the expected results with different and complementary perspectives (art4sea.eu, 2024).

Figure 1. Peristera Shipwreck (Greece). Photo by Matteo Collina (Source: MeDry-Dive, 2020b)

RESULTS AND DISCUSSION

3. The Elements of the Diving Destination System

The main elements of the Diving Destination System are considered to be the marine environment, the divers, the diving industry and the host community. The marine environment is the core of the system and all other elements that depend on it are required to co-exist as a social construct (Dimmock & Musa, 2015). For this system to work each element must responsibly serve its role and interact in a two-way manner promoting ecological and developmental goals.

Figure 2. The development of diving tourism as a sustainable development policy that contributes to social welfare (Dimmock & Musa, 2015· Brylske, 2023)

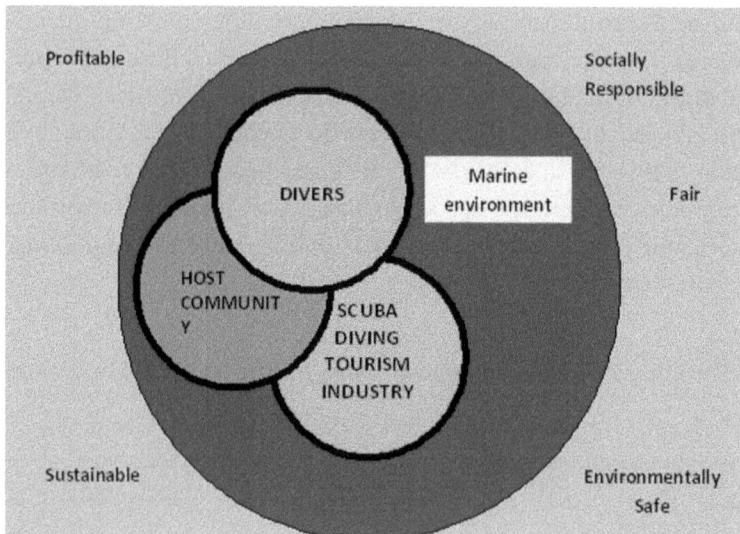

3.1 The Marine Environment

The marine environment as a valuable resource is the cornerstone on which the building block of the dive destination system is based. In particular, the diving industry relies on healthy marine environments where Marine Protected Areas (MPAs), created to protect marine life from the negative impacts of human activity such as overfishing, play an important role. As the conservation and management of the protection of the marine environment are critical factors for its sustainability, diving tourism offers a complementary solution to many problems. It is the antidote to the massive uncontrolled marine overtourism that destroys marine ecosystems. MPAs offer quality marine attractions and have a significant attraction for visitors. Diving tourism promotes responsibility for environmental stewardship, helps to research and record the image of the marine environment, corrects destructive human behaviors, and awakens the interest of the host community in the proper management of the resources (Brylske et al., 2023).

The island of Peristera (or Xero) extends east of the island of Allonissos in N. Aegean. It is located in Zone B within the National Marine Park of Alonissos - Northern Sporades which is the first marine park in Greece and was established in 1992 and is the largest protected marine area in Europe, covering an area of 2,260 sq km. The National Marine Park of Alonissos - Northern Sporades (NMPANS) belongs to the NATURA Habitat of the European Ecological Network Natura 2000 with code name GR1430004, a pan-European protection network whose main objective is to ensure the long-term conservation of biodiversity and habitats of endangered species in protected areas (Hellenic Republic, Ministry of Environment and Energy, 2024; NatureBank, 2024).

The National Marine Park of Alonissos - Northern Sporades consists of the marine area with a cluster of 7 islands (including Alonissos), 22 rocky islets and sea caves. It is an important habitat with extensive underwater Posidonia oceanicae meadows, coral reefs with red corals (Coraliu mrubrum), about 300 species of fish, more than 80 species of birds, reptiles and other mammals. The underwater fauna consists of many benthic and pelagic species such as the mediterranean seal (Monachus monachus), the Caretta caretta turtle (Caretta caretta), the green turtle (Chelonia mydas), the common dolphin (Delphinus delphis), the bottlenose dolphin (Tursiops truncatus), the striped dolphin (Stenella coeruleoalba), the Cuvier's beaked whale (Ziphius cavirostris) and the sperm whale (Physeter macrocephalus) (Alonissos Park, 2024).

In 1980, the professional fisherman Dimitrios Mavrikis discovered in the strait between Alonissos and Peristera at a depth of 22-32 meters, the largest in size and capacity shipwreck of the classical period (425-415 BC) that has been discovered to date, a large merchant ship carrying amphorae of wine from ancient Mendi of Chalkidiki and Perparithos (today's Skopelos) of the Sporades to Athens. Ten years after its declaration it was investigated and excavated by the Ephorate of Underwater Antiquities in 1992 - 1993 and 1999 by the diving archaeologist Dr. Hadjidaki Elpida with full photographic documentation and topographic mapping. The wreck site, an area 25 meters long and 12 meters wide, consists of a large concentration of mainly intact amphorae, forming a low hill of at least three successive layers up to the level of the ship's ballast and the first wooden masts of the hull. Approximately 1.000 amphorae were counted in the surface layer, while the total number of amphorae in the cargo is estimated to be more than 4.000 amphorae. Also, in the last layer, a large quantity of magnificent pottery and bronze vessels of Athenian identity in excellent condition were discovered and recovered. This wreck deserves exceptional importance because of its size for the hitherto prevailing views on ancient Greek shipbuilding (Odysseus.culture, 2024; Allovergreece, 2024; Anastasopoulou, 2024).

The Peristera Shipwreck is an underwater archaeological site and is the first underwater museum in Greece to be visited by guided diving from August 2020. It is an Accessible Underwater Cultural Heritage Site located within the largest Marine Protected Area in Europe.

The marine environment of the area offers a unique proposition: a cluster of islands of aesthetic, ecological, cultural and historical value that hosts rich and rare marine life in clear, accessible waters with meadows of Posidonia Oceanica (Neptune Grass) and coral reefs as well as a marine heritage site (Iosifidis, 2019).

It is a case study of how Accessible Underwater Heritage Sites (AUCHS) and Marine Protected Areas (MPAs) can be the tools for sustainable development and at the same time managing and preserving the marine environment and cultural heritage. Marine reserves and sites, whether natural or man-made, can support the development of sustainable tourism in a multidimensional way with economic, social, cultural and environmental benefits.

Diving tourism is a viable development option as diving activity contributes to the promotion and protection of the marine cultural heritage and the marine environment where it is located. It can contribute to changing the pattern of organized mass tourism and to the elimination of marine overtourism, as the development of diving tourism requires the spatial organization and development of marine leisure parks in areas with natural or man-made marine resources in accordance with the conditions and commitments relating to the protection of the environment.

The spatial organization and development of diving tourism requires the absolute and uninterrupted implementation of the terms, regulations and commitments regarding the sustainable development of coastal tourism such as the Greek Legal Framework (Law 4688/2020, Decision No.3000.0/31173/2023), European policies (Blue Development Policy), international interventions and practices (Ocean Decade 2021-2030, Agenda 30, The Mediterranean Strategy for Sustainable Development, UNEP, FEE, WWF, UNESCO, BEDF etc.) and trigger for the creation of an integrated marine planning strategy (REGINA MSP project, 2024, Worldbank, 2024).

Figure 3. Map of Classical Greece with Wreck Site (Hadjidaki, 1996).

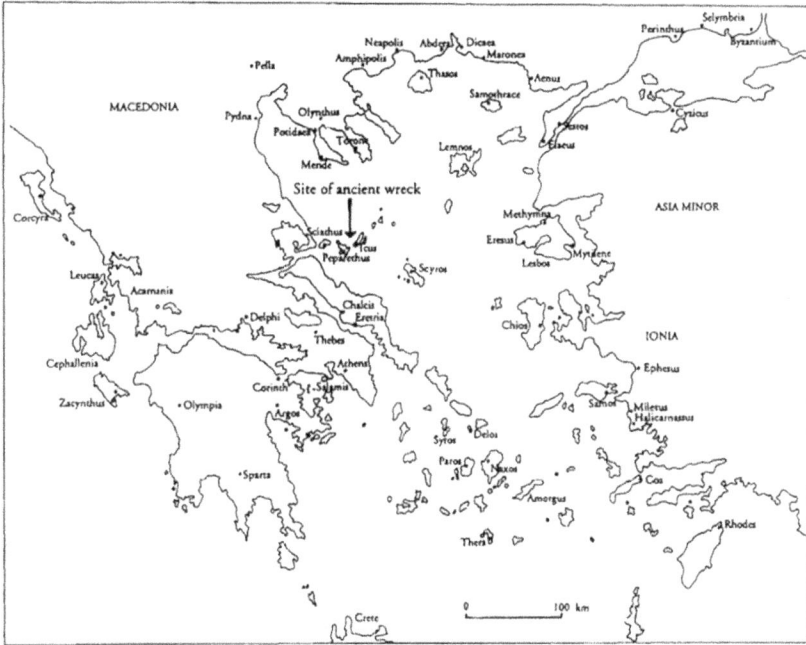

3.2 The Divers

The number of certified divers worldwide has reached 25.000.000, the number of active divers is 9.000.000, of which 4.000.000 are European and the number of certifications exceeds 1,000,000 every year. With 3.000.000 preferring Mediterranean destinations, the turnover of the diving industry in Europe is estimated at around 2 billion Euros per year. However, experts argue that this number could be much higher with the introduction of appropriate infrastructure, such as MPAs with underwater museums and diving parks (European Commission, 2017; DEMA, 2024; Kieran, 2024). The divers seek opportunities to see and experience unique experiences in underwater environments, creating demand that stems from their motivation and expectations. Divers focus on the water quality, marine life, reserves and landscapes of the underwater environment. The growing interest in travel experiences combined with environmental awareness and the knowledge that they can contribute to restoration programmes make them key contributors to eliminating the negative impacts of coastal economic development (Ferretti et al., 2023).

The proof of the achievement of sustainability of the destination is achieved through the presentation of a type of alternative tourism that is combined with other forms of alternative tourism as the profile of visitors who are specifically motivated by diving tourism are characterized as active and creative visitors who are involved with the local community. Divers in their 'surface intervals'[1] seek other creative ways to interact with the local community and are characterized by their active attitude to tourism.

One of the motivations that motivate divers is the uniqueness of the site (Musa & Dimmock, 2013c). Understanding the needs, desires and motivations of divers can ensure the development and promotion of the destination as it responds to the search for alternative tourism development patterns and contributes to sustainable coastal development as an opportune way of producing innovative tourism products and institutions.

3.3 The Diving Industry

The diving industry as a provider of diving tourism services and products focused in our study on diving centers that provide training and certification, and related businesses guarantee the safety and satisfaction of visiting divers based on quality services in the marine environment. Professional excellence combined with success-ful relationships and cooperation with local stakeholders promotes the success of their business objectives and builds their sustainability (Dimmock & Musa, 2015).

The wreck of Peristera is an impressive dive site. In order to dive the wreck one must contact one of the diving centers in the area that is licensed and has specially trained guides due to its peculiarities as an underwater heritage site and access to the site without their accompaniment is prohibited. For this very reason, the diving opportunity is given to divers of at least second level (Advanced Open Water - AOW - PADI or equivalent suitable for diving up to 30 m) and they may be asked to do a check dive before entering the wreck to make sure that they have a good buoyancy control in order to avoid any damage to the archaeological site. The wreck is accessible only by boat from the diving center due to the peculiarity of the geo-morphology of the island of Peristera and it is moored in the permanent moorings that have been built for the needs of its visit. The diving centre's managers help the visiting diver to prepare the equipment and dive safely in the water with their escort. After leaving the surface in a few meters the diver faces the impressive volume of the wreck and is only allowed to approach it peripherally and not to hover over it, to avoid any damage in case of loss of buoyancy. Due to fishing restrictions, marine life is at above average levels. By following the auxiliary signs the diver enjoys the exhibits and has enough time to process the wreck (Divelog, 2021).

The Hellenic Ministry of Culture aims to provide appropriately organized Accessible Underwater Cultural Heritage Sites (AUCHS) to the diving public. With the Visit Organization Study it has drawn up, it sets the framework for the preservation and proper management of the Peristera underwater archaeological site. Specifically, a maximum number of four dives per day had been set, with a maximum of ten people in two groups of four per dive with a guide escort from certified dive centers. The boats of the licensed diving centers by the Ministry of Culture sail from the port of Amaliapolis and the pier of Steni Vala Alonissos (departure and arrival points), after the necessary control by the staff of the Ephorate of Maritime Antiquities, which is the project's implementing agency. As soon as they arrive, they are moored to the moorings as the use of anchors is prohibited. The dive line starts at a short distance from the moorings and at a certain depth the designated underwater routes and tour stops begin. Underwater signs indicate the route, visitor stopping points and other points of interest. They contain basic information (depth, dating, type, shape) about the specific antiquities that visitors can observe at each stop. Divers are not allowed to approach within one and a half meters of the bottom and within one meter of the findings. It is forbidden to touch the findings, underwater signs, surveillance cameras and all operating facilities of the site. The above is ensured by a professional dive guide of each dive center, who is also certified as an escort. The Ministry of Culture has licensed three other UCHS that are open to visitors in the area. These are the wrecks of the bay of Tilegrafos (4th century AD wreck), the island of Kikynthos (11th century AD) and the Cape of Glaros with traces of at least four wrecks (one Hellenistic from the 3rd-2nd century BC, one Roman from the 1st-2nd century AD and two Byzantine, as well as findings of amphorae and anchors from the 12th-13th century AD) (Hellenic Republic, Ministry of Culture, 2024).

At least four certified diving centers are licensed and operating in the area of the wreck. Apart from the safe tour of the wreck of Peristera, they offer high quality services, multiple packages for beginners and experienced divers, diving in 17 dive sites and near the waters where the seal Monachus monachus swims, certifications etc. alternative tourism services.

Dive centers have a huge contribution to the development of diving tourism in the host society. Potential visitors eager to travel to a dive destination are looking for safe destinations and dive support from organized certified centers. Continuously trained and certified members from Open Water Divers to Course Directors form a "diving community" that interacts with each other through the digital services of the hyper-technological world. With the above communication tools they communicate with other members of the "diving community" around the world, they are informed, share their experiences and diving achievements, publish their work and hobbies, inform and be informed about unknown and unexplored places, communicate their ecological actions but also for commercial purposes by advertising their diving business and their interconnection with other diving and non-diving businesses, certification bodies and awards and promote the diving site for tourism. In summary, they are the ambassadors of the diving destination and contribute to its sustainability.

The diving community of the host society is the cornerstone that can support the creation and operation of such a project as the Marine Park and the Peristera Marine Museum. Visiting divers provide the economic boost to the protected area. Responsible dive tourism and Citizen Science efforts are awakening the international community to ocean conservation issues and mobilizing actions for the synergies needed as a link between visitors, the host community and the marine environment.

3.4 The Host Community

The host community plays a crucial role as it creates the arena where supply meets demand and the interaction that promotes socio-economic and environmental benefits is generated. Development prospects create potential employment opportunities for local people and curb labour mobility. Diving-related and other related occupations as well as purely tourism-related occupations create investment opportunities and infrastructure (Dimmock & Musa, 2015).

The development option of diving tourism is feasible as the destination has all those components that make it competitive, such as the natural and man-made environment and human resources, as they are the most important capital of the destination because their actions ensure the sustainability of the destination and the respect of its carrying capacity. It is the overall effort to specialize and create a unique proposal of an expanded and augmented tourism product characterized by many elements that make it unique, easily recognizable and competitive (Tsartas, 2021).

Tourism development in a host community is directly linked to its economic prosperity. It is generally acknowledged that there is a difficulty in defining tourism as a sector of the economy and this is due to the fact that the tourism product is heterogeneous and consists of individual component products and services that the visitors consume during their stay in the host society and which come from different productive sectors. We conclude, therefore, that tourism consumption supports the primary, secondary and tertiary sectors of the economy and that the tourism product is the result of the combination of the supply of many heterogeneous tourism by-products and services from hundreds of many small, medium and large enterprises directly or indirectly linked to the production of tourism products and services (Andriotis, 2005).

Economic impacts can be described as all those changes, positive or negative, that occur in the economy of the host country where tourism development takes place and are related to the specific characteristics of the operation of the tourism sector (Coccossis & Tsartas, 2001).

The positive economic effects of tourism are numerous, play a key role in the economic development of a host community and are a result of the relationship between tourism consumption and tourism production (Varvaresos, 2017).

3.4.1 Employment

Tourism is a labour-intensive sector that creates jobs of a mainly seasonal nature with the particular characteristics of unskilled and skilled labour. There is a high proportion of self-employed persons in tourism enterprises and the growth of family businesses. Often employment in tourism is combined with simultaneous employment in another sector of the economy (agriculture, livestock or craft business), resulting in an increase in family income. Finally, tourism is often the solution to unemployment of the local population, but to fill the jobs it often attracts workers from other regions of the country, both nationals and foreigners (Coccossis & Tsartas, 2001). The demand for goods and services from visitors in the host community creates seasonal jobs that also revitalize other sectors of the economy (agriculture, livestock, crafts, industry, commerce, transport, etc.), improving the level and quality of life of the parties involved.

3.4.2 Infrastructure and Superstructure Development

The development of tourism in a region brings regional growth and is highly dynamic. Incomes increase through employment, the productive base of the local economy expands, and investments are made in infrastructure that serve various forms of tourism and generate more and more revenue for the local economy. Reconstruction on superstructures, infrastructure projects such as road improvements, bridges, ports that facilitate access to geographically isolated, mountainous and rugged areas, often with a degraded agricultural sector, thus creating new destinations (Coccossis & Tsartas, 2001).

3.4.3 Increased Revenue for the State and the Region

Economic tourism activity generates revenue for the State through direct and indirect taxation (VAT, excise duties, income taxes on natural and legal persons, withholding taxes, airport taxes, etc.) as well as municipal and visitor taxes for the

municipalities of the Territory. Finally, the explosion of employment due to seasonality generates additional revenue for the country's insurance funds.

3.4.4 Multiplier Effects on Other Sectors of the Economy

Tourism consumption in a wide variety of tourism activities such as accommodation, trade, transport, services, food has multiplier effects on sectors seemingly
unrelated to tourism such as construction materials, furniture, electrical goods,
machinery, telecommunications, livestock, fisheries, agriculture, food and beverages, transport, trade, crafts, etc. Tourism is mainly a sector of services and final
consumption products and shows stability in its development, so its multiplier effects
are increasingly greater (Tsartas, 2010).

3.4.5 Health and Welfare

Tourism and seasonal population growth in a host society creates a need for
health and welfare services, both public and private. Pharmacies, Health Centers,
Hospitals, but also Private Clinics and Medical Companies are essential in tourist
destinations as they create a sense of security for the visitor and are a sign of extroversion and create ideal living conditions especially for high income visitors. The
host community also benefits.

In summary, by having a positive impact, tourism expenditure in a tourist destination has a multiplier effect on the whole economy through the links between
the tourism sector and other sectors of the economy. A strong host economy is able
to provide most of the goods and services required for tourism consumption. The
demand for locally produced goods and the use of local raw materials is able to
stimulate and strengthen other local productive sectors such as agriculture, livestock,
fisheries, handicrafts, crafts, retail and wholesale trade, construction, reconstruction,
transport and other services (Andriotis, 2005). The capacity of the host economy
lies in the balance of the tourism balance and its ability to plan the operation of
tourism so that the final result is positive, i.e. the burden that inevitably results from
the purchase of imported goods and the leakage of income is less than the positive
effect of tourism cash inflows which, as mentioned above, act as a multiplier (Coccossis & Tsartas, 2001).

But there can be no "profit" if there is no "cost". The coin of "tourism development" has two sides. Therefore, there are also negative effects on a visitor host
society, which can be summarized as the increase in the cost of living and social
services, inflation, the increase in property prices of real estate, the leakage of
income, the damage to the natural and man-made environment and the risk of
exceeding its carrying capacity. The burden on the natural and built environment

is caused by the mass form of tourism as the management of large numbers of visitors to a place creates needs for accommodation, transport and services that cause significant alterations to ecosystems, local natural resources, water, soil, air and energy. The carrying and assimilating capacity of a place is often violated and exacerbates its already acute environmental problems with consequences that are not easily reversible (Coccossis & Tsartas, 2001).

Tourism development inevitably brings about economic, social, environmental and cultural changes in the host region. They are often rapid and decisive and not easily managed by society. This is because the factors that interact and contribute to these changes are many, most of them are local entrepreneurs, national and international tourism businesses, domestic and foreign visitors, local and foreign workers as well as the exogenous workforce, government and international involvement with development programmes and strong promotion of the region.

Characteristics of tourism development are complex infrastructure and major tourism investments, infrastructure projects in the spatial and functional organization of the area with the ultimate aim of optimally serving the arriving visitors seeking the promotional image (Coccossis & Tsartas, 2001).

The development of diving tourism contributes to the sustainability of the destination as diving tourism is combined with other forms of alternative tourism, is of high quality and is usually characterized by multi-day stays and high per capita daily tourist expenditure. This creates a direct and multiplier economic and social impact. The synergies between tourism and non-tourism operators have been shown to achieve bottom-up development by combining the three productive sectors of the economy, primary, secondary and tertiary, thus revitalizing the local community economically, reducing seasonality, increasing the average daily per capita tourist expenditure per visitor and reducing the mobility of human resources.

The area of the Peristera Shipwreck and its host community offers all those characteristics, resources and competitive advantage that will add value to the sustainable development promotion of alternative forms of tourism in general and in particular to marine cultural and diving tourism, creating new expanded and combined alternative tourism products oriented to the needs of its visitors for the acquisition of unique experiences and responding to the challenge with a high added value development policy and low environmental footprint for its socio-economic, cultural and natural environment (Koutsi & Stratigea, 2019).

4. The Synergies Needed for the Exploitation of Maritime Cultural Heritage

The responsible exploitation of a UCHS can be a sustainable tourism development strategy with significant benefits for the host community of a coastal destination in terms of local economic and social development. Diving tourism activities in AUCHS in combination with other alternative tourism activities can generate revenue for the sustainable operation of both dive sites of interest and the businesses that support dive and coastal tourism. Small communities with rich water resources are looking for sustainable solutions to preserve and enhance them. The awareness of the host community brought about by the highlighting of a UCHS is achieved once individuals become familiar with their cultural heritage. The ability to be widely accessible on site (in situ), to be informed of its value and the need to protect it creates a strong local cultural identity of which they feel pride and contribute to its preservation (Manglis et al., 2021).

Accessibility to the UCHS may be accessible to the general public, divers or non-divers. The evolution of technologies in underwater topography, the digitization of the underwater environment, the integration of cutting-edge augmented reality (AR) technologies and virtual reality (VR) applications have created a new possibility of virtual accessibility and the possibility of remote diving. This feature not only increases accessibility to non-divers but also increases the number of visitors to the actual sites and serves educational purposes.

This is achieved through the iblueCulture project and the NOUS prototype system that created the UCHS real-time 24/7 detection and monitoring system, through a live video stream that has the ability to alert the user to the presence of large objects or the presence of unauthorized divers inside the wreck and to detect changes due to natural causes that may negatively affect the site. It provides an effective management strategy for continuous real-time monitoring down to -150 m and offers an immersive dry-diving experience to the public (Bruno et al., 2020; Manglis et al., 2021; Vlachos et al., 2023; NOUS, 2024).

The BLUEMED model is a project under the European Interreg Med 2014-2020 programme that aims to enhance the development of sustainable and responsible coastal and marine tourism in the Mediterranean region by focusing on the sustainable management and responsible promotion of AUCHS. It aims to protect both the marine cultural and natural heritage and to enhance sustainable tourism development in coastal areas and islands. The model is based on international best practices on legislation and management strategies for the protection and accessibility of the underwater cultural heritage (UCH) (Manglis et al., 2021).

One of the sites where the BLUEMED model has been piloted is the four accessible archaeological sites in Greece presented above in this chapter: the ancient shipwreck on the island of Peristera, near Alonissos, in the Northern Sporades and three ancient shipwreck sites on the west coast of the Pagasitikos Gulf, in the bay of Tilegrafos, on the island of Kikynthos and at Cape Glaros.

BLUEMED has created two Knowledge Awareness Centers (KACs) in the area. KAC is a new type of information center where it combines an exhibition and a visitor information point and integrates innovative applications to promote UCH to a wide audience, divers and non-divers alike. The first KAC is located in Chora, in Alonissos, near AUCHS of Peristera. The second Greek KAC is located in Amaliapoli, a seaside village on the west coast of the Pagasitikos Gulf, where the other three AUCHS are located nearby. Accessibility is ensured as non-divers, or those who may have diving limitations, are virtually dived through a system of VR media and applications that allows for virtual tours of the project's pilot sites. KACs provide information on the value of cultural and natural heritage, display replicas or actual excavated findings, educational videos and support the operation of AUCHS, contributing significantly to visitor awareness and thus contributing to the development of sustainable tourism in the area (Manglis et al., 2021, MedDive, 2024, Pehlivanides et al, 2020).

The BLUEMED model as it operates in Peristera is an integrated and flexible project that can be adapted to coastal areas and islands with underwater cultural and natural heritage and constitute a sustainable tourism development strategy. It focuses on issues related to the operation, management and promotion of AUCHS and sets out the key issues to be considered, such as site selection requirements, stakeholder engagement, integration of innovative technologies and KAC's creation. This development effort requires multi-sectoral synergies between relevant public authorities at local, regional and national levels and private sector stakeholders related to tourism, culture and diving (Manglis et al., 2021).

The case study of the Peristera Shipwreck creates a holistic framework for a review of the coastal tourism phenomenon.

The marine area with its marine resources needs protection and a different approach to its sustainable exploitation. The operation of an AUCHS and the KAC, combined with other places with cultural and environmental attractions offering the possibility of blue and green alternative tourism activities, becomes an attraction for visitors seeking soft tourism.

The role of the dive centers is crucial for the implementation of the model as they undertake and contribute to the sustainable operation of AUCHS and support the development of diving tourism with their services and facilities.

The other elements of the region's tourism system as offered as an extended set of products and services (accommodation, food, transfers, leisure, etc.) in a diving destination help to activate its productive fabric and reduce the mobility of human resources.

The development model of the Peristera region was based on a strong framework of synergies between different actors such as the Ministry of Culture, the Ministry of Tourism, the Ministry of Development and the Ministry of Environment and Energy, Municipal and Regional Authorities, Research and University Institutions, International organizations and associations for marine natural and cultural heritage, Destination Management Agencies, MPAs, AUCHS, underwater parks and museums, but also scientists archaeologists, marine biologists, ecologists, museologists, artists and experts in VR and AR technologies, economists, etc. Also travel agencies and tour operators, accommodation and catering and leisure establishments and transport service providers. The relevant authorities of the Ephorate of Marine Antiquities and dive centers ensure responsible access to the site and the KAC ensure accurate information and promotion in cooperation with other local cultural stakeholders (Manglis et al., 2021).

In summary, the case study of the Peristera Shipwreck has taken into account the various parameters that are affected by tourism development in a coastal destination and are social, economic, environmental and cultural as well as the technical and political aspects of the development context. Taking into account international trends and events, development policies to achieve 'Blue Growth' require that healthy competition between individual coastal destinations offering diving tourism be promoted. The actual situation creates a condition that requires a single long-term planning framework of "bottom up" and "top down" approaches and is a cross-sectoral and multidisciplinary effort based on the active participation of citizens, local communities, other stakeholders, competent authorities and tourism policy makers. Utilization of UCHS is a good practice for "Blue Growth", extends the tourism seasonality, has a low environmental impact and zero negative impact on the tourism profile of the destination, creates a competitive advantage recognizable on a global scale and a value chain with a high beneficial return directly attributable to the host community (Manglis et al., 2019; Manglis et al., 2020).

Figure 4. EUROMED Stamps for 2022: Maritime Archaeology of the Mediterranean (Source: Elta, 2022)

CONCLUSION

The development of diving tourism in a coastal destination, that until recently supported mass tourism by exceeding its carrying capacity and endangering its resources, is a new approach for the proper management, sustainability and resilience of the destination. A coastal destination that has a healthy marine environment, MPAs with underwater flora and fauna, marine antiquities, local diving centers and a coastal community that desires sustainable tourism development has all the tools oriented towards a holistic view of accessibility and equitable distribution of benefits.

It is scientifically accepted that the implementation of a management project focusing on the development of controlled recreational diving activities in MPAs could potentially: a) generate significant inputs to support surveillance and monitoring costs; b) multiplier multidimensional benefits to the host community by enhancing sustainable development; and finally, c) increase public awareness of the conservation of the marine environment (Gerovassileiou et al., 2009).

The cooperation of all stakeholders through the promotion of programmes and initiatives within a legislative framework that validates the importance of environmental protection as a tourism resource enhances the quality of the tourism product, mitigates seasonality, offers significant opportunities for modernization and restructuring of the state, activates the private sector, encourages participation and decentralization of responsibilities, maximizes the benefits to society as a whole by obeying the logic of co-responsibility (Coccossis & Tsartas, 2001).

Alternative forms of tourism can contribute to the sustainable development of a region rich in environmental and cultural resources as this can be achieved through rational planning, programming and organization and careful management of the local productive, social and environmental structure (Coccossis & Tsartas, 2001).

Sustainable management of Underwater Cultural Heritage requires synergies with the local community at its core. The holistic tourism development model for areas with rich underwater heritage is bringing to the fore good practices that are beginning to yield positive results in host communities. An inclusive synergy cluster benefits the destination in many ways and has positive effects at all levels of its social and economic fabric, preserving its resources and carrying capacity. At the same time, it contributes to the awakening, information and education of citizens and visitors on the proper management of resources and the development of policies and actions that reduce the negative impact of tourism. It sets the right basis for development, corrects distortions, mitigates the effects of climate change and achieves rational management of natural and man-made marine resources. Offering an expanded and enhanced tourism product with a synthesis of underwater and outdoor activities is the basis for development in response to the demands of the modern educated consumer who seeks healthy environments where a holistic approach to management and development is applied. The consumer as a creative visitor is looking for the proposal that will meet his needs and satisfy his motivation for a unique travel experience. This can be achieved when the destination rationally develops all those resources that contribute to the creation of a value chain capable of delivering a competitive advantage. Mediterranean destinations absorb 1/3 of global tourism activity and face major challenges in managing their fragile resources. The prospects of rational resource management following good practices of soft tourism development that respects carrying capacity is the requested and desired action plan by the contemporary international community. Wet and dry diving tourism can contribute to sustainable coastal development by setting the basis for the rational management of the environment, both natural and man-made, and its protection. The complex activities offered as a complementary activity create a framework that contributes to the image of the destination and the creation of a specific identity.

Dive Into the Wreck of Peristera, Greece

In summary, the development achieved through the proper management of resources with extroversion through flexible synergies between local, regional, national and international tourism and non-tourism stakeholders and the local community, without exclusion, is a case study worth discussing.

REFERENCES

Allovergreece. (n.d.). *Ναυάγιο Περιστέρα | Ναυάγια.* https://www.allovergreece.com/Wreck/Descr/25/el

Alonissos Park. (n.d.). *Χλωρίδα και Πανίδα – ΕΘΝΙΚΟ ΘΑΛΑΣΣΙΟ ΠΑΡΚΟ ΑΛΟΝΝΗΣΟΥ ΒΟΡΕΙΩΝ ΣΠΟΡΑΔΩΝ!*https://alonissos-park.gr/?page_id=63

Anastasopoulou, F. (n.d.) *ΝΑΥΑΓΙΟ ΠΕΡΙΣΤΕΡΑΣ (Αρχαιολογικός χώρος) | Αλόννησος | Σποράδες | Golden Greece.* Golden Greece. https://golden-greece.gr/archaeological/sporades/alonisos/alonperisteras

Andriotis, K. (2005). *Tourism Development and Planning.* Stamoulis.

art4sea.eu. (2024, March 21). *Home - Art4Sea.* Art4Sea -. https://art4sea.eu/#the-project

Archaeology Newsroom. (2020, December 15). Online. https://www.archaiologia.gr/blog/2020/12/15/%CF%80%CF%81%CF%8E%CF%84%CE%BF-%CE%B2%CF%81%CE%B1%CE%B2%CE%B5%CE%AF%CE%BF%CE%B3%CE%B9%CE%B1-%CF%84%CE%BF-%CF%85%CF%80%CE%BF%CE%B8%CE%B1%CE%BB%CE%AC%CF%83%CF%83%CE%B9%CE%BF-%CE%BC%CE%BF%CF%85%CF%83/

BLUEMED. (2020). https://bluemed.interreg-med.eu/fileadmin/user_upload/Sites/Sustainable_Tourism/Projects/BLUEMED/BLUEMED_BROCHURE-FINAL.pdf

Bruno, F., Ricca, M., Lagudi, A., Kalamara, P., Manglis, A., Fourkiotou, A., Papadopoulou, D., & Veneti, A. (2020). Digital technologies for the sustainable development of the accessible underwater cultural heritage sites. *Journal of Marine Science and Engineering*, 8(11), 955. 10.3390/jmse8110955

Brylske, A., McDougall, P., Popple, I., & Wagner, O. (2023). *Beneath the blue Planet: A Diver's Guide to the Ocean and Its Conservation.* Mango Media Inc.

Coccossis, Ch., & Tsartas, P. (2001). *Sustainable Tourism Development and the Environment.* Kritiki.

DEMA. (2024). dema.org. https://www.dema.org/store/download.aspx?id=7811B097-8882-4707-A160-F999B49614B6

Dimmock, K., & Musa, G. (2015). Scuba Diving Tourism System: A framework for collaborative management and sustainability. *Marine Policy*, 54, 52–58. 10.1016/j.marpol.2014.12.008

Dive Virtually - Peristera - MedDive. (n.d.). http://meddiveinthepast.eu/dive-virtually -peristera

Divelog. (2021, June 2). *Ναυάγιο Περιστέρας - DIVELOG | Your Secret Reef.* DIVELOG | Your Secret Reef - Plan Your Next Dive Here - Σχεδίασε Εδώ Την Επόμενή Σου Κατάδυση. https://www.divelog.gr/divepost/navagio-peristeras-2/

Elta. (2022, July 13). *EUROMED stamps for 2022: Maritime Archaeology of the Mediterranean.* (n.d.). https://www.elta.gr/en/singleblog/deltia-tupou/i-thalassia -archaiologia-tis-mesogeiou-sta-grammatosima-euromed-4

Euronews. (2021, May 31). Αλόννησος: Ανοίγει αύριο το πρώτο υποβρύχιο μουσείο της Ελλάδας. *Euronews.* https://gr.euronews.com/2021/05/31/alonnhsos-anoigei -aurio-to-prwto-upovruxio-mouseio-ths-elladas

European Commission. (2017). *Diving into underwater tourism in Greece.* https:// ec.europa.eu/regional_policy/en/newsroom/news/2017/10/10-04-2017-diving-into -underwater-tourism-in-greece

Ferretti, E., Thrush, S. F., Lewis, N., & Hillman, J. R. (2023). Restorative practices, marine ecotourism, and restoration economies: Revitalizing the environmental agenda? *Ecology and Society*, 28(4), art23. Advance online publication. 10.5751/ ES-14628-280423

Gerovassileiou, V., Koutsoubas, D., Sini, M., & Paikou, K. (2009). Marine protected areas and diving tourism in the Greek Seas: Practices and perspectives. *Tourismos: An International Multidisciplinary Journal of Tourism*, 4(4), 181–197.

Hadjidaki, E. (1996). Underwater Excavations of a Late Fifth Century Merchant Ship at Alonnesos, Greece : The 1991-1993 Seasons. *Bulletin De Correspondance HelléNique*, 120(2), 561–593. 10.3406/bch.1996.4619

Hellenic Republic, Ministry of Culture. (2016). *BLUEMED.* culture.gov.gr. https:// www.culture.gov.gr/en/service/SitePages/view.aspx?iID=3210

Hellenic Republic, Ministry of Culture Newsroom. (2024, February 29). Online https://www.culture.gov.gr/el/Information/SitePages/view.aspx?nID=4890

Hellenic Republic, Ministry of Environment and Energy. (2021, April 19). *Δίκτυο NATURA 2000.* https://ypen.gov.gr/perivallon/viopoikilotita/diktyo-natura-2000/

Iosifidis, S. (2019). The National Marine Park of Alonissos Northern Sporades. *ResearchGate.* https://www.researchgate.net/publication/332538725

Kieran, D. (2021). *Scuba diving industry Market Size & Statistics: 2021 Edition.*

Kieran, D. (2024, March 9). Survey results: State of the Dive Industry 2024 market reports. *Medium*. https://medium.com/scubanomics/survey-results-state-of-the-dive -industry-2024-market-reports-bcceccf8613a

Koutsi, D., & Stratigea, A. (2019). Ολοκληρωμένη συμμετοχική διαχείριση χερσαίων και ενάλιων πολιτιστικών πόρων ως πυλώνας ανάπτυξης. *ResearchGate*. https://www.researchgate.net/publication/336148494_Oloklēromene_symmetochike _diacheirise_chersaion_kai_enalion_politistikon_poron_os_pylonas_anaptyxes _apomonomenon_nesiotikon_periochon

Manglis, A., Fourkiotou, A., & Papadopoulou, D. (2019).Sustainable management and protection of Accessible Underwater Cultural Heritage sites; global practices and bottom-up initiatives. *International Conference in Management of Accessible Underwater, Cultural and Natural Heritage Sites: "Dive in Blue Growth", Athens, Greece, 16-18 October 2019*

Manglis, A., Fourkiotou, A., & Papadopoulou, D. (2020). The Accessible Underwater Cultural Heritage Sites (AUCHS) as a sustainable tourism development opportunity in the Mediterranean Region. *Tourism (Zagreb)*, 68(4), 499–503. 10.37741/t.68.4.9

Manglis, A., Fourkiotou, A., & Papadopoulou, D. (2021). A Roadmap for the Sustainable Valorization of accessible Underwater Cultural Heritage Sites. *Heritage*, 4(4), 4700–4715. 10.3390/heritage4040259

Manglis, A., Giatsiatsou, P., Papadopoulou, D., Drouga, V., & Fourkiotou, A. (2021). Implementing Multi-Criteria Analysis in the Selection of AUCHS for the Integration of Digital Technologies into the Tourism Offering: The Case of MeDryDive. *Heritage*, 4(4), 4460–4472. 10.3390/heritage4040246

MeDryDive. (2020b, April 28). *Peristera shipwreck (Greece)*. https://medrydive .eu/peristera-shipwreck-greece/

Miller, C., & Taylor, C. (2022). A Diver's Guide to the World. *National Geographic*.

Musa, G., & Dimmock, K. (2013c). *Scuba diving tourism*. https://doi.org/10.4324/ 9780203121016

NatureBank - Βιότοπος NATURA - ETHNIKO THALASSIO PARKO ALONNISOU - VOREION SPORADON, ANATOLIKI SKOPELOS. (n.d.). https://filotis.itia.ntua .gr/biotopes/c/GR1430004/

Odysseus.culture. (n.d.). http://odysseus.culture.gr/h/3/gh352.jsp?obj_id=19848

Pehlivanides, G., Monastiridis, K., Tourtas, A., Karyati, E., Ioannidis, G., Bejelou, K., Antoniou, V., & Nomikou, P. (2020). The VIRTUALDiver Project. Making Greece's underwater cultural heritage accessible to the public. *Applied Sciences (Basel, Switzerland)*, 10(22), 8172. 10.3390/app10228172

Peristera's ancient ship wreck – NOUS. (n.d.). https://nous.com.gr/naxly_project/ peristeras-ancient-ship-wreck/

REGINA-MSP project. (n.d.). REGINA-MSP. https://www.regina-msp.eu/projet

Staikos, A. (2020, August 1). Αλόννησος: Εγκαινιάστηκε το πρώτο υποβρύχιο μουσείο στην Ελλάδα - Ο «Παρθενώνας των ναυαγίων». *Euronews*. https://gr .euronews.com/2020/08/01/alonissos-egkainiastike-to-proto-ypovryxio-mouseio -stin-ellada-o-pathenonas-ton-nayagion

Tsartas, P. (2010). *Greek Tourism Development*. Characteristics, Clarifications, Proposals. Kritiki.

Tsartas, P. (2021, May 26). *Π. Τσάρτας (Χαροκόπειο Πανεπιστήμιο): 'Οι προορισμοί θα πρέπει να λειτουργούν και σε clusters'* TravelDailyNews Greece & Cyprus. https://traveldailynews.gr/columns/article/3823

Varvaresos, S. (2017). Religious Tourism: an economic approach. In Tsartas, P., & Lytras, P. (Eds.), *Contributions of Greek Scientists. Tourism, Tourism Development* (pp. 245–254). Papazisis.

Vlachos, A., Krinidis, S., Papadimitriou, K., Manglis, A., Fourkiotou, A., & Tzovaras, D. (2023). IBLUECULTURE: a novel system of real-time underwater image transmission in a virtual reality environment, as a new managerial approach for underwater cultural heritage. *The æInternational Archives of the Photogrammetry, Remote Sensing and Spatial Information Sciences/International Archives of the Photogrammetry, Remote Sensing and Spatial Information Sciences, XLVIII-1/ W2-2023*, 269–274. 10.5194/isprs-archives-XLVIII-1-W2-2023-269-2023

Worldbank. (2024). The Blue Economy Development Framework. https://thedocs .worldbank.org/en/doc/e5c1bdb0384e732de3cef6fd2eac41e5-0320072021/original/ BH023-BlueEconomy-FINAL-ENGLISH.pdf

ENDNOTE

[1] "Surface intervals" are the mandatory "breaks" between the maximum number of dives that divers can make during their stay at the destination.

Chapter 10
A Research on Factors Affecting Sustainable Competitive Advantage in the Tourism Sector

Edip Örücü
Bandırma Onyedi Eylül University, Turkey

Itir Hasirci
Inependent Researcher, Turkey

Ramazan Özkan Yildiz
 https://orcid.org/0000-0002-4382-2480
Bandırma Onyedi Eylül University, Turkey

ABSTRACT

The aim of this research is to identify the effects of organisational agility and electronic human resource management (E-HRM) on sustainable competitive advantage. The population of the research consists of 471,000 employees working in hotels in Turkey. Data were collected through an online survey. Therefore, the sample of the research is 421 employees working in these hotels. Frequency, factor, reliability, normality, correlation, and regression analysis were performed. When the regression analysis was analysed, it was determined that organisational agility and E-HRM have significant effects on sustainable competitive advantage. When the result of the regression analysis is evaluated, it is seen that organisational agility affects sustainable competitive advantage more than E-HRM. Therefore, in this sample, recommendations are presented in order to bring the importance of organisational agility to all employees.

DOI: 10.4018/979-8-3693-5405-6.ch010

Copyright © 2024, IGI Global. Copying or distributing in print or electronic forms without written permission of IGI Global is prohibited.

INTRODUCTION

The dynamic impact of technology and the environment, the rapid change of customers' demands, the desire to maximise customer satisfaction in order to respond to them, organisations need to adapt to changes in the environment in order to survive. In strategic management, organisations must maximise their organisational agility levels to ensure competitive advantage in such a dynamic environment. For sustainable success, it is essential for accommodation businesses to improve their organisational agility levels. The concept of agility is related to these behaviours. Agility, which is known as the ability of an organisation to adapt to unforeseen changes in the fastest way, supports organisations to gain and maintain competitive advantage (Akkaya ve Tabak, 2018). The idea of adapting to these sudden changes has led to the emergence of the concept of agility, one of the new concepts in business strategies. Agility has become an important driving force for all organisations over time, enabling organisations to survive and develop in uncertain and turbulent markets. In today's conditions of increasing competition, hotel businesses need to make a difference compared to their competitors in order to ensure continuity and gain sustainable competitive advantage. One of these differences they will create is to have organisational agility. Organisational agility is defined as the ability to identify and seize resources that provide competitive advantage in rapidly changing markets faster than competitors (Sağır and Aydın, 2017). Organisational agility fosters a culture of innovation and ongoing development inside organisations. Agile organisations promote and support experimentation, readily accept change, and empower people to share their ideas and viewpoints. The focus on innovation allows organisations to develop novel goods, services, and processes that align with evolving customer needs, enhance operational effectiveness, and enhance overall performance. By consistently introducing new ideas and making enhancements, organisations set themselves apart from their rivals, ultimately attaining a lasting edge in the market.

Today, developments in the global market environment accelerate the process of adaptation of organisations to information and communication technologies. Electronic human resources management has become important with the widespread use of computer and communication technologies in organisations and the increase in the accumulation of knowledge in intra-organisational networks. With the changes, regulations and increasing competition in communication technologies, organizations have turned to searching for new solutions (Ibrahim vd., 2023). Technological, economic and political changes and the effects of the social, cultural and business environment on consumer expectations and workforce have forced many organizations to change. In addition to human resources policies and practices, it has become necessary to question the understanding of responsibility, expectation and authority.

Among these functions transferred to the internet environment, features such as saving time, reducing bureaucracy and reducing costs come to the fore. With the increasing use of computer and communication technologies in organizations and the acceleration of database creation processes, applications for electronic human resources management have become widespread. Such applications have brought to the forefront the necessity for organisations to restructure their processes in order to take part in the competitive market economy and to expand their standards (Nyathi and Kekwaletswe, 2023).

Due to the increasing importance of the human element in organizations and increasing competition in today's conditions, training to empower employees as a management tool that imposes the responsibilities of their work for organizational success, encourages cooperation, creates a stable working environment through sharing, supports taking initiative, and gives sacrifice and decision-making skills. Many practices such as, teamwork, and emotional support have become very important. As has been the case since the beginning of humanity, from the primitive society to the information society, the ability of people to keep up with changing conditions is also valid for businesses. Since the basis of business is business and the people who run it, it is not a coincidence that the same characteristics that exist for people also exist for businesses. The ability to keep up with changing conditions is summarized by the concept of organizational agility, and it is seen that this feature positively affects the perception of sustainable quality regarding the products and services offered in the enterprise. The positive impact of sustainable quality perception reveals that quality managers and senior management should attach importance to agility in the business. From a strategic management perspective, it can be inferred that managers should take agility into consideration when determining their strategies in order for the business to achieve its goals and objectives. Strategic management covers analytical processes in which planning, organizing, execution and control functions are used effectively and efficiently, and speed and competence, which are the dimensions of organizational agility, are of great importance in these processes.

The concept of competitive advantage is defined as the tangible and intangible superiority of an organisation in the eyes of competitors and potential customers with the goods and services it offers (Demirel and Demirel, 2011). Competitive advantage is considered on two dimensions: cost and difference. Organisations have cost advantage when they can offer the benefits they offer to their customers at a lower cost compared to their competitors. If they can offer their customers benefits and values that the products they compete with do not have, they can have a difference advantage (Porter, 2008). Sustainable competition is defined as the competition process that emerges when organisations want to realise their economic interests and objectives in the market and their efforts to prevail. Organisations that want to excel in competition and sustain it try to imitate the successful solutions of their competitors and seek different ways of competition in the market. In the ever-changing market competition, organisations are engaged in continuous learning in order to follow innovations and reflect them to their practices. Competitive advantage is at the centre of the performance of organisations in competitive markets. In an environment of intensifying competition and environmental uncertainty, positive results can be achieved in the indicators of corporate performance by ensuring sustainable competitive advantage and preserving these advantages as much as possible (Klein, 2002). According to the resource-based approach, organisations' competitive advantage depends on their resources and capabilities. In addition, according to the market orientation approach; in order for organisations to achieve sustainable competitive advantage, it is essential to determine the current and potential customer needs in the market and to share the data obtained within all organisational functions. In addition, the needs must be met more effectively and efficiently compared to competitors. Both approaches are very important for organisations to gain sustainable competitive advantage. The resource-based approach emphasises the resources and capabilities of organisations as the critical factors for achieving competitive advantage and states that organisations should not only consider the factors determined by the external environment when determining their competitive strategies (Özbağ, 2016).

The hospitality and tourism industry is renowned for its swiftly evolving client demands and challenging market conditions. Hence, organisational agility, denoting the capacity to promptly and efficiently adapt to such alterations, is vital for attaining a competitive edge. Nevertheless, there is a dearth of study regarding the correlation between electronic human resource management, organisational agility, and sustained competitive advantage within the accommodation sector. Hence, it is imperative for organisations in the accommodation sector to analyse the impact of organisational agility and electronic human resource management on sustained competitive advantage. This analysis is essential for organisations to effectively adjust and expand their operations in the face of uncertainties and disruptions. The importance of this study rests in filling these knowledge gaps by offering valuable insights into the distinct impacts of electronic human resource management and organisational agility on sustained competitive advantage within the tourism and hospitality sector.

CONCEPTUAL BACKGROUND

In this part of the research, the conceptual backgroun regarding the variables will be presented.

ORGANIZATIONAL AGILTY

Agility is also expressed as a way of coping with environments where uncertainty and unpredictability exist. Initially focused on production, agility later evolved into an approach that also focuses on the production of products and services. In addition, agility requires adoption by utilising the necessary data, avoiding sticking to a single idea. It is explained as the ability of an organisation to adapt quickly, effectively and long-term to the continuous changes that occur as a result of its efficiency superiority. It is also stated that agility is an effective response to change and uncertainty. The most comprehensive model of organisational agility is divided into three parts: agility drivers, agility capabilities and agility enablers (Sharifi and Zhang, 1999). Agility drivers: The organisation's need to be agile and develop a strategy to be agile; agility capabilities such as speed, responsiveness, competence and flexibility; the ability to use agility capabilities is called agility enablers. Agility, which is expressed as the competitive advantage of the organisation, covers the entire organisation structure. Moreover, agility manifests itself when an organisation is able to see and adopt changes quickly. Based on this, effective knowledge management and learning skills are indispensable for agile organisations and agility encompasses all elements that make up the organisational structure such as technology, business processes, people, knowledge and strategy (Molla et al., 2012). In order to implement organisational agility in organisations, managers and employees in the organisation should be open to change and innovation. At the same time, it is important that the organisational culture has the characteristics to support this change. Agile organisations achieve success by providing competitive advantage over their competitors because they have the ability to respond and adapt quickly to unexpected and unpredictable changes, market opportunities and customer needs. Organizations with a high level of organizational agility quickly perceive the changes occurring in their environment. They also reduce their costs by minimizing unnecessary activities, focus on innovation, and integrate their talents and resources to ensure their competence. Against the uncertainties inherent in the accommodation sector, hotels need to adapt to environmental complexity and dynamism through various strategic decisions (Darvishmotevali et al., 2020). In constantly changing work environments, agility emerges as the dominant competitive tool for organizations that continue their activities. Agility is known as responding quickly to expected or unexpected changes in markets and turning these changes into opportunities. Based on these definitions, it can be stated that agility is necessary to meet customer demands in uncertain environments and increases innovation.

For the sake of continuity in organizations, it is necessary to adapt to changes quickly, and even act proactively, quickly and effectively before crises occur. Organizations that can achieve this will get through that period with minimum damage in the face of threats. By quickly evaluating possible opportunities, organizations that stand out in the competition will increase their market shares. The advantages of organizational agility include customer satisfaction, information and people, collaboration and the ability to follow change. Customer satisfaction is known as the trust and continuity that organizations give to their customers. As the welfare of customers increases, the quality, recognition and vision of the organization improve. In competitive conditions that develop and change day by day, the value to be given to employees is very important. With the employee's knowledge, skills and ideas, the organization will attribute greater productivity. With the continuous development of technology, the increasing differentiation of customer demands, and the huge increase in product demand, organizations are obliged to make various collaborations. An agile organization should be able to create more advanced collaborations through collaborations (Sharifi and Zhang, 1999). Being able to follow constantly changing competitive conditions and respond to organizations' moves in a timely and appropriate manner is a must for an agile organization. In times of stagnation or collapse of possible rival organizations, only an agile organization can survive with positive or negative change with different ideas and mindsets. In such situations, the agile organization gains great momentum by turning the negative situation into an advantage. Another advantage of being an agile organization is providing the opportunity to establish a sincere relationship with the customer. Another advantage is that the opinions of all individuals are given importance instead of the top-down approach. An organization that has achieved organizational agility will turn competition into opportunity and will be ready for different business partnerships to provide sustainable competitive advantage by creating a constantly evolving, flexible structure (Maskell, 2001).

Organizational agility is about an organization's ability to adapt and respond to an environment of rapid changes and uncertainty. It refers to the organization's ability to recognize and take advantage of opportunities, to quickly change strategies and operations, and to easily cope with the challenges it encounters (Walter, 2021). When examined concretely, it can be stated that it includes the ability of organizations to perceive environmental changes and easily respond to them by restructuring their resources, business processes and strategies. Additionally, Chakravarty et al. (2013) state that there are three interrelated dimensions that shape organizational agility. These; customer agility, which states that customers' opinions should be used to provide advanced market intelligence; partnership agility, which states that information should be obtained from different business partners to improve the organization's responses to market demands; and operational agility, which states that the process should be quickly redesigned to benefit from dynamic environment and market conditions. Organizational agility is expressed as the organization's conscious intervention ability, which makes it possible to act more efficiently even in complex situations (Charbonnier-Voirin, 2011). This behavior addresses not only the ability to respond quickly to change but also the organization's ability to anticipate and seize opportunities, especially through innovation and learning. Organizational agility shows that correct communication, continuous development, flexibility, self-awareness and self-discipline exist in organizations. For this reason, it is important to have leaders who share power, responsibilities and decision-making among their subordinates in order to ensure the trust and motivation of employees in organizations (Ramadan et al., 2023). Organizational agility is a structure that adds value to the activities of organizations and creates a basis for organizations to adapt to constantly changing market conditions by identifying gaps in business processes. It improves organizations' ability to detect inconsistencies. By addressing the problems in the market, it helps organizations with resource planning and production. It also supports organizations to adapt to real-time data and tools (Sun et al., 2022). Agile organizations adapt more quickly to fluctuations in the current market. Such organizations can immediately detect and react to possible sudden changes. Therefore, they reduce possible risks by taking advantage of opportunities. Organizations can gain a competitive advantage over their competitors by following market fluctuations. Thus, they can position themselves in the most advantageous way in the market (Alqarni et al., 2023).

ELECTRONIC HUMAN RESOURCES MANAGEMENT

The speed of access to information is of great importance for human beings, who by nature always tend to produce and improve themselves. In today's Information Age, electronic media are now included in almost every aspect of our lives and cause the letter "e" representing the word electronic to be added in front of many concepts. Examples of these are e-commerce, e-government, e-health, e-school and many other words. Electronic environments make our lives much easier and provide fast and easy access to information (Aydın, 2016).

Internet and information technologies has significantly affected the understanding and practices of human resources management. E-HRM is actually inspired by the popular term e-commerce. The prefix e- here refers to the word "electronic". E-human resources is actually a specific use of "networks". Therefore, it may be more accurate to use the term online human resources management instead of E-HRM (Panayotopoulou, 2007). E-HRM is the organisation's implementation of human resources strategies, policies and practices in a way that provides informed and direct support through the full use of web-technology based channels (Doğan, 2011). Electronic human resources management aims to ensure that human resources functions such as recruitment, dismissal, wage management, in-service training can be performed electronically and to adapt technological applications to human resources. Since human resources processes can be done anywhere and managed faster and more effectively, it is aimed to manage human resources transactions/ activities through the internet. Conducting human resources management processes in electronic environments creates advantages for organisations. These advantages include; eliminating paperwork and paperwork in human resources processes, providing convenience in processing and storing information, conducting applications without being bound to time and place, increasing quality by accessing information at any time and place, providing quick access to information, making employees feel valuable with e-mail, celebration and congratulation messages transmitted electronically and contributing to their performance and motivation (Altan, 2011). The time required for the installation of an electronic human resources management system can be very high. Since the system provides electronic communication instead of face-to-face communication, it prevents cooperation. Updating the software creates a disadvantage as a cost factor at this point. In this context, since the continuous developments in technology lead to the obsolescence of technology, it is necessary to purchase or use new technologies instead. In organisations, it is necessary to access old information that loses its validity in a short time with new equipment (Sullivan, 2005).

Electronic human resources is a technological application that allows practitioners and employees to directly access human resources and other organizational services for communication, performance reporting, team management, knowledge management and learning. This concept refers to the process of planning and implementing information technologies that network and assist at least two individual or collective actors in carrying out human resources activities collaboratively (De Alwis et al., 2022). In organizations, human resources practitioners interact with employees to provide both guidance services and human capital services and participate in human resources-related activities. Human resources practitioners are required to physically perform a great deal of administrative and paperwork. However, today the role of human resources practitioners has evolved along with technological developments (Beadles et al., 2005). Electronic human resources plays an important role in supporting sustainable innovation by encouraging knowledge sharing and making use of data analytics with the help of collaborative platforms. These capabilities enable organizations to identify and capitalize on sustainable improvement opportunities. In addition, electronic human resources facilitate effective communication and coordination by providing real-time access to information, enable agile decision-making, and strengthen organizational agility by responding quickly to market dynamics and competitive pressures (Singh and Koneru, 2022). Electronic human resources can support organizational agility. Thus, it can positively affect the organization's sustainable competitive advantage (Alkhodary, 2021). Organizations have comprehensive information about their employees through the use of electronic human resources. In addition, employees in organizations can access and use records and documents and provide necessary updates when needed. Among the advantages of electronic human resources: These include making comprehensive information about all employees accessible to employees themselves, assisting management in the decision-making process, making employees aware of the types of information that the organization can access about them, clarifying employees' positions within the organization, and online and up-to-date use of reports regarding intra-organizational functions (Nyathi, 2024). Electronic human resources management strategies facilitate the efficient acquisition, retention, and dissemination of information within an organisation. Online platforms provide employees with convenient access to information, facilitate the sharing of best practices, and enable collaboration on sustainability initiatives. Electronic HR management software enables effective knowledge management and cooperation, leading to a lasting competitive advantage. Workers can get advantages from the exchange of knowledge and cooperative endeavours to create inventive concepts and establish enduring human resources strategies that improve the organisation's competitive edge (Alqarni et al., 2023).

Aydın (2016) Elektronik expresses the advantages of human resources management as follows:

- It provides ease of processing and storing information by eliminating the paper and paperwork of human resources processes.
- With the transfer of human resources applications to electronic environments, applications are carried out regardless of time and place.
- Access to information anytime, anywhere increases the quality and efficiency of business processes.
- Provides fast and cheap access to accurate information.
- It has an important share in achieving strategic superiority by providing the ability to easily analyze, interpret and use information, and by increasing the time to focus on issues that create real added value to the business.
- It reduces the routine work of human resources and saves time.
- Electronic applications enable employees to take an active role in business processes.
- Thanks to electronic systems, e-mails, congratulatory and congratulatory messages sent to employees contribute to performance by significantly affecting the motivation of employees who feel special and valuable.

SUSTAINABLE COMPETITIVE ADVANTAGE

Competitiveness is a relative and multidimensional concept. In micro terms, it is generally defined as the ability to maintain and improve market position and market share relative to competitors (Listra, 2015). From a macro perspective, this concept is seen as a national problem and its main objective is to increase the real income level of societies. In this context, the competitiveness of a nation is a very broad construct that includes all economic, social, cultural and political variables that affect the performance of that nation in international markets. The competitiveness of a destination in tourism is defined as the ability to increase tourist expenditures, to attract an increasing number of visitors to the destination by providing memorable and satisfying experiences, and to do this profitably by improving the good living conditions of the people (Ritchie ve Crouch, 2000). Organisations offering similar goods and services to the same group of customers in the sector compete with each other. Competition, in a way, meets the needs of customers. On the other hand, it struggles in the market with strategies that realise their expectations and create value for them. Competitive advantage can only be achieved through value-creating strategies. Sustainable competitive advantage depends on the development of organisations and competitive advantages based on innovation and investment in improved factors of production. It is extremely important for the organisation to sustain the competitive advantage gained. However, it is not easy to maintain competitive advantage in a dynamic business environment, especially in the tourism and accommodation sector. The superiorities of successful organisations can be easily imitated by competitors and such superiority can be lost. Sustaining competitive advantage is only possible when the value-creating strategies of organisations cannot be imitated or implemented by competitors. Sustainability is the essence of maintaining competitive advantage. Without sustainability, the competitive advantage of a destination cannot be mentioned. Organisations can gain a sustainable competitive advantage through capabilities that cannot be easily imitated by competitors.

Competitive advantage refers to an organisation's capacity to achieve a favourable position in comparison to its competitors (Kim et al., 2020). Sustainable competitive advantage refers to an organisation's capacity to fulfil future competitive requirements without compromising its ability to fulfil present competitive demands. It is a dynamic process that effectively addresses current competitive needs (Mahdi and Nassar, 2021). Sustainable competitive advantages have been established through the use of the competitive advantage theory. They represent the enduring competitive advantages that an organisation can possess (Ge et al., 2018). Sustainable competitive advantage refers to the distinct and enduring superiority that an organisation possesses in comparison to its competitors. Furthermore, it enables organisations to sustain a dominant position in the market. This dominance encompasses a wide range of resources, including branding, customer services, technology, product design, and distribution networks. Sustainable competitive advantage refers to the ongoing ability of an organisation to consistently generate value for its customers. The ability of an organisation to maintain a sustainable competitive edge has a significant impact on its long-term performance in the market. Organisations lacking this edge are more susceptible to shifting demands and more prone to encountering heightened competition from new participants. An organisation's strategy should facilitate the enhancement of its enduring competitive advantage, enabling the creation of value for its consumers and the generation of profit (Remondino and Zanin, 2022).

METHOD

Aim, Importance, and Justification of the Research

The aim of this research is to examine the impact of electronic human resource management and organisational agility on sustainable competitive advantage in the hospitality sector. In particular, there is a research gap in exploring the relationships between these variables in the context of the hospitality sector. The rationale for this research is that it addresses these gaps in the literature and provides insights into the different effects of electronic human resource management and organisational agility on sustainable competitive advantage in the hospitality sector. Examining how electronic human resource management improves organisational agility and sustainable competitive advantage in the hospitality sector is important for organisations to successfully adapt to innovations, be agile and develop despite uncertainties and disruptions. This situation constitutes the importance of the study.

RESEARCH MODEL AND HYPOTHESES

Dynamic capabilities theory states that an organisation should take advantage of opportunities by adapting to evolving market dynamics. Electronic human resource management has the potential to increase sustainable competitive advantage by providing real-time data and valuable information about human resources. This enables organisations to respond quickly to fluctuations in the labour market and the need for talent (Kuo et al., 2022). In addition, dynamic capabilities theory enables the formation of a restructuring process by addressing an organisation's resources and capabilities to adapt to possible sectoral changes. Electronic human resource management is a valuable resource that can be flexibly reconfigured to adapt to evolving business strategies. Organisations can adapt their electronic human resource management systems to prioritise sustainability goals and develop a sustainable competitive advantage through innovative human resource practices (Iqbal et al., 2019). Dynamic capabilities theory emphasises the importance of continuous improvement and innovation. When used effectively, electronic human resource management allows organisations to improve their human resource practices and thus foster sustainable innovation. For example, organisations can use data analytics to optimise employee engagement, which can contribute to improved organisational performance (Alshibly & Alzubi, 2022). The hypotheses and model of the research, which are formed in the light of the literature review and dynamic capabilities theory, are presented below;

H$_1$: Organisational agility affects sustainable competitive advantage.

H$_2$: Electronic human resource management affects sustainable competitive advantage.

Figure 1. Research Model

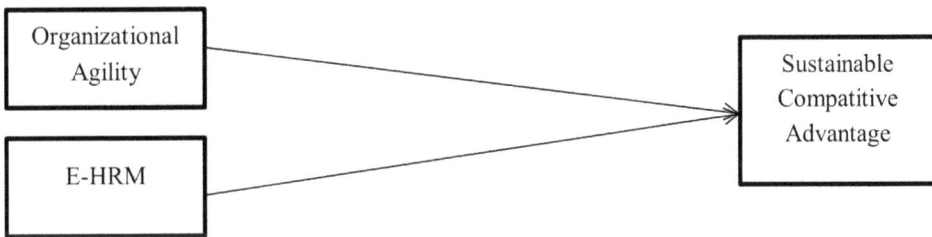

POPULATION AND SAMPLE OF THE STUDY

The population of the research consists of 471,000 employees working in all departments in hotels in Turkey. The data were obtained through an online survey. Therefore, the sample of the research consists of 421 personnel selected from these employees.

DATA COLLECTION TOOLS

The questionnaire form of the research consists of four sections. The first section includes questions on sustainable innovation, the second section includes questions on electronic human resource management, the third section includes questions on sustainable competitive advantage and the fourth section includes demographic questions to determine gender, education and income. For the measurement of electronic human resource management, the 6-question scale developed by Nyathi and Kekwaletswe (2023) was used. For the measurement of sustainable competitive advantage, the 4-question scale developed by Hossain et al. (2021) was used. For the measurement of organisational agility, the 4-question scale developed by Melián-Alzola et al. (2020) was used. The scale is one dimension. All scales are graded on a 5-point Likert scale and there are no reverse questions in the scales.

ANALYSIS

Demographic Findings

In this part of the research, information on the demographic characteristics of the individuals working in the hotels within the sample will be presented. This information obtained is given in the table;

Table 1. Frequency Analysis Findings

Variable		Frequency Value	%
Gender	Female	215	51.1
	Male	206	48.9
Education	Associate Degree	121	28.7
	Bachelor's degree	172	40.9
	Postgraduate	128	30.4
Income Status	18.000-22.000	90	21.4
	23.000-27.000	64	15.2
	28.000-32.000	73	17.3
	33.000-37.000	134	31.8
	38.000 TL	60	14.3

When the frequency analysis results given in Table 1 are analysed, it is seen that 215 female (51.1%) and 206 male (48.9%) hotel employees participated in the study. When the educational status of the participants was examined, it was determined that 121 (28.7%) had associate's degree, 172 (40.9%) had bachelor's degree and 128 (30.4%) had postgraduate degree. When the income status of the participants is analysed, it is seen that 90 (21.4%) of the participants have an income between 18,000-22,000, 64 (15.2%) of the participants have an income between 23,000-27,000, 73 (17.3%) of the participants have an income between 28,000-32,000, 134 (31.8%)

of the participants have an income between 33,000-37,000, and 60 (14.3%) of the participants have an income of 38,000 TL and above.

Reliability Analysis Findings

In social sciences, reliability analysis is performed to determine whether the scales make consistent measurements or whether there is consistency between the scale items. Reliability analysis shows how consistent a measurement tool measures. The alpha value, which is accepted as a measure of internal consistency, is used to determine the homogeneous structure of the items. It can be said that the items in the scale with high alpha coefficient have a consistent structure and calculate the same feature. Therefore, since the values in Table 2 are in the range of $0.80 < Alpha < 1.00$, it can be said that there is high reliability.

Table 2. Reliability Analysis Findings

Variables	Cronbach's Alpha	Mean	Standard Deviation
Organizational Agility (OA)	0.827	3.0053	1.07783
E-HRM	0.881	3.0484	1.02551
Sustainable Compatitive Advantage (SCA)	0.802	3.0196	1.02835

When Table 2 is analysed, it is seen that the internal consistency value between the scale items is acceptable. Since the alpha coefficient is above 0.70, the scales are accepted to be reliable.

Exploratory Factor Analysis Results

Exploratory factor analysis is conducted in order to define the observed variables, summarise these variables, and determine the factors at a manageable and workable level. The findings of the exploratory factor analyses for the variables are presented below;

Table 3. Exploratory Factor Analysis Findings for E-HRM

E-HRM		Factor Loadings
	E-HRM2	0.830
	E-HRM6	0.816
	E-HRM1	0.815
	E-HRM3	0.788

continued on following page

Table 3. Continued

E-HRM		Factor Loadings
	E-HRM5	0.753
	E-HRM4	0.750
KMO Value= 0.870		
Sig.= .000		
Chi Square Value= 1211.245		

When the CFA results for the electronic human resources management scale are analysed, it is seen that all items of the scale are gathered under a single factor, the KMO value is 0.870, and the single factor explains 62% of the total variance.

Table 4. CFA Findings for Sustainable Competitive Advantage

Sustainable Compatitive Advantage (SCA)		Factor Loadings
	SCA1	0.883
	SCA4	0.806
	SCA3	0.777
	SCA2	0.698
KMO Value= 0.754		
Sig.= .000		
Chi Square Value= 563.304		

When the CFA results for the sustainable competitive advantage scale are analysed, it is seen that all items of the scale are gathered under a single factor, the KMO value is 0.754, and the single factor explains 63% of the total variance.

Table 5. CFA Findings for Organisational Agility

Organizational Agility (OA)		Factor Loadings
	OA3	0.820
	OA4	0.819
	OA1	0.815
	OA2	0.794
KMO Value= 0.766		
Sig.= .000		
Chi Square Value= 617.054		

Normality Analysis Findings

George and Mallery (2010) state that data are normally distributed if kurtosis and skewness are between -2 and +2. When the normality test results given in Table 6 are analysed, the data are normally distributed.

Table 6. Skewness and Kurtosis Values

Variables	Kurtosis	Skewness
Organizational Agility (OA)	-.093	-1.768
E-HRM	-1.820	-.127
Sustainable Compatitive Advantage (SCA)	-1.738	-.132

The kurtosis and skewness values given in Table 6 were found to be between -2 and +2. This indicates that the scale scores show a normal distribution. Therefore, parametric analyses will be applied in order to test the hypotheses.

Correlation Analysis Findings

The results of the analyses conducted to find answers to the questions of whether there is a relationship between the variables, if any, whether this relationship is strong or weak, and whether one of the variables increases while the other increases or decreases are presented in Table 7;

Table 7. Relationships Between Variables

	OA	E-HRM	SCA
Organizational Agility (OA)	1		
E-HRM	,849**	1	
Sustainable Compatitive Advantage (SCA)	,912**	,841**	1

According to the results of the correlation analysis, there are positive relationships between organisational agility and electronic human resource management, between organisational agility and sustainable competitive advantage, and between electronic human resource management and sustainable competitive advantage.

Regression Analysis Findings

The aim of multiple regression analysis is to examine the effect of more than one independent variable on a dependent variable. The basic assumption is that there is a linear relationship between the dependent variable and the independent variables. Table 8 presents the results of the multiple regression analysis;

Table 8. Regression Analysis Findings

Dependent Variable	Independent Variable	B	Beta	Sig.	VIF
Sustainable Compatitive Advantage	Organizational Agility	.699	.706	.000	3.577
	E-HRM	.226	.242	.000	3.577
R^2= .847 Adjusted R^2= .848 F= 1161.367 Anova= .000					

The results of the regression analysis show that organisational agility and electronic human resource management affect sustainable competitive advantage. In line with these results, H_1 and H_2 hypotheses were accepted. The R^2 value obtained as a result of the analysis indicates that 84% of the change in the dependent variable sustainable competitive advantage is explained by the independent variables. The adjusted R^2 value shows that 84% of the variance in the dependent variable sustainable competitive advantage is explained by the independent variables. The overall significance (Anova) of the regression model was found to be less than 0.05. This indicates how well the variance in the dependent variable is explained by the model.

DISCUSSION AND CONCLUSION

As a result of the regression analysis conducted within the scope of the research, it was determined that organisational agility has a significant effect on sustainable competitive advantage. It fosters a culture of agility, innovation and continuous improvement in organisations and empowers people to share ideas and perspectives. Focusing on innovation enables organisations to develop new products, services and processes to meet changing customer needs and to improve overall performance. By consistently introducing new ideas and making enhancements, organisations set themselves apart from their rivals, ultimately attaining a lasting edge in the market. Similar to these results in the literature, there is a research conducted by Lee et al. (2008). According to the results obtained within the scope of the research, it is seen that organisational agility has a significant effect on sustainable competitive advantage

(SCA). In the research conducted by Sambamurthy et al. (2007), similar results were obtained in the research conducted by El Nsour (2021). In the research conducted by Almahamid et al. (2010) and in the research conducted by Medeiros and Maçada (2021), similar results were obtained. Notable research examples illustrating the correlation between e-HR and SCA consist of investigations conducted by Shamout et al. (2022) and Khammadee et al. (2023). These studies provide evidence that e-HR exerts a substantial influence on sustainable competitive advantage. These studies provide a basis for optimism that our research will provide similar outcomes. In a study conducted by Alqarni et al. (2023) with 313 employees of a firm in Egypt, it was determined that organisational agility and E-HRM affect SCA.

Electronic human resources in organisations is a factor that increases and facilitates the desire for skills, learning and development. In addition, organisational employees who have the chance to learn about new trends can develop a mindset that embraces competitive advantage. Based on these results, it is necessary to provide in-service training for the employees in order for the people working in the accommodation sector to contribute to the sustainable competitive advantage of the organisation they work for. In addition, it may be recommended to hold information meetings for employees to adopt the corporate governance approach. In order to increase the level of organisational agility in the accommodation sector, it is necessary to shape the management team accordingly and encourage employees to exhibit more agile behaviours. In addition, human resource professionals in organisations should encourage employee mobility, help discover unknown talent and create an adaptive, ethical and empowered culture. It is also important to create job descriptions that focus on rapid skills development rather than rigid job descriptions, and to support organisational redesign to enable problem solving. Human resource management in organisations can support the agile business model by hiring appropriate people. In addition, they can use performance appraisals that do not kill collaboration and implement work policies with appropriate flexibility. In addition, the steps to be taken by organisations for organisational agility should be to establish a strong communication network within the team, to make decisions at functional points instead of making decisions from a single centre, to make simple short-term plans, and to increase product and service quality.

Since every work done in organisations is ultimately done by human resources, in order for an organisation to be agile, it is important that all human resources, starting from the management level, adapt to the agile organisational structure and strategies. The main difference between inertial organisations and agile organisations emerges at this point. However, processes should also be designed to support the agility of human resources and functioning. Removing obstacles and bottlenecks in processes is an important way to eliminate inertia in organisations and people. Being an agile organisation and acting accordingly at every stage has become a requirement of today's competitive conditions. The innate agile processes that emerge every day lead organisations to get rid of inertia and to follow the latest technological developments more closely. With globalisation, international competition conditions as well as national competition conditions are changing rapidly. The most important question for the future is whether organizations can adopt agile management by abandoning old management approaches. It states that entrepreneurial activity in an environment where hospitality firms have varying levels of knowledge or (lack of) knowledge requires alertness to opportunities. In order for organisations in the hospitality sector to increase their agility, it is important that they continuously learn from their successes and failures and monitor previously unnoticed aspects of the market through trial and error experience, research and imagination. An agile organisation should have the flexibility to take advantage of every opportunity that will provide it with competitive advantage and should be open to all kinds of innovation and cooperation in order to gain these advantages.

In order for organisations to maintain their presence in the market by maintaining or increasing their profitability, they need to respond to customer demands with lower costs than their competitors, produce value for the customer, and be the first to offer the product change to the market by noticing the changing customer demands before the competitors. For this reason, there are some issues to create sustainable competitive advantage against competitors. Even if organisations offer the highest level product, quality will vary according to how much the product meets the needs of the customer. In other words, a customer who encounters a product that does not meet their needs will not be interested in the high level technology or modern product design used in the product. For this reason, if they want to meet the needs of their customers, they must constantly interact, learn what they demand, and create better products by working together. When it comes to creating sustainable competitive advantage, most managers focus on the features of their products or the value they create for their stakeholders, but if the employees are not given the necessary value and importance, it will not be possible to reach the desired point no matter how hard they work. One of the things that determines an organisation's reputation and therefore its attractiveness for investors is known as employee turnover rates. In order to have a profitable organisation in the long term and to maintain competitive advantage, it is essential to start from within. It is necessary to give employees the opportunity to stay in the organisation for a long time, to feel that they belong to the organisation and to create more value. Employees who feel that they belong to the organisation and believe that they are valued can develop projects that will create great value for their organisations in the long run. Employees who are open to sharing knowledge through activities such as continuous business development, open communication and mentoring are therefore making efforts to move their organisations forward. Therefore, before starting to think outside the organisation, it is necessary to satisfy the employees and give importance to creating a supportive ecosystem where they can express themselves, participate in the decision-making process and share authority and be proud of their achievements beyond being a business where they only receive their salaries. Nowadays, a large part of the activities that take place within an organisation can be done through computers and automation; even more value can be created by performing much more efficiently than people do. In order to enable employees to focus on areas where they can create higher value, we can reduce costs, increase efficiency and create much more value for all our stakeholders at the same time by regularly receiving and continuously analysing the data of activities such as production, transport, distribution, etc., where technology is used. In order for organizations to achieve sustainable success in the long term and to gain competitive advantage and protect their assets, it is important that they approach sustainability from a pluralistic perspective. In the final analysis, improvements in all these areas are necessary to increase and maintain profitability, which is the main purpose of an organization. Saving wasted time and resources by increasing efficiency rather than reducing costs to the lowest possible level in every field to ensure profitability. It becomes important to shift the saved resources and labor to different areas that will create more value. It is not possible for an organization operating in the tourism and accommodation sector to maintain its competitive advantage with physical resources for a long time. Because rival organizations are constantly changing physically. This tends to minimize the competitiveness of the organization. At the same time, many accommodation sector companies do not invest in human resources as they do in their physical resources. Human resources, which is a non-physical element and seen as a strategic resource, is considered the most important asset of organizations. The simultaneous production and delivery of services in the tourism and accommodation sector further increases the importance of human resources management. It is possible for organizations to gain competitive advantage in the long term, especially with the human resources capabilities they have. Therefore, it can be stated that tourism enterprises' long-term competitive advantage depends on the knowledge, talent and creativity of their human resources. An accommodation sector business with inimitable human resources capabilities provides sustainable competitive advantage and superior performance with organizational agility.

Agility increases customer satisfaction by continuously adapting to customers' changing priorities. It reduces risk by bringing the most valuable products and features to market in a more predictable way. It enhances the organisational experience by transforming multi-disciplinary team members into collaborative colleagues. It builds mutual respect and trust, greatly reducing the time wasted micromanaging unit roles and allowing senior managers to devote themselves to more value-added work that only they can do.

REFERENCES

Alkhodary, D. (2021). The impact of e-HRM on corporates sustainability: A study on the SMES in Jordan. *International Journal of Entrepreneurship*, 25(6), 1–15.

Almahamid, S., Awwad, A., & McAdams, A. C. (2010). Effects of organizational agility and knowledge sharing on competitive advantage: An empirical study in Jordan. *International Journal of Management*, 27(3), 387–408.

Alqarni, K., Agina, M. F., Khairy, H. A., Al-Romeedy, B. S., Farrag, D. A., & Abdallah, R. M. (2023). The Effect of Electronic Human Resource Management Systems on Sustainable Competitive Advantages: The Roles of Sustainable Innovation and Organizational Agility. *Sustainability (Basel)*, 15(23), 163–182. 10.3390/su152316382

Alshibly, H. H., & Alzubi, K. N. (2022). Unlock the black box of remote e-working effectiveness and e-HRM practices effect on organizational commitment. *Cogent Business & Management*, 9(1), 215–225. 10.1080/23311975.2022.2153546

Aydin, K. (2016). *Elektronik insan kaynakları yönetimi uygulamaları ve inovasyon performansı* (Master's thesis). Bahçeşehir University.

Beadles, N. A.II, Lowery, C. M., & Johns, K. (2005). The impact of human resource information systems: An exploratory study in the public sector. *Communications of the IIMA*, 5(4), 6–15.

Chakravarty, A., Grewal, R., & Sambamurthy, V. (2013). Information technology competencies, organizational agility, and firm performance: Enabling and facilitating roles. *Information Systems Research*, 24(4), 976–997. 10.1287/isre.2013.0500

Charbonnier-Voirin, A. (2011). The development and partial testing of the psychometric properties of a measurement scale of organizational agility. *M@n@gement*, 14(2), 119-156.

De Alwis, A. C., Andrlić, B., & Šostar, M. (2022). The Influence of E-HRM on modernizing the role of HRM context. *Economies*, 10(8), 181–202. 10.3390/economies10080181

El Nsour, J. A. (2021). 'Investigating the impact of organizational agility on the competitive advantage'. *Journal of Governance and Regulation*, 10(1), 10–22.

Ge, B., Yang, Y., Jiang, D., Gao, Y., Du, X., & Zhou, T. (2018). An empirical study on green innovation strategy and sustainable competitive advantages: Path and boundary. *Sustainability (Basel)*, 10(10), 3631–3652. 10.3390/su10103631

George, D., & Mallery, M. (2010). *SPSS for Windows step by step: A simple guide and reference*. Allyn & Bacon.

Hossain, M. A., Akter, S., & Yanamandram, V. (2021). Why doesn't our value creation payoff: Unpacking customer analytics-driven value creation capability to sustain competitive advantage. *Journal of Business Research*, 131, 287–296. 10.1016/j.jbusres.2021.03.063

Iqbal, A. (2019). The strategic human resource management approaches and organisational performance: The mediating role of creative climate. *Journal of Advances in Management Research*, 16(2), 181–193. 10.1108/JAMR-11-2017-0104

Khammadee, P. (2023). The Relationship Between E-HRM Practices and Organizational Performance: The Mediating Role of Organizational Agility and Sustainable Competitive Advantage. *SSRN*, 6(1), 1–21. 10.2139/ssrn.4546511

Kim, J. H., Seok, B. I., Choi, H. J., Jung, S. H., & Yu, J. P. (2020). Sustainable management activities: A study on the relations between technology commercialization capabilities, sustainable competitive advantage, and business performance. *Sustainability (Basel)*, 12(19), 7913–7923. 10.3390/su12197913

Kuo, Y. K., Khan, T. I., Islam, S. U., Abdullah, F. Z., Pradana, M., & Kaewsaeng-On, R. (2022). Impact of green HRM practices on environmental performance: The mediating role of green innovation. *Frontiers in Psychology*, 13, 1–12. 10.3389/fpsyg.2022.91672335774953

Lee, O. K. D., Sambamurthy, V., Lim, K., & Wei, K. K. (2008). IT-enabled organizational agility and sustainable competitive advantage. *Vallabhajosyula and Lim, Kai and Wei, KK, IT-Enabled Organizational Agility and Sustainable Competitive Advantage*.

Mahdi, O. R., & Nassar, I. A. (2021). The business model of sustainable competitive advantage through strategic leadership capabilities and knowledge management processes to overcome covid-19 pandemic. *Sustainability (Basel)*, 13(17), 9891–9912. 10.3390/su13179891

Medeiros, M. M. D., & Maçada, A. C. G. (2022). Competitive advantage of data-driven analytical capabilities: The role of big data visualization and of organizational agility. *Management Decision*, 60(4), 953–975. 10.1108/MD-12-2020-1681

Melián-Alzola, L., Domínguez-Falcón, C., & Martín-Santana, J. D. (2020). The role of the human dimension in organizational agility: An empirical study in intensive care units. *Personnel Review*, 49(9), 1945–1964. 10.1108/PR-08-2019-0456

Nyathi, M. (2024). The effect of electronic human resource management on electronic human resource management macro-level consequences: The role of perception of organizational politics. *African Journal of Economic and Management Studies*, 15(1), 1–14. 10.1108/AJEMS-04-2022-0168

Ramadan, M., Bou Zakhem, N., Baydoun, H., Daouk, A., Youssef, S., El Fawal, A., Elia, J., & Ashaal, A. (2023). Toward Digital Transformation and Business Model Innovation: The Nexus between Leadership, Organizational Agility, and Knowledge Transfer. *Administrative Sciences*, 13(8), 185–195. 10.3390/admsci13080185

Remondino, M., & Zanin, A. (2022). Logistics and agri-food: Digitization to increase competitive advantage and sustainability. Literature review and the case of Italy. *Sustainability (Basel)*, 14(2), 787–799. 10.3390/su14020787

Sambamurthy, V., Wei, K. K., Lim, K., & Lee, D. (2007). IT-enabled organizational agility and firms' sustainable competitive advantage. *ICIS 2007 proceedings*, 91-100.

Shamout, M., Elayan, M., Rawashdeh, A., Kurdi, B., & Alshurideh, M. (2022). E-HRM practices and sustainable competitive advantage from HR practitioner's perspective: A mediated moderation analysis. *International Journal of Data and Network Science*, 6(1), 165–178. 10.5267/j.ijdns.2021.9.011

Singh, P., & Koneru, K. (2022). A mediated moderation analysis of E-HRM practises and long-term competitive advantage from the perspective of HR practitioners. *Journal of Positive School Psychology*, 6(3), 4436–4458.

Sun, J., Sarfraz, M., Turi, J. A., & Ivascu, L. (2022). Organizational agility and sustainable manufacturing practices in the context of emerging economy: A mediated moderation model. *Processes (Basel, Switzerland)*, 10(12), 25–67. 10.3390/pr10122567

Walter, A. T. (2021). Organizational agility: Ill-defined and somewhat confusing? A systematic literature review and conceptualization. *Management Review Quarterly*, 71(2), 343–391. 10.1007/s11301-020-00186-6

Chapter 11
The Importance of Organizational Collaborative Strategic Actions of Independent Actors in Enhancing the Potential of Tourism Destination Management

Muhammed A. Yetgin
University of Karabük, Turkey

Kasım Yılmaz
University of Karabük, Turkey

Volkan Temizkan
https://orcid.org/0000-0002-1162-7912
University of Karabük, Turkey

ABSTRACT

On the UNESCO World Heritage List, Safranbolu is an essential tourist city in Turkey and internationally. Visited by thousands of tourists from Europe, the Far East, and other regions every year, Safranbolu is an attractive cultural tourism destination with its historic mansions, fountains, inns, baths, mosques, remarkable nature, traditional handicrafts, and local cuisine. Developing a city's tourism potential depends on the cooperation and coordination of stakeholders. Strategic

DOI: 10.4018/979-8-3693-5405-6.ch011

Copyright © 2024, IGI Global. Copying or distributing in print or electronic forms without written permission of IGI Global is prohibited.

cooperation increases efficiency and performance. The primary purpose of this study is to understand and reveal the importance of collaborative action styles of independent actors in expanding the potential of Safranbolu tourism destinations. In the study, data was collected through the qualitative interview method. According to the data obtained, it has been observed that stakeholders' collaborative action styles and techniques in Safranbolu tourism could be more effective at the expected level. For this reason, stakeholders need to act in coordination with an ordinary mind and develop effective strategies.

1. INTRODUCTION

In the 19th and 20th centuries, Safranbolu managed to preserve its historical texture and was included in the UNESCO World Heritage List in 1994 (Sevim et al., 2013). Safranbolu has become an important cultural tourism destination with its cultural heritage and its success in protecting this heritage. The known history of Safranbolu in antiquity dates back to 3000 BC (Kara, 2017). Traces of Hittite, Phrygian, Lydian, Persian, Hellenistic, Roman, Byzantine, and Ottoman civilizations can be seen in the region (Bozkurt, 2013). The Paflagonian region mentioned in Homer's Iliad epic is where Safranbolu is located (Bogenç & Sabaz, 2019). The city, a trade center during the Byzantine period, was known as "Dadybra," and Safranbolu, which joined the Ottoman lands in the 14th century, became an important trade center (Canbulat, 2020). Safranbolu, which produces and sells saffron and takes its name from this spice, has provided itself with an essential source of income (Khan, 2020). Today, the district continues producing saffron, the world's highest quality saffron.

In addition, Safranbolu's location on the transit route to the port of Bartın made it one of the resting routes for merchants (Özdemir, 2011a). Many mansions, mosques, madrasahs, baths, and fountains were built in the 17th and 18th centuries. Many existing mansions, which reflect the best examples of wooden architecture, were also built in this period.

Safranbolu's world fame is the preservation of Safranbolu Houses from the 18th and 19th centuries. Thus, the destination allows tourists to travel back in time with the preserved Ottoman Empire architecture and experience Turkish society's city life and culture. Today, the district, an "open-air museum," attracts many tourists, especially from the Far East. According to 2023 data, 1.2 million domestic and foreign tourists visited the district (Anadolu Agency, 2024). In addition to its historical values, Safranbolu has the potential to appeal to different tourism areas with its canyons, caves, ruins, and springs.

The Importance

Since Safranbolu has a cultural heritage from the past, it stands out not only with its architecture but also with its local cuisine, music, folk dances, and traditional handicrafts and crafts. Safranbolu has become a brand, especially in the production of Turkish delight, one of the most delicious and special desserts of Turkish cuisine (Diker et al., 2017). Safranbolu Turkish delight has been produced in this region using traditional methods since the 16th century and exported to many parts of the world.

Despite this potential, Safranbolu cannot attract enough tourists. Safranbolu has excellent potential beyond being a destination with its Ottoman houses, sidewalks, and Turkish delight. All local actors must develop projects on a common ground to unlock this potential. The same determination and cooperation should be maintained in realizing the projects on which consensus is reached. Support and investments such as transportation, accommodation, and promotion should be made in the region rather than just improving the current situation or creating new alternatives with the available opportunities.

In addition to its historic houses and cobblestones, Safranbolu has excellent potential for nature tourism. In its unique canyons and caves, climbing and trekking can be done. In addition, visitors can have different experiences with bungalow tourism facilities built around the canyons. One of Safranbolu's most significant advantages is that the locals have been familiar with tourism and tourists for years. For this reason, local people are incredibly polite and interested in tourists. For this reason, the local people will quickly adopt the projects produced in Safranbolu.

It is known that tourism cooperation makes a significant contribution to the economy of the city and the national income of the country. The ability of independent actors to make joint decisions is essential in increasing tourism potential. The adoption and applicability of joint choices are high. If this coordination among actors is not ensured, effective tourism policies cannot be produced, and there will be disruptions in implementing existing policies. Considering the contribution of tourism to national income, tourism policies need to be addressed not only on a local scale but also on a national scale. However, if local actors apply to national actors with the projects they produce, they will solve the problems more quickly and efficiently.

Despite their dedication, some local actors may need help to produce effective tourism policies. National authorities in the field of tourism are more seasoned and experienced, as they follow the performance and practices of many tourism destinations. National tourism decision-makers should prepare specific strategic plans for the country's major tourism destinations.

With its potential, Safranbolu is considered one of the places where a national strategic plan should be produced in this context. By acting together, Safranbolu's local actors can increase the competitiveness and diversity of the products and services offered in the destination. This cooperation will also improve the quality of the overall experience in Safranbolu. Conflicts of interest, different priorities, and goals of different actors in the destination are among the biggest obstacles to cooperation.

Furthermore, the lack of effective communication and trust among actors poses a significant challenge to sustaining such collaborations. While initial collaborations may show promise, they often falter or remain incomplete due to resource constraints. To fully realize the potential of cooperation, all actors must adopt a common mission and vision, a step that can help overcome these challenges and ensure the sustainability of collaborative efforts.

Transparent communication between actors will prevent trust issues and conflicts of interest. Actors motivated around a common goal will be willing to finance emerging projects. At this point, actors should first examine the destinations that have realized successful cooperation on a national scale.

Cappadocia is one of the most essential destinations we can point to as an example of successful cooperation in cultural tourism. All actors and local people in Cappadocia are motivated to work together to promote and develop regional tourism. Safranbolu could adopt this type of cooperation and increase its projects' and promotional activities' quality and diversity.

In this respect, the cooperation of local actors will contribute to ensuring sustainability by making tourism's environmental and socio-economic impacts manageable. Within Sustainable Tourism, cooperation plays a vital role in preserving Safranbolu's local architecture and texture, minimizing the adverse effects that may harm this texture, and ensuring that tourism continues in the long term. In this respect, cooperation is an essential element of sustainable tourism. Because all actors agree on the protection and development of the natural and cultural resources of the destination, the cooperation of local actors will contribute to sustainability in many aspects, such as reducing environmental impacts, managing socio-cultural impacts, increasing economic benefits, and developing capacity.

This study aims to reveal the need for independent actors to cooperate in realizing ideas and projects to increase Safranbolu's tourism potential. Data were collected through semi-structured interviews with 15 independent actors selected through Purposeful Sampling. The data were organized and content analyzed using MAX-QDA qualitative data analysis version 10.0 software.

The findings show that independent actors intend to cooperate in developing tourism in Safranbolu. However, since this cannot be organized under an institutional roof, ideas and projects must be undertaken individually. This leads to the failure to realize significant and essential projects with high effectiveness that will reveal Safranbolu's real potential and a single actor cannot overcome that. This study contributes to the literature showing the importance of independent actors cooperating to increase tourism potential.

Keywords: Safranbolu, Tourism actors, Collaborative behavior

2. THEORETICAL BACKGROUND

2.1. Tourism Potential of Safranbolu

Safranbolu, located in the Western Black Sea Region of Turkey, in the province of Karabük, is a historical city that is recognized on the world stage, stands out with its cultural tourism potential, and continues to attract more and more attention every day (Kara, 2017). While nature and sea tourism are available in many places, cultural tourism destinations with a historical background are limited (Bandeoğlu, 2015). For this reason, Safranbolu has excellent potential for cultural tourism due to its historical past and the preservation of the texture of this past. Especially in the city has many historical mansions, inns, baths, fountains, and mosques (Özmen & Eren, 2021). Yörük Village, which is also very close to Safranbolu, is a vital tourism center that complements Safranbolu with its historical streets, traditional houses, laundries, tombstones, square and fountains (Dönmez et al., 2015). In addition, the fact that Safranbolu is located in the middle of destinations with historical and natural beauties, such as Amasra and Kastamonu, expands the product range of tour operators. These destinations, which complement and strengthen Safranbolu, make Safranbolu the starting point of tour itineraries (Özdemir, 2011).

In addition, the fact that Safranbolu is in the category of calm/quiet cities (Cittaslow) has contributed to Safranbolu's world fame by enabling it to be included in both UNESCO and the calm city category (TRT Haber, 2024). The fact that Safranbolu is close to the Black Sea and has the characteristics of this Black Sea region makes this region rich in nature tourism. Its unique canyons, caves, plateaus, forests, and lakes create a favorable environment for nature and camping tourism. Safranbolu's unique traditional and local dishes and various types of handicrafts stand out as elements that increase and complement the cultural richness of this region (Ayyıldız, 2019). These handicrafts include Wood carving, blacksmithing, coppersmithing, saddlers, shoemaking, leatherwork, and coppersmithing (Sağır, 2013).

There are many other districts of Karabük close to this destination, located in the Safranbolu district of Karabük province. Different districts of Karabük have excellent tourism potential. However, they are not as well known as Safranbolu and cannot receive investment. If the necessary investments are made to reveal the existing potential of these districts in the future, their tourism potential will be shown. Especially the Hadrianapolis ruins and thermal water resources of Eskipazar district and the forest and nature flora of Yenicenin are essential locations that can increase the tourism diversity of Safranbolu tourism destination (Nayim & Yaman, 2019). Research was conducted on the development of agrotourism in Safranbolu. The city has fertile soils, mainly vineyards and fruit and vegetable cultivation. In this research, the areas of the city's natural and cultural features related to the use of agricultural tourism were queried and mapped in the Geographic Information System environment (Kiper & Arslan, 2009).

Local tourists contribute significantly to the development of sustainable tourism in Safranbolu. Local tourists' restaurants, accommodation, transportation, and shopping activities strengthen the local economy. Local tourists buying local products, visiting the historical and natural beauties of the country, and following the arts and crafts of the city with interest are among the factors affecting sustainable tourism in the region.

2.2. Obstacles to Safranbolu Tourism Potential

Various problems in tourism infrastructure (transportation, accommodation, food and beverage, infrastructure and facilities, entertainment activities, marketing, and promotion) are among the most critical obstacles to Safranbolu tourism (Diker & Çetinkaya, 2016). It is known that the idle capacity of hotels is very high except for national holidays. It is stated that the service quality of hotels operating with deficient capacities except for national holidays and weekends is not at the desired levels due to price competition. For this reason, the fact that the hotel's service quality is below the standards leads to a decrease in customer satisfaction. This indirectly affects Safranbolu's tourism potential. In addition, the fact that hotels often work with idle capacity, especially in the winter season, prevents the employment of qualified personnel (Selvi & Şahin, 2012). Again, this situation negatively affects customer satisfaction by reducing service quality.

There is no organization promoting Safranbolu other than tour operators, and apart from tour operators, Safranbolu is advertised by visitors through social media posts (Ceylan & Somuncu, 2016). Apart from these, no organization promotes Safranbolu tourism on a national and international scale. Although Safranbolu contains many types of tourism, it has not gone beyond cultural tourism. It cannot even fully sustain cultural tourism. Shopkeepers who focus on the sale of Turkish delights and souvenirs divert the attention of tourists who want to focus on the nature of cultural tourism. In addition, services to represent cultural tourism are not offered and products are not sold in this direction. For example, even a model of the Cinci Inn, which is identified with Safranbolu, is not sold (Karagöz, 2022). The products currently sold are both expensive and of low quality. In addition, it is seen that there is little diversity and similar products. It is observed that the products sold are ordinary products that can be found in almost every destination other than Safranbolu. If products specific to Safranbolu culture are designed and sold, this will both increase the sale of souvenirs and provide a better advertisement for Safranbolu.

The Importance

One of the most critical obstacles to Safranbolu's potential is the traffic problem (Dönmez et al., 2016). Although many attempts have been made to solve this problem, which everyone agrees on, a natural and permanent solution has not been produced. There is a significant traffic congestion and parking lot problem at the destination, where thousands of visitors flock, especially on weekends. This situation hinders tourists who want to shop comfortably and reach their hotels by car. On the other hand, attention is drawn to the lack of arrangements for disabled individuals (Diker & Çetinkaya, 2016). Considering the number of disabled people in our country, the number of disabled tourists constitutes a serious potential. Arrangements in this direction will increase the number of disabled tourists in the region.

One of Safranbolu tourism's biggest criticisms is that the destination's recreation and entertainment activities must be increased (Tipolojileri, 2020). Tourists who enjoy the region's historical beauties during the day complain that there are no activities to do after dark. The fact that both the hotels and the bazaar shopkeepers need to organize entertainment activities causes tourists to get bored throughout the night. This situation causes bored tourists not to want to stay in Safranbolu one more night.

Many complaints exist about the number of overnight stays tourists visit Safranbolu. However, this situation is also due to the nature of cultural tourism. Tourists usually visit the destinations they have visited for cultural tourism once in their lives. Because they have not seen the same region several times, like sea tourism, due to cultural tourism, the area cannot bring back the old customers, so it always has to find new visitors.

Potential hazards in Safranbolu tourism Özmen & Eren (2021): Inadequacy of infrastructure and superstructure works; insufficient infrastructure and superstructure work, parking problems at tourist spots, especially in the Old Bazaar area, some roads are broken, the lifting capacity can be exceeded during peak tourism periods, insufficient promotion, transportation problems, lack of an airport, environmental pollution, failure to evaluate the potential of tourism diversity, accommodation, and food and beverage venues are small and suitable for boutique demand, which may create problems in meeting large-scale tours, the active role of people with insufficient tourism education in tourism activities, destruction of historical sites, lack of investment. According to Koçan et al. (2023), the potential dangers in the tourism of the city are the lack of recreation areas, the neglect of the stream in the area, rural infrastructure inadequacies, the elderly population, insufficient emphasis on agriculture, inadequate public transportation, the migration of the young population from rural areas, the concentration of investments in education, health, etc. in the provincial center. According to Gürbüz (2003), one of the most critical problems experienced by Safranbolu tourism today is the short length of stay of visitors, so potential touristic products should be made suitable for use to extend the length of stay of visitors. According to Diker and Çetinkaya (2016), obstacles that make it difficult for disabled tourists to visit the city's tourist attractions are listed, and measures are recommended.

2.3. The Importance of Cooperative Action of Independent Actors in Increasing Tourism Potential

In tourism, companies engaged in transportation activities by land, air, and sea, tour operators, or accommodation businesses are the first to come to mind as the decisive actors that will bring success. These businesses do not motivate tourists to make their trips; they only facilitate their work. The factors that encourage tourists to visit are education, media, environmental management practices, governmental practices and policies, and technological factors (Coathup, 1999).

The purpose of education is to inform. It is necessary to reveal the elements of touristic value available at the destination and convey this to the target audiences. Information should be provided for the target tourist audience and the people living in the destination. Only in this way can tourist communication with local people be made healthy. To offer a healthy touristic product, it is imperative to understand what motivates tourists. It is essential to get the support of the press in tourism activities. This support can only be provided through sound management practices. Since the press is interested in what stands out and attracts attention due to its nature, a good product and practice can attract the media's attention, just as a bad event or practice can arouse interest similarly. Another critical issue in terms of tourism is physical and social environmental practices. Physical practices are related to nature conservation, while social practices are related to unfavorable human rights conditions. Tourism facilitators may be concerned about sending tourists to destinations that need better environmental practices. Governments and local practitioners are the actors that set the basic framework for tourism, and their practices are decisive in this respect. Finally, lagging behind technological innovations is an essential factor that can lead to losing interest in a destination over time. Constructive cooperation between facilitating and motivating actors is necessary for the success of tourism activities. Sustainable tourism is based on creating successful products/services and practical collaboration between stakeholders to achieve this result. The efforts of stakeholders in implementing the identified strategies are directly proportional to their expectations. Stakeholders are also actors in the tourism sector. These actors can include a wide range of institutions, organizations, businesses, and individuals. Figure 1 illustrates the dimensions of strategy development activities by independent actors concerning a tourist destination (Lopes et al., 2016).

Figure 1. Key Dimensions in Determining Tourism Destination Strategies (Lopes, 2016)

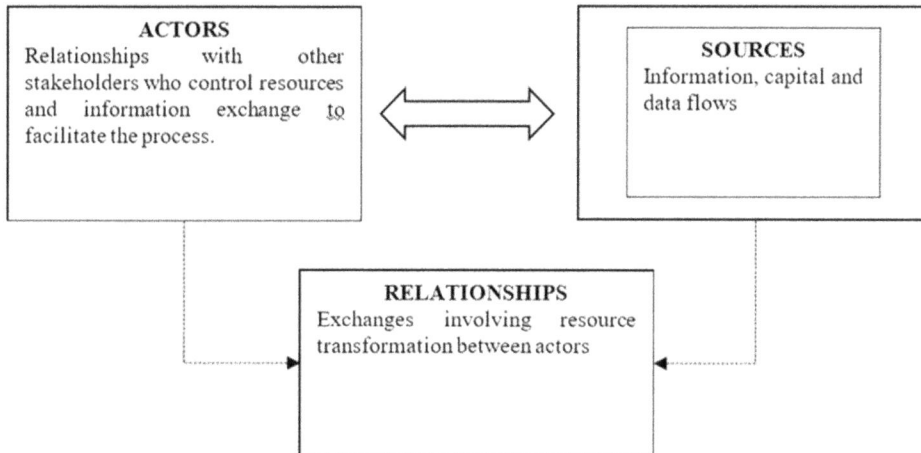

The interdependence of stakeholders in tourism requires these elements to participate in an effective network. The basis for creating management networks is cooperative actions and activities. This cooperation makes it possible to establish new organizations to ensure sustainable tourism. There are two types of management networks. The first is policy and planning networks, and the second is self-governing action networks. Policy and planning networks arise from the need to facilitate joint action and cooperation between ministries, local authorities, and all other stakeholders. Self-governing action networks are voluntary collaborations that occur in specific circumstances. Strategic tourism initiatives should be supported by the government, private sector, democratic mass organizations, professional and voluntary community organizations in cooperation (Erkuş-Öztürk & Eraydın, 2010).

Creating value for tourists in tourist areas is carried out directly or indirectly by many organizations and people. These include local authorities, businesses supplying goods and services, and people living there. Actors interacting at national, international, and local levels are mutually interdependent. At each stage of the value creation process, individual actors need the outputs of others as their inputs (March & Wilkinson, 2009). Proactive recognition of threats and opportunities that the sector may face is more easily realized through the interaction of actors, even if they are competitors. The cooperation of all actors contributes to tackling unemployment at the national level and developing and growing local resources.

On the topic of strategic cooperation in tourism, Gori, Fissi, and Romolini (2021) conducted a study in Tuscany, Italy, and concluded that if there is an opportunity for non-pressured dialogue between actors in the field of tourism, an environment of consensus can emerge, different viewpoints can appear. Strategic planning and expansions can be achieved in cooperation. This study has shown that the participation of public authorities plays a decisive role in determining and implementing appropriate strategies. Still, it is also essential to ensure that all stakeholders participate in decision-making, considering social, economic, cultural, and other multidimensional factors. It is also important to note that selecting a third party as the project leader in these initiatives effectively ensures that cooperation activities are not politicized (Gori, Fissi, and Romolini, 2021). The cooperation activities implemented in the Tuscany region took place within the framework of a communication protocol prepared in advance. They involved a large number of independent actors such as the airport authority, chamber of commerce, cultural association, destination observatory authority, municipality, port authority, non-profit organizations, private research organizations, public finance authority, social associations, sports organizations, sustainability and tourism-related organizations, trade unions, travel businesses, and universities.

Strategic cooperation efforts need to be carried out not only in the planning phase but also in the implementation phase. This necessity forces stakeholders to adopt a collaborative participatory management approach. According to Emerson et al. (2011), collaborative management is defined as 'constructively mobilizing people together through public institutions, various levels of government, and private organizations to constructively create public policy decision-making structures to achieve a societal goal that could not otherwise be achieved' (Emerson et al., 2012).

The main dimensions of collaborative management in tourism are accountability, transparency, participation, appropriate organizational structure, effectiveness, and authority (Zeppel, 2012). The core dimensions point to the characteristics that the stakeholders who will participate in collaborative activities in the field of tourism and the new organizations that may be formed as a result of cooperation should have. As a result, collaborative activities in tourism encourage participation and consensus in decision-making processes between public institutions and multiple stakeholder actors (Barandiaran et al., 2019).

3. METHOD

Primary data collection methods are widely used in exploratory research. This study conducted in-depth interviews to collect qualitative and direct data (Burns and Bush, 2017). In this way, ideas and opinions on "the importance of collaborative action styles of independent actors in increasing the potential of a tourism destination" can be obtained. In this study, where in-depth interviews were conducted using a qualitative approach, the researchers collected data and information from stakeholders who knew about Safranbolu tourism through semi-unstructured interviews. The interviewees were asked a single question to reveal their thoughts. This question was: Can you tell us about the importance of collaborative actions by independent actors in increasing the potential of Safranbolu tourism destination? The interviews ranged from 30 minutes to 1 hour on average. The sample of 8 people determined according to the purposive sampling method consists of the following people. Face-to-face interviews were conducted with eight people, 3 of whom were public institution managers, tourism company owners, tradespeople operating in the destination, academicians at Karabük University, foreign tourists, and local tourists. Interviews with the managers were conducted in their offices. The interviews were conducted between March 25 and April 7. In order not to distract the participants, a recording device was not used during the interviews. Still, the answers the participants gave were transferred to a piece of paper immediately after the interviews. This facilitated the content analysis process. The data were analyzed using MAXQDA 10.0 software.

4. FINDINGS AND DISCUSSIONS

Stakeholders were asked the following interview questions to understand the importance of collaborative action styles of independent actors in increasing a tourism destination's potential. The responses from 8 interviewees are given below. The answers of the interviewees are coded as Answer 1, Answer 2, Answer 8.

Question: Could you please tell us about the importance of independent actors' collaborative action styles in increasing the potential of Safranbolu Tourism Destination?

Answer 1 (Public Institution A): Safranbolu, like any other tourism region, faces a range of issues that require attention. As tourism managers and planners, we are actively involved in addressing these issues, often through frequent meetings with relevant stakeholders. However, the unique aspect of Safranbolu being a small district, coupled with the influence of powerful local families, can sometimes hinder institutional decision-making processes.

However, the protection of Safranbolu's historical texture and the investments made by these families in this region must be addressed. If the local authorities open the decisions to be taken about Safranbolu to public debate beforehand and take the opinions of the local people, the projects will be implemented faster. To ensure innovation and development, the current situation needs to change. Especially local people usually resist change. Change brings with it unknowns, and these unknowns cause fear. Therefore, if the reasons and benefits of structural changes are explained to the local people beforehand, this situation will be overcome faster. To make Safranbolu more valuable and to preserve its historical texture for many years, its supply should be restricted, and the necessary price tariffs should be adjusted. For this, the tradespeople operating in the tourism region must be trained to raise awareness. Faster and more effective results will be obtained when tradespeople, municipalities and non-governmental organizations, universities, district governorships, and other public and private institutions act together and make joint decisions to increase quality.

Answer 2 (Public Institution B): It is essential to produce public policies for tourism. However, this requires educated and dedicated staff. It is known that when human resources with this awareness are directed correctly, they will make significant contributions to the development and change of that city. Especially in tourism regions, the decisions to be taken will be more effective and appropriate when working with specialized and competent personnel in the field of tourism. Otherwise, tourism decision-makers who do not have a good command of the region will not produce effective policies and will not contribute positively to tourism development. It is essential to create statistics and information from data on tourism development. Information is the most crucial driving force in increasing the quality of the service to be provided. Developed countries, especially those leading in tourism, attach great importance to tourism statistics and improve their tourism potential by developing plans and projects based on these statistics. Public institutions showing themselves in the field will significantly contribute to the perception of a safe tourism region. Today's tourists attach importance to the security of the destination as much as the beauty of the destination. In this respect, when public institutions, local people, and tradespeople act together and join hands for the tourism destination's peace and security, they will attract more tourists by increasing the peace and attractiveness of the destination.

Answer 3 (Public Institution C): In places where cultural tourism is practiced, tourism guidance is as necessary as tourism. Guidance services should be provided not only to tourists coming with tour companies but also to independent tourists. Historical buildings and structures are essential in regions where cultural tourism is practiced. However, these structures need to be explained to visitors. With the development of technology, the history of significant buildings can be conveyed much more effectively and efficiently through digital tablets. In addition, if information on specific products sold can be provided in different languages, cultural tourism will be one step closer to its goal. If public and private institutions are open to cooperation in tourism development, the emerging ideas and products will benefit all segments. Because when the region develops and is in demand, all segments will help.

Answer 4 (Tourism company): Economic barriers, inadequate infrastructure, insufficient foreign language skills, and legal barriers hinder tourism development. Therefore, Safranbolu Tourism can strengthen by overcoming these obstacles through public and private sector cooperation. Price competition in Safranbolu sometimes leads to a decrease in service quality. Therefore, tourist satisfaction in Safranbolu decreases, affecting the destination's image and visitor loyalty. Safranbolu is a brand. However, very few activities and studies are carried out to increase the image of this brand. The only way to attract tourists to the region is not to offer low prices but to create a good promotion and image. If not only cheap cars but also luxury cars are breaking sales records today, everyone should think about it.

Answer 5 (Business Owner): Safranbolu is a significant source of livelihood for both Karabük and Safranbolu districts. Safranbolu tradespeople had many difficulties, especially during the pandemic. The recovery process is almost still ongoing. For this reason, I believe that more promotion is needed to attract more tourists and increase tourism revenues. The tourism season in Safranbolu is generally limited to the summer months, which prevents the income from being distributed evenly over 12 months. We need to generate revenue in winter. For this reason, activities that will attract tourists to the region in winter should be carried out. The Karabük/Keltepe ski center should be used and promoted more effectively. Stakeholders should collaborate to develop winter tourism and take action in this direction.

Answer 6 (Academician): For tourism to reach certain levels, basic infrastructure problems must be completely solved. Transportation, accommodation, and food and beverage facilities should also reach sufficient levels. More recreational areas need to be created for tourists who are on the move in the destination all day long to have a pleasant time. This requires financial planning and investments by institutional and private stakeholders.

Answer 7 (Korean Foreign Tourist): I had an adequate historical and cultural experience during my visit here. However, I could not get much information about Safranbolu's culture, traditions, and buildings because the shopkeepers needed to speak English better. It would be easier to get information if technological devices were used to explore destinations. We can have a pleasant and comfortable time during the day, but at night, we get bored in Safranbolu. If the hotels and decision-makers can overcome this deficiency, we will have a better evening time.

Answer 8 (Local Tourist): The local people I talked to told me about the area's many natural beauties and canyons, but they said that I would not be able to see them without my car. If Safranbolu tourism is to be developed and diversified, transportation facilities should be facilitated, and the routes I was told about should be opened to transportation by the authorities. They also mentioned that there are no places to stay around the canyons. I can spend more time in Safranbolu if transportation to the canyons is provided and facilities and hotels are built for accommodation. Maybe I will come to Safranbolu again to see the canyons.

According to the official of Public Institution-A, the fact that local solid families in Safranbolu have a say in the region slows down institutional decision-making mechanisms. For this reason, public opinion should be created by first taking the views of local people. This would help projects to be implemented faster.

According to the Public Institution-B official, educated and dedicated staff are required to produce public policies for tourism. In addition, decisions to be taken will be more effective and appropriate when working with personnel who are experts in their fields and competent in tourism.

According to Public Institution C, guidance services in cultural tourism should be expanded, and digital technologies should be utilized to provide more efficient and effective information transfer to visitors.

Tourism Company officials say economic barriers, inadequate infrastructure, insufficient foreign language skills, and legal barriers hinder tourism development. With the cooperation of the public and private sectors, these barriers can be overcome, and Safranbolu tourism can gain strength.

According to the shopkeeper, the tourism season in Safranbolu is limited to the summer months. For this reason, activities that will attract tourists to the region should be carried out to generate income in the winter months. More effective use and promotion of the Karabük/Keltepe ski center would be essential.

Academicians believe that for tourism to reach certain levels, basic infrastructure problems must be solved, and recreation areas should be created.

According to the opinion of a Korean foreign tourist, insufficient English knowledge of shopkeepers, inadequate use of technology for exploring the destination, and lack of activities that can be done in the evenings negatively affect the tourism experience.

According to local tourists, facilitating transportation to natural beauties and canyons and increasing accommodation facilities near the canyons will enable them to spend more time in Safranbolu.

5. CONCLUSION

Safranbolu is one of Turkey's most important tourist destinations, with its historical texture and natural beauty. To utilize the city's tourism potential to its total capacity, some obstacles must be overcome, and independent actors must adopt a cooperative attitude. This study examines the importance of independent actors' cooperative behavior in increasing Safranbolu's tourism potential. Interviews were conducted with relevant stakeholders to obtain information in this direction. For Safranbolu to fully utilize its potential, all independent actors, such as public institutions, the private sector, NGOs, and local people, should act cooperatively.

The Importance

This cooperation will enable concrete steps to improve infrastructure, explore new destinations, increase product diversity, and activate promotional activities. In this context, the following recommendations are offered: Involving local people and civil society organizations in decision-making processes by taking their views with a participatory management approach, coordination of public and private sector investments in cooperation with an ordinary mind, development of tourism education and awareness programs, active use of technology in the development of tourism services, discovering new destinations (canyons) and promoting them to tourists, facilitating transportation facilities and rapid construction of accommodation facilities in new destinations to be opened, diversification of tourism products and highlighting traditional products, development of an effective promotion strategy.

The importance of stakeholder cooperation for sustainable tourism development in Safranbolu is emphasized. In tourism, where there are many stakeholders, such as government agencies, tourism companies, local citizens, foreign tourists, and non-governmental organizations, stakeholders must act together with an ordinary strategic mind. The sustainable cooperation of stakeholders is essential for the implementation of sustainable tourism policies. Stakeholders following a sustainable policy with the same goal in planning and decision-making processes will ensure that the needs and expectations of tourists for tourism are better perceived and that the necessary products and services are developed more effectively. Miscommunication and conflict between stakeholders will harm the region's tourism development. Each stakeholder may have different resources, so combining resources for a common strategic goal and collaboration between stakeholders will enable the development of new ideas and innovative solutions. Stakeholders must trust each other and respect each other's business approaches. Anticipating and eliminating issues that lead to stakeholder conflicts will enable them to communicate more transparently, pursue equal participatory policies, and meet common goals. The ability of public and private stakeholders in Safranbolu to work together and to better promote Safranbolu through nationally and internationally supported projects gives hope for the future of tourism in Safranbolu.

With the implementation of these recommendations, Safranbolu will be able to become a tourism destination at international standards and fully utilize its potential.

Authors' Contribution

The authors contributed equally to the literature and research section.

REFERENCES

Anadolu Agency. (2024). *Safranbolu 2023'te yaklaşık 1 milyon 200 bin ziyaretçi ağırladı*. https://www.aa.com.tr/tr/ekonomi/safranbolu-2023te-yaklasik-1-milyon -200-bin-ziyaretci-agirladi/3112177

Ayyıldız, S. (2019). Turistik konak işletmelerinde mutfağın fiziksel koşullarının önemi: Safranbolu yöresel mutfak mimarisi üzerine bir araştırma. *Karabük Üniversitesi Sosyal Bilimler Enstitüsü Dergisi*, 9(2), 610–625.

Bandeoğlu, Z. (2015). Türkiye'de kültür turizmi potansiyeli üzerine bir değerlendirme. *Kahramanmaraş Sütçü İmam Üniversitesi İktisadi ve İdari Bilimler Fakültesi Dergisi*, 5(02), 155–168.

Barandiaran, X., Restrepo, N., & Luna, Á. (2019). Collaborative governance in tourism: Lessons from Etorkizuna Eraikiz in the Basque Country, Spain. *Tourism Review*, 74(4), 902–914. 10.1108/TR-09-2018-0133

Bogenç, Ç. & Sabaz, M. (2019). Dünya miras alanı Safranbolu'nun alan yönetim planının geliştirilmesi sürecinde; tema, hedef ve eylemlerin belirlenmesi. *İnsan ve Toplum Bilimleri Araştırmaları Dergisi, 8*(3), 1526-1544.

Bozkurt, G. S. (2013). 19. yy da Osmanlı konut mimarisinde iç mekan kurgusunun Safranbolu evleri örneğinde irdelenmesi. *Istanbul Üniversitesi Orman Fakültesi Dergisi*, 62(2), 37–70.

Burns, A. C., & Bush, R. F. (2017). *Marketing Research* (8th ed.). Pearson.

Canbulat, İ. (2020). Seyahatname ve Yazılı Kaynaklarda Safranbolu. *Kitap içi (bu kitap çalışması) Makale*, 70-91.

Ceylan, S., & Somuncu, M. (2016). Kültür turizmi alanlarında turizmin çeşitlendirilmesine eleştirel bir bakış: Safranbolu UNESCO Dünya miras alanı. *Uluslararası Türk Dünyası Turizm Araştırmaları Dergisi*, 1(1), 53–64.

Coathup, D. C. (1999). Dominant actors in international tourism. *International Journal of Contemporary Hospitality Management*, 11(2/3), 69–72. 10.1108/09596119910250689

Diker, O., & Çetinkaya, A. (2016). Erişilebilir Turizm Açısından Safranbolu Turizm Destinasyonunun Uygunluğunun Değerlendirilmesi. *Karabük Üniversitesi Sosyal Bilimler Enstitüsü Dergisi*, (2), 111–125. 10.14230/joiss186

Diker, O. & Türker, N. & Çetinkaya, A. & Kaya, F. B. (2017). Geleneksel türk tatlısı olarak lokum ve safranbolu lokumu. *Journal of Tourism & Gastronomy Studies,* 5(Special Issue 2), 333-344.

Dönmez, Y., Cabuk, S., Öztürk, M., & Gokyer, E. (2016). Safranbolu Kentsel Sit Alanında otopark sorunu ve çözüm alternatifleri. *Bartin Orman Fakültesi Dergisi,* 18(2), 137–145. 10.24011/barofd.270063

Dönmez, Y., Gökyer, E., & Aşkın, F. K. (2015). SWOT Analizi ile Safranbolu Yörük Köyü ve Yakın Çevresinin Ekoturizm Potansiyelinin Değerlendirilmesi. *Karabük Üniversitesi Sosyal Bilimler Enstitüsü Dergisi,* (5), 70–83.

Emerson, K., Nabatchi, T., & Balogh, S. (2012). An integrative framework for collaborative governance. *Journal of Public Administration: Research and Theory,* 22(1), 1–29. 10.1093/jopart/mur011

Erkuş-Öztürk, H., & Eraydın, A. (2010). Environmental governance for sustainable tourism development: Collaborative networks and organization building in the Antalya tourism region. *Tourism Management,* 31(1), 113–124. 10.1016/j.tourman.2009.01.002

Gori, E., Fissi, S., & Romolini, A. (2021). A collaborative approach in tourism planning: The case of Tuscany region. *European Journal of Tourism Research,* 29, 2907–2907. 10.54055/ejtr.v29i.2426

Gürbüz, A. (2003). Yerel Kalkınma Stratejisi İçinde Turizm ve Safranbolu. *Bilig,* (24), 29–48.

Haber, T. R. T. (2024). "Safranbolu'nun 'sakin şehir' listesine dahil olması sevinçle karşılandı". https://www.trthaber.com/haber/yasam/safranbolunun-sakin-sehir-listesine-dahil-olmasi-sevincle-karsilandi-846735.html

Kara, G. (2017). Kültürel Mirasın Turizm Amaçlı Kulanılmasında Turist Taleplerinin Belirlenmesi: Safranbolu Örneği. *Uluslararası Türk Kültür Coğrafyasında Sosyal Bilimler Dergisi,* 2(2), 40–50.

Karagöz, Z. C. (2022). *Endüstri Mirasının Evrensel Tasarım İlkeleri Kapsamında İncelenmesi: İzmit Seka Kağıt Müzesi Örneği* (Master's thesis, Fatih Sultan Mehmet Vakıf Üniversitesi, Lisansüstü Eğitim Enstitüsü).

Khan, A. A. (2020). Covid-19 salgınının turizme etkileri: Safranbolu miras kenti örneği. *İşletme ve İktisat Çalışmaları Dergisi,* 8(2), 28-37.

Kiper, T., & Arslan, M. (2009). Safranbolu-Yörükköyü Tarımsal Turizm Potansiyelinin Kırsal Kalkınma Açısından Değerlendirilmesi. *Turkish Journal Of Forestry*, 8(2), 145-158. Https://Doi.Org/10.18182/Tjf.92211

Koçan, N., Ozeren, A., Aktaş, E., & Köseoğlu, F. (2023). Değirmencik Köyünün (Safranbolu) Kırsal Turizm Potansiyelinin Araştırılması. *Kent Akademisi*, 16(1), 56–70. 10.35674/kent.1105332

Lopes, H., Remoaldo, P., Ribeiro, V., Ribeiro, J. C., & Silva, S. (2016). The creation of a new tourist destination in low-density areas: The Boticas case. *Journal of Tourism, Sustainability and Well-being*, 4(2), 118–131.

March, R., & Wilkinson, I. (2009). Conceptual tools for evaluating tourism partnerships. *Tourism Management*, 30(3), 455–462. 10.1016/j.tourman.2008.09.001

Nayim, Y. S., & Yaman, S. Ö. (2019). Eskipazar (Karabük) Peyzajının Ekoturizm Açısından Değerlendirilmesi. *Bartin Orman Fakültesi Dergisi*, 21(2), 336–349. 10.24011/barofd.579067

Özdemir, Ü. (2011). Safranbolu'nun Kültürel Miras Kaynakları Ve Korunması. *Doğu Coğrafya Dergisi*, 16(26), 129–142.

Özdemir, Ü. (2011a). Ulaşım Coğrafyası Açısından Önemli Bir Güzergâh: Karabük-Bartın Karayolu. *Doğu Coğrafya Dergisi*, 13(19), 213–230.

Özmen, N., & Eren, M. (2021). Safranbolu Destinasyonunun İnanç Turizmi Potansiyeline Yönelik SWOT Analizi Çalışması. *Ekonomi İşletme Ve Yönetim Dergisi*, 5(1), 62–82.

Sağır, A. (2013). Bir Ölüm Sosyolojisi Denemesi Bağlamında İktisadi Hayata Mezarlıklardan Bakmak: Safranbolu Örneği. *Electronic Turkish Studies, 8*(12).

Selvi, M. S., & Şahin, S. (2012). Yerel yönetimler perspektifinden sürdürülebilir turizm: Batı Karadeniz Bölgesi örneği. *International Journal of Social and Economic Sciences*, 2(2), 23–36.

Sevim, B., Seçilmiş, C., & Görkem, O. (2013). Algılanan Destinasyon İmajının Tavsiye Davranışı Üzerine Etkisi: Safranbolu'da Bir Araştırma. *Uluslararası Yönetim İktisat Ve İşletme Dergisi*, 9(20), 115–129.

Tipolojileri, T. (2020). Türk Turizm Araştırmaları Dergisi. *Journal of Turkish Tourism Research*, 4(2), 1060–1076.

Zeppel, H. (2012). Collaborative governance for low-carbon tourism: Climate change initiatives by Australian tourism agencies. *Current Issues in Tourism*, 15(7), 603–626. 10.1080/13683500.2011.615913

Chapter 12
Select the Best Place for Regenerative Practices in Tourism by Using the Fuzzy MABAC Method

Brajamohan Sahoo
https://orcid.org/0009-0001-9501-3570
Tezpur University, India

Bijoy Krishna Debnath
https://orcid.org/0000-0001-7215-9473
Tezpur University, India

ABSTRACT

Selecting the ideal location for regenerative tourism is vital for environmental preservation and sustainable progress. Destination choice significantly impacts regenerative initiatives' effectiveness, affecting ecological benefits and socio-economic outcomes. A well-selected site fosters ecosystem restoration and positive engagement with indigenous communities, leveraging tourism as a force for biodiversity preservation, carbon capture, and local empowerment. In this chapter, the fuzzy multi-attributive border approximation area comparison (MABAC) approach is utilized to select the optimal site for regenerative tourism initiatives, considering six criteria each with five alternatives and input from three decision-makers. Normalization occurs after forming the initial decision matrix, followed by weight normalization. Performance index and rank are determined using the fuzzy multi-attributive border approximation area comparison (MABAC) procedure. Ultimately, after careful evaluation and consideration, it becomes evident that the fifth alternative stands out as the most suitable location for implementing regenerative practices in the field of tourism.

DOI: 10.4018/979-8-3693-5405-6.ch012

Copyright © 2024, IGI Global. Copying or distributing in print or electronic forms without written permission of IGI Global is prohibited.

INTRODUCTION

Traveling for pleasure or work is known as tourism, and it includes a variety of experiences and activities that promote cross-cultural understanding, economic expansion, and personal development. There are a plethora of options provided by tourism for people to discover new places, extend their horizons, and make lifelong memories, from sampling foreign cuisine to touring historical buildings. The capacity of tourism to promote respect and knowledge of other cultures is among its most important features. Travelers are exposed to a variety of customs, languages, and lifestyles when they visit foreign places, which fosters empathy and tolerance among people from different backgrounds. Visitors learn about various worldviews and lifestyles via encounters with local people, which fosters a sense of connectivity and global citizenship.

The purpose of this chapter is to identify the optimal location for implementing regenerative practices within the tourism sector, employing the fuzzy MABAC (Multi-Attributive Border Approximation area Comparison) method. The objective is to systematically evaluate potential sites based on various criteria and determine the most suitable place for integrating regenerative practices in tourism. Through the application of the fuzzy MABAC method, this chapter aims to provide a structured approach to decision-making, considering the complex and uncertain nature of selecting the best location for regenerative tourism initiatives.

The primary research questions (RQ) that served as the basis for this study are as follows:

- RQ1: What are the primary difficulties facing the Regenerative Practices in Tourism?
- RQ2: What connections exist between these difficulties?
- RQ3: Why do we choose to best place for regenerative practices in tourism using this specific Fuzzy MABAC approach?
- RQ4: How could this research contribute to the tourism sector?

The subsequent research objectives (RO) will help this book chapter address the aforementioned research questions.

- RO1: Identify the key challenges to get a good place for Tourism.
- RO2: Determine the relationship between these challenges.
- RO3: Provide the benefits of using this particular fuzzy MABAC technique.
- RO4: Provide implications of this study.

Select the Best Place for Regenerative Practices

A nation lacking a tourism sector may encounter notable economic setbacks and forfeit chances for advancement. Tourism acts as a crucial income stream, employment generator, and contributor to foreign exchange reserves in numerous countries. The absence of tourism could hinder economic diversification, leaving countries dependent on restricted sectors. Moreover, the lack of tourism might obstruct cultural interchange, global cooperation, and international recognition. Additionally, communities reliant on tourism may confront joblessness and decreased earnings, affecting their standard of living. Overall, the nonexistence of a tourism industry could hinder a country's socio-economic progress and curtail its prospects for prosperity.

Tourism holds great significance and presents numerous advantages for individuals and communities worldwide. Essentially, tourism acts as a driver for economic growth, cultural interchange, and personal fulfillment. From an economic standpoint, tourism generates substantial revenue, boosts local enterprises, and creates job opportunities in sectors such as hospitality, transportation, and entertainment. The arrival of tourists injects funds into the economy, aiding in infrastructure enhancements, the development of small businesses, and the improvement of public services. Additionally, tourism facilitates cultural exchange by bringing together individuals from diverse backgrounds, fostering understanding, acceptance, and respect for various traditions and practices. Interactions with locals offer travelers valuable insights into distinct cultures, histories, and lifestyles, enhancing their journeys and broadening their horizons. Furthermore, tourism plays a crucial role in safeguarding cultural landmarks, natural environments, and ecosystems, emphasizing the significance of sustainable approaches and responsible management of tourism activities. By showcasing the allure and importance of destinations, tourism raises awareness about environmental preservation and motivates efforts to safeguard fragile ecosystems and areas rich in biodiversity. Moreover, tourism contributes to social progress by empowering communities, preserving indigenous wisdom, and promoting dialogue and collaboration across cultures. In essence, tourism stands as a potent instrument for fostering global connectivity, economic advancement, and mutual appreciation, rendering it an indispensable asset for individuals, communities, and nations alike.

When it comes to promoting sustainable development and maintaining the integrity of natural and cultural resources, choosing the ideal location for regenerative practices in tourism is crucial. Regenerative tourism aspires to improve visitor experiences, help local communities, and repair and rejuvenate ecosystems in addition to limiting adverse effects. Travelers can help achieve favorable social and environmental results by carefully selecting locations that emphasize regenerative concepts. Responsible tourism management, community involvement, and conservation are frequently given top priority in these locations. Furthermore, picking such locations sets an example for sustainable tourism growth globally and encourages other tourist stakeholders to embrace regenerative practices. After all, thoughtful location selection for regenerative tourism practices enhances visitor experiences, supports local economies, protects the environment, and guarantees the tourism sector's long-term sustainability.

The key features of our contribution to this manuscript are outlined as follows: This study identifies the essential criteria for the selection of the optimal place for regenerative practices in tourism. To address the uncertainty surrounding the selection of the best locations for implementing regenerative practices in tourism, researchers have employed the Multi-Attributive Border Approximation area Comparison (MABAC) methodology within a fuzzy environment. The normalization process is achieved by separating the criteria as beneficial and non-beneficial. In this chapter, the distance of each alternative from the boundary approximation area for the elements in the matrix is determined, and the sum of each row is evaluated to determine the overall performance index (S_i) for each alternative and rank them according to their performance index.

To achieve these objectives, the rest of this chapter is structured as follows: Section 3 undertakes a review of relevant literature. Section 4 explores the intricacies of the fuzzy Multi-Attributive Border Approximation area Comparison (MABAC) method. The case study and discussion of results are presented in section 5. Section 6 offers a sensitivity analysis. Section 7 discusses the implications of the study. Finally, Section 8 provides the concluding remarks and outlines the future directions for study in this chapter.

LITERATURE REVIEW

Regenerative tourism is becoming popular because it's a way to travel that doesn't harm the environment or the local communities you visit. Instead, it tries to make places even better than they were before. This is important because regular tourism can often hurt the environment, culture, and economy of the places people visit. Regenerative tourism wants to change that by helping nature, preserving culture, and making sure local people benefit too.

It's all about building a good relationship between travelers and the places they go. This kind of tourism encourages tourists to do things that help protect nature, share cultures, and support local businesses. By focusing on being sustainable and taking care of the places we visit, regenerative tourism brings benefits that last a long time for both the people who live there and those who come to visit.

In today's world, where more and more people care about the environment and want real experiences when they travel, regenerative tourism is a great way forward. It shows a shift towards traveling in a thoughtful way that looks after the Earth, cultures, and communities everywhere. This could change how tourism works and create new ways for people to travel responsibly in the future.

The importance of the Fuzzy MABAC (Multi-Attributive Border Approximation area Comparison) method stems from its capacity to handle the complexities inherent in decision-making through the integration of fuzzy sets theory. This approach empowers decision-makers to consider uncertainties in both criteria weights and performance assessments, providing a more accurate portrayal of real-world situations. With its structured approach to evaluating alternatives based on various criteria, it enables a comprehensive examination of both positive and negative factors, facilitating more informed decision-making.

Choosing the optimal location for regenerative tourism holds significant importance within sustainable development endeavors. Regenerative tourism emphasizes revitalizing natural and cultural assets, ensuring destinations not only manage their resources sustainably but actively contribute to their enhancement. The significance of selecting the right locale lies in its potential to set an example for other destinations, motivating them to embrace similar approaches. Typically, ideal sites for regenerative tourism initiatives feature diverse ecosystems, abundant cultural heritage, and a supportive local populace. These destinations provide avenues for visitors to partake in meaningful experiences while minimizing their environmental impact. Additionally, by prioritizing regenerative strategies, these areas can alleviate the adverse effects of tourism, encourage environmental stewardship, and stimulate socio-economic growth within the community. Ultimately, the careful selection of prime locations for regenerative practices in tourism is crucial for nurturing a more sustainable and adaptable tourism sector that benefits both current and future generations.

The fuzzy MABAC (Multi-Attributive Border Approximation area Comparison) method applies to real-world scenarios where decision-making grapples with multiple attributes or criteria that are uncertain or imprecise. Let's explore some practical examples where the Fuzzy MABAC method applied in real-world scenarios

1. Selecting the best supplier for a manufacturing company:

When choosing a supplier, the Manufacturing Company employs the fuzzy MABAC technique, which takes into account factors such as price, quality, delivery, and sustainability. Decision-makers evaluate each factor using fuzzy linguistic terms and pairwise comparisons. Supplier performance is then assessed against these factors using fuzzy criteria, and fuzzy weights are computed to indicate their significance. The method combines these assessments to rank suppliers, offering a reliable decision-making approach despite uncertainties.

2. Selecting a Location for a New Retail Store:

A retail corporation is preparing to launch a new store and must identify the optimal location. They analyze aspects like population density, income levels, market competition, and ease of access. Employing the Fuzzy MABAC approach, they evaluate each prospective site according to these factors. Decision-makers use fuzzy linguistic terms like 'high,' 'medium,' or 'low' to gauge population density and conduct pairwise comparisons to ascertain the significance of each factor. Through consolidating these assessments, the company can prioritize potential locations and select the most suitable one aligning with their goals, all while acknowledging uncertainties.

3. Selecting Tourist Destinations:

The task of a tourism board is to choose destinations for inclusion in travel packages. They take into account elements like scenic attractions, cultural richness, safety measures, and cost-effectiveness. Employing the fuzzy MABAC approach, they evaluate each destination against these standards, integrating personal assessments and the uncertainties that come with making decisions in the tourism industry.

Besides this, the fuzzy MABAC (Multi-Attributive Border Approximation area Comparison) method plays a crucial role in selecting the optimal location for regenerative tourism initiatives by offering a nuanced approach to decision-making in complex environments. Regenerative tourism focuses not just on minimizing negative impacts but actively contributing to the restoration and enhancement of ecosystems and communities. Given its holistic nature, identifying the most suitable site requires considering multiple criteria simultaneously, such as ecological sensitivity, cultural significance, economic viability, and social acceptance. Traditional decision-making methods often struggle to accommodate the inherent uncertainties and subjectivities involved in evaluating such diverse criteria. Here, the Fuzzy MABAC method excels by integrating fuzzy logic with the MABAC framework, allowing decision-makers to handle imprecise, ambiguous, or conflicting information more effectively. By employing fuzzy sets to represent linguistic terms like "high," "medium," or "low," it captures the inherent vagueness in human judgments and preferences. This approach enables decision-makers to navigate the complexities of regenerative tourism site selection more comprehensively, accounting for the diverse perspectives of stakeholders and the multifaceted nature of sustainability. By providing a structured yet flexible framework for decision analysis, the Fuzzy MABAC method empowers planners and policymakers to identify the most promising locations for regenerative tourism initiatives, thereby fostering sustainable development and positive socio-environmental impacts within the community.

In recent years, numerous researchers have directed their focus towards tourism and the exploration of the MABAC method, delving into various facets of this domain. Below are some significant contributions made in this domain.

Go and Kang (2023) wrote an article discussing Metaverse tourism for sustainable tourism development. Kumar and Singh (2019) also explored the seasonal effects on tourism in India. Rout et al. (2016) proposed a topic concerning the socio-economic impacts of tourism in India. Baerenholdt et al., (2017) contributed an article regarding performing tourist places. Xiang et al., (2021) introduced the Annals of Tourism Research curated collection focusing on designing tourism places. Büyüközkan, G., Mukul, E., & Kongar, E (2021) employed a fuzzy linguistic AHP-MABAC approach to select strategies for health tourism. Walker et al., (2019) discussed the role of Indigenous values and interpretation in promoting transformative change in tourists' place images and personal values. Hristoforova et al., (2019) examined the improvement of digital technologies in marketing communications of tourism and hospitality enterprises. Ghosh et al., (2022) employed an integrated IRN-SWARA-MABAC-based approach for the evaluation of tourism websites of the Indian states. Howard et al., (2023) proposed a review of exploratory factor analysis in tourism and hospitality research. Bellato et al., (2023) established a conceptual framework related to leveraging theory and practice. Duxbury et al., (2020) developed tourism development models for sustainable and regenerative tourism. Kemer, E. and Tyagi, P. K. (2023) explored the applications of Artificial Intelligence and Robotics in the field of Tourism and Hospitality Marketing. Żemła, M., & Staszewska, A. (2022) authored an article discussing the Use of Post-Industrial Heritage in the Construction of Competitive Tourist Products. Bhartiya, S et al., (2024) authored a book chapter related to "A Theory-Based Approach to Understanding Social Sustainability in Tourism". Saputro et al., (2023) evaluated the sustainability of rural tourism development with an integrated approach using MDS and ANP methods. Hassan, V., and Abou Fayad, S. (2023) contributed an article on slow tourism as a tool for sustainable tourism development post-pandemic. Chakraborty et al., (2023) suggested a combined method using FUCOM-MABAC to assess the effectiveness of Indian National Parks. Tomassini (2022) proposed a paper related to a paradigm to critically rethink sustainability in tourism and hospitality. Hassan, V. I., and Basheer, S. (2024) authored a research item exploring "The Impact of Advanced Technology on Medical Tourism Transformation".

METHODOLOGY

The decision-maker presently evaluates the available options or prerequisites by employing the linguistic expressions delineated in the provided Table 1.

Table 1. Linguistic Terms and the Corresponding Triangular Fuzzy Numbers

Linguistic Variable	Triangular Fuzzy Number
Equal importance	(1,1,1)
Very weak importance	(2,1,2)
Less importance	(3,2,1)
Moderately importance	(4,4,5)
Moderate	(5,6,6)
Moderately strong importance	(6,7,8)
Strong importance	(7,8,8)
Absolutely important	(8,9,9)

Fuzzy MABAC Method

This segment explores the nuances of the Multi Attributive Border Approxima-tion area Comparison (MABAC) method under a fuzzy environment, presenting a thorough strategy for systematically assessing and prioritizing diverse attributes. It is widely regarded as one of the most innovative methods in Multiple Criteria Decision Making (MCDM). The MABAC technique was initially introduced by Pamučar, D., & Ćirović, G. (2015), and subsequently, various researchers have ap-plied it in diverse contexts. In this section, we will explore the process of utilizing the MABAC method within a fuzzy environment. Several studies conducted in this realm focus on addressing uncertainty within the MABAC framework. Verma, R (2021) proposed a new variant of the MABAC method, utilizing exponential fuzzy information measures. Jokić, Ž, et al. (2021) Utilizing LBWA(Level Based Weight Assessment) and Fuzzy MABAC model for determining mortar unit fire positions.

The steps are given below

Step 1:

Considering qualitative information, the decision matrix constructed with tri-angular fuzzy numbers is provided below (Lotfi FH. 2023, Pamučar, D. & Ćirović, G. 2015)

$$Z = \begin{bmatrix} z_{11} & z_{12} & \cdots & z_{1n} \\ z_{21} & \cdots & \cdots & z_{2n} \\ \cdots & \cdots & \cdots & \cdots \\ \cdots & \cdots & \cdots & \cdots \\ z_{m1} & z_{m2} & \cdots & z_{mn} \end{bmatrix}$$

Where $z_{ij} = \left(z_{ij}^l, z_{ij}^m, z_{ij}^u \right)$ is a triangular fuzzy number.

Step 2: Normalized Decision Matrix(Bobar, Z. et al.2020)

The decision matrix in its normalized form is provided below.

$$N = \begin{bmatrix} n_{11} & n_{12} & \cdots & n_{1n} \\ n_{21} & \cdots & \cdots & n_{2n} \\ \cdots & \cdots & \cdots & \cdots \\ \cdots & \cdots & \cdots & \cdots \\ n_{m1} & n_{m2} & \cdots & n_{mn} \end{bmatrix}$$

The value of n_{ij} we get by using the following formula.
For Benefit type criteria (A greater value of the criterion is preferred):

Where

$$n_{ij} = \frac{\left(z_{ij} - z_i^-\right)}{\left(z_i^+ - z_i^-\right)} \tag{1}$$

Here $z_{(ij)} = \left[z_{(ij)}^l, z_{(ij)}^m, z_{(ij)}^u\right]$, $z_i^+ = max_i\{z_{ij}^u\}$; for i=1,2,....,m.
And $j = 1,2...,n.$

$z_i^- = min_i\{z_{ij}^l\}$; i=1,2,....,m and $j = 1,2...,n.$

For non-benefit type criteria (a lower value of the criterion is preferable)

Where

$$n_{ij} = \frac{\left(z_{ij} - z_i^+\right)}{\left(z_i^- - z_i^+\right)} \tag{2}$$

Here $z_i^+ = max_i\{z_{ij}^u\}$; $j = 1,2...,n.$

$z_i^- = min_i\{z_{ij}^l\}$; $j = 1,2...,n.$

Step3: The weighted Normalized Decision matrix (Pamučar, D., & Ćirović, G.2015).:
The elements of the weighted normalized decision matrix are obtained by using the following equation

$$v_{ij} = W_j \cdot \left(n_{ij} + 1\right); i = 1,....,m, j = 1,.....,n. \tag{3}$$

Where $W_1,....W_j$ are the weight vector obtained by using fuzzy AHP or any other MCDM method.
Using the above equation, the weight normalized decision matrix *V* represent below (Lotfi FH. 2023)

$$V = \begin{bmatrix} v_{11} & v_{12} & \cdots & v_{1n} \\ v_{21} & v_{22} & \cdots & v_{2n} \\ \cdots & \cdots & \cdots & \cdots \\ \cdots & \cdots & \cdots & \cdots \\ v_{m1} & v_{m2} & \cdots & v_{mn} \end{bmatrix}$$

$$=$$

$$\begin{bmatrix} W_1 \cdot (n_{11} + 1) & W_2 \cdot (n_{12} + 1) & \cdots & W_n \cdot (n_{1n} + 1) \\ W_1 \cdot (n_{21} + 1) & W_2 \cdot (n_{22} + 1) & \cdots & W_n \cdot (n_{2n} + 1) \\ \cdots & \cdots & \cdots & \cdots \\ \cdots & \cdots & \cdots & \cdots \\ W_1 \cdot (n_{m1} + 1) & W_2 \cdot (n_{m2} + 1) & \cdots & W_n \cdot (n_{mn} + 1) \end{bmatrix} \tag{4}$$

Here "v_{ij}" represent the corresponding elements of the weight-normalized decision matrix V.

Step 4: The Border Approximation Area Matrix

The BAA for each criterion is given below (Lotfi FH. 2023)

Where

$$g_j = \sqrt[m]{\prod_{i=1}^{m} v_{ij}} = \left(\sqrt[m]{\prod_{i=1}^{m} v_{ij}^l}, \sqrt[m]{\prod_{i=1}^{m} v_{ij}^m}, \sqrt[m]{\prod_{i=1}^{m} v_{ij}^u} \right) ; j = 1, \ldots, n \tag{5}$$

Here V represents the elements of the weighted matrix, where each element is denoted by v_{ij} and m signifies the number of alternatives.

Once the value g_j is calculated for each criterion, a matrix G is formed to represent the border approximation area, structured as an $n * 1$ matrix, where n denotes the total count of criteria employed in the selection of alternatives among the given options.

The BAA matrix is as below (Pamučar, D., & Ćirović, G. 2015).

$$G = \begin{matrix} C_1 & C_2 & \cdots & C_n \\ [g_1 & g_2 & \cdots & g_n] \end{matrix} \tag{6}$$

Step 5: Next determine the distance of each alternative from the boundary approximation area for the elements in the matrix(Q) (Lotfi FH. 2023).

$$Q = \begin{bmatrix} q_{11} & q_{12} & \cdots & q_{1n} \\ q_{21} & q_{22} & \cdots & q_{2n} \\ \cdots & \cdots & \cdots & \cdots \\ q_{m1} & q_{m2} & \cdots & q_{mn} \end{bmatrix}$$

Select the Best Place for Regenerative Practices

Here Q = V - G.

Where

$$q_{ij} = \begin{cases} d(v_{ij}, g_j) \text{ for } v_{ij} > g_j \\ o \text{ for } v_{ij} = g_j \\ -d(v_{ij}, g_j) \text{ for } v_{ij} < g_j \end{cases} \tag{7}$$

And

$$d(v_{ij}, g_j) = \sqrt[2]{\frac{1}{3}\left[\left(v_{ij}^l - g_j^l\right)^2 + \left(v_{ij}^m - g_j^m\right)^2 + \left(v_{ij}^u - g_j^u\right)^2\right]} \tag{8}$$

Here

$$v_{ij} = \left(v_{ij}^l, v_{ij}^m, v_{ij}^u\right) \text{ and } g_j = \left(g_j^l, g_j^m, g_j^u\right)$$

And if $\dfrac{\left(v_{ij}^l + 4v_{ij}^m + v_{ij}^u\right)}{6} > \dfrac{\left(g_j^l + 4v_j^m + v_j^u\right)}{6}$ then $v_{ij} > q_j$

Alternative A_i might be linked with the border approximation area. This region of approximation is divided into three segments: the border approximation area (denoted as G), the lower approximation area (denoted as G^-), and the upper approximation area (denoted as G^+).

$$A_i \in \begin{cases} G^+ \text{ if } q_{ij} > 0 \\ G \text{ if } q_{ij} = 0 \\ G^- \text{ if } q_{ij} < 0 \end{cases} \tag{9}$$

It clearly express that if the value of $g_{ij} > 0$, *then* $g_{ij} \in G^+$, then alternative A_i is near or equal to the ideal alternative. If the value $q_{ij} < 0$, then, $g_{ij} \in G^-$ then alternative A_i is near or equal to the anti-ideal alternative (Pamučar, D., & Ćirović, G. 2015).

Step 6: Ranking the alternatives

By calculating the sum of each row in the matrix, we obtain the ultimate values of the criterion functions for the alternatives (Pamučar, D., & Ćirović, G. 2015).

$$S_i = \sum_{j=1}^n q_{ij}, j = 1, 2, ..., n, i = 1, 2, ..., m \tag{10}$$

where n is the number of criteria, m is the number of alternatives.

CASE STUDY AND RESULTS DISCUSSION

In this study, we utilize the fuzzy MABAC method to choose the optimal location for implementing regenerative tourism practices. We consider five alternatives (A1, A2, A3, A4, and A5) and incorporate the preferences of three decision-makers. These decision-makers have collectively identified six criteria for evaluating the suitability of the chosen locations, as outlined below

- Environmental sustainability(C1):

Environmental sustainability in tourism evaluates the extent to which a destination or activity minimizes its ecological impact and promotes sustainability. Key factors include the integration of renewable energy sources, effective waste management techniques, conservation programs, and the protection of natural ecosystems. By prioritizing these initiatives, destinations can mitigate environmental harm and contribute positively to the preservation of the planet's resources for future generations.

- Social and cultural impacts(C2):

This criterion evaluates the impact of tourism activities on indigenous populations and local communities, taking into account factors like adherence to local customs and traditions, preservation of cultural heritage, empowerment and inclusion of community members, as well as efforts to mitigate adverse social effects such as cultural exploitation or displacement.

- Economic benefits(C3):

Economic benefits denote the financial gains derived from tourism endeavors, taking into account their fair distribution and long-term viability. This aspect encompasses elements such as the creation of employment opportunities, generation of income for local residents, support for local businesses within the tourism sector, and the fair sharing of tourism-derived income throughout the community.

- Accessibility and infrastructure(C4):

Assessing accessibility and infrastructure involves gauging the convenience of reaching the destination and the standard of infrastructure that facilitates tourism. This encompasses various elements such as transportation networks (e.g., roads, airports, public transit), lodging choices, healthcare services, and other essential amenities required by both visitors and locals.

• Community involvement(C5):

This criterion emphasizes the extent to which local communities are actively engaged and involved in decision-making processes concerning the development and management of tourism. It encompasses various mechanisms such as community consultation, participation in revenue-sharing programs, initiatives to enhance skills and capabilities, and the creation of opportunities for local entrepreneurship and employment within the tourism industry.

• Biodiversity preservation(C6):

Biodiversity conservation encompasses a range of efforts dedicated to safeguarding and preserving natural environments and their diverse ecosystems. This includes initiatives to protect endangered species, maintain ecological balance, promote responsible wildlife tourism, and prevent habitat degradation or fragmentation caused by tourism activities. These endeavors aim to ensure the long-term health and viability of ecosystems, fostering harmony between human activities and the natural world.

Figure 1. Best Place for Regenerative Practices in Tourism

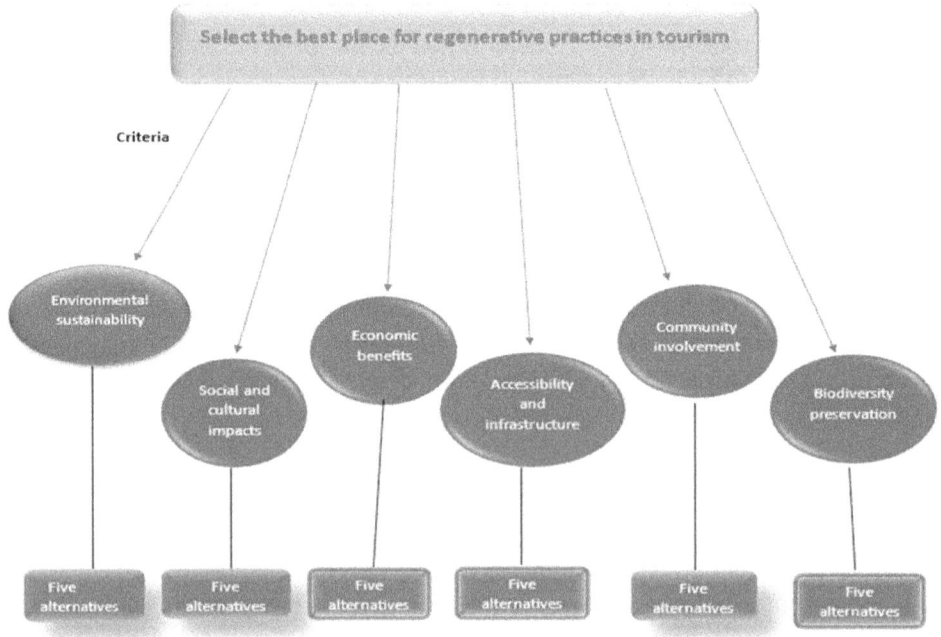

The figure above illustrates that to select the optimal location for implementing regenerative practices in tourism, decision-makers must evaluate six criteria, with each criterion having five alternative options.

For this case study, we use the following fuzzy weight of the decision criterion
$W_{Es}=0.12$, $W_{Sc}=0.15$, $W_{E}=0.16$, $W_{Ai}=0.20$ $W_{Ci}=0.19$, $W_{B}=0.18$

With the assistance of Table-1 and the opinions of decision-makers, an initial decision matrix is being constructed, as depicted in Table-2.

Table 2. Initial Decision Matrix

Alt	C1	C2	C3	C4	C5	C6
A1	5, 6, 6	7, 8, 8	5, 6, 6	4, 4, 5	7, 8, 8	6, 7, 8
A2	7, 8, 8	5, 6, 6	4, 4, 5	8, 9, 9	5, 6, 6	7, 8, 8
A3	4, 4, 5	6, 7, 8	7, 8, 8	5, 6, 6	7, 8, 8	5,6, 6
A4	8, 9, 9	6, 7, 8	5, 6, 6	6, 7, 8	6, 7, 8	4, 4, 5
A5	6, 7, 8	5, 6, 6	7, 8, 8	4, 4, 5	8,9,9	6, 7, 8

In this case study, the decision-makers regard all six criteria as beneficial criteria. Using Table 2 and equations 1 and 2, we obtain a normalized decision matrix displayed in Table 3. Next, employing Table 3, equations 3-4, and the value of the normalized weight attribute, we derive the required fuzzy weight normalized decision matrix present in Table 4. With the assistance of Equations 5-6 and Table 4, we generate the BAA or g matrix, displayed in Table 5. Subsequently, we arrive at the Q matrix, expressed in Table 6, with the help of equations 7-9 and Tables 4-5. Finally, by utilizing Equation 10 and Table 6, we obtain our required ranking matrix, which is displayed in Table 7.

Table 3. Normalized Decision Matrix

Alt.	C1	C2	C3	C4	C5	C6
A1	0.2,0.4,0.4	0.67,1,1	0.25,0.5,0.5	0,0,0.2	0.5,0.75,0.75	0.5,0.75,1
A2	0.6,0.8,0.8	0,0.33,0.33	0,0,0.25	0.8,1,1	0,0.25,0.25	0.75,1,1
A3	0,0,0.2	0.33,0.67,1	0.75,1,1	0.2,0.4,0.4	0.5,0.75,0.75	0.25,0.5,0.5
A4	0.8,1,1	0.33,0.67,1	0.25,0.5,0.5	0.4,0.6,0.8	0.25,0.5,0.75	0,0,0.25
A5	0.4,0.6,0.8	0,0.33,0.33	0.75,1,1	0,0,0.2	0.75,1,1	0.5,0.75,1

Table 4. Weight Normalized Decision Matrix

Alt.	C1	C2	C3	C4	C5	C6
A1	0.144,0.168,0.168	0.25,0.3,0.3	0.2,0.24,0.24	0.2,0.2,0.24	0.285,0.3325,0.3325	0.27,0.315,0.36
A2	0.192,0.216,0.216	0.15,0.2,0.2	0.16,0.16,0.2	0.36,0.4,0.4	0.19,0.2375,0.2375	0.315,0.36,0.36
A3	0.12,0.12,0.144	0.2,0.25,0.3	0.28,0.32,0.32	0.24,0.28,0.28	0.285,0.3325,0.3325	0.225,0.27,0.27
A4	0.216,0.24,0.24	0.2,0.25,0.3	0.2,0.24,0.24	0.28,0.32,0.36	0.2375,0.285,0.3325	0.18,0.18,0.225
A5	0.168,0.192,0.216	0.15,0.2,0.2	0.28,0.32,0.32	0.2,0.2,0.24	0.3325,0.38,0.38	0.27,0.315,0.36

Table 5. BAA Matrix

g_i	C1	C2	C3	C4	C5	C6
	0.165, 0.182, 0.193	0.186, 0.237, 0.255	0.219, 0.248, 0.259	0.2495, 0.2699, 0.29729	0.2613, 0.3096, 0.319	0.248, 0.280, 0.3094

Table 6. Q Matrix

Alt.	C1	C2	C3	C4	C5	C6
A1	-0.02	0.057	-0.016	-0.059	0.020397	0.0375
A2	0.028	-0.04	-0.07	0.1144	-0.074834	0.0666

Alt.	C1	C2	C3	C4	C5	C6
A3	-0.052	0.028	0.0643	0.0127	0.020397	-0.027
A4	0.0519	0.028	-0.016	0.0493	-0.021082	-0.085
A5	0.0143	-0.04	0.0643	-0.0592	0.067269	0.0375

Table 7. Ranking Matrix

Alt.	Score value(S_i)	Rank
A1	0.019897	4
A2	0.024166	3
A3	0.046397	2
A4	0.007118	5
A5	0.084169	1

Based on the ranking table above, we conclude that A5 is the optimal location for implementing regenerative practices in tourism.

SENSITIVITY ANALYSIS

Sensitivity analysis plays a pivotal role across diverse domains like finance, engineering, economics, and environmental science, assessing the repercussions of alterations in various variables on a model or system's outcome. Its fundamental objective is to gauge the resilience, dependability, and consistency of a model by pinpointing the pivotal factors shaping its results.

At its core, sensitivity analysis entails methodically adjusting the inputs of a model or system within defined parameters and noting the consequent shifts in outputs. This procedure aids in comprehending the interconnections among different variables and their impact on the ultimate result.

After standardizing the values, the alternatives are assigned weights as follows: A1 = 0.10948, A2 = 0.13297, A3 = 0.25528, A4 = 0.03916 and A5 = 0.46311. These numerical representations reflect the significance attributed to each alternative within the analysis. Table 8 provides a comprehensive overview of the values obtained at every stage of the sensitivity analysis, complemented by graphical and radar diagrams that visually depict the progression of the analysis.

Significantly, commencing from the 8th iteration, where the value stands at 0.35, the ranking order of the alternatives remains consistent without any alterations. Furthermore, beyond the 8th stage, alternative A5 maintains its lead position in the ranking, indicating its sustained prominence throughout the sensitivity analysis process.

The ranking order's consistency highlights the analysis's strength and supports the validity of the findings that are derived from it. It implies that the relative relevance of the options stays constant despite changes in input parameters and possible uncertainties, offering insightful information for decision-making procedures. Additionally, the analysis's graphical representations provide clear visualizations that enhance comprehension and make it easier to communicate the results to stakeholders.

Table 8. Sensitivity Analysis Matrix

Alt.	Original	0.05	0.1	0.15	0.2	0.25	0.3	0.35	0.4
A1	0.10948	0.193713	0.183518	0.173322	0.163127	0.152932	0.142736	0.132541	0.122345
A2	0.13297	0.235275	0.222892	0.21051	0.198127	0.185744	0.173361	0.160978	0.148595
A3	0.25528	0.451712	0.427938	0.404163	0.380389	0.356615	0.33284	0.309066	0.285292
A4	0.03916	0.069299	0.065652	0.062005	0.058357	0.05471	0.051063	0.047415	0.043768
A5	0.46311	0.05	0.1	0.15	0.2	0.25	0.3	0.35	0.4
Total	1	1	1	1	1	1	1	1	1

Figure 2. Graphical Representation of Sensitivity Analysis

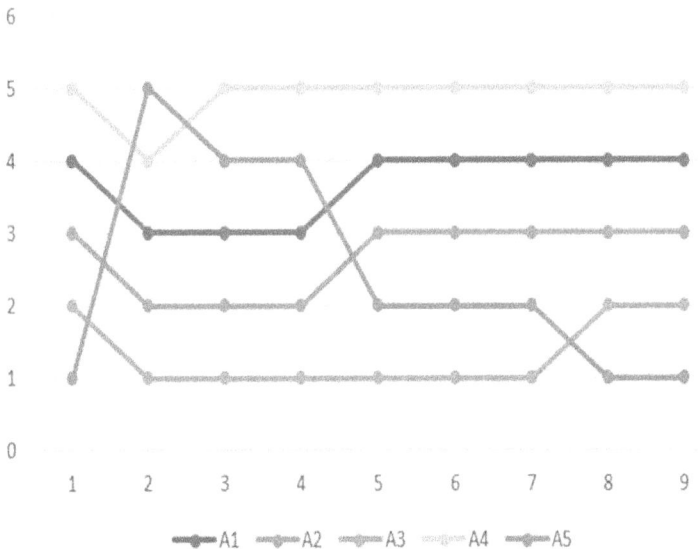

Figure 3. Radar Diagram of Sensitivity Analysis

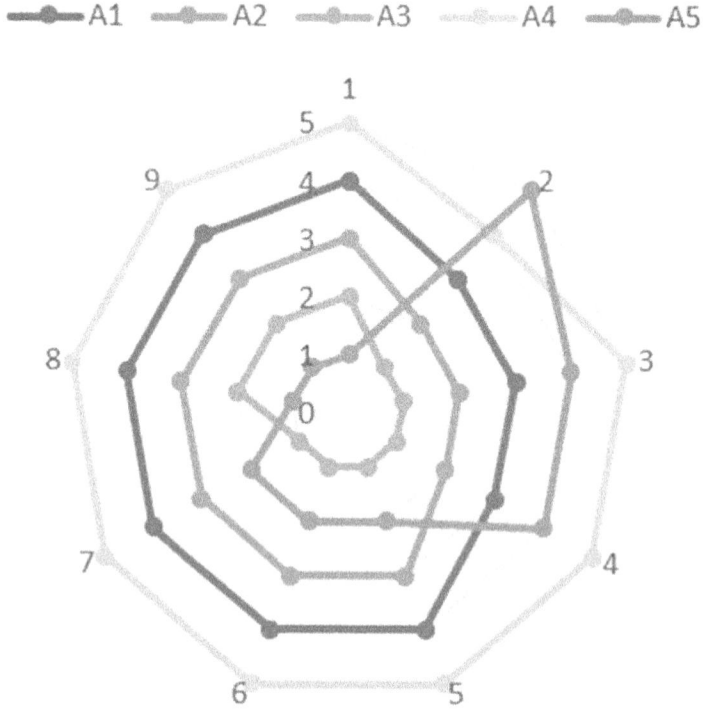

IMPLICATIONS OF THIS STUDY

The implications of using the fuzzy Multi-Attributive Border Approximation area Comparison (MABAC) method to select the best place for regenerative practices in tourism and hospitality are significant and far-reaching:

1. Sustainable Tourism Development:

The research underscores the significance of sustainability within the tourism and hospitality sectors. By giving preference to destinations that emphasize re-generative approaches, stakeholders actively contribute to safeguarding natural resources, preserving cultural heritage, and promoting socio-economic prosperity over the long term.

2. Environmental Conservation:

Introducing regenerative practices within tourism destinations aids in mitigating the adverse effects of tourism on the environment. These efforts encompass decreasing carbon emissions, preserving biodiversity, advocating for responsible waste disposal, and optimizing resource utilization. By implementing such initiatives, destinations can foster sustainable tourism models that prioritize environmental stewardship and long-term viability, ensuring the preservation of natural resources for future generations.

3. Cultural Preservation:

Choosing destinations that prioritize maintaining cultural authenticity and preserving traditions fosters admiration for local customs, traditions, and heritage, thereby enriching the travel experience. This approach not only aids in preserving cultural identity and fostering mutual understanding and appreciation between visitors and residents but also contributes to sustainable tourism development by safeguarding the unique cultural heritage of destinations. Embracing and celebrating cultural diversity strengthens social cohesion and promotes responsible travel practices, ensuring the long-term preservation of cultural treasures for future generations to enjoy.

4. Community Empowerment:

Regenerative approaches within tourism and hospitality have the potential to empower local communities through the establishment of economic avenues, bolstering small-scale enterprises, and engaging residents in decision-making endeavors. Consequently, this fosters heightened social integration, elevated standards of living, and fortified community resilience. By fostering economic diversification, regenerative tourism practices can mitigate the vulnerability of communities reliant solely on traditional industries. Furthermore, they promote cultural preservation, environmental stewardship, and the equitable distribution of benefits, ensuring sustainable development trajectories for destinations.

5. Enhanced Visitor Experience:

Choosing destinations that provide genuine and eco-friendly tourism opportunities allows travelers to immerse themselves in local culture, appreciate nature, and make positive contributions to the places they explore, resulting in richer and more satisfying travel experiences. By opting for such destinations, travelers not only minimize their environmental footprint but also support local communities and economies. Additionally, these destinations often offer unique and authentic experiences, fostering meaningful connections between travelers and their surroundings.

Ultimately, prioritizing eco-friendly tourism destinations aligns with sustainable travel practices, ensuring the preservation of natural resources and cultural heritage for future generations to enjoy.

6. Stakeholder Collaboration:

The research underscores the paramount importance of fostering cooperation and forging alliances among a diverse array of stakeholders, including government agencies, tourism entities, community groups, businesses, and travelers. By engaging in collaborative endeavors, these stakeholders can leverage their collective resources, exchange valuable expertise, and implement holistic strategies aimed at addressing the multifaceted challenges posed by sustainability issues in the tourism sector. Such collaborative initiatives are essential for fostering synergy and fostering a conducive environment for sustainable tourism development.

7. Promotion of Responsible Tourism:

The research advances the cause of responsible tourism principles, urging travelers to make informed decisions that not only minimize their environmental footprint but also respect and celebrate indigenous cultures while supporting sustainable development endeavors. By promoting awareness and advocating for ethical travel practices, this research seeks to foster a global mindset of responsible tourism, encouraging travelers to embrace a conscientious approach that prioritizes the preservation of natural resources, cultural heritage, and socio-economic well-being of local communities.

8. Socio-Economic Development:

Using the fuzzy Multi-Criteria Decision Making (MCDM) technique to locate places for regenerative initiatives in tourism and hospitality has the capacity to spark socio-economic advancement in surrounding communities. Through the identification of appropriate sites via MCDM, avenues for job creation, entrepreneurial endeavors, and infrastructure improvement can be pursued, thereby stimulating economic growth and enhancing residents' well-being. This method promotes sustainable development, guaranteeing that tourism benefits extend beyond environmental preservation to include socio-economic well-being.

9. Long-Term Economic Viability:

Supporting regenerative initiatives in tourism and hospitality is paramount for securing the enduring economic sustainability of destinations. By fostering regenerative practices, destinations attract conscientious travelers who prioritize environmental stewardship and community well-being. This not only enhances the destination's reputation but also improves its competitiveness in the global tourism market. Moreover, embracing regenerative principles helps mitigate the hazards associated with excessive tourism, such as overcrowding and environmental degradation, thus ensuring the long-term viability and resilience of tourism destinations.

In general, employing fuzzy Multi-Attributive Border Approximation area Comparison (MABAC) techniques to choose locations for regenerative initiatives in tourism and hospitality goes beyond singular destinations, encompassing wider sustainability aims, socio-cultural principles, and economic growth objectives. Embracing such practices enables stakeholders to generate enduring and favorable outcomes that serve the interests of current and future generations.

CONCLUSION AND FUTURE STUDY

In this chapter, the focus is on addressing the selection of the optimal location for implementing regenerative practices in tourism. A set of six criteria, each with five alternatives, is considered essential for this selection. To tackle the uncertainty surrounding this decision, the Multi-Attributive Border Approximation area Comparison (MABAC) methodology is applied within a fuzzy environment (Lotfi, F. H. 2023). The normalization process involves categorizing criteria as either beneficial or non-beneficial. Next, the distance of each alternative from the boundary approximation area in the matrix is determined, and the sum of each row is calculated to establish the overall performance index (Si) for each alternative, subsequently ranking them based on this index. The results, as presented in Table 7, indicate that A5 emerges as the optimal choice for implementing regenerative practices in the tourism industry. Leveraging the renowned efficiency of the fuzzy MABAC approach in decision-making, this method not only identifies the most suitable location but also provides insights into the intricate dynamics of decision-making within the tourism sector. Importantly, the applicability of the fuzzy MABAC method extends beyond tourism site selection, demonstrating its versatility across various industries, including manufacturing and healthcare. This underscores its significance as a valuable decision-making tool for navigating complex choice environments. The systematic approach offered by the fuzzy MABAC method ensures a comprehensive evaluation of alternatives(Keshavarz-Ghorabaee et al., 2021), thereby enabling informed and strategic decision-making processes across diverse domains. Thus, its utilization underscores the importance of deploying advanced methodologies to address the inherent complexities of decision-making processes, ultimately enhancing efficiency and effectiveness across multiple sectors.

Future research or practical advancements in the field of regenerative tourism can be driven by incorporating insights from the methodologies discussed in the preceding chapter. Through the application of the Multi-Attributive Border Approximation Area Comparison (MABAC) methodology within a fuzzy environment, researchers and practitioners can further enhance the process of selecting optimal locations for implementing regenerative practices in tourism. This approach facilitates a systematic evaluation of criteria and alternatives, taking into account uncertainties inherent in decision-making. Moreover, future studies could explore adapting this methodology to address specific challenges unique to regenerative tourism, such as evaluating the long-term sustainability and socio-economic impacts of regenerative initiatives. By harnessing advanced methodologies like fuzzy MABAC, researchers, and practitioners have the opportunity to refine decision-making processes, ultimately contributing to the sustainable development of tourism destinations and the preservation of natural and cultural resources. Additionally, the field of regenerative tourism can benefit from the utilization of various Multi-Criteria Decision Making (MCDM) methods within diverse fuzzy environments, including spherical fuzzy sets (Kahraman et al., 2021), T-spherical fuzzy sets (Shen et al., 2022), bipolar neutrosophic sets (Deli et al., 2015), Pythagorean fuzzy sets (Chaurasiya, R., & Jain, D., 2023), etc.

ACKNOWLEDGMENT

The authors express their gratitude to the editors and reviewers for their invaluable comments and suggestions, which greatly enhance this chapter.

REFERENCES

Bærenholdt, J. O., Haldrup, M., & Urry, J. (2017). *Performing tourist places*. Routledge. 10.4324/9781315247106

Bellato, L., Frantzeskaki, N., & Nygaard, C. A. (2023). Regenerative tourism: A conceptual framework leveraging theory and practice. *Tourism Geographies*, 25(4), 1026–1046. 10.1080/14616688.2022.2044376

Bhartiya, S., Bhatt, V., Rathore, A. H., & Khanam, T. (2024). A Theory-Based Approach to Understanding Social Sustainability in Tourism. In *Implementing Sustainable Development Goals in the Service Sector* (pp. 146–156). IGI Global.

Bobar, Z., Božanić, D., Djurić, K., & Pamučar, D. (2020). Ranking and assessment of the efficiency of social media using the fuzzy AHP-Z number model-fuzzy MABAC. *Acta Polytechnica Hungarica*, 17(3), 43–70. 10.12700/APH.17.3.2020.3.3

Büyüközkan, G., Mukul, E., & Kongar, E. (2021). Health tourism strategy selection via SWOT analysis and integrated hesitant fuzzy linguistic AHP-MABAC approach. *Socio-Economic Planning Sciences*, 74, 100929. 10.1016/j.seps.2020.100929

Chakraborty, S., Sarkar, B., & Chakraborty, S. (2023). A FUCOM-MABAC-based integrated approach for performance evaluation of the Indian National Parks. *OPSEARCH*, 60(1), 125–154. 10.1007/s12597-022-00611-2

Chaurasiya, R., & Jain, D. (2023). Hybrid MCDM method on Pythagorean fuzzy set and its application. *Decision Making: Applications in Management and Engineering*, 6(1), 379–398. 10.31181/dmame0306102022c

Deli, I., Ali, M., & Smarandache, F. (2015, August). Bipolar neutrosophic sets and their application based on multi-criteria decision making problems. In *2015 International conference on advanced mechatronic systems (ICAMechS)* (pp. 249-254). IEEE. 10.1109/ICAMechS.2015.7287068

Duxbury, N., Bakas, F. E., Vinagre de Castro, T., & Silva, S. (2020). Creative tourism development models towards sustainable and regenerative tourism. *Sustainability (Basel)*, 13(1), 2. 10.3390/su13010002

Ghosh, S., Chakraborty, S., & Chakraborty, S. (2022). An integrated IRN-SWARA-MABAC-based approach for evaluation of tourism websites of the Indian states. *OPSEARCH*, 59(3), 974–1017. 10.1007/s12597-022-00583-3

Go, H., & Kang, M. (2023). Metaverse tourism for sustainable tourism development: Tourism agenda 2030. *Tourism Review*, 78(2), 381–394. 10.1108/TR-02-2022-0102

Hassan, V., & Abou Fayad, S. (2023). Slow tourism as a tool for sustainable tourism development post-pandemic. *Uluslararası Sosyal Bilimler ve Eğitim Dergisi*, 5(8), 299–316.

Hassan, V. I., & Basheer, S. (2024). The Impact of Advanced Technology on Medical Tourism Transformation: Case Study of United Arabs of Emirates. In *Impact of AI and Robotics on the Medical Tourism Industry* (pp. 1–19). IGI Global. 10.4018/979-8-3693-2248-2.ch001

Howard, M. C., & Henderson, J. (2023). A review of exploratory factor analysis in tourism and hospitality research: Identifying current practices and avenues for improvement. *Journal of Business Research*, 154, 113328. 10.1016/j.jbusres.2022.113328

Hristoforova, I. V., Silcheva, L. V., Arkhipova, T. N., Demenkova, A. B., & Nikolskaya, E. Y. (2019). Improvement of digital technologies in marketing communications of tourism and hospitality enterprises. *Journal of Environmental Management and Tourism*, 10(4), 829–834. 10.14505//jemt.10.4(36).13

Jokić, Ž., Božanić, D., & Pamučar, D. (2021). Selection of fire position of mortar units using LBWA and Fuzzy MABAC model. *Operational Research in Engineering Sciences: Theory and Applications*, 4(1), 115–135.

Kahraman, C., & Gündogdu, F. K. (2021). Decision making with spherical fuzzy sets. *Studies in fuzziness and soft computing, 392*, 3-25.

Kemer, E., & Tyagi, P. K. (2023). Application of Artificial Intelligence and Robotics in Tourism and Hospitality Marketing. In *Embracing Business Sustainability Through Innovation and Creativity in the Service Sector* (pp. 125–140). IGI Global. 10.4018/978-1-6684-6732-9.ch008

Keshavarz-Ghorabaee, M., Amiri, M., Hashemi-Tabatabaei, M., & Ghahremanloo, M. (2021). Sustainable public transportation evaluation using a novel hybrid method based on fuzzy BWM and MABAC. *The Open Transportation Journal, 15*(1).

Kumar, A., & Singh, G. (2019). Seasonal effect on tourism in India. *Journal of Financial Economics*, 7(2), 48–51.

Lotfi, F. H. (2023). *Fuzzy Decision Analysis: Multi-Attribute Decision Making Approach*. Springer Nature. 10.1007/978-3-031-44742-6

Pamučar, D., & Ćirović, G. (2015). The selection of transport and handling resources in logistics centers using Multi-Attributive Border Approximation area Comparison (MABAC). *Expert Systems with Applications*, 42(6), 3016–3028. 10.1016/j. eswa.2014.11.057

Rout, H. B., Mishra, P. K., & Pradhan, B. B. (2016). Socio-economic impacts of tourism in India: An empirical analysis. *Journal of Environmental Management & Tourism*, 7(4 (16)), 762.

Saputro, K. E. A. (1835). Hasim, Karlinasari, L., & Beik, I. S. (2023). Evaluation of Sustainable Rural Tourism Development with an integrated approach using MDS and ANP methods: Case study in Ciamis, West Java, Indonesia. *Sustainability (New Rochelle, N.Y.)*, 15(3).

Shen, X., Sakhi, S., Ullah, K., Abid, M. N., & Jin, Y. (2022). Information measures based on T-spherical fuzzy sets and their applications in decision-making and pattern recognition. *Axioms*, 11(7), 302. 10.3390/axioms11070302

Tomassini, L., & Cavagnaro, E. (2022). Circular economy: a paradigm to critically rethink sustainability in tourism and hospitality. In *Planning and Managing Sustainability in Tourism: Empirical Studies, Best-practice Cases and Theoretical Insights* (pp. 1–12). Springer International Publishing. 10.1007/978-3-030-92208-5_1

Verma, R. (2021). Fuzzy MABAC method based on new exponential fuzzy information measures. *Soft Computing*, 25(14), 9575–9589. 10.1007/s00500-021-05739-9

Walker, K., & Moscardo, G. (2019). Moving beyond sense of place to care of place: The role of Indigenous values and interpretation in promoting transformative change in tourists' place images and personal values. In *Sustainable Tourism and Indigenous Peoples* (pp. 177–195). Routledge. 10.4324/9781315112053-11

Xiang, Z., Stienmetz, J., & Fesenmaier, D. R. (2021). Smart Tourism Design: Launching the annals of tourism research curated collection on designing tourism places. *Annals of Tourism Research*, 86, 103154. 10.1016/j.annals.2021.103154

Żemła, M., & Staszewska, A. (2022). The Use of Post-Industrial Heritage in the Construction of Competitive Tourist Products: The Case of the Upper Silesia-Zagłębie Metropolis, Poland. In *Tourism Planning and Development in Eastern Europe* (pp. 31-46). CABI.

Chapter 13
A Bibliometric Examination of Online Hotel Booking via OTA an AI and Tech–Driven Travel Solutions

Jagjit Singh
https://orcid.org/0000-0001-9753-4866
Chandigarh University, India

Shikha Sharma
https://orcid.org/0009-0001-3680-3556
Chandigarh University, India

ABSTRACT

Electronic commerce has changed travel product distribution and buyer behavior. Internet usage drives the online travel market's fast development and commercial potential. Online travel booking operators now account for many global travel sales. It is feasible to do this as a result of the fast development of high-speed internet and smart phones, both of which are readily available to any person in today's world.

INTRODUCTION

E-commerce transformed Indian business. The Indian e-commerce sector is predicted to reach US$200bn by 2026, up from US$38.5bn in 2017. Internet and smartphone usage have driven most industry growth. The government's 'Digital India'

DOI: 10.4018/979-8-3693-5405-6.ch013

Copyright © 2024, IGI Global. Copying or distributing in print or electronic forms without written permission of IGI Global is prohibited.

programme has boosted India's internet connections to 776.45 million by September 2020. 61% of Internet connections were urban, 97% wireless.. (E-Commerce in India: Industry Overview, Market Size & Growth| IBEF, n.d.). The internet's history dates back to the 1950s and 1960s, when computers were first invented. It has since evolved into a variety of businesses, including online travel agencies (OTAs), which have transformed travelers' needs into "one-stop shops" for all their travel needs. The online travel business did not commence on a specific day; however, it is possible to infer that consumer attitudes and behaviors regarding travel reservations have changed over the past five years. The traditional "brick and mortar" travel agency has been phased out in favor of internet trip booking. Rather than relying on travel agencies to organize their travels, travelers prefer to book and view their itinerary independently, and they desire direct access to rates. A travel portal is a highly integrated booking engine that connects providers in the travel and hospitality industries with customers on a single screen. Over the last decade, the growth of e-commerce in the hotel and tourism industries has affected product distribution networks. Technology has grown so quickly that Internet saturation is critical, allowing travel products to move primarily online. Growing online travel booking operators currently account for one-third of global travel sales. This fast-growing trend increased 50% in Asia-Pacific and 20% in Europe between 2010 and 2011. Online travel booking is considerably more prevalent in the US, where 83% of leisure and 76% of business travelers use the Internet to plan their trips. 9% greater than in 2011, US internet travel reservations earned $103 billion in 2012 (comScore, 2013). Since the internet is flexible and accessible, you may look for and purchase travel items and services with a few mouse clicks. The study examined the impact of travel suppliers' investments in generative AI on the booking share of online travel agencies (OTAs) in the US from 2023 to 2028, breaking down the data by scenario. In 2023, a study looked at how travel companies' investments in generative AI could affect online travel bookings in the US. The data shows that in 2023, 32% of all U.S. online travel reservations were made through OTAs. If travel suppliers do not invest in AI, the online travel agencies' booking share might increase to 46.7% by 2028, a growth of roughly 15%. The OTA booking share would fall to 29.1% in 2028 under a scenario where substantial investments are made in generative AI, which would lead to an increase in supplier-direct bookings.

1.1 Market Capability

From US$1.9 billion in 2019, the Indian online grocery business is expected to reach US$18.2 billion in 2024. In the fourth quarter of 2020, India's e-commerce orders rose 36%, with PCB&W benefitting most. The Indian e-commerce market is predicted to reach US$200bn by 2026, up from US$38.5bn in 2017. This surge is due to smartphone use, 4G network development, and increasing income. Flipkart, Amazon India, and Paytm Mall are predicted to boost India's online retail sales by 31% to US$32.70bn in 2018 (*Indian E-Commerce Industry Analysis | IBEF*, n.d.).

Indian smartphone sales surpassed 150 million in 2020, while 5G shipments topped 4 million owing to client demand after the shutdown. Indian e-commerce GMV reached $8.3 billion during the festive season CY20, up 66% from the previous holiday season. CY20's Christmas season, we had 88 million Indian e-commerce consumers, increasing 87% over the previous holiday season (E-Commerce in India: Industry Overview, Market Size & Growth| IBEF, n.d.).

Bibliometric analysis is a systematic and often-used method for studying and analyzing large amounts of scientific material. It enables us to investigate the complex evolutionary aspects of a certain discipline and shed light on the developing regions within it. Nevertheless, its use in business research is very new and sometimes lacks sufficient development. Hence, our objective is to provide a thorough exposition of the bibliometric methodology, focusing specifically on its many methodologies, and to furnish reliable, systematic directions for doing bibliometric analysis with precision. Furthermore, we provide guidance on the suitable use and timing of bibliometric analysis in relation to other similar approaches, such as systematic literature reviews and meta-analyses. Overall, this work is anticipated to serve as a beneficial resource for gaining a comprehensive grasp of the strategies and processes used in performing investigations via bibliometric analysis (Donthu et al., 2021)

The OTA and Hotel Business Model

Online travel agencies (OTAs) such as Expedia and Booking.com provide an easy booking platform for passengers, while simultaneously providing hotels with extensive consumer outreach. However, could you perhaps clarify the precise mechanics of the interaction between online travel agencies (OTAs) and hotels.OTAs collaborate with hotels to provide an internet-based platform for the sale of hotel accommodations. They get a commission for every reservation booked via their website. Hotels incur expenses for marketing, technology, and worldwide distribution. This tutorial provides an in-depth analysis of the OTA and hotel business model, including the intricacies of booking processes, the advantages and disadvantages for hotels, and the benefits for travelers (Kizielewicz, 2019).

Online vacation Agencies (OTAs) has fundamentally transformed the process of reserving vacation lodgings for individuals. These platforms serve as mediators between hotels and passengers, streamlining the booking process for enhanced speed and convenience. Now, let us delve into the intricacies of their business concept. Contractual agreements: Hotels establish a contractual agreement with an Online Travel Agency (OTA) to define the terms and circumstances of their collaboration.

This agreement has several facets, such as the commission structure, parity rate agreements, and other significant components. Online Travel Agencies (OTAs) often provide hotels with a comprehensive array of marketing services, such as showcasing their properties on their website, running advertising campaigns, and granting access to a large pool of potential customers. Hotels agree to remunerate the OTA platform by paying a commission for each booking facilitated via it (Wilson, 2011).

Commission structure plays a crucial role in the economic strategy of both OTAs and hotels. It calculates the proportion of income that hotels are required to provide to the OTA for every reservation. The commission fees may fluctuate based on variables like as the geographical location of the hotel, its star rating, and the quantity of reservations produced via the OTA platform. For instance, a high-end hotel in a renowned tourist hotspot may entail a greater commission rate in contrast to a low-cost hotel in a less frequented region. The prices are often negotiated between the online travel agency (OTA) and the hotel, and they have a substantial impact on the profitability of both parties. Reduced ability to manage and shape the perception of a brand's identity. Hotels compromise their brand identity when they form partnerships with OTAs. Online Travel Agencies (OTAs) sometimes own distinctive branding and design components that may outshine the hotel's own brand. Hotels often have difficulties in establishing a distinctive character and distinguishing themselves from their rivals. Moreover, hotels have little authority over the presentation of their property on the OTA's website, since the OTA has full control over the material and photos that are shown to prospective visitors. Hotels that want to highlight their property's distinctive characteristics and facilities may find it exasperating to have little control over the presentation (Rana & Sharma, 2015).

Advantages for Those Who Are Traveling Reservation Made via Online Travel Agencies (OTAs)

Effortlessly evaluate and contrast various hotel choices an advantageous aspect of reserving hotels via Online Travel Agencies (OTAs) is the convenience of readily comparing several hotel choices. By just clicking a few times, tourists can easily compare pricing, facilities, user ratings, and other significant variables. This enables consumers to save significant time and exertion by eliminating the need to do extensive research and navigate through several hotel websites. Online travel agencies (OTAs) provide a convenient interface that enables users to refine their search results by applying certain filters, such as location, price range, star rating, and other parameters. This greatly facilitates the task of guests in locating the ideal hotel that aligns with their specific tastes and financial constraints (J. Zhang et al., 2017).

Streamlined reservation process: Booking a hotel via an Online Travel Agency (OTA) provides a more efficient and organized booking process. Travelers may quickly and safely finalize their arrangements without the need to wade through several pages or endure protracted booking procedures. Online Travel Agencies (OTAs) provide a user-friendly booking platform that aims to streamline the whole process for maximum convenience. Frequently, they provide an extensive selection of payment alternatives, including credit cards, debit cards, and even mobile payment solutions. Furthermore, several online travel agencies (OTAs) provide round-the-clock customer support services, guaranteeing prompt help for passengers at any time (Punhani et al., 2021).

Customer loyalty programs and exclusive promotions: Several online travel agencies (OTAs) provide reward programs and exclusive offers for customers. These programs let regular customers to accumulate prizes, such as complimentary stays or unique price reductions, as a result of their ongoing loyalty. Travelers may avail themselves of these reward programs and reap extra advantages and benefits by making reservations via an Online Travel Agency (OTA).In addition, online travel agencies (OTAs) often engage in negotiations with hotels to secure advantageous agreements, leading to reduced prices or unique offers that may not be accessible when making a reservation directly via the hotel. This provides tourists with the chance to save and experience additional benefits when staying at the hotel (B.-D. Kim et al., 2001).

How the Hotel Industry Is Becoming Green for Sustainable Development

A Green Hotel is a kind of accommodation that is designed and operated in an environmentally sustainable manner, with a focus on reducing its carbon footprint and promoting eco-friendly practices.

A green hotel, also known as a sustainable or eco-hotel, prioritizes sustainability in its operations. The phrase "green hotel" comprises a diverse array of concepts, which show different levels of dedication to ecologically sustainable activities.

On one side of the scale, there are hotels intentionally built with a strong focus on sustainability in their design. These eco-hotels use sustainable construction principles from the beginning, reducing environmental harm throughout the development process. This involves using environmentally friendly building materials and energy-efficient technology. The finished property includes fixtures and systems that enable waste management, energy efficiency, and water conservation, such as solar power and water recycling systems. Hotels that use this holistic strategy often get certificates that acknowledge their dedication to sustainability, with many worldwide certifications being prevalent in the market (Gauvreau-Lemelin & Attia, 2017).

On the other side of the sustainability spectrum, existing hotels may adopt steps to enhance their environmental friendliness. Although some hotels may not have adhered to sustainable construction methods, they actively prioritize and implement sustainable principles in their operations. These activities may include implementing rainwater capture and reuse systems, installing low-flow toilets and LED lighting, and implementing guest programs that promote decreased laundry of towels and bedding (VanGeem et al., 2001).

Guide to Creating an Environmentally Sustainable Hotel

Developing your hotel's environmentally friendly credentials requires a deliberate and substantial commitment to sustainability, avoiding superficial actions that may be seen as deceptive marketing tactics. To achieve environmental sustainability in your hotel, take into account the following:

Enhance Sustainability: Prioritise the reduction of water use, the improvement of energy efficiency, and the implementation of efficient waste management strategies.

Community Benefits: Optimise the positive social and economic effects on your nearby community.

Environmental Impact: Implement measures to mitigate adverse environmental consequences linked to the activities of your hotel.

Supply Chain Sustainability: Evaluate and enhance the sustainability of your supply chain, since this will have a pivotal impact on any certification procedure.

To successfully direct your efforts, choose the certification(s) that are in line with your objectives. Every eco-hotel certification is accompanied by precise criteria, guaranteeing that your endeavors result in significant transformations and make you eligible for acknowledgment. By obtaining accreditation, you not only improve the reputation of your hotel but also attract environmentally aware travelers who are looking for hotels that prioritize sustainability(Alameeri et al., 2018).

LEED-Certified Hotel Around the World

Numerous hospitality businesses use the U.S. Green Building Council's LEED accreditation standard as a fundamental guideline for their sustainability initiatives. The prevailing method is the creation of hotels that are LEED-certified, starting from scratch(Sih, 2009). This requires incorporating the knowledge and skills of the hospitality industry in several aspects, including building design, construction, interior design, and construction systems.Marriott International is distinguished as a frontrunner in this aspect, having successfully certified a significant number of its properties.

The LEED Volume Programme, which it helped create, has played a substantial role in contributing to this achievement. This program employs pre-certified pro-totypes, which simplifies and accelerates the certification procedure for clusters of buildings. The benefits of using LEED from the first planning phases are clearly shown by cases like as the Palazzo Hotel in Las Vegas, which has achieved Silver certification. Composed mostly of 95% recycled steel and 26% recycled concrete, this structure exemplifies a fundamental dedication to environmentally-friendly ideals (Sipic, 2017)..The LEED Certification for Existing Buildings Operations & Maintenance method may also be used to effectively transform pre-existing buildings. Such instance is the Kempinski Hotel Mall of the Emirates in Dubai. Established in 2006, the facility obtained Silver certification in 2013 after thorough auditing and retrofitting endeavors.

These efforts led to a 9% decrease in energy and water use, even before the com-pletion of the certification procedure.The transition to renewable energy sources and improved energy efficiency is a major environmental project for U.S. hotels since energy expenses account for around 6% of their operating costs. Hotels often use advanced technology like smart systems and transition to sustainable energy suppliers. Some individuals or organizations take it a step further by producing energy directly at the location where it is needed.The MGM National Harbour in Maryland demonstrates the need for water conservation by collecting and treating rainwater for irrigation and restroom use. Hotels have issues in managing waste, particularly regarding food waste and single-use goods. The 1 Hotels Group im-plements strategies such as optimizing waste management, partnering with local organizations to recycle non-traditional goods, and using technology like Winnow Vision to track food waste and enhance menu development.The growing popularity of zero-energy buildings, such as Boutique Hotel Stadthalle in Vienna, which uses solar panels and groundwater heat pumps, indicates a promising trend for the future (Mondor et al., 2013).

LITERATURE REVIEW

E-Commerce in the Tourism Industry

Information technology has rapidly improved over the last two decades, con-tributing to the rapid growth of tourist e-commerce (S. Kim et al., 2021). Global distribution systems (GDS) played a crucial role in facilitating the coordination of activities between traditional travel agents and travel providers, including airlines and hotels, prior to the introduction of the Internet.

The development of the Internet and information communication technology since the late 1990s has greatly altered the operational approaches of hospitality organizations operating in the highly competitive worldwide market. Tourism firms, vacation destinations, and hospitality organizations have shifted their operations to electronic distribution. Leading hotel businesses have adopted proactive direct sales techniques via their websites instead of relying on traditional travel brokers. The process by which an organization takes back control of its distribution instead of relying on traditional travel middlemen is known as "disintermediation" (Calveras & Orfila-Sintes, 2019). Hotels and airlines often choose to use direct electronic distribution to save costs and enhance customer loyalty and pleasure.

Online Travel Agency

Online travel agencies (OTAs) like Orbitz.com, Expedia.com, Hotel.com, Travelocity.com, and Priceline.com are illustrative instances of such organizations. OTAs (online travel agencies) use one or more of the following business models: commissionable, merchant, or opaque selling (Schott & Nhem, 2018). The merchant model entails acquiring travel products or services through online travel agencies (OTAs). Acquire goods at a discounted price and then resell them to customers at a higher price. In contrast, a commission-based model involves OTAs arranging supplier meetings and receiving payment in the form of a commission, which is a proportion of the sale for each transaction (Arora et al., 2021). Users purchase travel items using the opaque selling approach, expressing their preferred pricing and receiving no further product information until the transaction is complete. Opaque selling offers significant savings due to the many constraints on the acquired goods. For instance, if a consumer is unaware of the hotel's name and exact location before making a purchase, they may face considerable risk if they cannot get a refund or exchange (Poinssot et al., 2013).

Websites That Use Meta-Search Functionality

Meta-search technologies collect data from several websites simultaneously based on user choices to provide a customized list of travel items (Hunold et al., 2018). Momondo.com, Kayak.com, Bookingbuddy.com, and Google.com are prominent meta-search engines. These websites streamline the search process for visitors by allowing them to simultaneously examine and compare information about different goods. Meta-search websites do not allow customers to complete reservation transactions; instead, they direct them to the specific travel website for completion. Researchers claim that some customers may perceive a product as of higher quality.

Social media sites include platforms and websites that allow users to communicate and interact online.

Social media platforms provide conduits for users to create and share material, such as personal experiences, product reviews, and travel-related information (Dhawale et al., 2020). Leading hotel chains have recognized the importance of social media as a marketing platform and created their own accounts on Twitter and Facebook. Their goal is to encourage customers to use the direct booking function (El Haddad et al., 2015).Tripadvisor.com, a popular social media network in the travel sector, combines information search features with user-generated content. Hotel guests provide assessments and rankings based on their level of pleasure, personal experience, and likelihood of returning (Akram et al., 2020). In addition, users have the option to perform hotel searches based on star rating, location, and price. Other social media sites, such as Biddingfortravel.com and Betterbidding. com, have a wealth of user-generated content provided by experienced customers who have booked their accommodations through online travel companies. These customers share their knowledge, guiding readers on how to find and buy travel items at a more affordable price over the Internet.

Exclusive Sales, Limited-Time Deals, and Time-Limited Websites

E-commerce platforms that facilitate flash sales and private sales provide reduced merchandise for a limited period, often ranging from twenty-four to forty-eight hours (TravelClick, 2012). Consumers must complete a membership registration in order to get daily discount offers by text message, email, or mobile application alerts. Flash and private sale websites sometimes provide cheap trip packages for sale. These internet platforms specifically target cost-conscious customers who are looking for comprehensive products at significant markdowns (Janani & Yuvaraj, 2019). Gilt-JetSetter, Groupon-Getaways, and Living Social-Escape are popular destinations for flash and private sales. Hotels utilize flash promotions for many purposes, such as boosting occupancy during the off-season, enhancing the hotel's exposure, attracting a new customer base, and competing with rivals (TravelClick1, 2012).

Online platforms Travelzoo.com and Lastminute.com offer last-minute deals and aim to sell perishable goods before they run out (Toh et al., 2011). These websites cater to users with flexible travel plans who prefer to wait for last-minute offers rather than incurring higher prices for prior bookings.

How Does the Internet Influence Pricing Strategies?

Price discrimination is a commonly documented occurrence in the hotel industry, used by businesses as a significant method to encourage demand and maximize income opportunities (Arya et al., 2019). Hotels, airlines, and other travel companies use various pricing schemes to obtain the desired profits. Hotels use a room rate structure that is based on customer demand and price sensitivity. Research indicates that online tourist suppliers often engage in price differentiation and dispersion (Dlacic et al., 2018). Online customers' easy access to accommodation prices and product information poses a significant challenge for hotels. Kimes (2009) conducted recent research where hotel revenue managers identified "price wars" as their primary concern. In order to retain a competitive advantage, hotels must carefully monitor market circumstances and make proportional adjustments to their room prices.

Consumer Decision Making Process (CDP)

The conventional model of the consumer decision-making process (CDP) suggests that consumers go through three separate phases before making a purchasing decision: recognizing their need, searching for information, and evaluating different options (Kalia & Paul, 2021). A cognitive process comprising three distinct phases influences consumers' buying choices. Consumers determine their desires and needs before beginning their search for items or services that satisfy them. By carefully assessing all possible options, consumers conduct an external inquiry, which is a critical phase in gathering information (Sano & Sano, 2019).

How Do Consumers Perceive and Understand Sales Promotions?

People have recognized the importance of customer perceived value in deciding pricing strategies. A value-based pricing approach focuses on enhancing customers' sense of value. Put simply, buyers should perceive the value of the product to be greater than the price they pay for it. Hospitality marketers often use this concept to create sales campaigns with the aim of improving customer happiness and increasing revenue (Raman & Aashish, 2021).

Hospitality e-commerce uses a variety of sales promotion formats, such as rebates, discount codes, premiums, sweepstakes, extra loyalty program points, mileage accumulation, and package aggregation (Toh et al., 2011).

Table 1. Depicts details summary of Literature Review can be seen in Table 1 which has Key terms, Authors & Year of publication along with Finding and Journal name. Airline tickets, automobile rentals, and accommodation can be researched, analyzed, and booked 24/7. Due to the range of product offerings, rapid price comparisons, time savings, and convenience when requesting services to fit their needs, online customers commonly use numerous websites as their primary instrument for travel planning. (Toh et al., 2011). Not only does Internet booking help clients streamline travel arrangements, and it also benefits businesses like airlines, hotels, and other tour providers by raising their income. Details summary of Literature Review can be seen in Table 1 which has Key terms, Authors & Year of publication along with Finding and Journal name.

Table 1. Summary of Literature Review

Key Terms	Author & Year	Finding	Journal Name
E-commerce	(Buhalis & Law, 2008)	As information technology has developed rapidly in the past twenty years, tourist e-commerce has increased substantially. Global distribution systems (GDS) were vital in coordinating operations between brick-and-mortar travel agents and travel providers before the advent of the internet era (i.e., airlines and hotels).	Tourism Management
E- commerce	(Tse, 2003)	Since the late 1990s, the Internet and ICT have become popular, transforming how hospitality firms operate in a worldwide competitive market. Hospitality groups, holiday locations, and tourism enterprises used electronic distribution. Major hotel firms used aggressive direct sales tactics via their websites rather than relying on travel intermediaries.	Hospitality Management
online travel agencies	(Lee & Law, 2012)	Yatra.com, Expedia.com, and Makemytrip.com are all examples of online travel agencies (OTAs). OTAs operate on one or more of the following business models: a merchant, commission-based, or opaque form of selling. OTAs acquire travel items at a discount in the merchant model and resell them to consumers at a premium price.	Journal of Travel and Tourism Market
Meta-search websites	(Anderson & Wilson, 2011)	Meta-search websites collect information from numerous websites depending on client preferences to provide the most appropriate travel items for specific consumers. E.g. Google.com site simplifies the customer search experience, allowing users to browse and compare information about several goods.	Journal of Hospitality Marketing & Management
Social media websites	(Jeong & Jeon, 2008)	Customers can use social media networks to discuss travel-related information, product assessments, and personal experiences. Major hotel chains have recognized social media as a vital marketing tool, creating their own Facebook and Twitter pages to entice clients to book directly.	Journal of Hospitality & Leisure Marketing

continued on following page

Table 1. Continued

Key Terms	Author & Year	Finding	Journal Name
Flash sales, private sales and last-minute websites	(Martinez & Kim, 2012)	Flash and private sales websites allow users to purchase items at a discounted price for a limited period, usually 24-48 hours. Consumers must sign up as members and receive daily discount announcements via email, text, or mobile app alerts. Vacation packages are often offered at a discount via flash and private websites.	Journal of Fashion Marketing and Management
Deal Searching	(E. M. Zhang, 2010)	Consumers may be active or passive. In active deal-searching, consumers notice sales promotions and seek bargains. Passive searching involves consumers waiting for company promotions. Passive customers react to marketers' direct contacts, such as e-mailing each client, rather than actively seeking deal-relevant information.	Psychology & Marketing
Consumers' proclivity towards deals	(Lichtenstein et al., 1993)	Price consciousness refers to consumers' preference for low pricing over product quality. Coupon and sale proneness measure customers' proclivity to use coupons and take advantage of promotional offers. Finally, "price mavens" refers to consumers' sensitivity to pricing information and their proclivity to share it with other customers.	Journal of Marketing Research
Evaluation and comparison process	(Sarkar, 2011)	Consumer aims to evaluate alternatives by seeking relevant information and weighing costs and advantages. However, some researchers claimed that customers' decision-making process is also impacted by emotional reactions, such as their feelings or encounters with product qualities.	International Management Review

Source:, Author compilation from Scopus data base

METHOD

3.1 Data Collection

According to PRISMA standards, the literature review involves developing research questions and choosing a search method. The following research questions inspired this analysis:

To address the following problems, a search method was developed to list and evaluate each study paper:

1. Define keywords and find relevant material.
2. Filtering documents.
3. Addressing potential prejudice.

Keywords are a vital step in the methodical investigation. We targeted hotels, restaurants, and the tourist business. Established keywords appear in Table 2. It shows common used key words in these studies.

Table 2. Target Keywords used in the Literature Search

Search	Target
1	online AND travel AND agency
2	online AND travel AND agencies
3	online AND travel AND agent
4	online AND travel AND intermediaries
5	hotel AND reservation

Source: Author compilation from Scopus data base

The eligibility criteria in this study were utilized to find other research and syntheses. OTA-related articles were kept, and others were abandoned. Scopus, Web of Sciences, provided data.

Table 2 includes search key words techniques for the acutance index. Other keywords were used to get further information. The methodologies and targeted subjects articles were not free between 2004 and 2021. Search engines include Google Scholar, Web of Science, and Science. This topic is evolving soon. Thus, Related Target Words were utilized to uncover 121 papers with content by the June 14, 2021 screening. A systematic omission and inclusion technique was applied as the archive still existed when the author identified all linked articles. Figure 1. shows following PRISMA rules, we found that after deleting duplicates (n = 51), a search of the listed records' titles, abstracts, results, and keywords excluded 23 articles due to their poor topic association. The 24 remaining publications were evaluated against eligibility, and 14 were rejected for failing to address the study's issues.

Figure 1. Chart Outlining the Collection Technique Following PRISMA Guideline

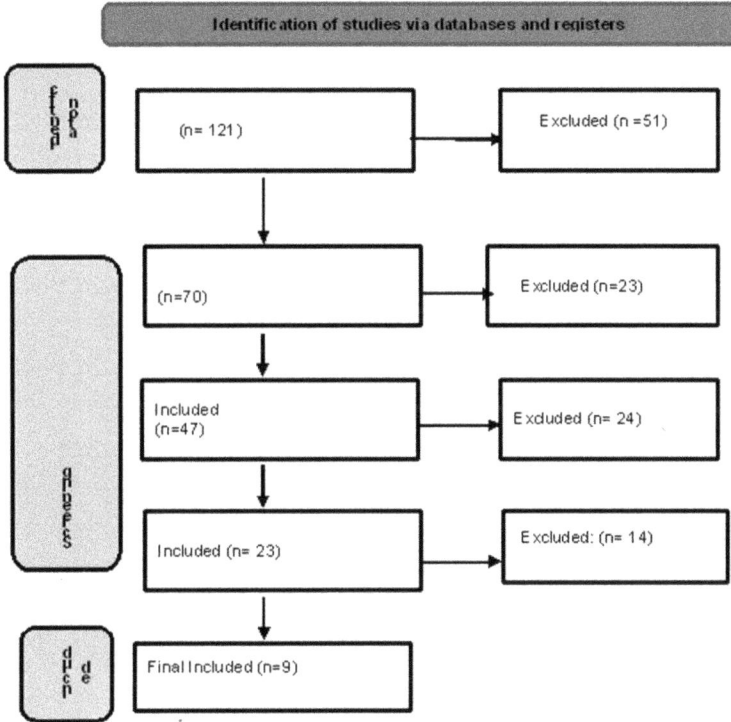

Source: Author compilation from Scopus data bas

DATA ANALYSIS

Figure 2 depicts co-citation analyses were used to determine the fundamental literature for the subject area, the most often referenced studies in chosen publications and to address the second research question. The investigation began with creating a chart depicting the rise in published figures. A review of the most influential newspapers, followed by a co-citation analysis, enables the identification of critical publications. Finally, a co-word study was conducted to determine the primary research subjects by examining keyword dimensions.

Figure 2. Bibliographic Map Based on Keywords Co-occurrence

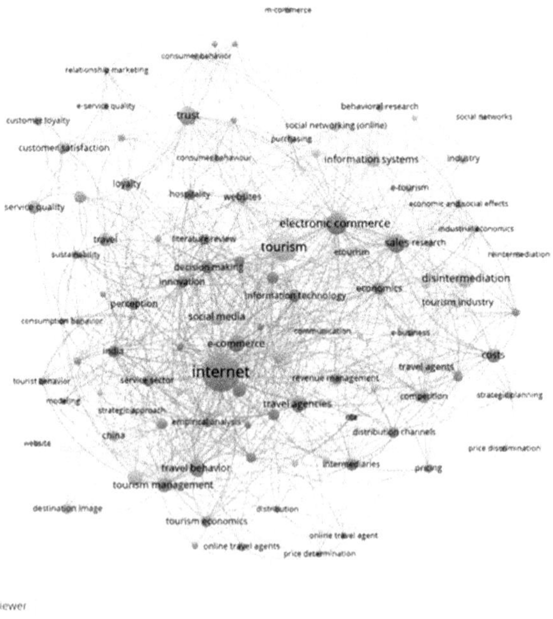

Source: Author compilation with (VOSviewer - Visualizing Scientific Landscapes, n.d.)

RESULTS

Figure 3. Document Category % Age-Wise

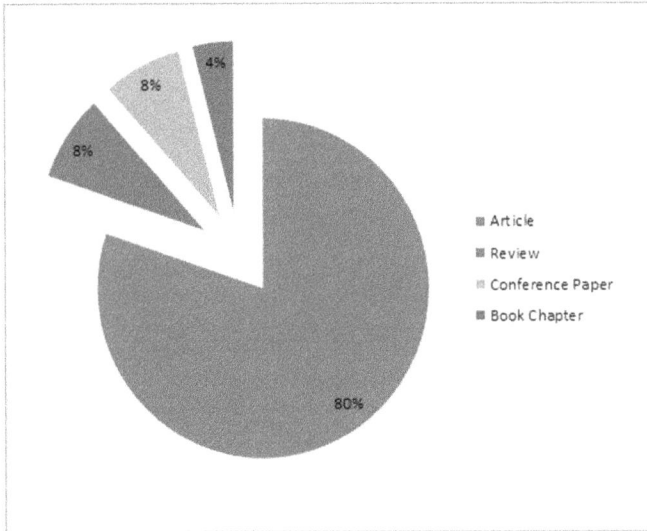

Source: Author compilation

Figure 3 shows document category-wise Publication from 2004 to 2021. 80% in articles, 8%- 8% in reviews and conference papers and 4% Book Chapters.

Figure 4. Year-wise Publications from 2004 to 2021

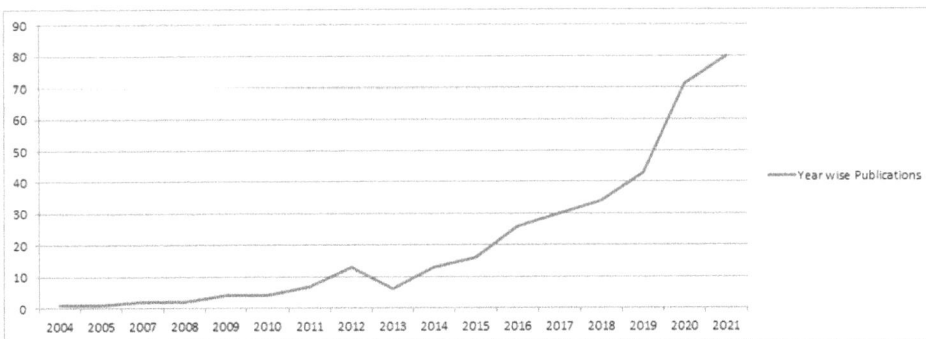

Source: Author compilation

Figure 4 illustrates the publishing increase throughout the study. Growth was constant from 2015 to 2021, dropped from 2004 to 2014, and accelerated from 2015.

Figure 5. Disciplinary Categories of Papers

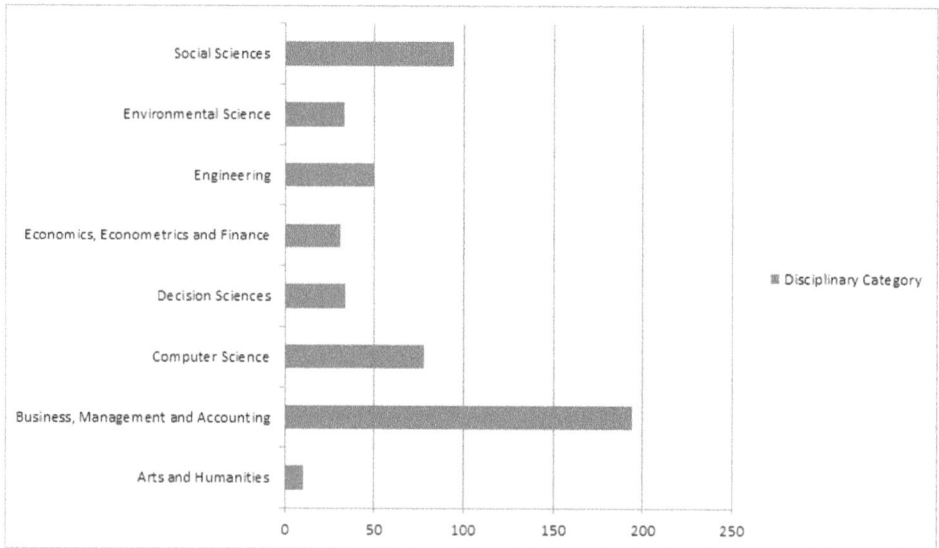

Source: Author compilation

Figure 5 shows articles had been published in different disciplinary categories in the year of 2004 to 2021.

CONCLUSION

Due to its rapid growth, online travel shopping has attracted researchers, and there is a growing body of literature in this field. This study examined nine articles published in prestigious tourism journals between 2004 and 2021, highlighting the significant contributions of these studies to the tourism field. In addition, a clear and complete examination of the components impacting online travel intermediaries was provided by categorizing all identified variables into three significant categories: client features, perceived channel features, and website and product features. This comprehensive examination resulted in the identification of several gaps and research opportunities. Indeed, several causes require additional investigation.

To begin with, certain essential variables of online trip purchases have been ignored. For example, the relationship between social media and online trip purchases has yet to be studied. Second, research should reconcile contradictory findings. In some instances, contradictory conclusions may result from researchers addressing the same construct differently (e.g., online shopping experience). However, it needs to be clarified how diverse research conceptualizes these constructs. This study thus suggests that researchers offer a comprehensive explanation of the components included in their studies and how they were operational to allow comparisons with other studies. Lastly, online travel purchase research has always been dispersed. Literature analysis showed a need for more research combining multiple factors to understand online travel buying better and determine which components are more important to buyers. A significant limitation of this study is that its literature review depends primarily on tourism and travel publishing papers. The examination may be strengthened by publishing online travel shopping from other academic journals.

On the other hand, while a systematic methodology has been employed to find eligible articles, some relevant articles may still need to be addressed. Indeed, publications may occasionally cover internet travel purchases, but the title or keywords may need to make this apparent, making identifying these pieces difficult. Despite these limitations, academics, tourism practitioners, and marketers may utilize this study to understand online travel purchase research better. Practitioners and marketers may discover characteristics that affect online travel purchases, enhancing their online travel distribution strategy. Understanding the purchase behavior of internet travellers is essential to successful online marketing techniques (Lee et al., 2007). This research is expected to contribute considerably to the current literature by extending information on internet travel purchases in the academic sector. Additionally, the study gaps revealed offer academic challenges for future research. Emerging regulatory frameworks requiring net-zero operations are driving the worldwide hotel sector to prioritize sustainability and ESG. Some hotel brands and stakeholders have pledged to improve their ESG performance and reach net-zero objectives, although slow economic development in the EU, UK, and Asia Pacific may slow progress. In addition, the expected U.S. recession may hinder short-term progress. Inflation, rising interest rates, and global uncertainty exacerbate these difficulties. These reasons may delay ESG measures for financially strapped hotel chains.

REFERENCES

Akram, M., Garg, H., & Zahid, K. (2020). Extensions of electre-i and topsis methods for group decision-making under complex pythagorean fuzzy environment. *Iranian Journal of Fuzzy Systems*, 17(5), 147–164. 10.22111/ijfs.2020.5522

Alameeri, A., Ajmal, M. M., Hussain, M., & Helo, P. (2018). Sustainable management practices in UAE hotels. *International Journal of Culture, Tourism and Hospitality Research*, 12(4), 440–466. 10.1108/IJCTHR-10-2017-0100

Anderson, C. K., & Wilson, J. G. (2011). Name-your-own price auction mechanisms-Modeling and future implications. *Journal of Revenue and Pricing Management*, 10(1), 32–39. 10.1057/rpm.2010.46

Arora, L., Singh, P., Bhatt, V., & Sharma, B. (2021). Understanding and managing customer engagement through social customer relationship management. *Journal of Decision Systems*, 30(2-3), 215–234. Advance online publication. 10.1080/12460125.2021.1881272

Arya, A. K., Chanana, S., & Kumar, A. (2019). Energy saving in distribution system using internet of things in smart grid environment. *International Journal of Computing and Digital Systems*, 8(2), 157–165. 10.12785/ijcds/080207

Buhalis, D., & Law, R. (2008). Progress in information technology and tourism management: 20 years on and 10 years after the Internet-The state of eTourism research. *Tourism Management*, 29(4), 609–623. 10.1016/j.tourman.2008.01.005

Calveras, A., & Orfila-Sintes, F. (2019). Intermediation in hospitality and transaction cost theory: Evidence from the Balearic Islands, 2001-2010. *Journal of Destination Marketing & Management*, 11, 281–291. 10.1016/j.jdmm.2018.05.004

Dhawale, A. D., Kulkarni, S. B., & Kumbhakarna, V. (2020). Survey of progressive era of text summarization for indian and foreign languages using natural language processing. *Lecture Notes on Data Engineering and Communications Technologies*, 46, 654–662. 10.1007/978-3-030-38040-3_74

Dlacic, J., Grbac, B., & Lazaric, M. (2018). Exploring relationship quality in the hospitality industry. *Tourism and Hospitality Management*, 24(2), 287–306. 10.20867/thm.24.2.3

Donthu, N., Kumar, S., Mukherjee, D., Pandey, N., & Lim, W. M. (2021). How to conduct a bibliometric analysis: An overview and guidelines. *Journal of Business Research*, 133(March), 285–296. 10.1016/j.jbusres.2021.04.070

E-commerce in India: Industry Overview, Market Size & Growth| IBEF. (n.d.). Retrieved June 16, 2021, from https://www.ibef.org/industry/ecommerce.aspx

El Haddad, R., Hallak, R., & Assaker, G. (2015). Price fairness perceptions and hotel customers' behavioral intentions. *Journal of Vacation Marketing*, 21(3), 262–276. 10.1177/1356766715573651

Gauvreau-Lemelin, C., & Attia, S. (2017). Benchmarking the environmental impact of green and traditional masonry wall constructions. In N. F. Brotas L. Roaf S. (Ed.), *Proceedings of 33rd PLEA International Conference: Design to Thrive, PLEA 2017* (Vol. 2, pp. 2856–2863). NCEUB 2017 - Network for Comfort and Energy Use in Buildings. https://www.scopus.com/inward/record.uri?eid=2-s2.0-85085915552& partnerID=40&md5=57dbc2846eeea66cf547cf84f6ee2168

Hunold, M., Kesler, R., Laitenberger, U., & Schluetter, F. (2018). Evaluation of best price clauses in online hotel bookings. *International Journal of Industrial Organization, 61*(SI), 542–571. 10.1016/j.ijindorg.2018.03.008

Indian E-commerce Industry Analysis | IBEF. (n.d.). https://www.ibef.org/industry/ ecommerce-presentation

Janani, M., & Yuvaraj, N. (2019). Social Interaction and Stress-Based Recommen-dations for Elderly Healthcare Support System—A Survey. *Advances in Intelligent Systems and Computing*, 750, 291–303. 10.1007/978-981-13-1882-5_26

Jeong, M., & Jeon, M. M. (2008). *Journal of Hospitality & Leisure Customer Reviews of Hotel Experiences through Consumer Generated Media (CGM).* 10.1080/10507050801978265

Kalia, P., & Paul, J. (2021). E-service quality and e-retailers: Attribute-based multi-dimensional scaling. *Computers in Human Behavior*, 115, 106608. Advance onlinc publication. 10.1016/j.chb.2020.106608

Kim, B.-D., Shi, M., & Srinivasan, K. (2001). Reward programs and tacit collusion. *Marketing Science*, 20(2), 99–120. 10.1287/mksc.20.2.99.10191

Kim, S., Bi, Y., & Kim, I. (2021). Travel website atmospheres inducing older trav-elers' familiarity: The moderating role of cognitive age. *International Journal of Environmental Research and Public Health*, 18(9), 4812. Advance online publication. 10.3390/ijerph1809481233946402

Kizielewicz, J. (2019). Human Resource Policies in Travel Companies Indexed on the Warsaw Stock Exchange. In C. Sousa, I. V. DeFreitas, & J. Marques (Eds.), Proceedings of the 2nd international conference on tourism research (ICTR 2019) (pp. 143–150). Academic Press.

Lee, H. A., & Law, R. (2012). Diversity in statistical research techniques: An analysis of refereed research articles in the journal of travel & tourism marketing between 1992 and 2010. *Journal of Travel & Tourism Marketing*, 29(1), 37–41. 10.1080/10548408.2012.638556

Lichtenstein, D. R., Ridgway, N. M., & Netemeyer, R. G. (1993). Price Perceptions and Consumer Shopping Behavior: A Field Study. *JMR, Journal of Marketing Research*, 30(2), 234–245. 10.1177/002224379303000208

Martinez, B., & Kim, S. (2012). Predicting purchase intention for private sale sites. *Journal of Fashion Marketing and Management*, 16(3), 342–365. 10.1108/13612021211246080

Mondor, C., Hockley, S., & Deal, D. (2013). The David Lawrence Convention Center: How green building design and operations can save money, drive local economic opportunity, and transform an industry. *Journal of Green Building*, 8(1), 28–43. 10.3992/jgb.8.1.28

Poinssot, C., Grandjean, S., Masson, M., Boullis, B., & Warin, D. (2013). Improving the actinides recycling in closed fuel cycles, a major step towards nuclear energy sustainability. *International Nuclear Fuel Cycle Conference, GLOBAL 2013: Nuclear Energy at a Crossroads, 1*, 672–677. https://www.scopus.com/inward/record.uri?eid=2-s2.0-84903217544&partnerID=40&md5=6f1471875a8844a7809594af7cda99b2

Punhani, R., Arora, V. P. S., Sabitha, S., & Kumar Shukla, V. (2021). Application of Clustering Algorithm for Effective Customer Segmentation in E-Commerce. In V. S. Naranje V. Singh B. (Ed.), *Proceedings of 2nd IEEE International Conference on Computational Intelligence and Knowledge Economy, ICCIKE 2021* (pp. 149–154). Institute of Electrical and Electronics Engineers Inc. 10.1109/ICCIKE51210.2021.9410713

Raman, P., & Aashish, K. (2021). To continue or not to continue: A structural analysis of antecedents of mobile payment systems in India. *International Journal of Bank Marketing*, 39(2), 242–271. 10.1108/IJBM-04-2020-0167

Rana, S., & Sharma, S. K. (2015). A literature review, classification, and simple meta-analysis on the conceptual domain of international marketing: 1990-2012. *Advances in International Marketing*, 25, 189–222. 10.1108/S1474-797920140000025009

Sano, K., & Sano, H. (2019). The effect of different crisis communication channels. *Annals of Tourism Research*, 79, 102804. Advance online publication. 10.1016/j.annals.2019.102804

Sarkar, A. (2011). *Impact of Utilitarian and Hedonic Shopping Values on Individual's Perceived Benefits and Risks in Online Shopping.* Academic Press.

Schott, C., & Nhem, S. (2018). Paths to the market: Analysing tourism distribution channels for community-based tourism. *Tourism Recreation Research*, 43(3), 356–371. 10.1080/02508281.2018.1447837

Sih, G. C. (2009). Sustainability aspects of large structures: Energy efficiency. *International Journal of Terraspace Science and Engineering*, 1(1), 1–7. https://www.scopus.com/inward/record.uri?eid=2-s2.0-77956343881&partnerID=40&md5=518120207245019ce3ec51e98a72095d

Sipic, T. (2017). Eco-labelling of marine recreation services: The case of Blue Flag price premium in Croatia. *Journal of Ecotourism*, 16(1), 1–23. 10.1080/14724049.2016.1194848

Toh, R. S., Raven, P., & DeKay, F. (2011). Selling rooms: Hotels vs. third-party websites. *Cornell Hospitality Quarterly*, 52(2), 181–189. 10.1177/1938965511400409

TravelClick. (2012). *Flash Sale Sites Lose Popularity with Hoteliers TravelClick survey shows dissatisfaction with group discount model.* https://www.travelclick.com/en/news-events/press-release/flash-sale-sites-lose-popularity-hoteliers-travelclick-survey-shows-dissatisfaction-group

Tse, A. C. B. (2003). Disintermediation of travel agents in the hotel industry. *International Journal of Hospitality Management*, 22(4), 453–460. 10.1016/S0278-4319(03)00049-532287843

VanGeem, M. G., Marceau, M. L., Gajda, J., & Nisbet, M. A. (2001). Partial environmental life-cycle inventory of single-family houses. *Thermal Performance of the Exterior Envelopes of Whole Buildings.* https://www.scopus.com/inward/record.uri?eid=2-s2.0-34248166867&partncrID=40&md5=07ae02d90a5680c82b9fb5f4d361c7d9

VOSviewer - Visualizing scientific landscapes. (n.d.). https://www.vosviewer.com/

Wilson, R. H. (2011). Internet Hotel Reservations: Recent Changes and Trends in the Enforcement of Click Wrap and Browse Wrap "Terms and Conditions/Terms of Use". *Cornell Hospitality Quarterly*, 52(2), 190–199. 10.1177/1938965510393734

Zhang, E. M. (2010). Understanding the Acceptance of Mobile SMS Advertising among Young Chinese Consumers. *Psychology and Marketing*, 30(6), 461–469. 10.1002/mar

Zhang, J., Zhou, Y., Tang, W., Gu, H., Yan, J., & Wang, H. (2017). An Agent-Mediated Tendering Mechanism for Intelligent Hotel Reservation. In *2017 IEEE 14th International Conference on E-Business Engineering (ICEBE 2017)* (pp. 307–311). 10.1109/ICEBE.2017.56

Compilation of References

Aas, C., Ladkin, A., & Fletcher, J. (2005). Stakeholder collaboration and heritage management. *Annals of Tourism Research*, 32(1), 28–48. 10.1016/j.annals.2004.04.005

Abdallah, F., & Khattib, K. (2020). Introduction to Business Law (2nd ed.). Academic Press.

Acharya, B. P., & Halpenny, E. A. (2016). Applying the Tourism Area Life Cycle and Small Tourism Enterprises' Growth Cycle Models to Explain Communities' Sustainability. 2016 *Conference. 4, University of Massachusetts* – Amherst, ScholarWorks@UMass Amherst.

Achim, M. V., Văidean, V. L., Sabau, A. I., & Safta, I. L. (2023). The impact of the quality of corporate governance on sustainable development: An analysis based on development level. *Economic Research-Ekonomska Istrazivanja*, 36(1). Advance online publication. 10.1080/1331677X.2022.2080745

Agbedahin, A. V. (2019). Sustainable development, Education for Sustainable Development, and the 2030 Agenda for Sustainable Development: Emergence, efficacy, eminence, and future. *Sustainable Development (Bradford)*, 27(4), 669–680. Advance online publication. 10.1002/sd.1931

Agyeiwaah, E., McKercher, B., & Suntikul, W. (2017). Identifying core indicators of sustainable tourism: A path forward? *Tourism Management Perspectives*, 24, 26–33. 10.1016/j.tmp.2017.07.005

Ahmed, S. (2020). Pancha rathas, the five stone temples of the Mahabalipuram site: Opportunity to revive its lost garden heritage through ecotourism. *Paranoá*, 13(28), 1–27. 10.18830/issn.1679-0944.n28.2020.07

Ahmed, S., Shamsuzzoha, A. T. M., & Zarif Rahman, M. (2023). Developing Inclusive Tourism in Chittagong Hill Tracts (CHT): A Case Study on Sajek Valley, Bangladesh. *Asian Review of Social Sciences*, 12(2), 1–9. 10.51983/arss-2023.12.2.3510

Akram, M., Garg, H., & Zahid, K. (2020). Extensions of electre-i and topsis methods for group decision-making under complex pythagorean fuzzy environment. *Iranian Journal of Fuzzy Systems*, 17(5), 147–164. 10.22111/ijfs.2020.5522

Alameeri, A., Ajmal, M. M., Hussain, M., & Helo, P. (2018). Sustainable management practices in UAE hotels. *International Journal of Culture, Tourism and Hospitality Research*, 12(4), 440–466. 10.1108/IJCTHR-10-2017-0100

Alänge, S., Clancy, G., & Marmgren, M. (2016). Naturalizing sustainability in product development: A comparative analysis of IKEA and SCA. *Journal of Cleaner Production*, 135, 1009–1022. 10.1016/j.jclepro.2016.06.148

Ali, A., & Frew, A. J. (2014). Technology innovation and applications in sustainable destination development. *Information Technology & Tourism*, 14(4), 265–290. 10.1007/s40558-014-0015-7

Ali, D. F., Zein, M., & Heragi, M. (2020). The Grand Egyptian Museum and its Role in Achieving Sustainable Tourism in the Memphite Necropolis. International Journal of Heritage. *Tourism and Hospitality*, 14(3 (Special Issue)), 175–193.

Ali, F., & Amin, M. (2014). The Influence of Physical Environment on Emotions, Customer Satisfaction and Behavioural Intentions in Chinese Resort Hotel Industry. *Journal for Global Business Advancement*, 7(3), 249–266. 10.1504/JGBA.2014.064109

Al-Jayyousi, O., Tok, E., Saniff, S. M., Wan Hasan, W. N., Janahi, N. A., & Yesuf, A. J. (2022). Re-Thinking Sustainable Development within Islamic Worldviews: A Systematic Literature Review. *Sustainability (Basel)*, 14(12), 7300. Advance online publication. 10.3390/su14127300

Alkhodary, D. (2021). The impact of e-HRM on corporates sustainability: A study on the SMES in Jordan. *International Journal of Entrepreneurship*, 25(6), 1–15.

Allovergreece. (n.d.). *Ναυάγιο Περιστέρα | Ναυάγια*. https://www.allovergreece.com/Wreck/Descr/25/el

Almahamid, S., Awwad, A., & McAdams, A. C. (2010). Effects of organizational agility and knowledge sharing on competitive advantage: An empirical study in Jordan. *International Journal of Management*, 27(3), 387–408.

Alonissos Park. (n.d.). *Χλωρίδα και Πανίδα – ΕΘΝΙΚΟ ΘΑΛΑΣΣΙΟ ΠΑΡΚΟ ΑΛΟΝΝΗΣΟΥ ΒΟΡΕΙΩΝ ΣΠΟΡΑΔΩΝ!*https://alonissos-park.gr/?page_id=63

Alouthah, D. (2023). Towards a Framework for the Socio-Spatial-Economic Regeneration of Historical Suqs (Doctoral dissertation, Effat University).

Alqarni, K., Agina, M. F., Khairy, H. A., Al-Romeedy, B. S., Farrag, D. A., & Abdallah, R. M. (2023). The Effect of Electronic Human Resource Management Systems on Sustainable Competitive Advantages: The Roles of Sustainable Innovation and Organizational Agility. *Sustainability (Basel)*, 15(23), 163–182. 10.3390/su152316382

Al-Sawi, M. (2018). The Effective Valorization of Resources for the Economic Development of Tyre. *MBA Thesis presented to the Lebanese International University.*

Alshibly, H. H., & Alzubi, K. N. (2022). Unlock the black box of remote e-working effectiveness and e-HRM practices effect on organizational commitment. *Cogent Business & Management*, 9(1), 215–225. 10.1080/23311975.2022.2153546

Compilation of References

Al-Yafei, H., Aseel, S., Kucukvar, M., Onat, N. C., Al-Sulaiti, A., & Al-Hajri, A. (2021). *A systematic review for sustainability of global liquified natural gas industry: A 10-year update* (Vol. 38). Energy Strategy Reviews.

Amoiradis, C., Velissariou, E., & Stankova, M. (2021). Tourism as a Socio-Cultural Phenomenon: A Critical Analysis. Social Sciences eJournal. .10.31014/aior.1991.04.02.271

Anadolu Agency. (2024). *Safranbolu 2023'te yaklaşık 1 milyon 200 bin ziyaretçi ağırladı.* https://www.aa.com.tr/tr/ekonomi/safranbolu-2023te-yaklasik-1-milyon-200-bin-ziyaretci-agirladi/3112177

Anastasopoulou, F. (n.d.) *ΝΑΥΑΓΙΟ ΠΕΡΙΣΤΕΡΑΣ (Αρχαιολογικός χώρος) | Αλόννησος | Σποράδες | Golden Greece.* Golden Greece. https://golden-greece.gr/archaeological/sporades/alonisos/alonperisteras

Anderson, C. K., & Wilson, J. G. (2011). Name-your-own price auction mechanisms- Modeling and future implications. *Journal of Revenue and Pricing Management*, 10(1), 32–39. 10.1057/rpm.2010.46

Andriotis, K. (2005). *Tourism Development and Planning.* Stamoulis.

Anggoro, D., Ramadhan, H., & Ngindana, R. (2022). *Public Private Partnership in Tourism: Build Up a Digitalization Financial Management Model.* Policy & Governance Review., 10.30589/pgr.v6i3.510

Annigeri, A. M. (1961). *A Guide to the Pattadakal Temples.* Dharwar: Archaeological Survey of India.

Ansari, A., Dutt, D., & Kumar, V. (2024). Catalyzing paradigm shifts in global waste Management: A case study of Saharanpur Smart city. *Waste Management Bulletin*, 2(1), 29–38. 10.1016/j.wmb.2023.12.003

Apostu, S. A., & Gigauri, I. (2023). Sustainable development and entrepreneurship in emerging countries: Are sustainable development and entrepreneurship reciprocally reinforcing? *Journal of Entrepreneurship. Management and Innovation*, 19(1), 41–77. Advance online publication. 10.7341/20231912

Archaeology Newsroom. (2020, December 15). Online. https://www.archaiologia.gr/blog/2020/12/15/%CF%80%CF%81%CF%8E%CF%84%CE%BF-%CE%B2%CF%81%CE%B1%CE%B2%CE%B5%CE%AF%CE%BF-%CE%B3%CE%B9%CE%B1-%CF%84%CE%BF-%CF%85%CF%80%CE%BF%CE%B8%CE%B1%CE%BB%CE%AC%CF%83%CF%83%CE%B9%CE%BF-%CE%BC%CE%BF%CF%85%CF%83/

Aref, F., & Gill, S. S. (2009). Rural tourism development though rural cooperatives. *Nature and Science*, 7(10), 68–73.

Arintoko, A., Ahmad, A. A., Gunawan, D. S., & Supadi, S. (2020). Communitybased Tourism Village Development Strategies: A Case of Borobudur Tourism Village Area, Indonesia. *Geo Journal of Tourism and Geosites*, 29(2), 398–413. 10.30892/gtg.29202-477

Arka, S. (2024). The role of institutions and globalization towards inclusive and sustainable green development (inclusive green growth). *Jurnal Ekonomi Kuantitatif Terapan*, 17(1), 145. 10.24843/JEKT.2024.v17.i01.p10

Arora, L., Singh, P., Bhatt, V., & Sharma, B. (2021). Understanding and managing customer engagement through social customer relationship management. *Journal of Decision Systems*, 30(2-3), 215–234. Advance online publication. 10.1080/12460125.2021.1881272

art4sea.eu. (2024, March 21). *Home - Art4Sea*. Art4Sea -. https://art4sea.eu/#the-project

Arya, A. K., Chanana, S., & Kumar, A. (2019). Energy saving in distribution system using internet of things in smart grid environment. *International Journal of Computing and Digital Systems*, 8(2), 157–165. 10.12785/ijcds/080207

Asgari, A., & Reza, A. (2021). How circular economy transforms business models in a transition towards circular ecosystem: The barriers and incentives. *Sustainable Production and Consumption*, 28, 566–579. 10.1016/j.spc.2021.06.020

Atta. (2018). Socio-economic Profile of Shina Community Subsisting on NTFPs in Gurez Valley of Kashmir. *International Journal of Advance Research in Science and Engineering*.

Attaran, M. (2020). Digital technology enablers and their implications for supply chain management. In *Supply Chain Forum. International Journal (Toronto, Ont.)*, 21(3), 158–172.

Avraham, E. (2021). Recovery strategies and marketing campaigns for global destinations in response to the Covid-19 tourism crisis. *Asia Pacific Journal of Tourism Research*, 26(11), 1255–1269. 10.1080/10941665.2021.1918192

Aydin, K. (2016). *Elektronik insan kaynakları yönetimi uygulamaları ve inovasyon performansı* (Master's thesis). Bahçeşehir University.

Ayyıldız, S. (2019). Turistik konak işletmelerinde mutfağın fiziksel koşullarının önemi: Safranbolu yöresel mutfak mimarisi üzerine bir araştırma. *Karabük Üniversitesi Sosyal Bilimler Enstitüsü Dergisi*, 9(2), 610–625.

Azazz, A., Elshaer, I., & Ghanem, M. (2021). Developing a Measurement Scale of Opposition in Tourism Public-Private Partnerships Projects. *Sustainability (Basel)*, 13(9), 5053. 10.3390/su13095053

Azrour, M., Dargaoui, S., Mabrouki, J., Guezzaz, A., Benkirane, S., Shafik, W., & Ahmad, S. (2024). A Survey of Machine and Deep Learning Applications in the Assessment of Water Quality. In *Technical and Technological Solutions Towards a Sustainable Society and Circular Economy* (pp. 471–483). Springer Nature Switzerland. 10.1007/978-3-031-56292-1_38

Babu, M. (2024, January 12). *10 Must-See Tourist Attractions in and Around Mahabalipuram*. Retrieved from Wander Wisdom: https://wanderwisdom.com/travel-destinations/must-see-attractions-in-mahabalipuram

Babu, A. S. (2008). *Tourism Development in India: A case study*. APH publishing.

Badoc-Gonzales, B. P., Mandigma, M. B. S., & Tan, J. J. (2022). SME Resilience as a Catalyst for Tourism Destinations: A Literature Review. *Journal of Global Entrepreneurship Research*, 12(1), 23–44. 10.1007/s40497-022-00309-1

Bærenholdt, J. O., Haldrup, M., & Urry, J. (2017). *Performing tourist places*. Routledge. 10.4324/9781315247106

Bagus, . (2019). Community Based Tourism as Sustainable Tourism Support. *Russian Journal of Agricultural and Socio-Economic Sciences*, 94(10), 70–78. 10.18551/rjoas.2019-10.09

Bajracharya, B., & Hastings, P. (2020). Stakeholder engagement for disaster management in master-planned communities. *Australian Journal of Emergency Management*, 35, 41–47.

Bali Swain, R., & Yang-Wallentin, F. (2020). Achieving sustainable development goals: Predicaments and strategies. *International Journal of Sustainable Development and World Ecology*, 27(2), 96–106. Advance online publication. 10.1080/13504509.2019.1692316

Bamzai, P. N. K. (1994). *Cultural and Political History of Kashmir* (Vol. 1). M. D. Publishers Private Limited.

Bandeoğlu, Z. (2015). Türkiye'de kültür turizmi potansiyeli üzerine bir değerlendirme. *Kahramanmaraş Sütçü İmam Üniversitesi İktisadi ve İdari Bilimler Fakültesi Dergisi*, 5(02), 155–168.

Banik, S., & Mukhopadhyay, M. (2020). Model-based strategic planning for the development of community based tourism: A case study of Ayodhya Hills in West Bengal, India. *GeoJournal*, 1–17.

Bansard, J., & Schröder, M. (2021). The Sustainable Use of Natural Resources: The Governance Challenge. Retrieved from: https://www.iisd.org/articles/deep-dive/sustainable-use-natural-resources-governance-challenge

Barandiaran, X., Restrepo, N., & Luna, Á. (2019). Collaborative governance in tourism: Lessons from Etorkizuna Eraikiz in the Basque Country, Spain. *Tourism Review*, 74(4), 902–914. 10.1108/TR-09-2018-0133

Barkin, D. (2013). Strengthening domestic tourism in Mexico: challenges and opportunities. The Native Tourist, 30-54.

Barkin, D., & Bouchez, C. P. (2002). NGO–community collaboration for ecotourism: A strategy for sustainable regional development. *Current Issues in Tourism*, 5(3-4), 245–253. 10.1080/13683500208667921

Barnes, S. J., Mattsson, J., & Sørensen, F. (2014). Destination brand experience and visitor behavior: Testing a scale in the tourism context. *Annals of Tourism Research*, 48, 121–139. 10.1016/j.annals.2014.06.002

Bazneshin, S. D., Hosseini, S. B., & Azeri, A. R. K. (2015). The physical variables of tourist areas to increase the tourists' satisfaction regarding the sustainable tourism criteria: Case study of Rudsar Villages, Sefidab in Rahim Abad. *Procedia: Social and Behavioral Sciences*, 201, 128–135. 10.1016/j.sbspro.2015.08.141

Beadles, N. A.II, Lowery, C. M., & Johns, K. (2005). The impact of human resource information systems: An exploratory study in the public sector. *Communications of the IIMA*, 5(4), 6–15.

Behera, S. K., Gautam, P., & Lenka, S. K. (2021). *Purchasing behavior of tourists toward prominent souvenirs of Odisha*. Vilakshan-XIMB Journal of Management. 10.1108/XJM-10-2020-0165

Belkayali, N., & Kesimoğlu, M. D. (2015). The stakeholders' point of view about the impact of recreational and tourism activities on natural protected area: A case study from Kure Mountains National Park, Turkey. *Biotechnology, Biotechnological Equipment*, 29(6), 1092–1103. 10.1080/13102818.2015.1072054

Bellato, L., & Cheer, J. M. (2021). Inclusive and regenerative urban tourism: Capacity development perspectives. *International Journal of Tourism Cities*, 7(4), 943–961. 10.1108/IJTC-08-2020-0167

Bellato, L., Frantzeskaki, N., & Nygaard, C. A. (2023). Regenerative tourism: A conceptual framework leveraging theory and practice. *Tourism Geographies*, 25(4), 1026–1046. 10.1080/14616688.2022.2044376

Bhartiya, S., Bhatt, V., Rathore, A. H., & Khanam, T. (2024). A Theory-Based Approach to Understanding Social Sustainability in Tourism. In *Implementing Sustainable Development Goals in the Service Sector* (pp. 146–156). IGI Global.

Bigne, E., Ruiz, C., & Curras-Perez, R. (2019). Destination appeal through digitalized comments. *Journal of Business Research*, 101, 447–453. 10.1016/j.jbusres.2019.01.020

Bigné, E., Zanfardini, M., & Andreu, L. (2020). How online reviews of destination responsibility influence tourists' evaluations: An exploratory study of mountain tourism. *Journal of Sustainable Tourism*, 28(5), 686–704. 10.1080/09669582.2019.1699565

Bishoge, O. K., Zhang, L., & Mushi, W. G. (2019). The Potential Renewable Energy for Sustainable Development in Tanzania: A Review. In *Clean Technologies* (Vol. 1, Issue 1). https://doi.org/10.3390/cleantechnol1010006

Blazeska, D., Strezovski, Z., & Klimoska, A. (2018). The influence of tourist infrastructure on the tourist satisfaction in Ohrid. *UTMS Journal*, 85-93.

BLUEMED. (2020). https://bluemed.interreg-med.eu/fileadmin/user_upload/Sites/Sustainable_Tourism/Projects/BLUEMED/BLUEMED_BROCHURE-FINAL.pdf

Bobar, Z., Božanić, D., Djurić, K., & Pamučar, D. (2020). Ranking and assessment of the efficiency of social media using the fuzzy AHP-Z number model-fuzzy MABAC. *Acta Polytechnica Hungarica*, 17(3), 43–70. 10.12700/APH.17.3.2020.3.3

Bogenç, Ç. & Sabaz, M. (2019). Dünya miras alanı Safranbolu'nun alan yönetim planının geliştirilmesi sürecinde; tema, hedef ve eylemlerin belirlenmesi. *İnsan ve Toplum Bilimleri Araştırmaları Dergisi, 8*(3), 1526-1544.

Compilation of References

Bogers, M., Biermann, F., Kalfagianni, A., Kim, R. E., Treep, J., & de Vos, M. G. (2022). The impact of the Sustainable Development Goals on a network of 276 international organizations. *Global Environmental Change*, 76, 102567. Advance online publication. 10.1016/j.gloenvcha.2022.102567

Bole, D. K. (2024). Sustainable Wine Tourism: Best Practices. In Martínez-Falcó, J., Marco-Lajara, B., Sánchez-García, E., & Millán-Tudela, L. A. (Eds.), *Wine Tourism and Sustainability* (pp. 95–122). Springer Nature Switzerland. 10.1007/978-3-031-48937-2_5

Bolton, M. (2021). Public sector understanding of sustainable development and the sustainable development goals: A case study of Victoria, Australia. *Current Research in Environmental Sustainability*, 3, 100056. Advance online publication. 10.1016/j.crsust.2021.100056

Bora, A. (2018). Archaeology, cultural heritage and tourism from the past to the future: on the cultural heritage of a dynasty from the Hellenistic period.

Boukas, N. (2008). *Cultural tourism, young people and destination perception: A case study of Delphi, Greece.* University of Exeter.

Bozkurt, G. S. (2013). 19. yy da Osmanlı konut mimarisinde iç mekan kurgusunun Safranbolu evleri örneğinde irdelenmesi. *Istanbul Üniversitesi Orman Fakültesi Dergisi*, 62(2), 37–70.

Bramwell, B. (1994). Rural tourism and sustainable rural tourism. *Journal of Sustainable Tourism*, 2(1-2), 1–6. 10.1080/09669589409510679

Bramwell, B., & Lane, B. (2011). Critical research on the governance of tourism and sustainability. *Journal of Sustainable Tourism*, 19(4-5), 411–421. 10.1080/09669582.2011.580586

Braun, V., & Clarke, V. (2013). *Successful qualitative research: A practical guide for beginners.* Sage.

Bruno, F., Ricca, M., Lagudi, A., Kalamara, P., Manglis, A., Fourkiotou, A., Papadopoulou, D., & Veneti, A. (2020). Digital technologies for the sustainable development of the accessible underwater cultural heritage sites. *Journal of Marine Science and Engineering*, 8(11), 955. 10.3390/jmse8110955

Brylske, A., McDougall, P., Popple, I., & Wagner, O. (2023). *Beneath the blue Planet: A Diver's Guide to the Ocean and Its Conservation.* Mango Media Inc.

Buckley, R. (2012). Sustainable tourism: Research and reality. *Annals of Tourism Research*, 39(2), 528–546. 10.1016/j.annals.2012.02.003

Budeanu, A. (2005). Impacts and responsibilities for sustainable tourism: A tour operator's perspective. *Journal of Cleaner Production*, 13(2), 89–97. 10.1016/j.jclepro.2003.12.02432288344

Buhalis, D., & Law, R. (2008). Progress in information technology and tourism management: 20 years on and 10 years after the Internet-The state of eTourism research. *Tourism Management*, 29(4), 609–623. 10.1016/j.tourman.2008.01.005

Burns, A. C., & Bush, R. F. (2017). *Marketing Research* (8th ed.). Pearson.

Buturlina, O., Dovhal, S., Hryhorov, H., Lysokolenko, T., & Palahuta, V. (2021). Stem education in Ukraine in the context of sustainable development. *European Journal of Sustainable Development*, 10(1), 323. Advance online publication. 10.14207/ejsd.2021.v10n1p323

Büyüközkan, G., Mukul, E., & Kongar, E. (2021). Health tourism strategy selection via SWOT analysis and integrated hesitant fuzzy linguistic AHP-MABAC approach. *Socio-Economic Planning Sciences*, 74, 100929. 10.1016/j.seps.2020.100929

Calveras, A., & Orfila-Sintes, F. (2019). Intermediation in hospitality and transaction cost theory: Evidence from the Balearic Islands, 2001-2010. *Journal of Destination Marketing & Management*, 11, 281–291. 10.1016/j.jdmm.2018.05.004

Canbulat, İ. (2020). Seyahatname ve Yazılı Kaynaklarda Safranbolu. *Kitap içi (bu kitap çalışması) Makale*, 70-91.

Carrillo-Barrios-Gómez, E., & Herrmann-Martinez, H. (1989). Sian Ka'an: A new biosphere reserve model in Mexico. In Worldwide Conservation: Proceedings of the Symposium on Biosphere Reserves (p. 223). US Department of the Interior, National Park Service, Science Publications Office.

Carvache-Franco, M., Pérez-Orozco, A., Carvache-Franco, O., Víquez-Paniagua, A., & Carvache-Franco, W. (2020). The perceived value in ecotourism related to satisfaction and loyalty: A study from Costa Rica., 24, 229-243. .10.5937/gp24-25082

Castro, C., & Lopes, C. (2022). Digital Government and Sustainable Development. *Journal of the Knowledge Economy*, 13(2), 880–903. Advance online publication. 10.1007/s13132-021-00749-2

Cetin, G., & Bilgihan, A. (2016). Components of cultural tourists' experiences in destinations. *Current Issues in Tourism*, 19(2), 137–154. 10.1080/13683500.2014.994595

Ceylan, S., & Somuncu, M. (2016). Kültür turizmi alanlarında turizmin çeşitlendirilmesine eleştirel bir bakış: Safranbolu UNESCO Dünya miras alanı. *Uluslararası Türk Dünyası Turizm Araştırmaları Dergisi*, 1(1), 53–64.

Chakraborty, S., Sarkar, B., & Chakraborty, S. (2023). A FUCOM-MABAC-based integrated approach for performance evaluation of the Indian National Parks. *OPSEARCH*, 60(1), 125–154. 10.1007/s12597-022-00611-2

Chakravarty, A., Grewal, R., & Sambamurthy, V. (2013). Information technology competencies, organizational agility, and firm performance: Enabling and facilitating roles. *Information Systems Research*, 24(4), 976–997. 10.1287/isre.2013.0500

Chambers, W. (1869). *The Seven Pagodas on the Coromandel Coast*. Archaeological Survey of India.

Charbonnier-Voirin, A. (2011). The development and partial testing of the psychometric properties of a measurement scale of organizational agility. *M@n@gement*, 14(2), 119-156.

Compilation of References

Chauhan, E. (2023). Role Of Community In Managing Cultural Heritage Tourism In Historical Quarters Of Delhi (Doctoral Dissertation, Brandenburg University Of Technology Cottbus).

Chauhan, C., Kaur, P., Arrawatia, R., Ractham, P., & Dhir, A. (2022). Supply chain collaboration and sustainable development goals (SDGs). Teamwork makes achieving SDGs dream work. *Journal of Business Research*, 147, 290–307. Advance online publication. 10.1016/j.jbusres.2022.03.044

Chaurasiya, R., & Jain, D. (2023). Hybrid MCDM method on Pythagorean fuzzy set and its application. *Decision Making: Applications in Management and Engineering*, 6(1), 379–398. 10.31181/dmame0306102022c

Chavan, R. R., & Bhola, S. S. (2016). Assessment of Variables in Measuring Tourist Infrastructure. *Vishwakarma Business Review*, 105–115.

Cheng, Z., Wang, R., Li, Y., & Dai, J. (2023). Paving the Way for a Sustainable Society: Assessing the Inclusive Tourism Development in Transition China. *Journal of Environment & Development*, 32(4), 323–342. 10.1177/10704965231197672

Chen, W., & Wu, M. (2024). Exploring the role of psychological ownership in tourists' shift toward sustainable behavior in cultural tourism. *Journal of Sustainable Tourism*, 1–20. 10.1080/09669582.2024.2341890

Choo, H., Ahn, K., & Petrick, J. F. (2016). An integrated model of festival revisit intentions: Theory of planned behavior and festival quality/satisfaction. *International Journal of Contemporary Hospitality Management*, 28, 818–838. 10.1108/IJCHM-09-2014-0448

Clark, W. C., Van Kerkhoff, L., Lebel, L., & Gallopin, G. C. (2016). Crafting usable knowledge for sustainable development. In *Proceedings of the National Academy of Sciences of the United States of America* (Vol. 113, Issue 17). 10.1073/pnas.1601266113

Clawson, M., & Knetsch, J. L. (1966). *Economics of outdoor recreation*. Johns Hopkins Press.

Coathup, D. C. (1999). Dominant actors in international tourism. *International Journal of Contemporary Hospitality Management*, 11(2/3), 69–72. 10.1108/09596119910250689

Coccossis, Ch., & Tsartas, P. (2001). *Sustainable Tourism Development and the Environment*. Kritiki.

Coelho, P. M., Corona, B., Ten Klooster, R., & Worrell, E. (2020). *Sustainability of reusable packaging–Current situation and trends. Resources, Conservation & Recycling, (6).*

Cohen, E. (2004). *Contemporary tourism: Diversity and change*. Elsevier.

Collins-Kreiner, N., & Wall, G. (2015). Tourism and religion: Spiritual journeys and their consequences. The changing world religion Map: Sacred places, identities, practices and politics, 689-707.

Dangi, T., & Jamal, T. (2016). An Integrated Approach to Sustainable Community-Based Tourism. *Sustainability (Basel)*, 8(5), 475. 10.3390/su8050475

Danilov, Y. A. (2022). Coalitions for Sustainable Finance and Sustainable Development. *Herald of the Russian Academy of Sciences*, 92(S2), S91–S99. Advance online publication. 10.1134/S1019331622080032

Dar, H. & Islam, N., (2018). Tourism Development in Kashmir: The Policy Perspective. *International Research Journal of Management Science & Technology*.

Dar, H. (2014). The potential of Tourism in border destinations: A study of Jammu and Kashmir. *African Journal of Hospitality, Tourism and Leisure*, 4(2).

Dar, H. (2018a). Tourists satisfaction of tourism services in Kashmir valley. PhD thesis submitted in *Kurukshetra University Kurukshetra University*.

Dar, H. (2018b). Satisfaction of domestic tourists visiting Gulmarg in Jammu and Kashmir, India. *International Journal on Recent Trends in Business and Tourism*, 2(1), 16–22.

Dar, H. (2020). Hindu religious motivations in Kashmir valley. *International Journal of Religious Tourism and Pilgrimage*, 8(3), 2.

Dar, H. (2024). Sustainable Measures Deterring Ethical and Decent Dilemmas in Tourism. In *Managing Tourism and Hospitality Sectors for Sustainable Global Transformation* (pp. 219–229). IGI Global. 10.4018/979-8-3693-6260-0.ch016

Das, S. (2019). Towards the Development of Sustainable Tourism in Sikkim, India: Issues and Challenges. *International Journal of Research in Social Sciences*, 9(2), 575–592.

De Alwis, A. C., Andrlić, B., & Šostar, M. (2022). The Influence of E-HRM on modernizing the role of HRM context. *Economies*, 10(8), 181–202. 10.3390/economies10080181

Degai, T. S., & Petrov, A. N. (2021). Rethinking Arctic sustainable development agenda through indigenizing UN sustainable development goals. *International Journal of Sustainable Development and World Ecology*, 28(6), 518–523. Advance online publication. 10.1080/13504509.2020.1868608

Dehejia, V. (2019). The Future of India's Past: Conservation of Cultural Heritage. In *India Briefing, 1990* (pp. 131–157). Routledge. 10.4324/9780429033636-6

Del Soldato, E., & Massari, S. (2024). Creativity and digital strategies to support food cultural heritage in Mediterranean rural areas. *EuroMed Journal of Business*, 19(1), 113–137. 10.1108/EMJB-05-2023-0152

Deli, I., Ali, M., & Smarandache, F. (2015, August). Bipolar neutrosophic sets and their application based on multi-criteria decision making problems. In *2015 International conference on advanced mechatronic systems (ICAMechS)* (pp. 249-254). IEEE. 10.1109/ICAMechS.2015.7287068

DEMA. (2024). dema.org. https://www.dema.org/store/download.aspx?id=7811B097-8882-4707-A160-F999B49614B6

Dessai, A. G. (2023). Sustainable Tourism. In *Environment, Resources and Sustainable Tourism* (pp. 187–228). Springer Nature Singapore. 10.1007/978-981-99-1843-0_7

Compilation of References

Dewan, P. (2011). *The people and culture of Jammu-Kashmir-Ladakh*. Manas Publication.

Dhaoui, I. (2022). E-Government for Sustainable Development: Evidence from MENA Countries. *Journal of the Knowledge Economy*, 13(3), 2070–2099. Advance online publication. 10.1007/s13132-021-00791-0

Dhawale, A. D., Kulkarni, S. B., & Kumbhakarna, V. (2020). Survey of progressive era of text summarization for indian and foreign languages using natural language processing. *Lecture Notes on Data Engineering and Communications Technologies*, 46, 654–662. 10.1007/978-3-030-38040-3_74

DHNS. (2019, August 11). *Heritage sites Hampi, Pattadakal besieged by water*. Retrieved from Deccan Herald: https://www.deccanherald.com/india/karnataka/heritage-sites-hampi- pattadakal-besieged-by-water-753728.html

Díaz-Andreu, M. (2013). Ethics and archaeological tourism in Latin America. *International Journal of Historical Archaeology*, 17(2), 225–244. 10.1007/s10761-013-0218-1

Diker, O. & Türker, N. & Çetinkaya, A. & Kaya, F. B. (2017). Geleneksel türk tatlısı olarak lokum ve safranbolu lokumu. *Journal of Tourism & Gastronomy Studies*, 5(Special Issue 2), 333-344.

Diker, O., & Çetinkaya, A. (2016). Erişilebilir Turizm Açısından Safranbolu Turizm Destinasyonunun Uygunluğunun Değerlendirilmesi. *Karabük Üniversitesi Sosyal Bilimler Enstitüsü Dergisi*, (2), 111–125. 10.14230/joiss186

Dimmock, K., & Musa, G. (2015). Scuba Diving Tourism System: A framework for collaborative management and sustainability. *Marine Policy*, 54, 52–58. 10.1016/j.marpol.2014.12.008

Ditta-Apichai, M., Sroypetch, S., & Caldicott, R. W. (2024). A critique of community-based tourism development: The comparative case of Betong and Pho Tak Districts, Thailand. *Community Development (Columbus, Ohio)*, 55(1), 67–84. 10.1080/15575330.2022.2144921

Dive Virtually - Peristera - MedDive. (n.d.). http://meddiveinthepast.eu/dive-virtually-peristera

Divelog. (2021, June 2). *Ναυάγιο Περιστέρας - DIVELOG | Your Secret Reef*. DIVELOG | Your Secret Reef - Plan Your Next Dive Here - Σχεδίασε Εδώ Την Επόμενή Σου Κατάδυση. https://www.divelog.gr/divepost/navagio-peristeras-2/

Dlacic, J., Grbac, B., & Lazaric, M. (2018). Exploring relationship quality in the hospitality industry. *Tourism and Hospitality Management*, 24(2), 287–306. 10.20867/thm.24.2.3

Dolnicar, S. (2020). Designing for more environmentally friendly tourism. Annals of Tourism Research. https://doi.org/10.31235/osf.io/s76mj

Doni, F., & Johannsdottir, L. (2020). *Environmental social and governance (ESG) ratings*. Climate Action. 10.1007/978-3-319-95885-9_36

Dönmez, Y., Cabuk, S., Öztürk, M., & Gokyer, E. (2016). Safranbolu Kentsel Sit Alanında otopark sorunu ve çözüm alternatifleri. *Bartin Orman Fakültesi Dergisi*, 18(2), 137–145. 10.24011/barofd.270063

Dönmez, Y., Gökyer, E., & Aşkın, F. K. (2015). SWOT Analizi ile Safranbolu Yörük Köyü ve Yakın Çevresinin Ekoturizm Potansiyelinin Değerlendirilmesi. *Karabük Üniversitesi Sosyal Bilimler Enstitüsü Dergisi*, (5), 70–83.

Donthu, N., Kumar, S., Mukherjee, D., Pandey, N., & Lim, W. M. (2021). How to conduct a bibliometric analysis: An overview and guidelines. *Journal of Business Research*, 133(March), 285–296. 10.1016/j.jbusres.2021.04.070

Dossou, T. A. M., Asongu, S. A., Kambaye, E. N., Dossou, K. P., & Alinsato, A. S. (2023). Governance, tourism and inclusive growth in Africa. *International Social Science Journal*. 10.1111/issj.12476

DULT. (2016). *City Service Bus Evaluation - Badami*. Bengaluru: Urban Development Department. Filliozat, V. (2015). *Saiva Monument at Pattadakal*. Unpublished manuscript.

Dunn, S. (2007). Toward empowerment: Women and community-based tourism in Thailand. Master Thesis, *University of Oregon*, The Faculty of Graduate Studies USA.

Duvnjak, B., & Kohont, A. (2021). The role of sustainable hrm in sustainable development. *Sustainability (Basel)*, 13(19), 10668. Advance online publication. 10.3390/su131910668

Duxbury, N., Bakas, F. E., Vinagre de Castro, T., & Silva, S. (2020). Creative tourism development models towards sustainable and regenerative tourism. *Sustainability (Basel)*, 13(1), 2. 10.3390/su13010002

Dwipayanti, N. M. U., Nastiti, A., Johnson, H., Loehr, J., Kowara, M., De Rozari, P., Vada, S., Hadwen, W., Nugraha, M. A. T., & Powell, B. (2022). Inclusive WASH and sustainable tourism in Labuan Bajo, Indonesia: Needs and opportunities. *Journal of Water, Sanitation, and Hygiene for Development : a Journal of the International Water Association*, 12(5), 417–431. 10.2166/washdev.2022.222

Dwyer, L., & Kim, C. (2003). Destination competitiveness: Determinants and indicators. *Current Issues in Tourism*, 6(5), 369–414. 10.1080/13683500308667962

Eagles, P. F., McCool, S. F., & Haynes, C. D. (2002). *Sustainable tourism in protected areas: Guidelines for planning and management (No. 8)*. Iucn.

E-commerce in India: Industry Overview, Market Size & Growth| IBEF. (n.d.). Retrieved June 16, 2021, from https://www.ibef.org/industry/ecommerce.aspx

Edgell, D. L.Sr. (2019). *Managing sustainable tourism: A legacy for the future*. Routledge.

El Azazy, S. A. (2022). Tourism development of the cultural heritage and archaeological sites within the national project for urban sustainable development in Egypt. *International Journal of Humanities and Education Development*, 4(2), 53–68. 10.22161/jhed.4.2.8

El Haddad, R., Hallak, R., & Assaker, G. (2015). Price fairness perceptions and hotel customers' behavioral intentions. *Journal of Vacation Marketing*, 21(3), 262–276. 10.1177/1356766715573651

Compilation of References

El Nsour, J. A. (2021). 'Investigating the impact of organizational agility on the competitive advantage'. *Journal of Governance and Regulation*, 10(1), 10–22.

Eleftheriou, V., Lembidaki, E., & Kaimara, I. (2020). Forty-five Years in Engaging the Public with the Restoration of the Acropolis of Athens. Material Cultures in Public Engagement, 21.

Elkington, J. (1999). *Cannibals with forks: the triple bottom line of 21st century business*. Capstone.

Elmo, G., Arcese, G., Valeri, M., Poponi, S., & Pacchera, F. (2020). Sustainability in Tourism as an Innovation Driver: An Analysis of Family Business Reality. *Sustainability (Basel)*, 12(15), 6149. Advance online publication. 10.3390/su12156149

El-Rifai, A. (2021). "What is Sutainability"? In *The Sustainable 'Triple Bottom Line' Approach*. Retrieved June 26, 2024, from: https://cose-eu.org/2021/05/02/the-sustainable-triple-bottom-line-approach

Elta. (2022, July 13). *EUROMED stamps for 2022: Maritime Archaeology of the Mediterranean*. (n.d.). https://www.elta.gr/en/singleblog/deltia-tupou/i-thalassia-archaiologia-tis-mesogeiou-sta-grammatosima-euromed-4

Ely, P. A. (2013). Tourism Management Perspectives. *Tourism Management*, 8, 80–89.

Emerson, K., Nabatchi, T., & Balogh, S. (2012). An integrative framework for collaborative governance. *Journal of Public Administration: Research and Theory*, 22(1), 1–29. 10.1093/jopart/mur011

Erkuş-Öztürk, H., & Eraydın, A. (2010). Environmental governance for sustainable tourism development: Collaborative networks and organization building in the Antalya tourism region. *Tourism Management*, 31(1), 113–124. 10.1016/j.tourman.2009.01.002

Esser, F., & Steppat, D. (2017). News media use: International comparative research. The international encyclopedia of media effects, 1-17.

Euronews. (2021, May 31). Αλόννησος: Ανοίγει αύριο το πρώτο υποβρύχιο μουσείο της Ελλάδας. *Euronews*. https://gr.euronews.com/2021/05/31/alonnhsos-anoigei-aurio-to-prwto-upovruxio-mouseio-ths-elladas

European Commission. (2017). *Diving into underwater tourism in Greece*. https://ec.europa.eu/regional_policy/en/newsroom/news/2017/10/10-04-2017-diving-into-underwater-tourism-in-greece

Ezeah, C., Fazakerley, J., & Byrne, T. (2015). Tourism waste management in the European Union: Lessons learned from four popular EU tourist destinations. *American Journal of Climate Change*, 4(5), 431–445. 10.4236/ajcc.2015.45035

Farnhan, P. (2015). *Economics for Managers* (Global Edition). Pearson.

Fei, W., Opoku, A., Agyekum, K., Oppon, J. A., Ahmed, V., Chen, C., & Lok, K. L. (2021). The critical role of the construction industry in achieving the sustainable development goals (Sdgs): Delivering projects for the common good. *Sustainability (Basel)*, 13(16), 9112. Advance online publication. 10.3390/su13169112

Feraday, S. (2022). 5 Sustainability Challenges and How to Overcome Them. Retrieved from: https://www.apriori.com/blog/five-sustainability-challenges-and-how-to-overcome-them

Ferguson, T., Roofe, C., & Cook, L. D. (2021). Teachers' perspectives on sustainable development: The implications for education for sustainable development. *Environmental Education Research*, 27(9), 1–17. Advance online publication. 10.1080/13504622.2021.1921113

Ferretti, E., Thrush, S. F., Lewis, N., & Hillman, J. R. (2023). Restorative practices, marine ecotourism, and restoration economies: Revitalizing the environmental agenda? *Ecology and Society*, 28(4), art23. Advance online publication. 10.5751/ES-14628-280423

Fonseca, L. M., Domingues, J. P., & Dima, A. M. (2020). Mapping the sustainable development goals relationships. *Sustainability (Basel)*, 12(8), 3359. Advance online publication. 10.3390/su12083359

Francis, E. (2024). Pallavas (D. Potts, E. Harkness, J. Neelis, & R. McIntosh, Eds.). *The Encyclopedia of Ancient History*, 1-4.

Fu, B., Meadows, M. E., & Zhao, W. (2022). Geography in the Anthropocene: Transforming our world for sustainable development. In *Geography and Sustainability* (Vol. 3, Issue 1). 10.1016/j.geosus.2021.12.004

Futures, T. Sustainable Tourism Futures.

Gauvreau-Lemelin, C., & Attia, S. (2017). Benchmarking the environmental impact of green and traditional masonry wall constructions. In N. F. Brotas L. Roaf S. (Ed.), *Proceedings of 33rd PLEA International Conference: Design to Thrive, PLEA 2017* (Vol. 2, pp. 2856–2863). NCEUB 2017 - Network for Comfort and Energy Use in Buildings. https://www.scopus.com/inward/record.uri?eid=2-s2.0-85085915552&partnerID=40&md5=57dbc2846eeea66cf547cf84f6ee2168

Gavin, M. (2019). How to create social change: 4 business strategies. Retrieved April 14, 2021, from https://online.hbs.edu/blog/post/how-can-business-drive-social-change

Ge, B., Yang, Y., Jiang, D., Gao, Y., Du, X., & Zhou, T. (2018). An empirical study on green innovation strategy and sustainable competitive advantages: Path and boundary. *Sustainability (Basel)*, 10(10), 3631–3652. 10.3390/su10103631

Geddes, P. (1915). *Cities in Evolution: An Introduction to the Town Planning Movement and to the Study of Civics*. University of Michigan Library.

Gemar, G., Soler, I. P., & Moniche, L. (2023). Exploring the impacts of local development initiatives on tourism: A case study analysis. *Heliyon*, 9(9), e19924. 10.1016/j.heliyon.2023.e1992437809430

Compilation of References

George, D., & Mallery, M. (2010). *SPSS for Windows step by step: A simple guide and reference*. Allyn & Bacon.

Georgoula, V., & Terkenli, T. (2017). Tourism Impacts of International Arts Festivals in Greece. The Cases of the Kalamata Dance Festival and Drama Short Film Festival. *Innovative Approaches to Tourism and Leisure: Fourth International Conference IACuDiT, Athens 2017* (pp. 101-114). Athens: Springer International Publishing.

Gerovassileiou, V., Koutsoubas, D., Sini, M., & Paikou, K. (2009). Marine protected areas and diving tourism in the Greek Seas: Practices and perspectives. *Tourismos: An International Multidisciplinary Journal of Tourism*, 4(4), 181–197.

Ghobakhloo, M., Iranmanesh, M., Mubarak, M. F., Mubarik, M., Rejeb, A., & Nilashi, M. (2022). Identifying industry 5.0 contributions to sustainable development: A strategy roadmap for delivering sustainability values. *Sustainable Production and Consumption*, 33, 716–737. Advance online publication. 10.1016/j.spc.2022.08.003

Ghosh, S., Chakraborty, S., & Chakraborty, S. (2022). An integrated IRN-SWARA-MABAC-based approach for evaluation of tourism websites of the Indian states. *OPSEARCH*, 59(3), 974–1017. 10.1007/s12597-022-00583-3

Giampiccoli, A., & Saayman, M. (2018). Community-Based Tourism Development Model and Community Participation. African Journal of Hospitality, Tourism and Leisure, 7(4).

Giampiccoli, A., & Saayman, M. (2018). Community-based tourism development model and community participation. *African Journal of Hospitality, Tourism and Leisure*, 7(4), 1–27.

Giangrande, N., White, R. M., East, M., Jackson, R., Clarke, T., Coste, M. S., & Penha-Lopes, G. (2019). A competency framework to assess and activate education for sustainable development: Addressing the UN sustainable development goals 4.7 challenge. *Sustainability (Basel)*, 11(10), 2832. Advance online publication. 10.3390/su11102832

Gigauri, I., Popescu, C., & Palazzo, M. (2024). Sustainability initiatives in tourism and marketing of sustainable tourism destination. In *Contemporary Marketing and Consumer Behaviour in Sustainable Tourism* (1st ed., pp. 121–140). Routledge. 10.4324/9781003388593-9

Gimouki, E. (2022, November). Sustainable Tourism Development in Less Touristy Destinations; The Case of Epirus, Greece. In The International Conference on Cultural Sustainable Tourism (pp. 13-20). Cham: Springer Nature Switzerland.

Glavič, P. (2020). Identifying key issues of education for sustainable development. *Sustainability (Basel)*, 12(16), 6500. Advance online publication. 10.3390/su12166500

Go, H., & Kang, M. (2023). Metaverse tourism for sustainable tourism development: Tourism agenda 2030. *Tourism Review*, 78(2), 381–394. 10.1108/TR-02-2022-0102

Gohori, O., & van der Merwe, P. (2024). Barriers to community participation in Zimbabwe's community-based tourism projects. *Tourism Recreation Research*, 49(1), 91–104. 10.1080/02508281.2021.1989654

Goodwin, H., & Santilli, R. (2009). Community-Based Tourism: a success? *ICRT* Occasional Paper 11, 1-37.

Gori, E., Fissi, S., & Romolini, A. (2021). A collaborative approach in tourism planning: The case of Tuscany region. *European Journal of Tourism Research*, 29, 2907–2907. 10.54055/ejtr. v29i.2426

Gössling, S. (2006). Tourism and water. In *Tourism and global environmental change* (pp. 180–194). Routledge. 10.4324/9780203011911-12

Gratacap, L. P. (1883). Ancient Mexican Civilization. The American Antiquarian And Oriental Journal, 5(3), 255.

Grima, R. (2017). Presenting archaeological sites to the public. Key concepts in public archaeology, 73-92.

Grimm, I. J., Alcântara, L., & Sampaio, C. A. C. (2018). Tourism under climate change scenarios: impacts, possibilities, and challenges. Revista Brasileira de Pesquisa em Turismo, 12, 1-22.

Group, B. M. W. (2020). BMW Group named sector leader in Dow Jones Sustainability Indices 2020. https://www.press.bmwgroup.com/global/article/detail/T0321071EN/bmw-group-named -sector-leader-in-dow-jones-sustainability-indices-2020?language=en

Grynspan, R. (2012). The Role of Natural Resources in promoting Sustainable Development. *Presented on the occasion of the Opening of the 67th UN General Assembly side event on the Role of Natural Resources in Promoting Sustainable Development*. Retrieved from: http://www .ar.undp.org

Guarini, E., Mori, E., & Zuffada, E. (2022). Localizing the Sustainable Development Goals: A managerial perspective. *Journal of Public Budgeting, Accounting & Financial Management*, 34(5), 583–601. Advance online publication. 10.1108/JPBAFM-02-2021-0031

Gunasekaran, N., & Anandkumar, V. (2012). Factors of influence in choosing alternative accommodation: A study with reference to Pondicherry, a coastal heritage town. *Procedia: Social and Behavioral Sciences*, 62, 1127–1132. 10.1016/j.sbspro.2012.09.193

Gupta, R., & Mohd Ear, M. (2024). *Sustainable Tourism Development: Balancing Economic Growth And Environmental Conservation*. 10.13140/RG.2.2.18018.34245

Gupta. (2018). Community Based Tourism Development amid Complex Mountain Issues: A Strategic Analysis of Chakrata Region of Uttarakhand. *International Journal of Hospitality& Tourism Systems, 12.*

Gupta, J., & Vegelin, C. (2016). Sustainable development goals and inclusive development. *International Environmental Agreement: Politics, Law and Economics*, 16(3), 433–448. Advance online publication. 10.1007/s10784-016-9323-z

Gürbüz, A. (2003). Yerel Kalkınma Stratejisi İçinde Turizm ve Safranbolu. *Bilig*, (24), 29–48.

Compilation of References

Haber, T. R. T. (2024). "Safranbolu'nun 'sakin şehir' listesine dahil olması sevinçle karşılandı". https://www.trthaber.com/haber/yasam/safranbolunun-sakin-sehir-listesine-dahil-olmasi-sevincle -karsilandi-846735.html

Hadjidaki, E. (1996). Underwater Excavations of a Late Fifth Century Merchant Ship at Alonnesos, Greece : The 1991-1993 Seasons. *Bulletin De Correspondance HelléNique*, 120(2), 561–593. 10.3406/bch.1996.4619

Hailemariam, A., & Erdiaw-Kwasie, M. O. (2023). Towards a circular economy: Implications for emission reduction and environmental sustainability. *Business Strategy and the Environment*, 32(4), 1951–1965. 10.1002/bse.3229

Hák, T., Janoušková, S., & Moldan, B. (2016). Sustainable Development Goals: A need for relevant indicators. *Ecological Indicators*, 60, 565–573. Advance online publication. 10.1016/j.ecolind.2015.08.003

Hall, C. M., & Jenkins, J. (2004). Tourism and public policy. A companion to tourism, 523-540.

Hall, C. M. (2013). Policy learning and policy failure in sustainable tourism governance: From first-and second-order to third-order change? In *Tourism governance* (pp. 239–261). Routledge.

Hall, C. M., & Lew, A. A. (2009). *Understanding and managing tourism impacts: An integrated approach*. Routledge. 10.4324/9780203875872

Hall, C. M., & Page, S. J. (2009). Progress in tourism management: From the geography of tourism to geographies of tourism–A review. *Tourism Management*, 30(1), 3–16. 10.1016/j.tourman.2008.05.014

Han, H. (2021). Consumer behavior and environmental sustainability in tourism and hospitality: A review of theories, concepts, and latest research. *Journal of Sustainable Tourism*, 29(7), 1021–1042. 10.1080/09669582.2021.1903019

Han, H., Eom, T., Ansi, A., Ryu, H. B., & Kim, W. (2019). Community-Based Tourism as a Sustainable Direction in Destination Development: An Empirical Examination of Visitor Behaviors. *Sustainability (Basel)*, 11(10), 2864. 10.3390/su11102864

Hariyadi, B. R., Rokhman, A., Rosyadi, S., Yamin, M., & Runtiko, A. G. (2024). The Role of Community-Based Tourism in Sustainable Tourism Village In Indonesia. *Revista de Gestão Social e Ambiental*, 18(7), e05466. 10.24857/rgsa.v18n7-038

Hasan, A. (2021). *Green Tourism*. Media Wisata. 10.36276/mws.v12i1.195

Hassan, V., & Abou Fayad, S. (2023). Slow tourism as a tool for sustainable tourism development post-pandemic. *Uluslararası Sosyal Bilimler ve Eğitim Dergisi*, 5(8), 299–316.

Hassan, T. H., Almakhayitah, M. Y., & Saleh, M. I. (2024). Sustainable Stewardship of Egypt's Iconic Heritage Sites: Balancing Heritage Preservation, Visitors' Well-Being, and Environmental Responsibility. *Heritage*, 7(2), 737–757. 10.3390/heritage7020036

Hassan, V. I., & Basheer, S. (2024). The Impact of Advanced Technology on Medical Tourism Transformation: Case Study of United Arabs of Emirates. In *Impact of AI and Robotics on the Medical Tourism Industry* (pp. 1–19). IGI Global. 10.4018/979-8-3693-2248-2.ch001

Hawass, Z. (2015). *Magic of the Pyramids: My adventures in Archeology.* Leonardo Paolo Lovari.

He, Z. (2019). Increasing challenges for world heritage sites protection as a result of the development of sustainable tourism: a case of The Old Town of Lijiang, China (Master's thesis, Universitat Politècnica de Catalunya).

Hellenic Republic, Ministry of Culture Newsroom. (2024, February 29). Online https://www .culture.gov.gr/el/Information/SitePages/view.aspx?nID=4890

Hellenic Republic, Ministry of Culture. (2016). *BLUEMED.* culture.gov.gr. https://www.culture .gov.gr/en/service/SitePages/view.aspx?iID=3210

Hellenic Republic, Ministry of Environment and Energy. (2021, April 19). *Δίκτυο NATURA 2000.* https://ypen.gov.gr/perivallon/viopoikilotita/diktyo-natura-2000/

Helmy, E. (2004). Towards integration of sustainability into tourism planning in developing countries: Egypt as a case study. *Current Issues in Tourism, 7*(6), 478–501. 10.1080/1368350050408668199

Heshmati, A., & Rashidghalam, M. (2021). Assessment of the urban circular economy in Sweden. *Journal of Cleaner Production, 310,* 127475. 10.1016/j.jclepro.2021.127475

Hoang, K. V. (2021). The benefits of preserving and promoting cultural heritage values for the sustainable development of the country. In *E3S Web of Conferences* (Vol. 234, p. 00076). EDP Sciences. 10.1051/e3sconf/202123400076

Hodambia, M., & Dandala, S. (2020). Impact of Global Warming on Public Health. *Impact of Global Warming on Public Health., 1*(2), 65–70. 10.48173/jwh.v1i2.35

Holden, E., Linnerud, K., & Banister, D. (2017). The Imperatives of Sustainable Development. *Sustainable Development (Bradford), 25*(3), 213–226. Advance online publication. 10.1002/sd.1647

Holley-Kline, S., & Papazian, S. (2020). Heritage Trekking: Toward an Integrated Heritage Studies Methodology. *Journal of Field Archaeology, 45*(7), 527–541. 10.1080/00934690.2020.1807241

Ho, S. J., Hsu, Y. S., Lai, C. H., Chen, F. H., & Yang, M. H. (2022). Applying Game-Based Experiential Learning to Comprehensive Sustainable Development-Based Education. *Sustainability (Basel), 14*(3), 1172. Advance online publication. 10.3390/su14031172

Hossain, M. A., Akter, S., & Yanamandram, V. (2021). Why doesn't our value creation payoff: Unpacking customer analytics-driven value creation capability to sustain competitive advantage. *Journal of Business Research, 131,* 287–296. 10.1016/j.jbusres.2021.03.063

Howard, M. C., & Henderson, J. (2023). A review of exploratory factor analysis in tourism and hospitality research: Identifying current practices and avenues for improvement. *Journal of Business Research, 154,* 113328. 10.1016/j.jbusres.2022.113328

Compilation of References

Hristoforova, I. V., Silcheva, L. V., Arkhipova, T. N., Demenkova, A. B., & Nikolskaya, E. Y. (2019). Improvement of digital technologies in marketing communications of tourism and hospitality enterprises. *Journal of Environmental Management and Tourism*, 10(4), 829–834. 10.14505//jemt.10.4(36).13

Huby, G., Avery, A., & Sheikh, A. (2011). The case study approach. *BMC Medical Research Methodology*, 11(1), 100. 10.1186/1471-2288-11-10021707982

Hummels, H., & Argyrou, A. (2021). Planetary demands: Redefining sustainable development and sustainable entrepreneurship. *Journal of Cleaner Production*, 278, 123804. Advance online publication. 10.1016/j.jclepro.2020.123804

Hung, K.-P., Peng, N., & Chen, A. (2019). Incorporating on-site activity involvement and sense of belonging into the Mehrabian-Russell model—The experiential value of cultural tourism. *Tourism Management Perspectives*, 30, 43–52. 10.1016/j.tmp.2019.02.003

Hunold, M., Kesler, R., Laitenberger, U., & Schluetter, F. (2018). Evaluation of best price clauses in online hotel bookings. *International Journal of Industrial Organization, 61*(SI), 542–571. 10.1016/j.ijindorg.2018.03.008

Ibrahim, R., & Ajide, K. (2021). Nonrenewable and renewable energy consumption, trade openness, and environmental quality in G-7 countries: The conditional role of technological progress. *Environmental Science and Pollution Research International*, 28(33), 45212–45229. 10.1007/s11356-021-13926-233860425

Iftikhar, H., Chen, P., Ullah, S., & Ullah, A. (2022). Impact of tourism on sustainable development in BRI countries: The moderating role of institutional quality. *PLoS One*, 17(4), e0263745. Advance online publication. 10.1371/journal.pone.026374535436304

Iftikhar, H., Ullah, A., & Pinglu, C. (2024). *From Regional Integrated Development towards Sustainable Future: Evaluating the Belt and Road Initiative's Impact between Tourism, Fintech and Inclusive Green Growth.* 10.21203/rs.3.rs-3841996/v1

Iliopoulou-Georgudaki, J., Theodoropoulos, C., Konstantinopoulos, P., & Georgoudaki, E. (2017). Sustainable tourism development including the enhancement of cultural heritage in the city of Nafpaktos–Western Greece. *International Journal of Sustainable Development and World Ecology*, 24(3), 224–235. 10.1080/13504509.2016.1201021

Imon, S. S. (2013). Issues of sustainable tourism at heritage sites in Asia. In *Asian Heritage Management* (pp. 253–268). Routledge.

Inbakaran, R., & Jackson, M. (2005). Understanding Resort Visitors through Segmentation. *Tourism and Hospitality Research*, 6(1), 53–71. 10.1057/palgrave.thr.6040044

Indian E-commerce Industry Analysis | IBEF. (n.d.). https://www.ibef.org/industry/ecommerce-presentation

Iosifidis, S. (2019). The National Marine Park of Alonissos Northern Sporades. *ResearchGate*. https://www.researchgate.net/publication/332538725

Iqbal, A. (2019). The strategic human resource management approaches and organisational performance: The mediating role of creative climate. *Journal of Advances in Management Research*, 16(2), 181–193. 10.1108/JAMR-11-2017-0104

Jagić, I. (2017). Natural and cultural heritage interpretation for the sustainable development of local communities. Models of valorisation of cultural heritage in sustainable tourism, 228.

Janani, M., & Yuvaraj, N. (2019). Social Interaction and Stress-Based Recommendations for Elderly Healthcare Support System—A Survey. *Advances in Intelligent Systems and Computing*, 750, 291–303. 10.1007/978-981-13-1882-5_26

Jeong, M., & Jeon, M. M. (2008). *Journal of Hospitality & Leisure Customer Reviews of Hotel Experiences through Consumer Generated Media (CGM).* 10.1080/10507050801978265

Jeong, E., Lee, T., Brown, A., Choi, S., & Son, M. (2021). Does a National Park Enhance the Environment-Friendliness of Tourists as an Ecotourism Destination? *International Journal of Environmental Research and Public Health*, 18(16), 8321. Advance online publication. 10.3390/ijerph1816832134444073

Jha, S., Nanda, S., Acharya, B., & Dalai, A. K. (2024). Introduction to sustainability science in addressing energy security and achieving sustainable development goals. In *Biomass to Bioenergy* (pp. 1–14). Woodhead Publishing. 10.1016/B978-0-443-15377-8.00001-1

Jilcha, K., & Kitaw, D. (2017). Industrial occupational safety and health innovation for sustainable development. *Engineering Science and Technology, an International Journal, 20*(1). 10.1016/j.jestch.2016.10.011

Joensuu, T., Edelman, H., & Saari, A. (2020). Circular economy practices in the built environment. *Journal of Cleaner Production*, 276, 276. 10.1016/j.jclepro.2020.124215

Jokić, Ž., Božanić, D., & Pamučar, D. (2021). Selection of fire position of mortar units using LBWA and Fuzzy MABAC model. *Operational Research in Engineering Sciences: Theory and Applications*, 4(1), 115–135.

Jong, A. (2019). How to develop community-based tourism? Blog. Retrieved on 30/11/2020 from: https://fairsayari.com/blog/how-to-develop-community-based tourism#:~:text=Community%2Dbased%20tourism%20is%20a,their%20culture%20and%20daily%20lives.&text=These%20types%20of%20activities%20create,its%20beliefs%20 and%20social%20norms

Joshi, R. (2010). Eco-tourism as a viable option for wildlife conservation: Need for policy initiative in Rajaji National Park, North-West India. *Global Journal of Human Social Science Research*, 10(5), 19–30.

Jovanovic, S., & Ilic, I. (2016). Infrastructure as important determinant of tourism development in the countries of Southeast Europe. *Ecoforum Journal, 5*(1), 288-294.

Juma, L. O., & Khademi-Vidra, A. (2019). Community-Based Tourism and Sustainable Development of Rural Regions in Kenya; Perceptions of the Citizenry. *Sustainability (Basel)*, 11(17), 4733. 10.3390/su11174733

Compilation of References

Jun, H, & Minseok K. (2021). From stakeholder communication to engagement for the sustainable development goals (SDGs): A case study of LG electronics. *Sustainability,13*(15), 8624.

Kahraman, C., & Gündogdu, F. K. (2021). Decision making with spherical fuzzy sets. *Studies in fuzziness and soft computing, 392*, 3-25.

Kalia, P., & Paul, J. (2021). E-service quality and e-retailers: Attribute-based multi-dimensional scaling. *Computers in Human Behavior*, 115, 106608. Advance online publication. 10.1016/j.chb.2020.106608

Kaligotla, S. (2019). *A Temple without a Name: Deccan Architecture and the Canon for Sacred Indian Buildings. Canons and Values: Ancient to Modern.* Academia.

Kara, G. (2017). Kültürel Mirasın Turizm Amaçlı Kulanılmasında Turist Taleplerinin Belirlenmesi: Safranbolu Örneği. *Uluslararası Türk Kültür Coğrafyasında Sosyal Bilimler Dergisi*, 2(2), 40–50.

Karagöz, Z. C. (2022). *Endüstri Mirasının Evrensel Tasarım İlkeleri Kapsamında İncelenmesi: İzmit Seka Kağıt Müzesi Örneği* (Master's thesis, Fatih Sultan Mehmet Vakıf Üniversitesi, Lisansüstü Eğitim Enstitüsü).

Kargabayeva, S. T., Tuleubayeva, M. K., Makenova, G. U., & Kirichok, O. V. (2023). International tourism as a tool for inclusive development of region. *Bulletin of "Turan" University*, 4(4), 293–307. 10.46914/1562-2959-2023-1-4-293-307

Karoubi, M., & Ferdowsi, S. (2021). Impact of Perceived Social Apathy on Tourists' Behavioral Intentions. *Leisure Studies*, 40(5), 628–644. 10.1080/02614367.2021.1888308

Kaul, A. K. (2014). *Studies in geography of Jammu and Kashmir.* Rawat Publications.

Kaul, H., & Gupta, S. (2009). Sustainable tourism in India. *Worldwide Hospitality and Tourism Themes*, 1(1), 12–18. 10.1108/17554210910949841

Kavitha, K., & Ravi, G. R. (2024). Culinary Heritage as a Sustainable Tourism Product: A Review. In Bhartiya, S., Bhatt, V., & Jimenez Ruiz, A. E. (Eds.), *Advances in Hospitality, Tourism, and the Services Industry* (pp. 60–76). IGI Global. 10.4018/979-8-3693-4135-3.ch004

Kemer, E., & Tyagi, P. K. (2023). Application of Artificial Intelligence and Robotics in Tourism and Hospitality Marketing. In *Embracing Business Sustainability Through Innovation and Creativity in the Service Sector* (pp. 125–140). IGI Global. 10.4018/978-1-6684-6732-9.ch008

Keshavarz-Ghorabaee, M., Amiri, M., Hashemi-Tabatabaei, M., & Ghahremanloo, M. (2021). Sustainable public transportation evaluation using a novel hybrid method based on fuzzy BWM and MABAC. *The Open Transportation Journal, 15*(1).

Khadaroo, J., & Seetanah, B. (2007). Transport infrastructure and tourism development. *Annals of Tourism Research*, 34(4), 1021–1032. 10.1016/j.annals.2007.05.010

Khammadee, P. (2023). The Relationship Between E-HRM Practices and Organizational Performance: The Mediating Role of Organizational Agility and Sustainable Competitive Advantage. *SSRN*, 6(1), 1–21. 10.2139/ssrn.4546511

Khan, A. A. (2020). Covid-19 salgınının turizme etkileri: Safranbolu miras kenti örneği. *İşletme ve İktisat Çalışmaları Dergisi, 8*(2), 28-37.

Khan, I. S., Ahmad, M. O., & Majava, J. (2021). Industry 4.0 and sustainable development: A systematic mapping of triple bottom line, Circular Economy and Sustainable Business Models perspectives. In *Journal of Cleaner Production* (Vol. 297). 10.1016/j.jclepro.2021.126655

Khan. (2019). Gurez Valley: The Most Comprehensive Travel Guide. Retrieved on 26/11/2020 from: https://vargiskhan.com/log/gurez-valley/

Khan, I. S., Ahmad, M. O., & Majava, J. (2023). Industry 4.0 innovations and their implications: An evaluation from sustainable development perspective. *Journal of Cleaner Production*, 405, 137006. Advance online publication. 10.1016/j.jclepro.2023.137006

Khoury, G. (2022a). Estimating the Influence of Obsolete Curricula on the Effective Tourism Education. *Abstract presented at the 5th International Conference on Multi-Disciplinary Research Studies and Education.*

Khusainova, I., Gasimova, A. A., Mammadova, I. I., Yekimov, S., Tahirzade, J. F., Khalilova, R. F., & Sobirov, B. (2024). Studying the principles of sustainable tourism development in Karabakh. *BIO Web of Conferences, 93*, 05003. 10.1051/bioconf/20249305003

Kieran, D. (2021). *Scuba diving industry Market Size & Statistics: 2021 Edition.*

Kieran, D. (2024, March 9). Survey results: State of the Dive Industry 2024 market reports. *Medium*. https://medium.com/scubanomics/survey-results-state-of-the-dive-industry-2024-market-reports-bccceccf8613a

Kim, B.-D., Shi, M., & Srinivasan, K. (2001). Reward programs and tacit collusion. *Marketing Science*, 20(2), 99–120. 10.1287/mksc.20.2.99.10191

Kim, E. E. K., Mattila, A. S., & Baloglu, S. (2011). Effects of gender and expertise on consumers' motivation to read online hotel reviews. *Cornell Hospitality Quarterly*, 52(4), 399–406. 10.1177/1938965510394357

Kim, J. H., Ritchie, J. R. B., & Tung, V. W. S. (2010). The effect of memorable experience on behavioral intentions in tourism: A structural equation modeling approach. *Tourism Analysis*, 15(6), 637–648. 10.3727/108354210X12904412049776

Kim, J. H., Seok, B. I., Choi, H. J., Jung, S. H., & Yu, J. P. (2020). Sustainable management activities: A study on the relations between technology commercialization capabilities, sustainable competitive advantage, and business performance. *Sustainability (Basel)*, 12(19), 7913–7923. 10.3390/su12197913

Compilation of References

Kim, S., Bi, Y., & Kim, I. (2021). Travel website atmospheres inducing older travelers' familiarity: The moderating role of cognitive age. *International Journal of Environmental Research and Public Health*, 18(9), 4812. Advance online publication. 10.3390/ijerph1809481233946402

Kiper, T., & Arslan, M. (2009). Safranbolu-Yörükköyü Tarımsal Turizm Potansiyelinin Kırsal Kalkınma Açısından Değerlendirilmesi. *Turkish Journal Of Forestry*, 8(2), 145-158. Https://Doi .Org/10.18182/Tjf.92211

Kizielewicz, J. (2019). Human Resource Policies in Travel Companies Indexed on the Warsaw Stock Exchange. In C. Sousa, I. V. DeFreitas, & J. Marques (Eds.), Proceedings of the 2nd international conference on tourism research (ICTR 2019) (pp. 143–150). Academic Press.

Knio, M. S. (2020a). The effect of e-commerce richness on consumer behaviour. *Abstract presented at the İstanbul Aydın Üniversitesi Conference.*

Knio, M. S. (2020b). Estimating the impact of the effective valorization of cultural and natural resources for the economic growth of Beirut. *Abstract presented at the İstanbul Aydın Üniversitesi Conference.*

Koçan, N., Ozeren, A., Aktaş, E., & Köseoğlu, F. (2023). Değirmencik Köyünün (Safranbolu) Kırsal Turizm Potansiyelinin Araştırılması. *Kent Akademisi*, 16(1), 56–70. 10.35674/kent.1105332

Kopnina, H. (2020). Education for the future? Critical evaluation of education for sustainable development goals. *The Journal of Environmental Education*, 51(4), 280–291. Advance online publication. 10.1080/00958964.2019.1710444

Korov, T., Šostar, M., & Andrlić, B. (2024). The model of strategic management of a religious tourism destination in function of sustainable development. *International Journal of Professional Business Review*, 9(4), e04599. 10.26668/businessreview/2024.v9i4.4599

Kota, H. B., Singh, G., Mir, M., Smark, C., & Kumar, B. (2021). Sustainable development goals and businesses. *Australasian Accounting, Business and Finance Journal, 15*(5 Special Issue). 10.14453/aabfj.v15i5.1

Kotler, P., & Keller, K. (2009). *Marketing Management.* Pearson Education.

Koutsi, D., & Stratigea, A. (2019). Ολοκληρωμένη συμμετοχική διαχείριση χερσαίων και ενάλιων πολιτιστικών πόρων ως πυλώνας ανάπτυξης. *ResearchGate*. https://www.researchgate .net/publication/336148494_Olokleromene_symmetochike_diacheirise_chersaion_kai_enalion _politistikon_poron_os_pylonas_anaptyxes_apomonomenon_nesiotikon_periochon

Koutsouris, A. (2009). Social learning and sustainable tourism development; local quality conventions in tourism: A Greek case study. *Journal of Sustainable Tourism*, 17(5), 567–581. 10.1080/09669580902855810

Kozak, M., & Buhalis, D. (2019). Cross–border tourism destination marketing: Prerequisites and critical success factors. *Journal of Destination Marketing & Management*, 14, 1–9. 10.1016/j. jdmm.2019.100392

Kozinets, R. V. (2010). Netnography: The marketer's secret weapon. *White paper*, 1-13.

Kozinets, R. V. (2002). The field behind the screen: Using netnography for marketing research in online communities. *JMR, Journal of Marketing Research*, 39(1), 61–72. 10.1509/jmkr.39.1.61.18935

Kubiszewski, I., Costanza, R., Franco, C., Lawn, P., Talberth, J., Jackson, T., & Aylmer, C. (2013). Beyond GDP: Measuring and achieving global genuine progress. *Ecological Economics*, 93, 57–68. 10.1016/j.ecolecon.2013.04.019

Kulavuz-Onal, D., & Vásquez, C. (2013). Reconceptualising fieldwork in a netnography of an online community of English language teachers. *Ethnography and Education*, 8(2), 224–238. 10.1080/17457823.2013.792511

Kumar, R. B., & Dar, H. (2014). Developmental shift of tourism in Kashmir. *Abhinav International Monthly Refereed Journal of Research in Management & Technology, 3*(11).

Kumar, A., & Singh, G. (2019). Seasonal effect on tourism in India. *Journal of Financial Economics*, 7(2), 48–51.

Kumar, R. B. (2009). Indian heritage tourism: Challenges of identification and preservation. *International Journal of Hospitality and Tourism Systems*, 2(1), 120.

Kumar, S., Talukder, M. B., Kabir, F., & Kaiser, F. (2023). Challenges and Sustainability of Green Finance in the Tourism Industry: Evidence From Bangladesh. In Taneja, S., Kumar, P., Grima, S., Ozen, E., & Sood, K. (Eds.), (pp. 97–111). Advances in Finance, Accounting, and Economics. IGI Global. 10.4018/979-8-3693-1388-6.ch006

Kuo, Y. K., Khan, T. I., Islam, S. U., Abdullah, F. Z., Pradana, M., & Kaewsaeng-On, R. (2022). Impact of green HRM practices on environmental performance: The mediating role of green innovation. *Frontiers in Psychology*, 13, 1–12. 10.3389/fpsyg.2022.91672335774953

Kusumah, E. P. (2023). Sustainable tourism concept: Tourist satisfaction and destination loyalty. *International Journal of Tourism Cities*. 10.1108/IJTC-04-2023-0074

Lama, R. (2014). Community Based Tourism Development: A Case Study of Sikkim. *PhD thesis submitted*, Department of Tourism and Hotel Management Kurukshetra University, Kuruksetra.

Landorf, C. (2009). Managing for sustainable tourism: A review of six cultural World Heritage Sites. *Journal of Sustainable Tourism*, 17(1), 53–70. 10.1080/09669580802159719

Langergaard, L. L., & Krøjer, J. (2024). Social Sustainability in Unsustainable Times: Introduction of One Book and Many Problems. In *Social Sustainability in Unsustainable Society: Concepts, Critiques and Counter-Narratives* (pp. 1–13). Springer International Publishing.

Lanzara, G., & Minerva, G. A. (2018). Tourism, amenities, and welfare in an urban setting. *Journal of Regional Science*, 59(3), 452–479. 10.1111/jors.12440

Larsen, S. (2007). Aspects of a psychology of the tourist experience. *Scandinavian Journal of Hospitality and Tourism*, 7(1), 7–18. 10.1080/15022250701226014

Larson, L. R., & Poudyal, N. C. (2012). Developing sustainable tourism through adaptive resource management: A case study of Machu Picchu, Peru. *Journal of Sustainable Tourism*, 20(7), 917–938. 10.1080/09669582.2012.667217

Leal Filho, W., Azeiteiro, U., Alves, F., Pace, P., Mifsud, M., Brandli, L., Caeiro, S. S., & Disterheft, A. (2018). Reinvigorating the sustainable development research agenda: The role of the sustainable development goals (SDG). *International Journal of Sustainable Development and World Ecology*, 25(2), 131–142. Advance online publication. 10.1080/13504509.2017.1342103

Leal Filho, W., Yang, P., Eustachio, J. H. P. P., Azul, A. M., Gellers, J. C., Gielczyk, A., Dinis, M. A. P., & Kozlova, V. (2023). Deploying digitalisation and artificial intelligence in sustainable development research. *Environment, Development and Sustainability*, 25(6), 4957–4988. Advance online publication. 10.1007/s10668-022-02252-335313685

Lee, O. K. D., Sambamurthy, V., Lim, K., & Wei, K. K. (2008). IT-enabled organizational agility and sustainable competitive advantage. *Vallabhajosyula and Lim, Kai and Wei, KK, IT-Enabled Organizational Agility and Sustainable Competitive Advantage.*

Lee, H. A., & Law, R. (2012). Diversity in statistical research techniques: An analysis of refereed research articles in the journal of travel & tourism marketing between 1992 and 2010. *Journal of Travel & Tourism Marketing*, 29(1), 37–41. 10.1080/10548408.2012.638556

Lee, J. W. (2020). Green finance and sustainable development goals: The case of China. *Journal of Asian Finance. Economics and Business*, 7(7), 577–586. Advance online publication. 10.13106/jafeb.2020.vol7.no7.577

Lee, S., Lee, N., Lee, T. J., & Hyun, S. S. (2024). The influence of social support from intermediary organizations on innovativeness and subjective happiness in community-based tourism. *Journal of Sustainable Tourism*, 32(4), 795–817. 10.1080/09669582.2023.2175836

Leiper, N. (1990). Tourist attraction systems. *Annals of Tourism Research*, 17(3), 367–384. 10.1016/0160-7383(90)90004-B

Le, T. H., Arcodia, C., Novais, M. A., & Kralj, A. (2019). What we know and do not know about authenticity in dining experiences: A systematic literature review. *Tourism Management*, 74, 258–275. 10.1016/j.tourman.2019.02.012

Lichtenstein, D. R., Ridgway, N. M., & Netemeyer, R. G. (1993). Price Perceptions and Consumer Shopping Behavior: A Field Study. *JMR, Journal of Marketing Research*, 30(2), 234–245. 10.1177/002224379303000208

Liengpunsakul, S. (2021). Artificial Intelligence and Sustainable Development in China. *Chinese Economy*, 54(4), 235–248. Advance online publication. 10.1080/10971475.2020.1857062

Lim, C. K., Haufiku, M. S., Tan, K. L., Farid Ahmed, M., & Ng, T. F. (2022). Systematic Review of Education Sustainable Development in Higher Education Institutions. *Sustainability (Basel)*, 14(20), 13241. Advance online publication. 10.3390/su142013241

Lim, M. M. L., Søgaard Jørgensen, P., & Wyborn, C. A. (2018). Reframing the sustainable development goals to achieve sustainable development in the anthropocene—A systems approach. *Ecology and Society*, 23(3), art22. Advance online publication. 10.5751/ES-10182-230322

Li, T., Dong, Y., & Liu, Z. (2020). A review of social-ecological system resilience: Mechanism, assessment and management. *The Science of the Total Environment*, 723, 138113. 10.1016/j.scitotenv.2020.13811332224405

Li, X., Abbas, J., Wang, D., Baig, N., & Zhang, R. (2022). From Cultural Tourism to Social Entrepreneurship: Role of Social Value Creation for Environmental Sustainability. *Frontiers in Psychology*, 13, 925768. Advance online publication. 10.3389/fpsyg.2022.92576835911048

Locher, J. L., Yoels, W. C., Maurer, D., & van Ells, J. (2005). Comfort foods: An exploratory journey into the social and emotional significance of food. *Food & Foodways*, 13(4), 273–297. 10.1080/07409710500334509

Lopes, H., Remoaldo, P., Ribeiro, V., Ribeiro, J. C., & Silva, S. (2016). The creation of a new tourist destination in low-density areas: The Boticas case. *Journal of Tourism, Sustainability and Well-being*, 4(2), 118–131.

Lotfi, F. H. (2023). *Fuzzy Decision Analysis: Multi-Attribute Decision Making Approach*. Springer Nature. 10.1007/978-3-031-44742-6

Loureiro, S., & Nascimento, J. (2021). Shaping a View on the Influence of Technologies on Sustainable Tourism. *Sustainability (Basel)*, 13(22), 12691. Advance online publication. 10.3390/su132212691

Lu, Y., Chen, M., & Xue, J. (2020). Water Culture in the Development of National Cultural Tourism under the New Ecological Environment. *Journal of Coastal Research*, 104(sp1), 746–750. 10.2112/JCR-SI104-130.1

Lyaskovskaya, E., & Khudyakova, T. (2021). Sharing economy: For or against sustainable development. *Sustainability (Basel)*, 13(19), 11056. Advance online publication. 10.3390/su131911056

Macleod, D. V., & Carrier, J. G. (Eds.). (2009). *Tourism, power and culture: Anthropological insights*. Multilingual Matters. 10.21832/9781845411268

Mahapatra, B. (2011). *Ethnic Dances and Music of Western Orissa: An Anthropological Study Towards Promoting Ecotourism*. Concept Publishing Company.

Mahdi, O. R., & Nassar, I. A. (2021). The business model of sustainable competitive advantage through strategic leadership capabilities and knowledge management processes to overcome covid-19 pandemic. *Sustainability (Basel)*, 13(17), 9891–9912. 10.3390/su13179891

Maka, A. O. M., & Alabid, J. M. (2022). Solar energy technology and its roles in sustainable development. *Clean Energy*, 6(3), 476–483. Advance online publication. 10.1093/ce/zkac023

Makhdoomi, A., & Khaki, A. A. (2023). Journey to Resilience: Sustainable Tourism and Community Participation in Jammu and Kashmir. *International Journal of Management and Development Studies*, 12(12), 41–48. 10.53983/ijmds.v12n12.005

Managi, S., Chen, S., Kumar, P., & Dasgupta, P. (2024). Sustainable matrix beyond GDP: Investment for inclusive growth. *Humanities & Social Sciences Communications*, 11(1), 185. 10.1057/s41599-024-02659-5

Mandić, A., Mrnjavac, Ž., & Kordić, L. (2018). Tourism infrastructure, recreational facilities and tourism development. *Tourism and Hospitality Management*, 24(1), 41–62. 10.20867/thm.24.1.12

Manglis, A., Fourkiotou, A., & Papadopoulou, D. (2019). Sustainable management and protection of Accessible Underwater Cultural Heritage sites; global practices and bottom-up initiatives. *International Conference in Management of Accessible Underwater, Cultural and Natural Heritage Sites: "Dive in Blue Growth", Athens, Greece, 16-18 October 2019*

Manglis, A., Fourkiotou, A., & Papadopoulou, D. (2020). The Accessible Underwater Cultural Heritage Sites (AUCHS) as a sustainable tourism development opportunity in the Mediterranean Region. *Tourism (Zagreb)*, 68(4), 499–503. 10.37741/t.68.4.9

Manglis, A., Fourkiotou, A., & Papadopoulou, D. (2021). A Roadmap for the Sustainable Valorization of accessible Underwater Cultural Heritage Sites. *Heritage*, 4(4), 4700–4715. 10.3390/heritage4040259

Manglis, A., Giatsiatsou, P., Papadopoulou, D., Drouga, V., & Fourkiotou, A. (2021). Implementing Multi-Criteria Analysis in the Selection of AUCHS for the Integration of Digital Technologies into the Tourism Offering: The Case of MeDryDive. *Heritage*, 4(4), 4460–4472. 10.3390/heritage4040246

March, R., & Wilkinson, I. (2009). Conceptual tools for evaluating tourism partnerships. *Tourism Management*, 30(3), 455–462. 10.1016/j.tourman.2008.09.001

Marcouiller, D. W., Kim, K. K., & Deller, S. C. (2004). Natural amenities, tourism and income distribution. *Annals of Tourism Research*, 31(4), 1031–1050. 10.1016/j.annals.2004.04.003

Martínez Rodríguez, M. C., & Moreno, C. N. (2023). Perspectives for Resilience, Social Inclusion, and Sustainable Tourism in Mexico. In Aguilar-Rivera, N., Borsari, B., De Brito, P. R. B., & Andrade Guerra, B. (Eds.), *SDGs in the Americas and Caribbean Region* (pp. 49–74). Springer International Publishing. 10.1007/978-3-031-16017-2_49

Martinez, B., & Kim, S. (2012). Predicting purchase intention for private sale sites. *Journal of Fashion Marketing and Management*, 16(3), 342–365. 10.1108/13612021211246080

Mathers, A. & Deonandan, R. (2018). Are the Sustainable Development Goals Realistic and Effective: A Qualitative Analysis of Key Informant Opinions. *OIDA International Journal of Sustainable Development,* 11(3).

Matteis, F., Notaristefano, G., & Bianchi, P. (2021). Public—Private Partnership Governance for Accessible Tourism in Marine Protected Areas (MPAs). *Sustainability (Basel)*, 13(15), 8455. Advance online publication. 10.3390/su13158455

Mauri, A. G., & Minazzi, R. (2013). Web reviews influence on expectations and purchasing intentions of hotel potential customers. *International Journal of Hospitality Management*, 34, 99–107. 10.1016/j.ijhm.2013.02.012

Mayaka, M., Croy, W. G., & Cox, J. W. (2019). A dimensional approach to community-based tourism: Recognising and differentiating form and context. *Annals of Tourism Research*, 74, 177–190. 10.1016/j.annals.2018.12.002

Mazza, B. (2023). A Theoretical Model of Strategic Communication for the Sustainable Development of Sport Tourism. *Sustainability (Basel)*, 15(9), 7039. 10.3390/su15097039

McIntyre, G. (1993). *Sustainable tourism development: guide for local planners.*

Medeiros, M. M. D., & Maçada, A. C. G. (2022). Competitive advantage of data-driven analytical capabilities: The role of big data visualization and of organizational agility. *Management Decision*, 60(4), 953–975. 10.1108/MD-12-2020-1681

Medium, G. R. I. (2020). The business value of sustainability reporting. Retrieved from: https://globalreportinginitiative.medium.com/the-business-value-of-sustainability-reporting-a7a29992a074

MeDryDive. (2020b, April 28). *Peristera shipwreck (Greece)*. https://medrydive.eu/peristera-shipwreck-greece/

Mehrotra, D. S., Subramanian, D., Krishnan, Dr. S., Bharat, Dr. A., & Garg, Dr. Y. K. (Eds.). (2024). *Calibrating Urban Livability in the Global South*. B P International. 10.9734/bpi/mono/978-81-971889-1-6

Melián-Alzola, L., Domínguez-Falcón, C., & Martín-Santana, J. D. (2020). The role of the human dimension in organizational agility: An empirical study in intensive care units. *Personnel Review*, 49(9), 1945–1964. 10.1108/PR-08-2019-0456

Melo, R. H., Pambudi, M. R., & Niode, A. (2024). Socioeconomic status, lake knowledge, and community participation in the sustainable Lake Limboto management, Gorontalo Regency. *Journal of Water and Land Development*, 177–182. https://doi.org/10.24425/jwld.2024.149119

Mendes, H. J. D. A., Paiva, T. M. D. D., Felgueira, T. M. M., Alves, C. A., & Costa, A. A. (2024). The need for business models in accessible, inclusive and sustainable tourism. *International Journal of Professional Business Review*, 9(4), e04542. 10.26668/businessreview/2024.v9i4.4542

Menon, S. M. (2020, September 26). *Megaliths of Pattadakal*. Retrieved from Deccan Herald: deccanherald.com/spectrum/megaliths-of-pattadakal-893182.html

Mensah, J. (2019). Sustainable development: Meaning, history, principles, pillars, and implications for human action: Literature review. *Cogent Social Sciences*, 5(1), 1653531. Advance online publication. 10.1080/23311886.2019.1653531

Compilation of References

Miah, J. H., Griffiths, A., McNeill, R., Poonaji, I., Martin, R., Morse, S., & Sadhukhan, J. (2015). Creating an environmentally sustainable food factory: A case study of the Lighthouse project at Nestlé. *Procedia CIRP*, 26, 229–234. 10.1016/j.procir.2014.07.030

Miller, K. (2020). The Triple Bottom Line: What it is & why it's important. Retrieved April 14, 2021, from https://online.hbs.edu/blog/post/what-is-the-triple-bottom-line

Miller, C., & Taylor, C. (2022). A Diver's Guide to the World. *National Geographic*.

Milman, A. (2015). Preserving the cultural identity of a World Heritage Site: The impact of Chichen Itza's souvenir vendors. *International Journal of Culture, Tourism and Hospitality Research*, 9(3), 241–260. 10.1108/IJCTHR-06-2015-0067

Mintzberg, H. (2009, July– August). Rebuilding Companies as Communities. *Harvard Business Review*.

Mishra, A., & Maitra, R. (2022). Sustainable Tourism At Lonar Lake. In *Maharashtra: A Geopark Approach*. Impact And Policy Research.

Mkono, M. (2012). Netnographic tourist research: The internet as a virtual fieldwork site. *Tourism Analysis*, 17(4), 553–555. 10.3727/108354212X13473157390966

Mkono, M. (2013). Using net-based ethnography (Netnography) to understand the staging and marketing of "authentic African" dining experiences to tourists at Victoria Falls. *Journal of Hospitality & Tourism Research (Washington, D.C.)*, 37(2), 184–198. 10.1177/1096348011425502

Mkono, M., & Markwell, K. (2014). The application of netnography in tourism studies. *Annals of Tourism Research*, 48, 289–291. 10.1016/j.annals.2014.07.005

Mohajan, H. K. (2018). Qualitative research methodology in social sciences and related subjects. Journal of economic development, environment and people, 7(1), 23-48.

Mohamad Taghvaee, V., Assari Arani, A., Nodehi, M., Khodaparast Shirazi, J., Agheli, L., Neshat Ghojogh, H. M., Salehnia, N., Mirzaee, A., Taheri, S., Mohammadi Saber, R., Faramarzi, H., Alvandi, R., & Ahmadi Rahbarian, H. (2023). Sustainable development goals: Transportation, health and public policy. *Review of Economics and Political Science*, 8(2), 134–161. Advance online publication. 10.1108/REPS-12-2019-0168

Mohammad, B. T., & Mokarram Hossain, M. (2021). Prospects of future tourism in Bangladesh: An evaluative study. *I-Manager's. Journal of Management*, 15(4), 31. 10.26634/jmgt.15.4.17495

Mohanty, P., Chandran, A., & Mathew, R. (2018). Branding Odisha as a rural tourism destination: An alternate approach. *International Journal of Creative Research Thoughts*, 6. Advance online publication. 10.5281/zenodo.1164173

Moldovan, L., & Moldovan, F. (2024). Inclusive Innovation and Inclusive Growth Tools for Eliminating the Gaps Created by Economic Growth. In L. Moldovan & A. Gligor (Eds.), *The 17th International Conference Interdisciplinarity in Engineering* (Vol. 926, pp. 542–551). Springer Nature Switzerland. 10.1007/978-3-031-54664-8_46

Mondor, C., Hockley, S., & Deal, D. (2013). The David Lawrence Convention Center: How green building design and operations can save money, drive local economic opportunity, and transform an industry. *Journal of Green Building*, 8(1), 28–43. 10.3992/jgb.8.1.28

Monroy-Rodríguez, S., & Caro-Carretero, R. (2023). Congress tourism: Characteristics and application to sustainable tourism to facilitate collective action towards achieving the SDGs. *Cogent Business & Management*, 10(3), 2286663. 10.1080/23311975.2023.2286663

Morton, S., Pencheon, D., & Squires, N. (2017). Sustainable Development Goals (SDGs), and their implementation. In *British Medical Bulletin* (Vol. 124, Issue 1). 10.1093/bmb/ldx031

Moscardo, G. (2015). Tourism and sustainability: Challenges, conflict and core knowledge. Education for Sustainability in Tourism: A Handbook of Processes, Resources, and Strategies, 25-43.

Moscardo, G. (2018). Rethinking the role and practice of destination community involvement in tourism planning. In *Tourism policy and planning implementation* (pp. 36–52). Routledge. 10.4324/9781315162928-3

Mtapuri, O., & Giampiccoli, A. (2013). Interrogating the role of the state and non-state actors in community-based tourism ventures: Toward a model for spreading the benefits to the wider community. *The South African Geographical Journal*, 95(1), 1–15. 10.1080/03736245.2013.805078

Mtapuri, O., & Giampiccoli, A. (2016). Towards a comprehensive model of community-based tourism development. *The South African Geographical Journal*, 98(1), 154–168. 10.1080/03736245.2014.977813

MTC. (2024, April 15). *Bus route from Mahabalipuram to Thirupporur*. Retrieved from MTC Chennai: https://mtcbus.tn.gov.in/Home/bustimingsearch

Mukhuty, S., Upadhyay, A., & Rothwell, H. (2022). Strategic sustainable development of Industry 4.0 through the lens of social responsibility: The role of human resource practices. *Business Strategy and the Environment*, 31(5), 2068–2081. Advance online publication. 10.1002/bse.3008

Munt, I. (1998). *Tourism and sustainability: new tourism in the third world*. Routledge.

Murnane, W. (1995). The History of Ancient Egypt: An Overview. *Civilizations of the Ancient Near East*, 2, 712–714.

Musa, G., & Dimmock, K. (2013c). *Scuba diving tourism*. https://doi.org/10.4324/9780203121016

Mustafa, M. H. (2021). Cultural heritage: A tourism product of Egypt under risk. *Journal of Environmental Management and Tourism*, 12(1(49)), 243–257. 10.14505/jemt.v12.1(49).21

Na Thongkaew, B., Ruksapol, A., & Brewer, P. (2024). The Role of Local Networks in Supportive Mechanisms Model for Sustainable Community-based Tourism Administration. *Tourism Planning & Development*, 1-23.

Compilation of References

Nair, B., & Sathiyabamavathy, K. (2020). Visitor perception and expectation of heritage tourism at Mahabalipuram monuments. *Strategies for promoting sustainable hospitality and tourism services*, 191-210.

Najar, P. A., Dar, H., Singh, P., & Najar, A. H. (2022). Anti-Social Factors Influence the Decision Making of Tourists: A Study of Kashmir. *International Journal of Cyber Warfare & Terrorism*, 12(1), 1–14. 10.4018/IJCWT.315590

Narangajavana Kaosiri, Y., Callarisa Fiol, L. J., Moliner Tena, M. A., Rodríguez Artola, R. M., & Sanchez Garcia, J. (2019). User-generated content sources in social media: A new approach to explore tourist satisfaction. *Journal of Travel Research*, 58(2), 253–265. 10.1177/0047287517746014

NatureBank - Βιότοπος NATURA - ETHNIKO THALASSIO PARKO ALONNISOU - VOREION SPORADON, ANATOLIKI SKOPELOS. (n.d.). https://filotis.itia.ntua.gr/biotopes/c/GR1430004/

Nayim, Y. S., & Yaman, S. Ö. (2019). Eskipazar (Karabük) Peyzajının Ekoturizm Açısından Değerlendirilmesi. *Bartin Orman Fakültesi Dergisi*, 21(2), 336–349. 10.24011/barofd.579067

Nestlé. (2017). The Circular Economy: These are the world's most sustainable companies. Retrieved from: https://www.corporate.nestle.ca/en/stories/world-most-sustainable-companies-henniez

Ngo, T. H., Tournois, N., Dinh, T. L. T., Chu, M. T., & Phan, C. S. (2024). Sustainable Community-Based Tourism Development: Capacity Building for Community; The Case Study in Cam Kim, Hoi An, Vietnam. *Journal of Sustainability Research*, 6(2).

Niemets, K., Kravchenko, K., Kandyba, Y., Kobylin, P., & Morar, C. (2021). World cities in terms of the sustainable development concept. In *Geography and Sustainability* (Vol. 2, Issue 4). 10.1016/j.geosus.2021.12.003

Noronha, L. (2010). Tourism products, local host communities and ecosystems in Goa, India. Sustainable Production Consumption Systems: Knowledge, Engagement and Practice, 237-249.

Noroozi, H. (2023). *Sustainable tourism development in iranian nomadic areas: Study of Socio-cultural, Economy, Environment and Political of Iranian Pastoral Nomads, and Development of Sustainable Tourism in Nomadic Areas of Iran.* 10.13140/RG.2.2.18025.47207

Nousheen, A., Yousuf Zai, S. A., Waseem, M., & Khan, S. A. (2020). Education for sustainable development (ESD): Effects of sustainability education on pre-service teachers' attitude towards sustainable development (SD). *Journal of Cleaner Production*, 250, 119537. Advance online publication. 10.1016/j.jclepro.2019.119537

Noy, C. (2007). The poetics of tourist experience: An autoethnography of a family trip to Eilat. *Journal of Tourism and Cultural Change*, 5(3), 141–157. 10.2167/jtcc085.0

Nunkoo, R., Sharma, A., Rana, N. P., Dwivedi, Y. K., & Sunnassee, V. A. (2023). Advancing sustainable development goals through interdisciplinarity in sustainable tourism research. *Journal of Sustainable Tourism*, 31(3), 735–759. Advance online publication. 10.1080/09669582.2021.2004416

Nutsugbodo, R. (2016). Tourist accommodation. *Tourism development in Ghana's Brong-Ahafo Region: Demand and supply dynamics*, 73-88.

NWKRTC. (2024, April 16). *Bus Time Table*. Retrieved from North Western Karnataka Road Transport Corporation: https://nwkrtc.karnataka.gov.in/info-3/Bus+Time+Table/en

Nyathi, M. (2024). The effect of electronic human resource management on electronic human resource management macro-level consequences: The role of perception of organizational politics. *African Journal of Economic and Management Studies*, 15(1), 1–14. 10.1108/AJEMS-04-2022-0168

Odysseus.culture. (n.d.). http://odysseus.culture.gr/h/3/gh352.jsp?obj_id=19848

Ogryzek, M. (2023). The Sustainable Development Paradigm. *Geomatics and Environmental Engineering*, 17(1), 5–18. Advance online publication. 10.7494/geom.2023.17.1.5

Ojha, A. K. (2022). Strategies for Sustainable Tourism Business Development: A Comprehensive Analysis. *Journal of Social Responsibility. Tourism and Hospitality*, 24(24), 25–30. 10.55529/jsrth.24.25.30

Okazaki, E. (2008). A community-based tourism model: Its conception and use. *Journal of Sustainable Tourism*, 16(5), 511–529. 10.1080/09669580802159594

Oppermann, M. (1997). First-time and repeat visitors to New Zealand. *Tourism Management*, 18(3), 177–181. 10.1016/S0261-5177(96)00119-7

Organization for Economic Cooperation and Development (OECD). (1994). *Tourism Strategies and Rural Development*.

Özdemir, Ü. (2011). Safranbolu'nun Kültürel Miras Kaynakları Ve Korunması. *Doğu Coğrafya Dergisi*, 16(26), 129–142.

Özdemir, Ü. (2011a). Ulaşım Coğrafyası Açısından Önemli Bir Güzergâh: Karabük-Bartın Karayolu. *Doğu Coğrafya Dergisi*, 13(19), 213–230.

Özmen, N., & Eren, M. (2021). Safranbolu Destinasyonunun İnanç Turizmi Potansiyeline Yönelik SWOT Analizi Çalışması. *Ekonomi İşletme Ve Yönetim Dergisi*, 5(1), 62–82.

Page, S. J. (2014). *Tourism management*. Routledge. 10.4324/9781315768267

Palinkas, L., & Wong, M. (2020). Global climate change and mental health. *Current Opinion in Psychology*, 32, 12–16. 10.1016/j.copsyc.2019.06.02331349129

Pamučar, D., & Ćirović, G. (2015). The selection of transport and handling resources in logistics centers using Multi-Attributive Border Approximation area Comparison (MABAC). *Expert Systems with Applications*, 42(6), 3016–3028. 10.1016/j.eswa.2014.11.057

Pan, X., Shao, T., Zheng, X., Zhang, Y., Ma, X., & Zhang, Q. (2023). Energy and sustainable development nexus: A review. In *Energy Strategy Reviews* (Vol. 47). https://doi.org/10.1016/j.esr.2023.101078

Compilation of References

Panigrahi, N. (2005). Development of eco-tourism in tribal regions of Orissa: potential and recommendations. *CEWCES Research Papers*, 9.

Parakh, N. (2022). Understanding the importance of ecotourism by supporting eco-design principles. *International Journal for Research in Applied Science and Engineering Technology*, 10(6), 4865–4872. Advance online publication. 10.22214/ijraset.2022.45085

Park, H. Y. (2013). *Heritage tourism*. Routledge. 10.4324/9781315882093

Patel, V., Pauli, N., Biggs, E., Barbour, L., & Boruff, B. (2021). Why bees are critical for achieving sustainable development. *Ambio*, 50(1), 49–59. Advance online publication. 10.1007/s13280-020-01333-932314266

Pearce, D. (1989). *Tourism Development* (2nd ed.). Longman Scientific and Technical with John Wiley and Sons.

Pechlaner, H., Innerhofer, E., & Erschbamer, G. (Eds.). (2019). *Overtourism: Tourism management and solutions*. Routledge.

Pehlivanides, G., Monastiridis, K., Tourtas, A., Karyati, E., Ioannidis, G., Bejelou, K., Antoniou, V., & Nomikou, P. (2020). The VIRTUALDiver Project. Making Greece's underwater cultural heritage accessible to the public. *Applied Sciences (Basel, Switzerland)*, 10(22), 8172. 10.3390/app10228172

Peredo, A. M., & Chrisman, J. J. (2006). Toward a Theory of Community-Based Enterprise. *Academy of Management Review*, 31(2), 309–328. 10.5465/amr.2006.20208683

Peristera's ancient ship wreck – NOUS. (n.d.). https://nous.com.gr/naxly_project/peristeras-ancient-ship-wreck/

Peterson, R. R., DiPietro, R. B., & Harrill, R. (2020). In search of inclusive tourism in the Caribbean: Insights from Aruba. *Worldwide Hospitality and Tourism Themes*, 12(3), 225–243. 10.1108/WHATT-02-2020-0009

Pine, B. J., & Gilmore, H. J. (1998). *The experience economy: Work is theatre & every business a stage*. Harvard Business School Press., 10.4337/9781781004227.00007

Pine, B. J., & Gilmore, J. H. (2002, June). Differentiating Hospitality Operations via Experiences. *The Cornell Hotel and Restaurant Administration Quarterly*, 43(3), 87–96. 10.1016/S0010-8804(02)80022-2

Pizam, A. (2010). Creating memorable experiences. *International Journal of Hospitality Management, 29*(3), 343. 10.1016/j.ijhm.2010.04.003

Pjero, E., & Gjermëni, O. (2020). Tourist's satisfaction in terms of accommodation: A case study in Vlore, Albania. *Business Perspectives and Research*, 8(1), 67–80. 10.1177/2278533719860022

Poinssot, C., Grandjean, S., Masson, M., Boullis, B., & Warin, D. (2013). Improving the actinides recycling in closed fuel cycles, a major step towards nuclear energy sustainability. *International Nuclear Fuel Cycle Conference, GLOBAL 2013: Nuclear Energy at a Crossroads, 1*, 672–677. https://www.scopus.com/inward/record.uri?eid=2-s2.0-84903217544&partnerID=40&md5=6f 1471875a8844a7809594af7cda99b2

Polnyotee, M., & Thadaniti, S. (2015). Community-Based Tourism: A Strategy for Sustainable Tourism Development of Patong Beach, Phuket Island, Thailand. *Asian Social Science*, 11(27), 90. Advance online publication. 10.5539/ass.v11n27p90

Pradahan, P., Costa, L., Rybski, D., Lucht, W., & Kropp, J. P. (2017). *A Systematic Study of Sustainable Development Goal (SDG) Interactions*. AGU Publications.

Prideaux, B. (2000). The Role of the Transport System in Destination Development. *Tourism (Zagreb)*, 53–63.

Prieto-Jiménez, E., López-Catalán, L., López-Catalán, B., & Domínguez-Fernández, G. (2021). Sustainable development goals and education: A bibliometric mapping analysis. *Sustainability (Basel)*, 13(4), 2126. Advance online publication. 10.3390/su13042126

Profillidis, V., Botzoris, G., & Galanis, A. (2018, May). Traffic noise reduction and sustainable transportation: A case survey in the cities of Athens and Thessaloniki, *Greece. In Conference on Sustainable Urban Mobility* (pp. 402-409). Cham: Springer International Publishing.

Pulido-Fernández, J., & Cárdenas-García, P. (2020). Analyzing the Bidirectional Relationship between Tourism Growth and Economic Development. *Journal of Travel Research*, 60(3), 583–602. 10.1177/0047287520922316

Punhani, R., Arora, V. P. S., Sabitha, S., & Kumar Shukla, V. (2021). Application of Clustering Algorithm for Effective Customer Segmentation in E-Commerce. In V. S. Naranje V. Singh B. (Ed.), *Proceedings of 2nd IEEE International Conference on Computational Intelligence and Knowledge Economy, ICCIKE 2021* (pp. 149–154). Institute of Electrical and Electronics Engineers Inc. 10.1109/ICCIKE51210.2021.9410713

Puwanendram, G., Silva, S., & Ganeshan, K. (2023). *Sustainable Tourism for Development and Value Chain Analysis Analyzing the Potential and Prospects for Agritourism Development in Sri Lanka: An Inclusive and Integrated Approach with Tea Industry and Homestay Services*. 10.13140/RG.2.2.24204.49281

Qiu, M., Sha, J., & Scott, N. (2021). Restoration of Visitors through Nature-Based Tourism: A Systematic Review, Conceptual Framework, and Future Research Directions. *International Journal of Environmental Research and Public Health*, 18(5), 2299. Advance online publication. 10.3390/ijerph1805229933652652

Rageh, A., Melewar, T. C., & Woodside, A. (2013). Using netnography research method to reveal the underlying dimensions of the customer/tourist experience. *Qualitative Market Research*, 16(2), 126–149. Advance online publication. 10.1108/13522751311317558

Compilation of References

Rahma, H., Fauzi, A., Juanda, B., & Widjojanto, B. (2019). Development of a composite measure of regional sustainable development in Indonesia. *Sustainability (Basel)*, 11(20), 5861. Advance online publication. 10.3390/su11205861

Ramadan, M., Bou Zakhem, N., Baydoun, H., Daouk, A., Youssef, S., El Fawal, A., Elia, J., & Ashaal, A. (2023). Toward Digital Transformation and Business Model Innovation: The Nexus between Leadership, Organizational Agility, and Knowledge Transfer. *Administrative Sciences*, 13(8), 185–195. 10.3390/admsci13080185

Raman, P., & Aashish, K. (2021). To continue or not to continue: A structural analysis of antecedents of mobile payment systems in India. *International Journal of Bank Marketing*, 39(2), 242–271. 10.1108/IJBM-04-2020-0167

Rana, S., & Sharma, S. K. (2015). A literature review, classification, and simple meta-analysis on the conceptual domain of international marketing: 1990-2012. *Advances in International Marketing*, 25, 189–222. 10.1108/S1474-797920140000025009

Rani, H., Afifuddin, M., & Akbar, H. (2017). Tourism infrastructure development prioritization in Sabang Island using analytic network process methods. *AIP Conference Proceedings*, 1-6.

Rasethuntsa, B. C., & Perks, S. (2022). Travel and tourism policies and enabling conditions: An analysis of strategies in Mauritius and Egypt. *Turyzm (Lódz)*, 32(1), 159–183. 10.18778/0867-5856.32.1.08

Rasoolimanesh, S. M., Ramakrishna, S., Hall, C. M., Esfandiar, K., & Seyfi, S. (2023). A systematic scoping review of sustainable tourism indicators in relation to the sustainable development goals. *Journal of Sustainable Tourism*, 31(7), 1497–1517. Advance online publication. 10.1080/09669582.2020.1775621

Rauf, J. (2021). Sustainable Tourism. 10.4135/9781483368924.n438

REGINA-MSP project. (n.d.). REGINA-MSP. https://www.regina-msp.eu/projet

Remondino, M., & Zanin, A. (2022). Logistics and agri-food: Digitization to increase competitive advantage and sustainability. Literature review and the case of Italy. *Sustainability (Basel)*, 14(2), 787–799. 10.3390/su14020787

Responsible Travel Handbook (2006).

Richards, G. (2000). Tourism and the World of Culture and Heritage. *Tourism Recreation Research*, 25(1), 9–17. 10.1080/02508281.2000.11014896

Richards, G. (2007). *Cultural tourism: Global and local perspectives*. Psychology Press.

Rokka, J. (2010). Netnographic inquiry and new translocal sites of the social. *International Journal of Consumer Studies*, 34(4), 381–387. 10.1111/j.1470-6431.2010.00877.x

Romero–Medina, N., Flores–Tipán, E., Carvache-Franco, M., Carvache-Franco, O., Carvache-Franco, W., & González-Núñez, R. (2024). Organizational design for strengthening community-based tourism: Empowering stakeholders for self-organization and networking. *PLoS One*, 19(1), e0294849. 10.1371/journal.pone.029484938261593

Rout, H. B., Mishra, P. K., & Pradhan, B. B. (2016). Socio-economic impacts of tourism in India: An empirical analysis. *Journal of Environmental Management & Tourism*, 7(4 (16)), 762.

Ruggerio, C. A. (2021). Sustainability and sustainable development: A review of principles and definitions. In *Science of the Total Environment* (Vol. 786). 10.1016/j.scitotenv.2021.147481

Runyowa, D. (2017). Community-based tourism development in Victoria Falls, Kompisi Cultural Village: An entrepreneur's model. *African Journal of Hospitality, Tourism and Leisure*, 6(2), 1–7.

Sağır, A. (2013). Bir Ölüm Sosyolojisi Denemesi Bağlamında İktisadi Hayata Mezarlıklardan Bakmak: Safranbolu Örneği. *Electronic Turkish Studies, 8*(12).

Sahu, V. K., Baral, S. K., & Singh, R. (2024). Financial Empowerment of Tribal Women: An Inquiry into Sustainable Economic Justice Initiatives and Pathways towards Inclusive Development. *Asian Journal of Economics. Business and Accounting*, 24(4), 182–194. 10.9734/ajeba/2024/v24i41272

Saini, N., & Shri, C. (2024). Environmental, social, and governance reporting adoption factors for sustainable development at the country level. *Environment, Development and Sustainability*, 1–40.

Salazar, N. B. (2017). Community-based cultural tourism: Issues, threats and opportunities. In *Tourism and Poverty Reduction* (pp. 131–144). Routledge.

Sambamurthy, V., Wei, K. K., Lim, K., & Lee, D. (2007). IT-enabled organizational agility and firms' sustainable competitive advantage. *ICIS 2007 proceedings*, 91-100.

Sampedro, R. (2021). The Sustainable Development Goals (SDG). *Carreteras*, 4(232), 38–46. Advance online publication. 10.1201/9781003080220-8

Sano, K., & Sano, H. (2019). The effect of different crisis communication channels. *Annals of Tourism Research*, 79, 102804. Advance online publication. 10.1016/j.annals.2019.102804

Saputro, K. E. A. (1835). Hasim, Karlinasari, L., & Beik, I. S. (2023). Evaluation of Sustainable Rural Tourism Development with an integrated approach using MDS and ANP methods: Case study in Ciamis, West Java, Indonesia. *Sustainability (New Rochelle, N.Y.)*, 15(3).

Sarkar, A. (2011). *Impact of Utilitarian and Hedonic Shopping Values on Individual's Perceived Benefits and Risks in Online Shopping*. Academic Press.

Sautter, E. T., & Leisen, B. (1999). Managing stakeholders a tourism planning model. *Annals of Tourism Research*, 26(2), 312–328. 10.1016/S0160-7383(98)00097-8

Scheyvens, R. (2002). *Tourism for development: Empowering communities*. Pearson Education.

Compilation of References

Scheyvens, R., Carr, A., Movono, A., Hughes, E., Higgins-Desbiolles, F., & Mika, J. P. (2021). Indigenous tourism and the sustainable development goals. *Annals of Tourism Research*, 90, 103260. Advance online publication. 10.1016/j.annals.2021.103260

Schott, C., & Nhem, S. (2018). Paths to the market: Analysing tourism distribution channels for community-based tourism. *Tourism Recreation Research*, 43(3), 356–371. 10.1080/02508281.2018.1447837

Seaton, A. V., Jenkins, L. L., Wood, R. C., Picke, P. U. C., Bennett, M. M., & MacLellan, L. R. (1994). *Tourism the State of Art*. John Wiley and Sons Ltd.

Seervi, D. (2023). *Ecotourism and Sustainable Development*. International Journal For Multidisciplinary Research. 10.36948/ijfmr.2023.v05i05.7049

Selvi, M. S., & Şahin, S. (2012). Yerel yönetimler perspektifinden sürdürülebilir turizm: Batı Karadeniz Bölgesi örneği. *International Journal of Social and Economic Sciences*, 2(2), 23–36.

Sever, S. D., & Tok, M. E. (2023). Education for Sustainable Development in Qatar. In *Gulf Studies* (Vol. 9). 10.1007/978-981-19-7398-7_17

Sevim, B., Seçilmiş, C., & Görkem, O. (2013). Algılanan Destinasyon İmajının Tavsiye Davranışı Üzerine Etkisi: Safranbolu'da Bir Araştırma. *Uluslararası Yönetim İktisat Ve İşletme Dergisi*, 9(20), 115–129.

Shackley, M. (2009). *Visitor management*. Routledge. 10.4324/9780080520681

Shafik, W. (2023). IoT-Based Energy Harvesting and Future Research Trends in Wireless Sensor Networks. *Handbook of Research on Network-Enabled IoT Applications for Smart City Services*, 282-306. 10.4018/979-8-3693-0744-1.ch016

Shafik, W. (2024b). Industry 4.0 Technologies' Opportunities and Challenges for Realising Net-Zero Economy. *Net Zero Economy, Corporate Social Responsibility and Sustainable Value Creation: Exploring Strategies, Drivers, and Challenges*, 19-41. 10.1007/978-3-031-55779-8_2

Shafik, W. (2024c). Industry Revolution 4.0 and Beyond: Abilities and Perils for Sustainable Zero Net Economy Development. In *Powering Industry 5.0 and Sustainable Development Through Innovation* (pp. 292-316). IGI Global. 10.4018/979-8-3693-3550-5.ch020

Shafik, W. (2024d). Shaping the Next Generation Smart City Ecosystem: An Investigation on the Requirements, Applications, Architecture, Security and Privacy, and Open Research Questions. In Smart Cities: Innovations, Challenges and Future Perspectives (pp. 3-52). Cham: Springer Nature Switzerland. 10.1007/978-3-031-59846-3_1

Shafik, W., & Kalinaki, K. (2023). Smart City Ecosystem: An Exploration of Requirements, Architecture, Applications, Security, and Emerging Motivations. In *Handbook of Research on Network-Enabled IoT Applications for Smart City Services* (pp. 75-98). IGI Global. 10.4018/979-8-3693-0744-1.ch005

Shafik, W. (2024a). Artificial Intelligence Models to Prevent Forest Fires. In *AI and IoT for Proactive Disaster Management* (pp. 78–106). IGI Global. 10.4018/979-8-3693-3896-4.ch005

Shafik, W. (2024e). Toward a More Ethical Future of Artificial Intelligence and Data Science. In *The Ethical Frontier of AI and Data Analysis* (pp. 362–388). IGI Global. 10.4018/979-8-3693-2964-1.ch022

Shafik, W., & Azrour, M. (2024). Building a Greener World: Harnessing the Power of IoT and Smart Devices for Sustainable Environment. In Mabrouki, J., & Mourade, A. (Eds.), *Technical and Technological Solutions Towards a Sustainable Society and Circular Economy. World Sustainability Series*. Springer, 10.1007/978-3-031-56292-1_3

Shah, C., & Trupp, A. (2021). Trends in consumer behaviour and accommodation choice: perspectives from India. *Tourism in India*, 68-83.

Shaheen, . (2017). Disadvantaged Mountain Farmers of Gurez Valley in Kashmir: Issues of Livelihood, Vulnerability, Externality and Sustainability. *Indian Journal of Agricultural Economics*, 72(3).

Shamout, M., Elayan, M., Rawashdeh, A., Kurdi, B., & Alshurideh, M. (2022). E-HRM practices and sustainable competitive advantage from HR practitioner's perspective: A mediated moderation analysis. *International Journal of Data and Network Science*, 6(1), 165–178. 10.5267/j.ijdns.2021.9.011

Sharma, S., & Bains, H. (2021). Tourism System: Components, Elements and Models. In *S. o. (SOTHSM), BTMC-135: Concept and Impacts of Tourism* (pp. 81–96). IGNOU.

Sharpley, R. (2020). Tourism, sustainable development and the theoretical divide: 20 years on. *Journal of Sustainable Tourism*, 28(11), 1932–1946. Advance online publication. 10.1080/09669582.2020.1779732

Sharpley, R., & Telfer, D. J. (Eds.). (2014). *Tourism and development: Concepts and issues*. Multilingual Matters. 10.21832/9781845414740

Shen, X., Sakhi, S., Ullah, K., Abid, M. N., & Jin, Y. (2022). Information measures based on T-spherical fuzzy sets and their applications in decision-making and pattern recognition. *Axioms*, 11(7), 302. 10.3390/axioms11070302

Shi, L., Han, L., Yang, F., & Gao, L. (2019). The Evolution of Sustainable Development Theory: Types, Goals, and Research Prospects. *Sustainability (Basel)*, 11(24), 7158. Advance online publication. 10.3390/su11247158

Shiri, A., Howard, D., & Farnel, S. (2022). Indigenous digital storytelling: Digital interfaces supporting cultural heritage preservation and access. *The International Information & Library Review*, 54(2), 93–114. 10.1080/10572317.2021.1946748

Compilation of References

Shulla, K., Filho, W. L., Lardjane, S., Sommer, J. H., & Borgemeister, C. (2020). Sustainable development education in the context of the 2030 Agenda for sustainable development. *International Journal of Sustainable Development and World Ecology*, 27(5), 458–468. Advance online publication. 10.1080/13504509.2020.1721378

Shulla, K., Voigt, B. F., Cibian, S., Scandone, G., Martinez, E., Nelkovski, F., & Salehi, P. (2021). Effects of COVID-19 on the Sustainable Development Goals (SDGs). *Discover Sustainability*, 2(1), 15. Advance online publication. 10.1007/s43621-021-00026-x35425922

Shunali & Arora, M. (2014). Gastronomy Tourism and Destination Image Formation. *Indian Journal of Applied Hospitality & Tourism Research, 6*, 68-75.

Shu-Yuan Pan, M., Gao, M., Kim, H., Shah, K. J., Pei, S.-L., & Chiang, P.-C. (2018). Advances and challenges in sustainable tourism toward a green economy. *The Science of the Total Environment*, 635, 452–469. 10.1016/j.scitotenv.2018.04.13429677671

Sih, G. C. (2009). Sustainability aspects of large structures: Energy efficiency. *International Journal of Terraspace Science and Engineering*, 1(1), 1–7. https://www.scopus.com/inward/record.uri?eid=2-s2.0-77956343881&partnerID=40&md5=518120207245019ce3ec51e98a72095d

Simarmata, J., Yuliantini, Y., & Keke, Y. (2016). The influence of travel agent, infrastructure and accommodation on tourist satisfaction. *International Conference on Tourism, Gastronomy, and Tourist Destination (ICTGTD 2016)* (pp. 281-283). Atlantis Press.

Simons, I., & de Groot, E. (2015). Power and empowerment in community-based tourism: Opening Pandora's box? *Tourism Review*, 70(1), 72–84. 10.1108/TR-06-2014-0035

Sinakou, E., Boeve-de Pauw, J., Goossens, M., & Van Petegem, P. (2018). Academics in the field of Education for Sustainable Development: Their conceptions of sustainable development. *Journal of Cleaner Production*, 184, 321–332. Advance online publication. 10.1016/j.jclepro.2018.02.279

Singh, P., & Koneru, K. (2022). A mediated moderation analysis of E-HRM practises and long-term competitive advantage from the perspective of HR practitioners. *Journal of Positive School Psychology*, 6(3), 4436–4458.

Sipic, T. (2017). Eco-labelling of marine recreation services: The case of Blue Flag price premium in Croatia. *Journal of Ecotourism*, 16(1), 1–23. 10.1080/14724049.2016.1194848

Sita & Nor. (2012). Community-Based Tourism (CBT): Local Community Perceptions toward Social & Cultural Impacts. Proceedings of the Tourism and Hospitality International Conference. Retrieved on 26/11/2020 from: https://www.researchgate.net/publication/275953671_Communitybased_Tourism_CBT_Local_Community_Perceptions_toward_Social_and_Cultural_Impacts

Sita, S. E. D., & Nor, N. A. M. (2015). Degree of Contact and Local Perceptions of Tourism Impacts: A Case Study of Homestay Programme in Sarawak. *Procedia: Social and Behavioral Sciences*, 211, 903–910. 10.1016/j.sbspro.2015.11.119

Sivaramamurthy, C. (2004). *Mahabalipuram*. Archaeological Survey of India.

Siwek, M., Kolasińska, A., Wrześniewski, K., & Zmuda Palka, M. (2022). Services and amenities offered by city hotels within family tourism as one of the factors guaranteeing satisfactory leisure time. *International Journal of Environmental Research and Public Health*, 19(14), 1–18. 10.3390/ijerph1914832135886167

Slaper, T., & Hall, T. J. (2011). The Triple Bottom Line: What is it and how does it work. *Indiana Business Review*, 86(1), 4–8.

Smith, S. L. (1994). The tourism product. *Annals of Tourism Research*, 21(3), 582–595. 10.1016/0160-7383(94)90121-X

Snyder, H. (2019). Literature review as a research methodology: An overview and guidelines. *Journal of Business Research*, 104, 333–339. 10.1016/j.jbusres.2019.07.039

Sofield, T. (2006). Border Tourism and Border Communities: An Overview. *Tourism Geographies*, 8(2), 102–121. 10.1080/14616680600585489

Sofield, T. H. (Ed.). (2003). *Empowerment for sustainable tourism development*. Emerald Group Publishing.

Soliman, D. M. (2010). Managing visitors via demarketing in the Egyptian world heritage site: Giza pyramids. *Journal of Association of Arab Universities for Tourism and Hospitality*, 7(1), 15–20.

Som, J., Chatterjee, S., & Suklabaidya, P. (2020). Stakeholders' Perspective on Tourism Infrastructure at Khajuraho Dance Festival. *Global Journal of Enterprise Information System*, 12(2), 82–90.

Sonko, K. N., & Sonko, M. (2023). *Demystifying Environmental, Social and Governance (ESG)*. Palgrave Studies in Impact Finance. 10.1007/978-3-031-35867-8

Sonuç, N. (2020). Culture, tourism and sustainability (cultural heritage and sustainable tourism, social sustainability of tourism, socio-cultural sustainability of tourism). In *Encyclopedia of sustainable management* (pp. 1–7). Springer International Publishing. 10.1007/978-3-030-02006-4_457-1

Spaiser, V., Ranganathan, S., Swain, R. B., & Sumpter, D. J. T. (2017). The sustainable development oxymoron: Quantifying and modelling the incompatibility of sustainable development goals. *International Journal of Sustainable Development and World Ecology*, 24(6), 457–470. Advance online publication. 10.1080/13504509.2016.1235624

Spenceley, A., & Rylance, A. (2019). The contribution of tourism to achieving the United Nations Sustainable Development Goals. A research agenda for sustainable tourism, 107-125.

Staikos, A. (2020, August 1). Αλόννησος: Εγκαινιάστηκε το πρώτο υποβρύχιο μουσείο στην Ελλάδα - Ο «Παρθενώνας των ναυαγίων». *Euronews*. https://gr.euronews.com/2020/08/01/alonissos-egkainiastike-to-proto-ypovryxio-mouseio-stin-ellada-o-pathenonas-ton-nayagion

Stamboulis, Y., & Skayannis, P. (2003). Innovation strategies and technology for experience-based tourism. *Tourism Management*, 24(1), 35–43. 10.1016/S0261-5177(02)00047-X

Compilation of References

Stanikzai, I. U., Seerat, D. A. H., & Humdard, W. U. (2024). Role of Sustainable Tourism in Preserving Cultural Heritage of Afghanistan: A Comprehensive Review. *Society & Sustainability*, 5(2), 30–38. 10.38157/ss.v5i2.594

Stawicka, E. (2021). Sustainable development in the digital age of entrepreneurship. *Sustainability (Basel)*, 13(8), 4429. Advance online publication. 10.3390/su13084429

Steiger, R., Posch, E., Tappeiner, G., & Walde, J. (2020). The impact of climate change on demand of ski tourism - a simulation study based on stated preferences. *Ecological Economics*, 170, 106589. 10.1016/j.ecolecon.2019.106589

Štreimikienė, D., Švagždienė, B., Jasinskas, E., & Simanavicius, A. (2020). Sustainable tourism development and competitiveness: The systematic literature review. *Sustainable Development (Bradford)*, 29(1), 259–271. 10.1002/sd.2133

Strelnikova, M., Ivanova, R., Skrobotova, O., Polyakova, I., & Shelopugina, N. (2023). Development of inclusive tourism as a means of achieving sustainable development. *Journal of Law and Sustainable Development*, 11(1), e0273. 10.37497/sdgs.v11i1.273

Subramaniam, N., Akbar, S., Situ, H., Ji, S., & Parikh, N. (2023). Sustainable development goal reporting: Contrasting effects of institutional and organisational factors. *Journal of Cleaner Production*, 411, 137339. Advance online publication. 10.1016/j.jclepro.2023.137339

Suebsantiwongse, S. (2023). Frozen sentiments: The transformation of Kālidāsa's Drama to sacred art at the Cālukya Court. *Humanities, Arts and Social Sciences Studies*, 49-56.

Sugandini, D., Effendi, M. I., Aribowo, A. S., & Utami, Y. S. (2018). Marketing strategy on community based tourism in special region of Yogyakarta. *Journal of Environmental Management and Tourism*, 9(4), 733–774. 10.14505//jemt.v9.4(28).06

Sugiama, A. G., Oktavia, H. C., & Karlina, M. (2022). The Effect of Tourism Infrastructure Asset Quality on Tourist Satisfaction: A Case on Forest Tourism in Tasikmalaya Regency. *International Journal of Applied Sciences in Tourism and Events*, 6(1), 65–71. 10.31940/ijaste.v6i1.65-71

Suksmawati, H., Nuryananda, P. P., & Rahmatin, L. S. (2024). Local Community Awareness in Inclusive Tourism Development in Tegaren Village, Trenggalek. *Nusantara Science and Technology Proceedings*, 52-58.

Sumardani, R., & Wiramatika, I. G. (2023). The Sustainable Tourism Implementation in Bonjeruk Tourism Village, Central Lombok. *Jurnal Manajemen Pelayanan Hotel*, 7(2), 846. 10.37484/jmph.070213

Sun, J., Sarfraz, M., Turi, J. A., & Ivascu, L. (2022). Organizational agility and sustainable manufacturing practices in the context of emerging economy: A mediated moderation model. *Processes (Basel, Switzerland)*, 10(12), 25–67. 10.3390/pr10122567

Swarbrooke, J. (2001). Key challenges for visitor attraction managers in the UK. *Journal of Retail & Leisure Property*, 1(4), 318–336. 10.1057/palgrave.rlp.5090130

Talukder, M. B., Kumar, S., Kaiser, F., & Mia, Md. N. (2024). Pilgrimage Creative Tourism: A Gateway to Sustainable Development Goals in Bangladesh. In M. Hamdan, M. Anshari, N. Ahmad, & E. Ali (Eds.), *Advances in Public Policy and Administration* (pp. 285–300). IGI Global. 10.4018/979-8-3693-1742-6.ch016

Talukder, M. B., & Das, I. R. (2024). The Technology Impacts and AI Solutions in Hospitality. *i-Manager's Journal on Artificial Intelligence &Machine Learning*, 2(1), 56–72. 10.26634/jaim.2.1.20291

Talukder, M. B., Das, I. R., & Kumar, S. (2024). Implementing Digital Marketing Channels on BTHM Admission: Evidence from Dhaka City. *IUBAT Review*, 7(1), 142–170. 10.3329/iubatr.v7i1.74361

Talukder, M. B., Hoque, M., & Das, I. R. (2024). Opportunities of Tourism and Hospitality Education in Bangladesh: Career Perspectives. i-manager's. *Journal of Management*, 18(3), 21–34. 10.26634/jmgt.18.3.20385

Talukder, M. B., Kabir, F., Kaiser, F., & Lina, F. Y. (2024). Digital Detox Movement in the Tourism Industry: Traveler Perspective. In Grima, S., Chaudhary, S., Sood, K., & Kumar, S. (Eds.), (pp. 91–110). Advances in Marketing, Customer Relationship Management, and E-Services. IGI Global. 10.4018/979-8-3693-1107-3.ch007

Talukder, M. B., & Kaiser, F. (2023). Economic Impact of River Tourism: Evidence of Bangladesh. *i-manager's. Journal of Management*, 18(2), 47–60. 10.26634/jmgt.18.2.20235

Talukder, M. B., & Kumar, S. (2024). The Development of ChatGPT and Its Implications for the Future of Customer Service in the Hospitality Industry. In Derbali, A. (Ed.), *Blockchain Applications for Smart Contract Technologies* (pp. 100–126). IGI Global. 10.4018/979-8-3693-1511-8.ch005

Talukder, M. B., Kumar, S., & Das, I. R. (2024). Mindful Consumers and New Marketing Strategies for the Restaurant Business: Evidence of Bangladesh. In Ramos, C., Costa, T., Severino, F., & Calisto, M. (Eds.), *Social Media Strategies for Tourism Interactivity* (pp. 240–260). IGI Global. 10.4018/979-8-3693-0960-5.ch010

Talukder, M. B., & Muhsina, K. (2024). Prospect of Smart Tourism Destination in Bangladesh. In Correia, R., Martins, M., & Fontes, R. (Eds.), *AI Innovations for Travel and Tourism* (pp. 163–179). IGI Global. 10.4018/979-8-3693-2137-9.ch009

Tan, J., Tan, F. J., & Ramakrishna, S. (2022). Transitioning to a circular economy: A systematic review of its drivers and barriers. *Sustainability (Basel)*, 14(3), 1757. 10.3390/su14031757

TechnoFunc - Social & Cultural Impact of Tourism. (n.d.). https://www.technofunc.com/index.php/domain-knowledge/travel-and-tourism-domain/item/social-cultural-impact

Theodora, Y. (2020). Cultural heritage as a means for local development in Mediterranean historic cities—The need for an urban policy. *Heritage*, 3(2), 152–175. 10.3390/heritage3020010

Timothy, D. J. (2014). Contemporary cultural heritage and tourism: Development issues and emerging trends. *Public Archaeology*, 13(1-3), 30–47. 10.1179/1465518714Z.00000000052

Compilation of References

Tipolojileri, T. (2020). Türk Turizm Araştırmaları Dergisi. *Journal of Turkish Tourism Research*, 4(2), 1060–1076.

Toh, R. S., Raven, P., & DeKay, F. (2011). Selling rooms: Hotels vs. third-party websites. *Cornell Hospitality Quarterly*, 52(2), 181–189. 10.1177/1938965511400409

Tomassini, L., & Cavagnaro, E. (2022). Circular economy: a paradigm to critically rethink sustainability in tourism and hospitality. In *Planning and Managing Sustainability in Tourism: Empirical Studies, Best-practice Cases and Theoretical Insights* (pp. 1–12). Springer International Publishing. 10.1007/978-3-030-92208-5_1

Tosun, C. (2000). Limits to community participation in the tourism development process in developing countries. *Tourism Management*, 21(6), 613–633. 10.1016/S0261-5177(00)00009-1

Tran, L. T. T. (2024). Metaverse-driven sustainable tourism: A horizon 2050 paper. *Tourism Review*. Advance online publication. 10.1108/TR-12-2023-0857

TravelClick. (2012). *Flash Sale Sites Lose Popularity with Hoteliers TravelClick survey shows dissatisfaction with group discount model.*https://www.travelclick.com/en/news-events/press -release/flash-sale-sites-lose-popularity-hoteliers-travelclick-survey-shows-dissatisfaction-group

TripAdvisor. (2024, April 18). *Restaurants in Mahabalipuram*. Retrieved from TripAdvisor: https://www.tripadvisor.in/FindRestaurants?geo=1162480&broadened=true

Tristanti, T., Nurhaeni, I. D. A., Mulyanto, M., & Sakuntalawati, R. D. (2024). Model of Women's Empowerment in the Economic Aspects of the Tourism Field Through Community-Based Education in Gunungkidul. *International Journal of Religion*, 5(1), 702–710. 10.61707/vnck6s02

Tsartas, P. (2021, May 26). *Π. Τσάρτας (Χαροκόπειο Πανεπιστήμιο): 'Οι προορισμοί θα πρέπει να λειτουργούν και σε clusters'* TravelDailyNews Greece & Cyprus. https://traveldailynews.gr/ columns/article/3823

Tsartas, P. (2010). *Greek Tourism Development*. Characteristics, Clarifications, Proposals. Kritiki.

Tse, A. C. B. (2003). Disintermediation of travel agents in the hotel industry. *International Journal of Hospitality Management*, 22(4), 453–460. 10.1016/S0278-4319(03)00049-532287843

Ullah, N., Khan, J., Saeed, I., Zada, S., Xin, S., Kang, Z., & Hu, Y. (2022). Gastronomic Tourism and Tourist Motivation: Exploring Northern Areas of Pakistan. *International Journal of Environmental Research and Public Health*, 19(13), 1–17. 10.3390/ijerph1913773435805393

UNESCO. (2024, March 21). *UNESCO*. Retrieved from Group of Monuments at Mahabalipuram: https://whc.unesco.org/en/list/249

Unknown. (2024, April 15). *Chennai City Bus*. Retrieved from Chennai Bus Route & Timings (MTC): https://chennaicitybus.in/

UNWTO. (2020). Tourism and Poverty Alleviation. Project report, *World Tourism Organization*. https://www.e-unwto.org/doi/pdf/10.18111/9789284405497

Valjakka, M. (2013). CSR and Company Reputation-Case study of Nike. PhD thesis, University of Wolverhampton.

van Vuuren, D. P., Zimm, C., Busch, S., Kriegler, E., Leininger, J., Messner, D., Nakicenovic, N., Rockstrom, J., Riahi, K., Sperling, F., Bosetti, V., Cornell, S., Gaffney, O., Lucas, P. L., Popp, A., Ruhe, C., von Schiller, A., Schmidt, J. O., & Soergel, B. (2022). Defining a sustainable development target space for 2030 and 2050. In *One Earth* (Vol. 5, Issue 2). 10.1016/j.oneear.2022.01.003

van Zanten, J. A., & van Tulder, R. (2021). Improving companies' impacts on sustainable development: A nexus approach to the SDGS. *Business Strategy and the Environment*, 30(8), 3703–3720. Advance online publication. 10.1002/bse.2835

VanGeem, M. G., Marceau, M. L., Gajda, J., & Nisbet, M. A. (2001). Partial environmental life-cycle inventory of single-family houses. *Thermal Performance of the Exterior Envelopes of Whole Buildings*. https://www.scopus.com/inward/record.uri?eid=2-s2.0-34248166867&partnerID=40&md5=07ae02d90a5680c82b9fb5f4d361c7d9

Varvaresos, S. (2017). Religious Tourism: an economic approach. In Tsartas, P., & Lytras, P. (Eds.), *Contributions of Greek Scientists. Tourism, Tourism Development* (pp. 245–254). Papazisis.

Vashkevich, N., & Barykin, S. (2023). Methodological Approaches Towards the Use of Inclusive Tourism as a Tool of Economic Development of Russian Federation. *Research of Economic and Financial Problems*, 4(4), 10–10. 10.31279/2782-6414-2023-4-7

Velichkina, A. V. (2014). The assessment of the regional tourism infrastructure development. Ehkonomicheskie i sotsialnye peremeny: fakty, tendentsii, prognoz, 239-250.

Verma, A., & Rajendran, G. (2017). The effect of historical nostalgia on tourists' destination loyalty intention: An empirical study of the world cultural heritage site – Mahabalipuram, India. *Asia Pacific Journal of Tourism Research*, 22(9), 977–990. 10.1080/10941665.2017.1357639

Verma, R. (2021). Fuzzy MABAC method based on new exponential fuzzy information measures. *Soft Computing*, 25(14), 9575–9589. 10.1007/s00500-021-05739-9

Virkar, A. R., & Mallya, P. D. (2018). A review of dimensions of tourism transport affecting tourist satisfaction. *Indian Journal of Commerce and Management Studies*, 9(1), 72–80. 10.18843/ijcms/v9i1/10

Visseren-Hamakers, I. J. (2020). The 18th Sustainable Development Goal. In *Earth System Governance* (Vol. 3). 10.1016/j.esg.2020.100047

Vlachos, A., Krinidis, S., Papadimitriou, K., Manglis, A., Fourkiotou, A., & Tzovaras, D. (2023). IBLUECULTURE: a novel system of real-time underwater image transmission in a virtual reality environment, as a new managerial approach for underwater cultural heritage. *The œInternational Archives of the Photogrammetry, Remote Sensing and Spatial Information Sciences/International Archives of the Photogrammetry, Remote Sensing and Spatial Information Sciences, XLVIII-1/W2-2023*, 269–274. 10.5194/isprs-archives-XLVIII-1-W2-2023-269-2023

Compilation of References

Vora & Sundaresh. (2003). Mahabalipuram: A Saga of Glory to Tribulations. *Migration & Diffusion, 4,* 67-80.

VOSviewer - Visualizing scientific landscapes. (n.d.). https://www.vosviewer.com/

Wahhab Ajeena, D. (2022, May). Sustainable Tourism and Its Role in Preserving Archaeological Sites. In *International Symposium: New Metropolitan Perspectives* (pp. 2485–2495). Springer International Publishing. 10.1007/978-3-031-06825-6_237

Waligo, V. M., Clarke, J., & Hawkins, R. (2013). Implementing sustainable tourism: A multi-stakeholder involvement management framework. *Tourism Management*, 36, 342–353. 10.1016/j.tourman.2012.10.008

Walker, K., & Moscardo, G. (2019). Moving beyond sense of place to care of place: The role of Indigenous values and interpretation in promoting transformative change in tourists' place images and personal values. In *Sustainable Tourism and Indigenous Peoples* (pp. 177–195). Routledge. 10.4324/9781315112053-11

Walter, A. T. (2021). Organizational agility: Ill-defined and somewhat confusing? A systematic literature review and conceptualization. *Management Review Quarterly*, 71(2), 343–391. 10.1007/s11301-020-00186-6

Wang, M., Su, M. M., Gan, C., Peng, X., Wu, Z., & Voda, M. (2023). Does digital inclusive finance matter in sustainable tourism development at the county level? Evidence from the Wuling Mountain area in China. *Sustainable Development*. 10.1002/sd.2838

Weaver, D. (2007). *Sustainable tourism*. Routledge. 10.4324/9780080474526

Weiland, S., Hickmann, T., Lederer, M., Marquardt, J., & Schwindenhammer, S. (2021). The 2030 agenda for sustainable development: Transformative change through the sustainable development goals? In *Politics and Governance* (Vol. 9, Issue 1). 10.17645/pag.v9i1.4191

Wibowo, J. M., & Hariadi, S. (2022). Indonesia sustainable tourism resilience in the COVID-19 pandemic era (Case study of five Indonesian super-priority destinations). Millennial Asia.

Wilson, R. H. (2011). Internet Hotel Reservations: Recent Changes and Trends in the Enforcement of Click Wrap and Browse Wrap "Terms and Conditions/Terms of Use". *Cornell Hospitality Quarterly*, 52(2), 190–199. 10.1177/1938965510393734

Witchayakawin. (2020). Factors on Development of Community-Based Tourism (CBT) in Phitsanulok Province of Thailand. *Journal of Critical Reviews*.

Wood.Hey, P. (1990). Truth and Beauty in hand space-Trends in landscape and Leisure. *Land Space Australia*, 12(1), 43–47.

Worldbank. (2024). The Blue Economy Development Framework. https://thedocs.worldbank.org/en/doc/e5c1bdb0384e732de3cef6fd2eac41e5-0320072021/original/BH023-BlueEconomy-FINAL-ENGLISH.pdf

Woyo, E., & Amadhila, E. (2018). Desert tourists experiences in Namibia: A netnographic approach. *African Journal of Hospitality, Tourism and Leisure*, 7(3), 1–13.

Wu, L., & Jin, S. (2022). Corporate Social Responsibility and Sustainability: From a Corporate Governance Perspective. *Sustainability (Basel)*, 14(22), 1–15. 10.3390/su142215457

Wu, M.-Y., & Pearce, P. L. (2014). Chinese recreational vehicle users in Australia: A netnographic study of tourist motivation. *Tourism Management*, 43, 22–35. 10.1016/j.tourman.2014.01.010

Wu, Y., & Tham, J. (2023). The impact of environmental regulation, Environment, Social and Government Performance, and technological innovation on enterprise resilience under a green recovery. *Heliyon*, 9(10), e20278. 10.1016/j.heliyon.2023.e2027837767495

Xiang, Z., Schwartz, Z., Gerdes, J. H.Jr, & Uysal, M. (2015). What can big data and text analytics tell us about hotel guest experience and satisfaction? *International Journal of Hospitality Management*, 44, 120–130. 10.1016/j.ijhm.2014.10.013

Xiang, Z., Stienmetz, J., & Fesenmaier, D. R. (2021). Smart Tourism Design: Launching the annals of tourism research curated collection on designing tourism places. *Annals of Tourism Research*, 86, 103154. 10.1016/j.annals.2021.103154

Xiao, Y., & Watson, M. (2019). Guidance on conducting a systematic literature review. *Journal of Planning Education and Research*, 39(1), 93–112. 10.1177/0739456X17723971

Xu, L., Ao, C., Liu, B., & Cai, Z. (2023). Ecotourism and sustainable development: a scientometric review of global research trends. In *Environment, Development and Sustainability* (Vol. 25, Issue 4). 10.1007/s10668-022-02190-0

Yassine, D. (2015). Principles of Accounting II. Academic Press.

Yellowhom, E. (2000). Indians, archaeology and the changing world.

Yin, R. K. (2018). *Case study research and applications* (Vol. 6). Sage.

Youness, H. (2017). Trends of Business (1st ed.). Academic Press.

Yun, H. (2014). Spatial Relationships of Cultural Amenities in Rural Tourism Areas. *Tourism Planning & Development*, 11(4), 452–462. 10.1080/21568316.2014.894557

Zakari, A., Khan, I., Tan, D., Alvarado, R., & Dagar, V. (2022). Energy efficiency and sustainable development goals (SDGs). *Energy*, 239, 122365. Advance online publication. 10.1016/j.energy.2021.122365

Zapata, M. J., Hall, C. M., Lindo, P., & Vanderschaeghe, M. (2013). Can community-based tourism contribute to development and poverty alleviation? Lessons from Nicaragua. In Tourism and the Millennium Development Goals (pp. 98-122). Routledge.

Zapata, , Hall, C. M., Lindo, P., & Vanderschaeghe, M. (2011). Can community-based tourism contribute to development and poverty alleviation? Lessons from Nicaragua. *Current Issues in Tourism*, 14(8), 725–749. 10.1080/13683500.2011.559200

Compilation of References

Żemła, M., & Staszewska, A. (2022). The Use of Post-Industrial Heritage in the Construction of Competitive Tourist Products: The Case of the Upper Silesia-Zagłębie Metropolis, Poland. In *Tourism Planning and Development in Eastern Europe* (pp. 31-46). CABI.

Zeng, Z., & Wang, X. (2021). Spatial Effects of Domestic Tourism on Urban-Rural Income Inequality. *Sustainability (Basel)*, 13(16), 9394. Advance online publication. 10.3390/su13169394

Zeppel, H. (2012). Collaborative governance for low-carbon tourism: Climate change initiatives by Australian tourism agencies. *Current Issues in Tourism*, 15(7), 603–626. 10.1080/13683500.2011.615913

Zhang, J., Zhou, Y., Tang, W., Gu, H., Yan, J., & Wang, H. (2017). An Agent-Mediated Tendering Mechanism for Intelligent Hotel Reservation. In *2017 IEEE 14th International Conference on E-Business Engineering (ICEBE 2017)* (pp. 307–311). 10.1109/ICEBE.2017.56

Zhang, C., & Xiao, H. (2014). Destination development in China: Towards an effective model of explanation. *Journal of Sustainable Tourism*, 22(2), 214–233. 10.1080/09669582.2013.839692

Zhang, E. M. (2010). Understanding the Acceptance of Mobile SMS Advertising among Young Chinese Consumers. *Psychology and Marketing*, 30(6), 461–469. 10.1002/mar

Zhang, G., Chen, X., Law, R., & Zhang, M. (2020). Sustainability of Heritage Tourism: A Structural Perspective from Cultural Identity and Consumption Intention. *Sustainability (Basel)*, 12(21), 9199. 10.3390/su12219199

Zhang, J., & Walsh, J. (2021). Tourist experience, tourist motivation and destination loyalty for historic and cultural tourists. *Pertanika Journal of Social Science & Humanities*, 28(4), 3277–3296. 10.47836/pjssh.28.4.43

Zhao, X. R., Wang, L., Guo, X., & Law, R. (2015). The influence of online reviews to online hotel booking intentions. *International Journal of Contemporary Hospitality Management*, 27(6), 1343–1364. Advance online publication. 10.1108/IJCHM-12-2013-0542

Zhu, F., & Zhang, X. (2010). Impact of online consumer reviews on sales: The moderating role of product and consumer characteristics. *Journal of Marketing*, 74(2), 133–148. 10.1509/jm.74.2.133

Zwolińska, K., Lorenc, S., & Pomykała, R. (2022). Sustainable Development in Education from Students' Perspective—Implementation of Sustainable Development in Curricula. *Sustainability (Basel)*, 14(6), 3398. Advance online publication. 10.3390/su14063398

About the Contributors

Viana Hassan is actively involved in academic and research work in Tourism & Cultural Management in Lebanon and Malta. She got her Ph.D. in Tourism Management and Cultural from Saint Joseph University, Beirut. Her Thesis was entitled "Medical Tourism in Lebanon". She has more than 15 years of tourism experience in many related Travel and Tourism Fields, varying from airline sales experience (MEA), to Co-management several Lebanese Travel agencies. She is an Experienced Lecturer with more than 13 years' experience at several universities in Lebanon (Lebanese University, A.U. L, Lebanese International University, Islamic University) and the Institute of Tourism Studies, Malta, with a demonstrated history of working in the Higher education industry, Skilled in Tourism Management, Customer service, Branding, Event Management, and Medical Tourism. Dr. Viana has participated in international conferences in multiple countries, including Athens, Paris, Vienna, Dubai, Beirut, Valencia, and has published papers in peer review journals.

Anna Staszewska, an Assistant Professor and Secretary of the Department of Tourism at the Upper Silesian Academy, holds a doctoral degree in management sciences from the Cracow University of Economics. She works closely with organizations such as the Polish Chamber of Tourism, the Silesian Tourist Organization, and the Silesian Chamber of Tourism. Additionally, she serves as the Chancellor of the Jurassic Folk University in Ogrodzieniec and is a member of the Silesian Marketing Association and the Zagłębie Association. Her work on sustainable development includes giving lectures to various educational institutions and teaching a related subject at her alma mater. She is also an Ambassador of the European Climate Pact and actively participates in expert work on Climate Education. Dr. Staszewska's research interests primarily revolve around industrial tourism, tourism management, and sustainable tourism. Attended in Europe's influential climate adaptation conference, ECCA 2023, takes place from 19 to 21 June 2023, and will be held in Dublin, Ireland, Operational organization and challenges of Climate Pact Ambassadors in the European Union by Anna Staszewska (Akademia Górnośląska).

Shivam Bhartiya is an esteemed professional working as an assistant professor in the field of tourism management in the department of commerce and management. Data analysis, research and development, problem solving, administrative and teaching expertise—Shivam's wide skill set makes him a vibrant contributor to the academic world. Publications of his important research papers in esteemed journals and his position as publisher of books indexed by Scopus attest to his dedication to research excellence. Shivam has not only made significant contributions to academia, but he has also been a sought-after speaker, giving guest lectures at prestigious universities and organizations throughout the world. His participation in scientific committees, along with his other notable accomplishments, has solidified his position as an invaluable resource to the field of academia and research.

* * *

About the Contributors

Gaurav Bathla is having over thirteen years of experience in Academia & Industry and presently working as Professor in School of Hotel Management, Airlines and Tourism at CT University Punjab. He has received his Doctorate (PhD) in Hotel Management and Tourism from GNA University, Punjab. Dr. Bathla has authored more than 30 research papers in Scopus Indexed, UGC Approved and Peer Review Journals. He has been associated with many universities and hotel management institutions for their curriculum development and examination system. Dr. Bathla is editorial / reviewer board member of more than 8 National & International Journals. He has also organized various conferences and Faculty Development Programs in the field of Hospitality and Tourism.

Vaibhav Bhatt is an assistant professor in the Department of Tourism and Hospitality Management at the Central University of Tamil Nadu. Dr. Bhatt holds a Ph.D. in Tourism from HNB Garhwal (A Central) University, where he researched the planning and development strategies for the promotion of nature tourism in the Indian Himalayas. With ten years of professional experience in tourism and hospitality, he has garnered practical industry experience through long research and teaching stints. In his research, he focuses on sustainable tourism planning and development, wherein he seeks to aid the tourism sector by crafting sustainability strategies to transform theoretical concepts into practice. Dr. Bhatt is an active researcher and has published numerous research articles in prestigious national and international journals and books. He has been a reviewer of various national and international journals and also delivers guest lectures at academic conferences and faculty development programs.

Mudasir Ahmad Dar is a bakery chef by profession. Currently, he is working with Vivanta by Taj hotel, Kashmir-India. He has obtained post graduate degree in hotel management. Besides, keeping he academic passion alive, he is pursuing post graduate degree in tourism management. He is actively involved in research activities for impactful practical research implications.

Bijoy Krishna Debnath is currently working as Assistant Professor in the dept of Applied Sciences, School of Engineering, Tezpur University, India from 2019. Prior to that he worked as an Assistant Professor under MHRD project (TEQIP III) at Government College of Engineering Kalahandi, Odisha, India. He did Ph.D. in Operations Research from NIT Agartala in the year 2019. He has published many papers in his credits in EAAI, Applied Energy, IJFS, IJOR, IJLSM, HJMS, JAIHC, etc.

Suja John is a Professor of Tourism Studies with the School of Business and Management, CHRIST (Deemed to be University). She has been associated with Christ University for over 20 years in various capacities. To her credit, she has received copyright ownership for her work titled 'Bamboo the "Green Gold": A Strategic Resilient to Control Climate Change Issues Catalyst to attain Sustainable Development Goals. She has published two books, 'Community-Based Decentralized Waste Management for Sustainable Tourism' and 'Tourists Behaviour in the Age of Climate Change.' Dr Suja is a subject expert for the Tourism E-Content Development Project -National Mission on Education through ICT, Ministry of Human Resource Development, Government of India. As a part of the project, she developed two core papers: Hygiene and Sanitation and Geography for Tourism. She has also published research articles in International and national referred journals and participated and presented papers in various conferences and seminars in India and abroad.

Musfiqur Rahoman Khan is an accomplished author and Teaching Assistant at the Department of Tourism and Hospitality Management at Daffodil Institute of IT (DIIT), Dhaka, Bangladesh. He holds a Bachelor's degree in Business Administration (BBA), majoring in Tourism and Hospitality Management, from the same institute. With a strong academic background and a passion for exploring the intersection of travel and culture, Musfiq's diverse areas of interest include Adventure tourism, Cultural tourism, and Wildlife tourism. Through his teaching and writing, he strives to inspire others to discover the richness and diversity of the world through travel.

Erietta Kiachidou is a Ph.D. Candidate at the Department of Tourism Economics and Management of the University of the Aegean. She is working on the marine tourism and more specifically on the diving tourism and its development in Greece. Her research interests include, apart from diving tourism, sustainable tourism and the Blue Economy and has presented her research in international conferences.

Amit Kumar is currently serving as an Assistant Professor in the Department of Tourism and Hotel Management at Central University of Haryana. Dr. Kumar is a distinguished figure in the field of tourism and hospitality management, with a prolific academic and research career. He is a well-structured academic professional and researcher demonstrating proven success in fostering student learning outcomes through creative and innovative curriculum delivery methods. He Adepts at driving thought-provoking class debates to promote student engagement and learning. He has more than 70 research paper publications in International and National Journals of repute along with 02 Authored Books, 02 Edited Books and 03 Patents to his credit.

Sanjeev Kumar is an accomplished expert in Food and Beverage. He currently holds the positions of Professor in Lovely Professional University, Punjab, India. With over a decade of experience in the field, food Service Industry, his research focuses on Alcoholic beverages, Event management and Sustainable Management Practices, Metaverse and Artificial Intelligence. He has published more than 40 research papers, articles and chapters in Scopus Indexed, UGC Approved and peer reviewed Journals and books. Dr. Sanjeev Kumar participated and acted as resource person in various National and International conferences, seminars, research workshops and industry talks and his work has been widely cited.

Sreshtaa S. Kumar is a research scholar in the Tourism Department at CHRIST (Deemed to be University), Bangalore. She is doing her Ph.D. on "Evaluation of Event-based Tourism Infrastructure for Dance Festival Venues." She has completed her post-graduation in hotel management from IHM Chennai. She has three years of teaching experience in a reputed college in SRM University Chennai, where she taught Front Office and other allied subjects such as Tourism and Nutrition for undergraduate students. With this research, Sreshtaa hopes to reach out to professionals interested in cultural tourism and the promotion & marketing of dance festivals.

Shreeansh Mishra is working as an Assistant Professor of Tourism in Central University of Tamil Nadu, India. His research highlights the transformative role of self-help groups, microfinance, and community readiness in advancing community-based tourism and fostering sustainable development. His work examines factors that synergize marginalized communities and foster sustainable development. With a commitment to global collaboration and continuous efforts, Shreeansh Mishra continues his mission to create a more inclusive and equitable tourism landscape, where gender disparities are addressed and women's empowerment takes center stage, catalyzing a brighter future for all.

Pallavi Mohanan is a dedicated research scholar at the Amity Institute of Social Sciences, Amity University, Noida, Uttar Pradesh, focusing on ancient civilizations, trans-national communities, globalization in the ancient world, socio-cultural history, and historical archaeology. Currently pursuing her Ph.D. in History, Pallavi's passion for understanding the intricacies of ancient societies drives her research endeavors. With a strong academic background and extensive writing experience, she has contributed significantly to scholarly discourse with numerous papers published in esteemed journals and books. Pallavi's work has been recognized through various awards and accolades, highlighting her commitment to advancing knowledge in her areas of expertise. Her interdisciplinary approach and deep insights into historical narratives make her a valuable asset to the academic community, fostering meaningful discussions and contributing to a better understanding of our shared human heritage.

Edip Örücü is a business administration professor. He works in the field of organizational behavior. He teaches at the Business Administration Department of Bandırma Onyedi Eylül University. His area of expertise is strategic management.

Georgia Papadopoulou is an Assistant Professor of Tourism Economics and Operations Management at the Department of Tourism Economics and Management, University of the Aegean, Greece. She is teaching courses in Tourism Economics, Regional Development and Operations Management. Her research interests include tourism economics, marine tourism, tourists' behavior, tourism management and cruise transport. She has published papers in international journals and chapters in books. She has also presented her work at international conferences.

About the Contributors

Brajamohan Sahoo is a research scholar in the dept of Applied Sciences, School of Engineering, Tezpur University, India under the guidance of Dr. Bijoy Krishna Debnath. He completed Master of Science from Central University of Jharkhand, India in the year 2020 and did Bachelor of Science from Fakir Mohan University in the year 2018. His current research interest include Fuzzy MCDM techniques for complex real life problems, etc.

Wasswa Shafik (Member, IEEE) received a Bachelor of Science degree in information technology engineering with a minor in mathematics from Ndejje University, Kampala, Uganda, a Master of Engineering degree in information technology engineering (MIT) from Yazd University, Iran, and a Ph.D. degree in computer science with the School of Digital Science, Universiti Brunei Darussalam, Brunei Darussalam. He is also the Founder and a Principal Investigator of the Dig Connectivity Research Laboratory (DCRLab) after serving as a Research Associate at Network Interconnectivity Research Laboratory, Yazd University. Prior to this, he worked as a Community Data Analyst at Population Services International (PSI-Uganda), Community Data Officer at Programme for Accessible Health Communication (PACE-Uganda), Research Assistant at the Socio-Economic Data Centre (SEDC-Uganda), Prime Minister's Office, Kampala, Uganda, an Assistant Data Officer at TechnoServe, Kampala, IT Support at Thurayya Islam Media, Uganda, and Asmaah Charity Organization. He has more than 60 publications in renowned journals and conferences. His research interests include Computer Vision, AI-enabled IoT/IoMTs, Smart Cities.

Pramendra Singh has earned his PhD from Jiwaji University, Gwalior in India in 2018 and currently working as Assistant Professor and Head of the department of Tourism & Airlines department, School of Hotel Management & Tourism in Lovely Professional University, Punjab. He has also earned three masters degrees, two in Tourism & Travel Management and another in History. He has more than ten years of teaching and research experience. He has in his credit more than twenty research papers and book chapters published by publishers of international repute. He has edited two books on tourism & sustainability related themes being published by Emerald Publishing and is also currently editing another book on Niche tourism & sustainability being published by CABI and Religious tourism and technology being published by Emerald. His research interest includes heritage tourism, cultural tourism, sustainable tourism, tourism education, tourism and technology.

Mohammad Badruddoza Talukder is an Associate Professor, College of Tourism and Hospitality Management, IUBAT - International University of Business Agriculture and Technology, Dhaka-1230, Bangladesh. He holds PhD in Hotel Management from Lovely Professional University, India. He has been teaching various courses in the Department of Tourism and Hospitality at various universities in Bangladesh since 2008. His research areas include tourism management, hotel management, hospitality management, food & beverage management, and accommodation management, where he has published research papers in well-known journals in Bangladesh and abroad. Mr. Talukder is one of the executive members of the Tourism Educators Association of Bangladesh. He has led training and consulting for a wide range of hospitality organizations in Bangladesh. He just became an honorary facilitator at the Bangladesh Tourism Board's Bangabandhu international tourism and hospitality training institution.

Ranjeeta Tripathi is presently working as an Assistant Professor in Amity University, Lucknow. Completed her Doctorate (PhD) in Hospitality from CT University, Ludhiana and Masters in Hotel Management from Uttarakhand open University, Haldwani Uttarakhand. She obtained her Diploma in Hotel Management from Madras University in 2001 and later completed her Bachelors in Hotel management from Uttarakhand open University, Haldwani Uttarakhand. She has over 22 years of experience in Academia and Industry. She has provided her services Carnival Cruise Line, Miami Florida USA for almost 10 years. She switched to academics in 2011 and started teaching from IHM Meerut and later went to IHM Lucknow. She is also a member of nodal body of Indian Culinary Forum (ICF). She has published 28 Research papers in National and International Conference. She has served as jury member of Skill India Competition in 2019.

Ramazan Yıldız works as an assistant professor at the Maritime Faculty. He works in the field of organizational behavior.

Index

Publishing Tomorrow's Research Today

IGI Global
Publishing Tomorrow's Research Today
www.igi-global.com

Uncover Current Insights and Future Trends in
Business & Management
with IGI Global's Cutting-Edge Recommended Books

Print Only, E-Book Only, or Print + E-Book.
Order direct through IGI Global's Online Bookstore at **www.igi-global.com** or through your preferred provider.

Premier Reference Source
Developmental Language Disorders in Childhood and Adolescence

ISBN: 9798369306444
© 2023; 436 pp.
List Price: US$ 230

Premier Reference Source
The Sustainable Fintech Revolution
Building a Greener Future for Finance

ISBN: 9798369300084
© 2023; 358 pp.
List Price: US$ 250

Premier Reference Source
Cases on Enhancing Business Sustainability Through Knowledge Management Systems

ISBN: 9781668458594
© 2023; 366 pp.
List Price: US$ 240

Premier Reference Source
5G, Artificial Intelligence, and Next Generation Internet of Things
Digital Innovation For Green and Sustainable Economies

ISBN: 9781668486344
© 2023; 256 pp.
List Price: US$ 280

Premier Reference Source
The Use of Artificial Intelligence in Digital Marketing
Competitive Strategies and Tactics

ISBN: 9781668493243
© 2024; 318 pp.
List Price: US$ 250

Premier Reference Source
AI and Emotional Intelligence for Modern Business Management
Bridging the Gap and Nurturing Success

ISBN: 9798369304181
© 2023; 415 pp.
List Price: US$ 250

Do you want to stay current on the latest research trends, product announcements, news, and special offers?
Join IGI Global's mailing list to receive customized recommendations, exclusive discounts, and more.
Sign up at: www.igi-global.com/newsletters.

Scan the QR Code here to view more related titles in Business & Management.

www.igi-global.com   Sign up at www.igi-global.com/newsletters   facebook.com/igiglobal   twitter.com/igiglobal   linkedin.com/igiglobal

Ensure Quality Research is Introduced to the Academic Community

Become a Reviewer for IGI Global Authored Book Projects

Premier Reference Source

The Use of Artificial Intelligence in Digital Marketing

IGI Global

Premier Reference Source

Innovations in Materials Chemistry, Physics, and Engineering Research

Eugene de Silva and Pranlad Abeydeera

IGI Global

Premier Reference Source

Experimental and Clinical Evidence of the Neuropathology of Parkinson's Disease

Ahmed Draoui, Omar El Hiba, and Anushyami R. Jayakumar

IGI Global

Premier Reference Source

Balance and Boundaries in Creating Meaningful Relationships in Online Higher Education

Sarah H. Jarvie and Cara Metz

IGI Global

The overall success of an authored book project is dependent on quality and timely manuscript evaluations.

Applications and Inquiries may be sent to:
development@igi-global.com

Applicants must have a doctorate (or equivalent degree) as well as publishing, research, and reviewing experience. Authored Book Evaluators are appointed for one-year terms and are expected to complete at least three evaluations per term. Upon successful completion of this term, evaluators can be considered for an additional term.

If you have a colleague that may be interested in this opportunity, we encourage you to share this information with them.

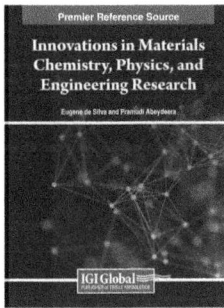

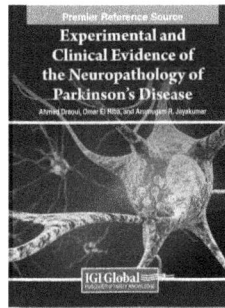

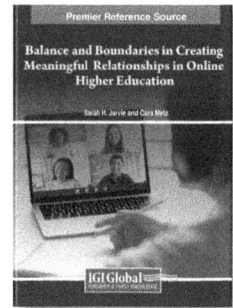

IGI Global
Publishing Tomorrow's Research Today
www.igi-global.com

IGI Global
Open Access
Journal Program

Publishing Tomorrow's Research Today
IGI Global's Open Access Journal Program
Including Nearly 200 Peer-Reviewed, Gold (Full) Open Access Journals across IGI Global's Three Academic Subject Areas:
Business & Management; Scientific, Technical, and Medical (STM); and Education

Consider Submitting Your Manuscript to One of These Nearly 200 Open Access Journals for to Increase Their Discoverability & Citation Impact

| Web of Science Impact Factor | **6.5** | Web of Science Impact Factor | **4.7** | Web of Science Impact Factor | **3.2** | Web of Science Impact Factor | **2.6** |

JOURNAL OF
Organizational and End User Computing

JOURNAL OF
Global Information Management

INTERNATIONAL JOURNAL ON
Semantic Web and Information Systems

JOURNAL OF
Database Management

Choosing IGI Global's Open Access Journal Program Can Greatly Increase the Reach of Your Research

Higher Usage
Open access papers are 2-3 times more likely to be read than non-open access papers.

Higher Download Rates
Open access papers benefit from 89% higher download rates than non-open access papers.

Higher Citation Rates
Open access papers are 47% more likely to be cited than non-open access papers.

Submitting an article to a journal offers an invaluable opportunity for you to share your work with the broader academic community, fostering knowledge dissemination and constructive feedback.

Submit an Article and Browse the IGI Global Call for Papers Pages

We can work with you to find the journal most well-suited for your next research manuscript.
For open access publishing support, contact: journaleditor@igi-global.com

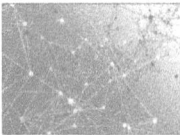

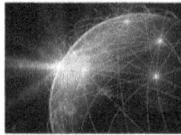

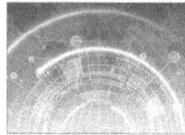